Cultural Atlas of
AFRICA

Editor Graham Speake
Art Editor Andrew Lawson
Map editor Liz Orrock
Text editor Jennifer
Drake-Brockman
Design Adrian Hodgkins
Production Clive Sparling
Index Barbara James

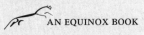 AN EQUINOX BOOK

Published in North America by
Facts on File, Inc., 460 Park Avenue South
New York, N.Y. 10016, 1981

Planned and produced by
Equinox (Oxford) Ltd,
Littlegate House,
St Ebbe's Street, Oxford OX1 1SQ

Copyright © Equinox (Oxford) Ltd, 1981
Reprinted 1982, 1985

Origination by Chapman Brothers, Oxford;
M.B.A. Ltd, Chalfont St Peter, Bucks

Filmset by Keyspools Ltd,
Golborne, Lancs

Printed in Spain by Heraclio Fournier, S.A.
Vitoria

Library of Congress Cataloging
in Publication Data
Murray, Jocelyn.
Cultural atlas of Africa.

Bibliography: p.
Includes index.
1. Africa-Civilization. I. Title.
DT14.M84 960 80-27762
ISBN 0-87196-558-5

Frontispiece A miscellany of
African masks. Left to right:
Biombo, Zaïre; Bedu, Ghana;
Ngi, Zaïre; Chokwe, Zaïre;
N'tomo, Mali. Overleaf, left to
right: Kota reliquary head,
Gabon; Dan, Liberia; Bwani,
Zaïre; Pende, Congo.

Cultural Atlas of
AFRICA

edited by Jocelyn Murray

Facts On File Publications
New York

CONTENTS

Pende mask, Congo.

Special Features

List of Maps

INTRODUCTION

The continent of Africa is so vast and so rich in contrasts that a lifetime's traveling in it could scarcely skim the surface of its diversity. For hundreds of years fabulous tales of the dark continent fired the imagination of Europe. Where was the land of Punt to which the ancient Egyptians traded for spices? Was there really a great Christian emperor called Prester John ruling in the African heartland? Where did the Nile rise, and what was the secret of its annual flooding? The early Portuguese sailors, edging their way along inhospitable coasts, were far from answering any of these questions, and the mapmakers who largely relied upon their accounts could draw only the outline of the shores and had to fill the unknown interior with pictures of monstrous men and beasts. Thus Africa became known through myths, rather than by facts, and new myths still spring up to replace the old: the 19th-century picture of "the African jungle" is now supplanted, it seems, by another fallacious image – Africa as a vast safari park.

Myths about physical geography are in the end less damaging than the myths about the African people and their "primitiveness," but both varieties must be fought. For misconceptions persist at every level and even within Africa itself there is lack of knowledge in one area or region about the basic historical and geographical facts of another region. Ignorance has been compounded by the presence of differing colonial regimes, knowledge of different European languages, and consequent restriction of access to information for linguistic reasons. Moreover, the story of man in Africa can be traced over millions of years, and the tall pastoralist Maasai of East Africa and the forest-dwelling pygmies of central Africa demonstrate man's physical ability to adapt to different environments and ways of life. Africa gave birth to one of man's first essays in civilization in the astonishing flowering of arts and sciences in Egypt in the third millennium BC; at the other end of the scale of man's cultural experience, Kalahari hunters still lead the precarious existence of their Stone Age forebears. The 19th-century Zulu king Chaka organized his armies into one of the most efficient fighting machines the world has ever seen. The serene artistry of the Benin bronze heads suggests a totally different spiritual dimension. Faced with these contrasts, we are forced to ask if there is, indeed, something "African" to discover – négritude, the "authenticity" of Zaïre, the ujamaa of Tanzania – which links and binds together the people of vastly separated countries and cultures. If we emphasize the variety that Africa encompasses we are in danger of not even looking for, let alone finding, the unity.

Africans themselves are still wrestling with the question of identity after emerging from 60, 70 or 80 (seldom longer) years of colonial rule. A vast continent was divided up by lines ruled on maps in European offices. Kingdoms, clans, families, were split up. Assorted educational systems, alien languages, new religions, and varying versions of all these have resulted in modern African nations having distinct national characters which owe as much, or nearly as much, to the colonial regime under which their borders were defined as to preexisting ethnic and cultural factors.

To understand the context and significance of events and processes in Africa today, facts are needed to replace the myths. Both within and outside Africa there is a need for a book that will provide an introduction to the continent as a whole. The *Cultural Atlas of Africa* aims to do just this, by a combination of text, illustrations and maps. The maps are perhaps the key contribution: whatever is said about Africa needs to be grounded in the physical realities of the continent. The book is first of all an atlas, but it is an atlas set within the historical context. It draws upon the knowledge of experts in many fields in its endeavor to be true to the diversity, while seeking to present the unity, of the continent.

Africa's plains have been surveyed, its mountains climbed, its rivers harnessed for hydroelectricity, its minerals exploited, and its inhabitants drawn into the mainstream of 20th-century life, but its future presents a formidable challenge, not only for the African peoples themselves, but for the whole of mankind. This atlas is an interim report on the nature of the challenge and the response to it.

Acknowledgments

I should like to thank a number of people whose advice and support have been of great help to me in the preparation of this book. Contacting so many authors and potential authors was not easy. Kent and Nancy Rasmussen in Los Angeles gave me hospitality at an early stage. In Aberdeen Roy Bridges and Jeffrey Stone were constant critics and friends. Many others could be named, but behind everything else lie the continuing work and wisdom of Graham Speake, who with his wife Jennifer also gave hospitality.   J.M.

PART ONE
THE PHYSICAL BACKGROUND

THE GEOGRAPHY OF AFRICA

The continent of Africa is exceeded in area by Asia alone. With an area of 30 420 000 square kilometers, it is three times the size of Europe and four times the size of the USA. Moreover, it is a remarkably compact continent. The islands have a total area of only some 624 000 square kilometers and 95 per cent of that figure is accounted for by the fourth largest island in the world, Madagascar. The mainland is regular in outline, with no great gulfs or other deep embayments, so that the coastline is shorter in total length than that of any other continent.

Africa lies astride the equator; three-quarters of its surface area is within the tropics. Despite the fact that the total latitudinal extent of over 61° is approximately bisected by the equator, some two-thirds of the area of Africa lies in the northern hemisphere. The maximum longitudinal extent, from Senegal to Somalia, is some 69°. At the equator, the longitudinal distance between coasts is less than half that figure, and the distance diminishes with distance southward. The continent is all but an island. The boundary between Africa and Asia lies not at the northwest part of the isthmus north of the Gulf of Suez, but stretches the 240 kilometers or so between the Gulf of Aqaba and the Mediterranean Sea.

The shape of the African continent is the product of its evolution through geological time. About 180 million years ago, proto-Africa lay at the heart of a super-continent consisting of several of the great mobile plates that comprise the earth's crust. During the Cretaceous period the plates began to drift apart, leaving the African plate isolated, except for a few offshore remnants of continental rock such as Madagascar. With the passage of time, the African plate was increasingly isolated, except in the northwest where collision with the Eurasian plate gave rise to great earth movements and to mountain ranges. Elsewhere, isolation produced its own stresses in the African plate. Rift systems, whose origin may date to the breakup of the super-continent, remained active; extensive basins were the product of gentle upwarping of the intervening surfaces. In addition, the attritional action of wind and water, which had shaped the surface of the super-continent, continued to act on its isolated remnant, redistributing material and creating stress by sheer weight of sediments or by relieving the underlying strata. The relative altitude of land and sea has changed on an unknown number of occasions. A range of interconnected processes are therefore responsible for the primary component of African landscapes, the extensive plateau surfaces. These are sometimes separately discernible at different altitudes, often merging, but higher in the south and east and lower in the north and west.

Gradual change of altitude over distance characterizes much of Africa. Where depression and upwarping of the surface are relatively recent, then great shallow basins remain discernible at the continental scale. These are not necessarily totally enclosed basins nor are they features that can be demarcated by lines on maps. At their margins they merge imperceptibly into the adjacent higher plateau surfaces, but by means of contours and drainage lines, they can easily be identified. Lake Chad and the Okavango Swamp are local inland drainage basins within two of the great shallow depressions that cover much of the surface of Africa.

Movement in the earth's crust also gives rise to more dramatic relief features. Where crustal movements, either vertical or horizontal, have induced tension exceeding the strength of the subsurface strata, then faults occur, either singly or in pairs or clusters. These sometimes cause slopes whose steepness is in sharp contrast to the adjacent plateau surfaces and the slopes occur as individual escarpments or as great trenches or uplifted blocks of varying width. One of the earth's longest rift systems passes from the Red Sea, through the Ethiopian highlands and through East Africa where it bifurcates before reappearing in southern Africa. The Great Rift Valley is best known in East Africa, where its location is emphasized by the alignment of some of the East African lakes, but it is equally well seen in the Luangwa valley of Zambia or in the Ethiopian highlands east of Addis Ababa.

Steep slopes are not solely the product of faulting. At quite different periods of geological time, violent crustal movements on the continent's periphery, associated with the drift of the African tectonic plate, have led to folding and uplift of strata in the Cape ranges and the Atlas Mountains. Subsequent

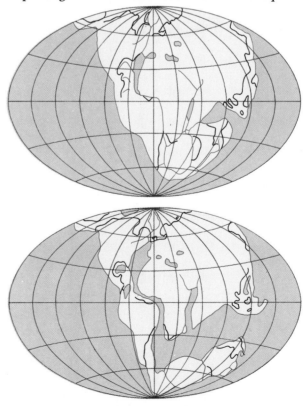

Right: The political and physical geography of Africa Broad plateau surfaces are the most extensive relief feature of the African continent, occurring at a relatively high altitude in the south and east but at a much lower altitude in the north and west. Changes in altitude tend to be either extremely abrupt or very gradual. The almost imperceptible inclines of the five great basins give rise to the major drainage alignments.

Left In the early Mesozoic era (*above*) the African continental plate lay at the center of the proto-continent named Pangaea (all land). During the Cretaceous era (*below*) South America and Africa began to drift apart and the Indian Ocean opened up between the African and Asian land masses. Fossils provide evidence of former land connections between the southern continents. For example, a fossil plant (*Glossopteris*) occurs in late Paleozoic deposits in South America, South Africa, Madagascar, India and Australia.

erosion has sharpened the relief. The stability of the African continent was tested in what were major phases of mountain building in Eurasia and America, when little lasting impact was made on the interior of the continent. The Benue trough, with its dissected scarp topography, is one of the few examples of disruption of the inexorable leveling of the interior.

Landforms characteristic of erosion by water and wind also disrupt the extensive flat surfaces, although it is their intermittent occurrence as much as their outward forms that makes them so noticeable. One such form is the tabular landform epitomized in Table Mountain near Cape Town and occurring across southern Africa in association with hardened sediments and lavas. Further types include the dome-shaped inselbergs with widespread occurrences across Africa, also steep-sided ridges associated with veins of especially resistant rock, well seen in Zimbabwe, and the dune forms and blow-outs of the sand deserts. Lavas and dolerites give rise to level surfaces and adjacent very steep slopes, for instance in Nigeria, Libya and in Africa south of the equator, where they underlie the Victoria Falls and its gorges. Perhaps the most striking single erosional feature is the Great Escarpment, an almost continuous feature around southern Africa, from Zimbabwe to Angola, cut through rocks of varying resistance and in places more than 2000 meters high, forming a formidable barrier to movement. Depositional features are as significant as eroded forms. These vary from the great spreads of ancient sandstones that underlie the Sahara and much of southern Africa, to unconsolidated sediments that are still being laid down in the great river basins, such as the Barotse Plain and the Kafue Flats of the Zambezi basin, and in the Kalahari. These features extend the nearly level surfaces produced elsewhere by erosion, accentuating already widespread planation.

One further process which has created some of Africa's best-known landscapes is volcanism. Volcanic forms include such well-known cones as Kilimanjaro and Mount Cameroon. Volcanism is often associated with the tensions and stresses of the rift system, which allow molten material or ash to penetrate the earth's crust and sometimes to reach the surface, as is still occurring, for example, in Zaïre, Cameroon and Kenya. Volcanic explosions in the past have left vast steep-sided depressions or calderas, such as Ngorongoro in Tanzania, or clusters of much smaller lake-filled depressions, as in southwest Uganda. The remnants of dikes, sills and ancient volcanic necks add to the array of volcanic forms which in parts diversify the flat surface of the continent.

The main drainage alignments of Africa are remarkable in that the great rivers appear to take the most indirect route to the sea. The upper Niger aims for the center of the Sahara before it eventually turns seaward. The upper Zambezi heads south towards the arid Kalahari before turning eastward to the Indian Ocean. The controlling factor is the great sequence of down-warped basins which draw excess surface water from their flanks towards the center before allowing an outlet to be explored. The marginal escarpments of the central plateaus mean that the lower courses of rivers are characterized by waterfalls and cataracts. The great natural lakes of Africa, like most of its physical attributes, are very unevenly distributed and are almost exclusive to the trenches and basins of the east.

Africa's coastline has been presented in a historical context as forbidding. In fact there is a diversity of coastal forms. One consistent feature is that indentations of any size or economic significance are few. Sand bars maintained by longshore drift and mangroves shield much of West Africa, as do coral reefs in East Africa. Heavy swell is continuous on many coasts facing great expanses of open ocean, and river mouths are marked by great sedimentary deltas rather than estuaries. Shingle is not a common tropical beach material and the extent of sand beaches from the Mediterranean to the extreme south of the continent far exceeds any conceivable tourist market.

Climate

The availability of water is a powerful determinant to man's activities in Africa, and African climatology is dominated by the study of rainfall. Average rainfall is a familiar concept, particularly in temperate climates, but in Africa the pattern of mean annual rainfall is a statistical abstraction that hides the most significant characteristics of the rainfall regime. Certainly, the map of mean annual rainfall locates the great deserts and the limited extent of areas with high annual rainfall totals. It also emphasizes north–south gradients in rainfall amounts along the southern margins of the Sahara, but elsewhere it obscures the marked zonal (east–west) alignment of the isohyets.

The really significant features of African rainfall regimes are to be seen by examining the sequence of monthly charts. Only then is it apparent that, in the depths of the northern hemisphere winter, almost the entire continent north of the equator, except the Mediterranean shoreline, is arid. Six months later, the situation is reversed, but between these two extremes, the zonal belt of rainfall appears to have marched from one hemisphere to the other, although this requires qualification. The underlying causes in the southern hemisphere atmosphere of January rainfall maxima from Mozambique to Angola have ceased to exist, and circumstances conducive to rainfall in July occur independently in the northern hemisphere from Ethiopia to Gambia. In the intervening periods, conditions giving rise to cloud formation in depth, and therefore the possibility of rainfall, occur erratically in the equatorial belt but with particular uncertainty in the east, thus giving characteristic variability to low-latitude rainfall in April and October.

The great deserts of Africa are not the products of purely African circumstances. They result from atmospheric processes on a global scale. The Sahara, including arid Somalia, is a part of an immense desert stretching from Morocco to Baluchistan. This is the result of subtropical subsidence of air which prevents cloud formation in depth and is a major feature of the general atmospheric circulation of the globe. The Namib Desert is a product of the same processes in mirror image in the southern hemisphere, aided by the local factor of a cold offshore current. The fact that southeast Africa is seasonally rather than permanently arid points to the fact that where the altitude of the surface is great enough to raise the land surface above the intensely persistent

Top In the eastern Transvaal, horizontally bedded rocks have been uplifted to heights in excess of 2000 meters and have then been deeply dissected to form the rugged landscape of the northern Drakensberg. The Blyde river, a tributary of the Olifants river, has cut a gorge 1000 meters deep to create scenery in spectacular contrast to the great expanse of almost level plateau surface to the west.

Above Most African deserts are flat and featureless expanses of gravel and sand but the Namib Desert of southwestern Angola and western Namibia has extensive occurrences of sand dunes. The dune forms are constantly changing and are the product of the direction and strength of the wind and the supply of sand.

high pressure of subtropical sea level conditions, then rain is possible at the time of year when atmospheric pressure is, in any case, not so high. This is confirmed in the northern hemisphere by the wetter Ethiopian highlands which are in a latitude otherwise associated with aridity.

Rainfall in Africa usually originates in one of several types of quite severe atmospheric disturbances. These include thunderstorms, but also assemblages of many individual thunderstorms in, for example, the cloud clusters now recognized through satellite observations as a major feature of the global circulation. In south central Africa, summer rain occurs in outbreaks of several days in duration with intervening clearer spells. Occasional tropical cyclones bring intense rainfall to southeast Africa. Elsewhere, atmospheric pressure conditions which encourage rainfall are brought about irregularly throughout the wetter season, so that an important characteristic of African rainfall is its intensity and short duration within the so-called wet seasons. This is clearly seen in the relative small number of rain days and the high thunderstorm incidence over much of the continent.

Temperature is less of a variable factor in African climates. In a compact continent, altitude is as important as latitude in understanding temperature regimes. Mean monthly maxima in excess of 32°C are found over most of Africa, with a tendency for an increase with distance from the sea. There is not a great range of variations in maximum temperature. Similarly, there is only a small range of minimum temperatures and indeed of annual temperature regimes. By contrast, much of the continent experiences diurnal temperature ranges in excess of 15°, so that the differences between night and day are more pronounced than between seasons.

Scarcity of recording stations means that atmospheric observations other than rainfall and temperature are available only in a few local situations. It is, however, possible to consider factors such as sunshine and wind speed by use of observed distributions of vegetation, the plant being taken as a barometer not only of commonly recorded meteorological elements but also of those not readily available. This has the advantage of presenting climate as it really is, as an interrelated set of phenomena forming a single complex, rather than as individual elements, separated as an artificial device of convenience. The best-known scheme of this kind for the classification of climate into types is that of Köppen. This scheme applied to Africa provides a useful synopsis at the continental scale, if not for local areas. The system uses rainfall and temperature values to locate the limits of occurrence of certain groups of plants, which are themselves in part a reflection of all of the elements that comprise a climate. The resultant distribution demonstrates the extent of seasonality as a primary factor in African climates. Most of the continent beyond the deserts or semideserts (B category) experiences a pronounced dry season (w or s subcategory). The continuously watered parts of this continent (f subcategory) are confined to the extreme southeast and to a restricted equatorial occurrence in low Africa. The seasonal wet-and-dry regimes dominate Africa, an environmental fact of great economic significance.

The disastrous sahel drought in the 1970s means that Africa looms large in current concern about climatic change. The drought has been ascribed solely to environmental mismanagement by man because the years of low rainfall are within the bounds of expectation on the basis of existing statistics of sub-Saharan rainfall. However, major fluctuations in rainfall amounts from year to year, or over short periods of several years, are a feature of the climates of the arid margins. Although no long-term cyclic change is evidenced by recent droughts in the sahel, as well as in East and southern Africa, they highlight the fact that in the desert margins long-term averages have little meaning. Much more important is variation from the average, especially where the averages are in themselves so low as to make many agricultural practices marginal.

Soils

African soils are the consequence of four interacting factors. First, the form of the land determines whether an area experiences net loss or net accumulation of loose material, or whether it is an area of transference. Areas of overall removal have steep slopes where loose material is raw and the soils imperfectly developed. Accumulation occurs in valley bottoms, the centers of the great basins, and along coastal margins. In between, the character of the soil is in part controlled by the local rate of accumulation as opposed to removal, that is, the local nature of transference.

Climate is the second factor influencing soil development. Nonbiological reactions increase in speed in proportion to the increase in temperature while biological reactions are facilitated within limits by warmth. This is seen in Africa in the exceptional depth achieved by soil-forming processes and the extensive transformations that take place in the material, although both of these attributes are only achieved where rainwater is adequate.

The close correlation between the distribution of soil and vegetation is an indication of the importance of plant cover in soil formation. A plant cover regulates the supply and removal of loose material, adds organic matter throughout the soil, facilitates the movement of minerals and the subsequent creation of horizons within the soil and assists in the breakdown of solid particles through the production of acids and other compounds. The complexity of the interaction between soils and vegetation means that very different processes are initiated under such differing vegetative associations as rain forest or savanna.

The fourth factor is the nature of the parent material. In areas of overall removal, underlying basalt, for instance, will yield a very different spectrum of minerals from, say, schist or granite, though the mineral composition of any one rock type is far from constant. In areas of transference or accumulation the situation is greatly complicated by the likelihood of mixed origins, and in both of these areas soils are frequently residues of prolonged and active weathering and leaching of the minerals, much reducing the potential utility of the soil to man. With some notable exceptions in areas of volcanic ash and recent alluvia, African soils are poor in the minerals valuable in agriculture.

The single most extensive soil type is the raw

mineral soil of the deserts where biological activity is at a minimum. These cover some 28 per cent of the continent. A further 20 per cent of the continent is covered by soils that are weakly developed due to lack of either moisture, movement or, in situations of relatively rapid accumulation or removal, time. Such shallow soils cover large areas of southern, eastern and northern Africa. Almost as extensive are the ferrallitic soils which have suffered extensive leaching. These acid clay soils, extensive in wetter zones, frequently exhibit the tendency towards horizontal accumulation of certain oxides, which in its fully developed form is known as laterite. Between the mineral soils of the deserts and the ferrallitic soils lie the ferruginous soils, and the brown-red soils of the desert margins. Together they cover about the same area as the ferrallitic soils, but they are the soils of the seasonally wet and dry climatic regimes of Africa. Under short but intense periods of leaching, the movements of minerals vary according to their particular properties, producing a soil with a characteristic profile and often of low fertility. On the desert margins the increasing deficit in soil moisture is in part counteracted by and leads to the development of deep root systems which have the effect of distributing organic matter through the profile.

At the continental scale, there is clear correlation between vegetation and climate, particularly the seasonal distribution and amount of rainfall. Starting from parts of the continent with highest annual rainfall totals and very short dry seasons, there are tall rain forests characterized by great variety of species, grouped by height, but with a lower density than is sometimes suggested. Several subtypes of rain forest are recognized. As the length of the dry season increases on the rain forest margins, these give way to mosaics of woodland and grassland. Deciduous tree species replace the evergreens of the rain forest and canopies are characteristically lower and less dense. Variety is provided in the form of denser tree cover along watercourses but the moist woodland savanna, typified by the *miombo* woodland of East Africa, is extensive. On its drier margins, tussocky grasses are increasingly predominant and the forested margins of water courses are even more apparent. As the length of the dry season further increases, short grasses predominate and widely dispersed tree species capable of withstanding long dry periods, such as *acacia*, occur. On the desert margins, savanna gives way to desert steppe characterized by sparsely distributed succulents and species with deep root systems. True desert vegetation varies according to location. In the Sahara vast areas exhibit only very few shrubs or grasses, according to the nature of the underlying surface. In the western Namib Desert dew provides a water source to the benefit of the abundant succulents. The temperate margins of the continent, north and south of the desert, have their own characteristic vegetative associations, as do the upper slopes of mountains in tropical Africa. On Mount Kenya, for example, above the cultivation level, montane forest gives way to bamboo, heather, alpines and finally to lichens at the summit. The tree ferns and giant groundsel of the upper slopes of Ruwenzori are particularly spectacular.

The above generalizations are perhaps valid at the continental scale, but these zonations are now so disrupted on the ground that they are fast becoming conceptual rather than real. There has long been debate about the role of deliberate burning in producing the vegetative characteristics of much of seasonally wet and dry Africa. Fire is used to induce new growth of grass for cattle or to prepare for cultivation. Man has probably been a major influence on African vegetation for a very long time, but the substantial increase in the area under domesticated livestock with uniform grazing habits or under cultivation means that the vegetation over much of Africa is becoming as man-made as it is in Europe. To map vegetation on the ground is to map land use and, in areas of dense population, climax vegetation is not to be found. For example, in southern Nigeria, patches of secondary forest are almost the only visible reminder of formerly extensive rain forest.

The vegetation cover of Africa is therefore increasingly the product of human activity, primarily of agricultural systems. All systems may be categorized as either fallow or permanent, depending on whether or not land is allowed to lie fallow. Two common subtypes of fallow systems are shifting cultivation and bush fallow. The first is a long fallow system in which the farmer may not return to land he has cultivated, whereas bush fallow is a form of rotation within a finite area of land and may not involve the movement of the homestead. Permanent farming may be further subdivided into small- and large-scale systems. Small-scale systems include specialized horticulture, adjacent to urban areas, mixed livestock and land husbandry with the cattle aiding the maintenance of fertility of permanently utilized land, a mixture of bush fallow and permanent cultivation incorporating particular crop sequences and the application of refuse to aid maintenance of fertility in permanently cultivated areas, and commercial tree crop farming. Permanent large-scale systems include the long-standing plantation agriculture characterized by high yields from large areas by means of sophisticated technology and management, often expatriate in origin. A similar system has recently been introduced under state control in many African countries to meet rapidly increased demand for food from urban dwellers. Farm settlements with a degree of cooperative control and centralized decision-making are a third subtype of permanent large-scale farming.

A major determinant upon agricultural practices is the incidence of trypanosomiasis, that is the infection of many of the vertebrates of Africa, including man, by trypanosomes or parasites of the blood and sometimes of other tissues. The consequent disease takes a variety of forms, including sleeping sickness in man and nagana in cattle. Absence of cattle due to prevalence of the disease is a major control on the type of agriculture that can be practiced, since cattle are beasts of burden. The ecology of trypanosomes is extremely complex. More than 50 species of wild animals, together with some birds and reptiles, are known to host the parasites. Transmission from one animal to another may be carried out by any one of 34 species, subspecies and races of tsetse fly (*Glossina*) and the distribution of these vectors is the only clear determining factor on the incidence of the diseases.

Top Fishing festival at Argungu, northwest Nigeria. Every stream or pond is a potential source of fish for protein-deficient diets and communally organized netting and trapping in Africa are common, often by people who have traditionally established rights to particular waters. Some larger lakes and rivers have considerable commercial fisheries based on urban markets. However, in the seasonally wet and dry tropics, fishing may not be possible all the year around. It is particularly prone to disruption at times of high water.

Above The scenery of much of southern Africa is epitomized in the nearly level surfaces of the upper Zambezi basin, which is in part inundated seasonally by the Zambezi river. However, at the Victoria Falls, the character of the river changes. The river is eroding intersecting fractures in successive horizontal beds of basalt and plunges into the Batoka gorge, spanned by the combined road and rail bridge linking Zambia to Zimbabwe. The gorge tightly confines the river to a narrow course for some 100 kilometers before opening out into the fault-controlled Zambezi valley now occupied by the man-made Lake Kariba. The falls are an escape route for the Zambezi river from the great down-warped inland basin of southern Africa, which successfully retains the drainage of much of southern Angola in the Okavango Swamps of northeast Botswana.

Game parks and fisheries

While some wild animals do suffer from trypanosomiasis and deaths occur in endemic areas, survivors probably acquire a natural immunity. The fact that wild animals are able to maintain their populations in infected areas has to some degree shielded them from competition by man. It is in these areas not usually coveted for agriculture that many of the game conservation projects were originally established. The other pronounced feature of the parks of Africa is their preponderance in the seasonal wet and dry climates of Africa. The open savannas are the home of most of the spectacular fauna of Africa. Almost every African country has designated one or more national parks. These represent a significant part of the total land use, but outright protection is no longer the prime objective. Increasingly, national parks are considered to be a special kind of land utilization, affording not only tourist and recreational facilities, but also acting as sources of meat to be culled on a sustained yield basis. They are also locations for other controlled usages, such as timber extraction, afforestation, pastoralism and fishing. In some parks illegal hunting for meat, ivory and skins has severely reduced the large fauna although there are also instances of population explosions in the protected environments of the parks, beyond the carrying capacity of the park area.

While the sea fisheries of West Africa, Angola, Namibia and South Africa have attracted increasing international attention, the freshwater fisheries of Africa are valuable sources of protein for a great many people. The great lakes and swamps of Africa, including man-made lakes such as Kariba, in most cases have fisheries, often operated by a great many small producers and served by many private vehicle owners who transport the fish to urban markets. The great rivers have commercial fisheries, where adequate transport is accessible to take the fresh or dried fish to market. But elsewhere in rural Africa, almost any stream or pond is a potential source of fish to supplement starch-based diets.

Population

The population distribution of Africa is the product of economic, social and political factors, variously operating in the past as well as at present, but always within the constraints and conducive features of the diverse physical environment. The climatic factor undeniably explains the extremely low population densities in the great Sahara and Namib/Kalahari deserts of Africa, and, to a lesser extent, in the Horn of Africa. Mountain ranges such as the Drakensberg, Ruwenzori and the Atlas also occasion low population densities. On the other hand, the lower slopes of Kilimanjaro and Mount Cameroon provide conditions attracting high densities. In other areas population densities are extremely variable. High densities may change to low densities quite suddenly, as they do in parts of Nigeria or Kenya, and often more abruptly than can be explained by any corresponding physical environmental changes. In such circumstances the past is probably the clue to the present.

The quality of census data in Africa varies greatly from country to country. Costs of enumeration, unskilled enumerators, illiteracy, census evasion and the impermanence of people's homes are among the problems of taking a census in Africa. International comparison is therefore difficult. Nevertheless, there is an extraordinary diversity of population totals and densities in Africa. On the mainland densities range from 1 per square kilometer to more than 150. Totals range from not many more than 50000 people to more than 60 million, though a great many countries have fewer than 10 million. There is no typical population size in African countries and high density does not imply pressure upon resources any more than low density implies an absence of population pressure.

Mineral resources and energy

The diverse but unequally distributed mineral resources of Africa are a product of its geological history. Underlying almost the entire continent and outcropping over about half of its surface area is the complex basement group of rocks over 500 million years old. These Precambrian rocks vary greatly in type, but the metamorphic rocks of the upper Precambrian contain many valuable minerals such as copper, chrome and gold. Four main series of younger sedimentary rocks rest upon the basement. The oldest are Paleozoic and occur extensively in North Africa and the Cape ranges, but are not heavily mineralized. The Karoo series of Carboniferous and later date is extensive and largely undeformed in southern Africa, and includes enormous reserves of coal. In the Mesozoic era, continental and marine sediments were deposited widely in northern Africa and have been found to contain not only valuable mineral and oil deposits, but also water-bearing strata. Tertiary and Quaternary strata are found in the great basins and along coasts. They contain the oil deposits of West Africa.

Africa's mineral resources are exceeded only by those of North America, and what the North American continent lacks, Africa can provide. In base metals Africa's resources are unbalanced; copper resources far exceed those of lead, zinc or tin. In light metals the position is similar, with high-grade bauxite reserves far in excess of magnesite or titanium. Proven resources of strategic metals are not always readily divulged, but substantial reserves of uranium, lithium, columbium and tantalum are known. Data on precious minerals are also not always available, but the continent's gold and platinum reserves are renowned, as are the reserves of gem and industrial diamonds. Many semiprecious stones and abrasives are known in significant quantities. Reserves of industrial metals such as mercury, sulfur, antimony and arsenic are small, but there are large known reserves of minerals used in agriculture, such as phosphate, potash and salt. There are abundant supplies of the raw materials of the cement industry and also of other building materials such as gypsum, asbestos and vermiculite. Overall, the continent is well endowed, but the resource bases of individual nations vary from great extent and diversity to almost total paucity. Known reserves of iron ore have increased recently, but where an energy source is available production of iron and steel may gradually assume a more widespread distribution. The potential for growth in the steel industry is emphasized by the very large proportion of world reserves of other steel industry metals such as ferrochromium, manganese, cobalt and vanadium.

Africa has a number of extensive coal deposits. Seams are often thick and undisturbed by comparison with Europe but quality is often low. In the past, immediate access was often not available and large resources remained uneconomic. The quickening pace of development, including the utilization of available resources, has increased the number of mines in operation. The extreme imbalance in the distribution of coal reserves, which are largely confined to southern Africa, is mirrored by the distribution of oil and natural gas, located in the coastal states of North and West Africa. Petroleum is even more valuable than coal to a developing country and hence the major discoveries since 1956 have been particularly opportune. Once a field has been brought into production, a refinery is an attractive proposition to reduce foreign exchange expenditure, despite small local markets for refined products. Even countries without their own oil reserves have built refineries to process imported crude oil in order to reduce the cost of the finished product. The result is that some refineries operate at less than their optimum economic level.

The great river systems of Africa are developed in shallow basins in the extensive plateau surfaces so that the run-off from vast catchment areas, channeled into single great streams, descends to sea level in short distances by means of falls and rapids. This provides enormous potential for the generation of power, a potential which has already been in part tapped in such spectacular schemes as Kariba, Aswan, Kainji, Akosombo, Cabora Bassa and the Orange River scheme. In a continent with approximately 10 per cent of the world's population, it has been estimated that the potential for hydroelectric power generation is more than a third of the global potential. In relation to the size of its population, the continent has slightly more than its share of coal and oil reserves and substantially more of its share of natural gas reserves; yet annual per capita energy consumption is substantially lower than any other continent. The development potential is therefore great. Consumption of energy varies greatly from country to country. South Africa is by far the greatest consumer of energy; elsewhere the countries with high rates of energy consumption tend to be those with large extraction industries such as Libya, Gabon, Zambia and Zimbabwe.

Transportation and communications

The transportation network of Africa is more rudimentary and less integrated than in any other continent. Since an efficient transportation system is a prerequisite, if not a catalyst, for economic development, Africa's transportation map is changing more rapidly than elsewhere. In particular, the network of railroads is increasing. There are, however, five different gauges of track in operation, even after the abandonment of some very small gauges; hence problems of interrupted flow remain even after separate systems are linked. Also, existing lines were sometimes constructed to meet needs that no longer exist, such as an exhausted mineral deposit, so that there are problems of wrong location as well as inadequate density. The rate at which further lines will be constructed depends on the rate of development of processing industries which reduce the need for long-distance haulage of bulky and heavy raw materials.

Inland waters are relatively insignificant in Africa's transportation network. Distances are too great for canal construction and the large rivers are frequently unsuitable for navigation because of rapids, large seasonal variation in flow and impeded mouths, so that they are used as transportation arteries only locally. The East African lakes have regular services operating over distances similar to the limited riverine transportation. The great rivers are impediments, particularly to road transportation, which must use time-consuming ferries in the absence of costly bridges (costly either because of the width of the rivers or the low density of the traffic).

In a continent where distances are great and economic activity concentrated, air transportation would seem to have great potential. However, the products of Africa are frequently bulky and would-be travelers live at income levels at which saving of time is less important than savings in cost. Nevertheless, a proliferation of internal airlinks and a great increase in the numbers of airports of international standards have come about due to the formation of national airlines. Internal flights are often by small passenger craft, and the transcontinental components of national airline fleets are often very small and maintained on a contract basis by Western airlines.

Increasing international air traffic has not posed any significant threat to the traditional surface routing of trade through the major seaports of Africa. Sophisticated port facilities are recognized as imperative even to severely undeveloped economies, since the cost of delay in handling both imports and exports is high. Transshipment by boats standing off shore is no longer acceptable, and a modern African port must provide deepwater berthing for rapid handling of general cargo, in part containerized, and it may also have to provide specialized terminals for the handling of specific commodities such as petroleum, phosphate, iron ore and timber. Occasionally, such commodities are moved to and from the port by pipeline or conveyor, adding a new component to the transportation network.

Road transportation is the major component of the network because of flexibility. Both vehicles and services can be readily adapted to local needs, reaching areas inaccessible by any other means. Cost of road construction and maintenance is high. Long distances and low traffic densities make the high costs of bridges, culverts, drains and hard surfacing uneconomic, particularly in high-rainfall areas. Tarred routes have been disparately constructed with national needs in mind, usually the main arteries connecting the capital to regional centers, but international roads are often of a lower standard. International programs of upgrading are under way, including the Trans-Sahara and Trans-Africa (east–west) highways.

International comparison of road vehicles in use is a reflection of relative personal prosperity and economic activity. A car is an economic and social asset and road haulage is so important that many state road transportation corporations have been formed. South Africa and the North African countries are high on the list. In this respect, as in so many others, the distribution of material well-being across the continent is very uneven. J.C.S.

Geology and (inset) rift systems and volcanoes
The ancient Precambrian basement complex of extremely resistant rocks underlies much of the continent and outcrops extensively. It is widely overlain by Tertiary or even more recent sediments, although the earlier sedimentary strata of the Karoo system are widespread in southern Africa, and North Africa has its own pre-Tertiary sedimentary series. Chronological gaps in the form of unconformities are frequent in such an ancient landmass.

The rift valleys of East Africa form the largest rift valley system in the world. It has evolved over millions of years, resulting in many different valley forms including single faults, stepped faults and secondary faulting. It has been partly infilled by great flat spreads of volcanic rocks but the many volcanic cones in East Africa are also associated with the rift system. By contrast, the great basins are scarcely discernible to the observer on the ground but their vast expanse implies significant relief amplitude.

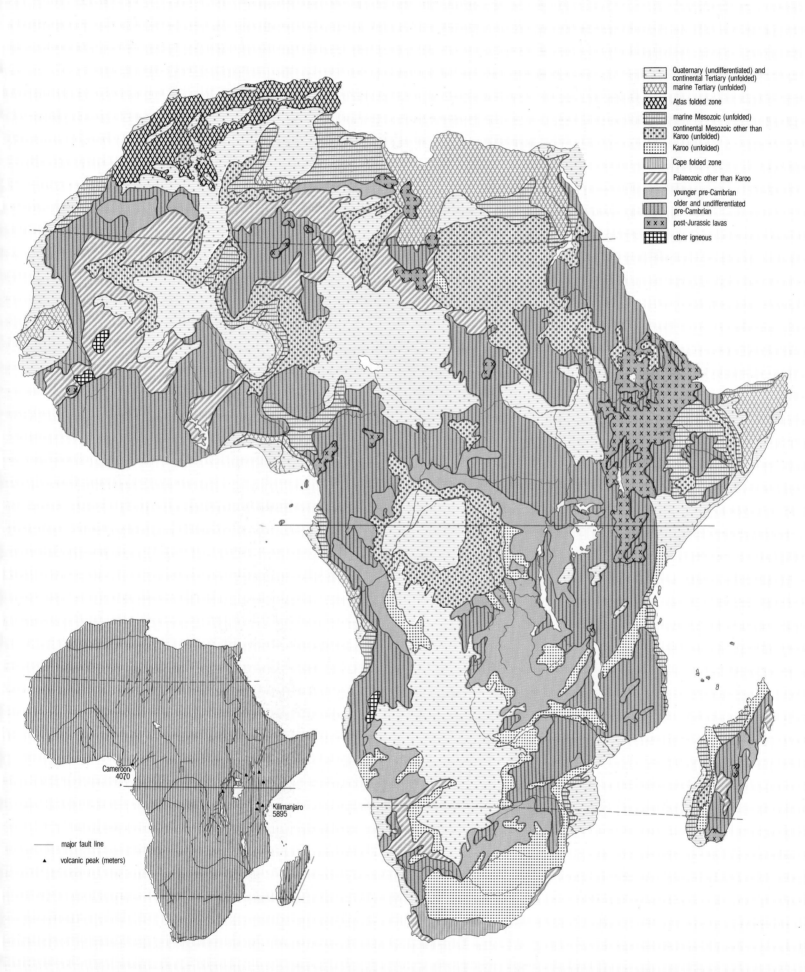

Quaternary (undifferentiated) and
continental Tertiary (unfolded)

marine Tertiary (unfolded)

Atlas folded zone

marine Mesozoic (unfolded)

continental Mesozoic other than
Karoo (unfolded)

Karoo (unfolded)

Cape folded zone

Palaeozoic other than Karoo

younger pre-Cambrian

older and undifferentiated
pre-Cambrian

post-Jurassic lavas

other igneous

Cameroon
4070

Kilimanjaro
5895

major fault line

volcanic peak (meters)

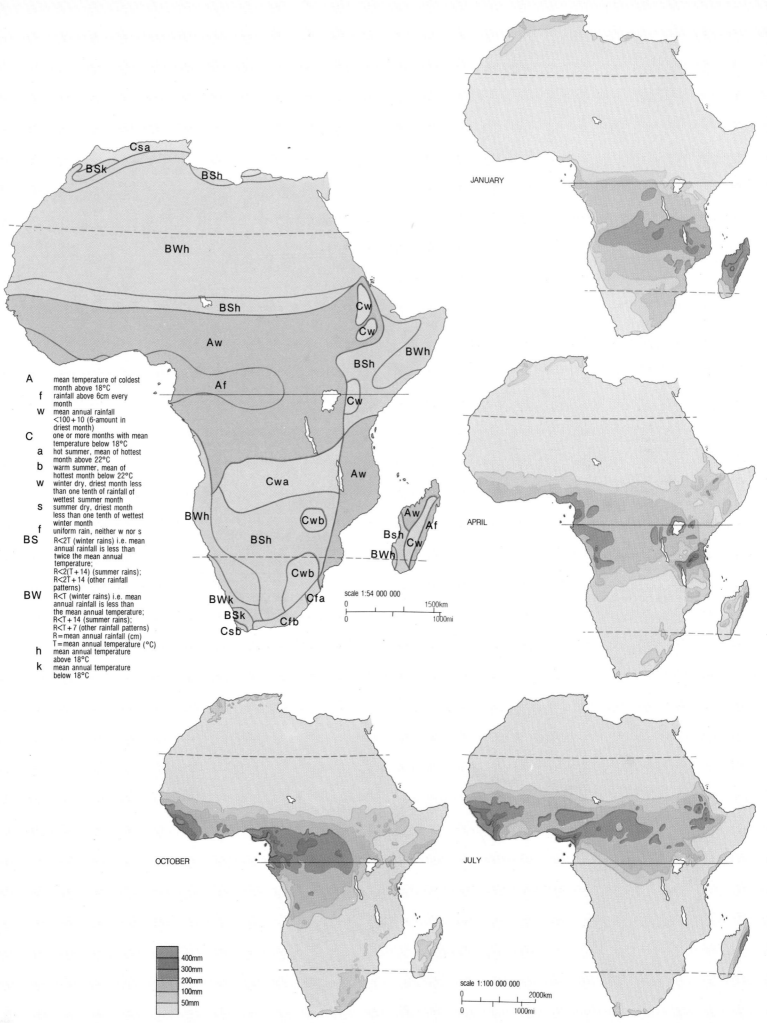

Csa
BSk
BSh
BWh
BSh
Cw
Cw
Aw
BWh
BSh
Af
Cw
A   mean temperature of coldest
     month above 18°C
f   rainfall above 6cm every
     month
w   mean annual rainfall
     <100 + 10 (6-amount in
     driest month)
C   one or more months with mean
     temperature below 18°C
a   hot summer, mean of hottest
     month above 22°C
b   warm summer, mean of
     hottest month below 22°C
w   winter dry, driest month less
     than one tenth of rainfall of
     wettest summer month
s   summer dry, driest month
     less than one tenth of wettest
     winter month
f   uniform rain, neither w nor s
BS   R<2T (winter rains) i.e. mean
     annual rainfall is less than
     twice the mean annual
     temperature;
     R<2(T + 14) (summer rains);
     R<2T + 14 (other rainfall
     patterns)
BW   R<T (winter rains) i.e. mean
     annual rainfall is less than
     the mean annual
     temperature;
     R<T + 14 (summer rains);
     R<T + 7 (other rainfall patterns)
     R=mean annual rainfall (cm)
     T=mean annual temperature (°C)
h   mean annual temperature
     above 18°C
k   mean annual temperature
     below 18°C

Cwa
Aw
BWh
Cwb
Aw
Af
Bsh
Cw
BWh
BSh
Cwb
Cfa
BWk
BSk
Cfb
Csb

scale 1:54 000 000
0   1500km
0   1000mi

JANUARY

APRIL

OCTOBER

JULY

400mm
300mm
200mm
100mm
50mm

scale 1:100 000 000
0   2000km
0   1000mi

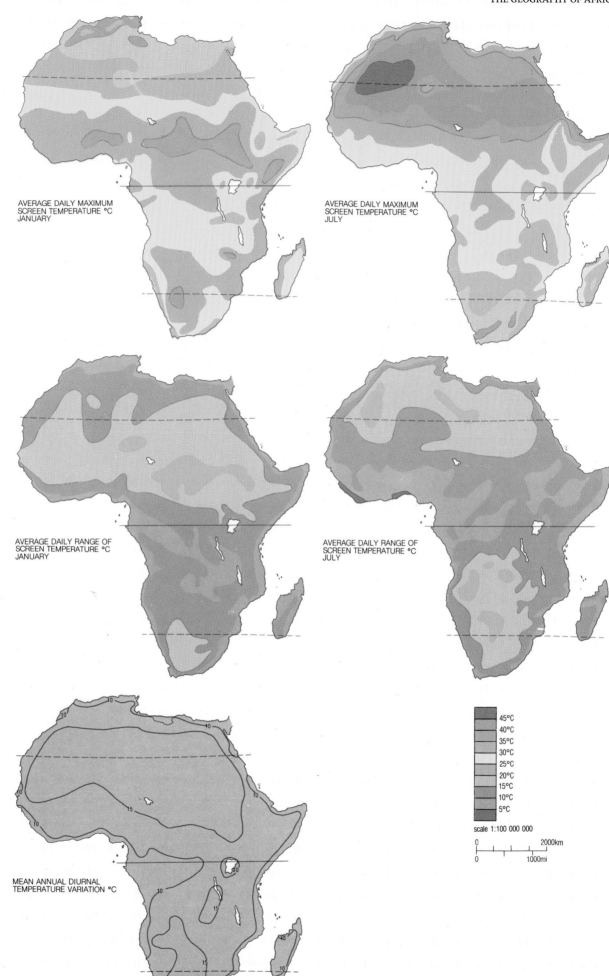

Far left: Climatic types (after Köppen)
Apart from the extensive hot deserts (BW), African climates are predominantly seasonally wet and dry (BS, Aw, Cw, Cs). The extent of rain forest climatic regimes (Af) is much more confined than is frequently supposed. Temperate regimes with rain all year (Cf) are even more restricted.

Left: Rainfall: monthly mean for January, April, July and October
The marked seasonality of African rainfall regimes is apparent in the almost total aridity of the continent north of the equator (except for the Mediterranean littoral) in January, by comparison with the absence of rainfall south of the equator (except at the Cape) in July. The midseason months of April and October are times of particularly great uncertainty in occurrence and amount of rainfall.

Right: Temperature: average daily maximum, January and July; average daily range, January and July; mean annual diurnal temperature variation
The principal characteristic of African temperature regimes is high diurnal range, so much so that mean daily temperature (usually obtained from the mean of the maximum and minimum temperatures) has very little significance. Temperature maxima vary markedly from one half of the year to the next in all but the lowest latitudes, so that most of Africa has a winter. Also the average daily range tends to be more marked in winter, but the compact shape of the continent and the lack of maritime influence on temperatures are stressed by the sharp increase in daily range away from coasts.

AVERAGE DAILY MAXIMUM
SCREEN TEMPERATURE °C
JANUARY

AVERAGE DAILY MAXIMUM
SCREEN TEMPERATURE °C
JULY

AVERAGE DAILY RANGE OF
SCREEN TEMPERATURE °C
JANUARY

AVERAGE DAILY RANGE OF
SCREEN TEMPERATURE °C
JULY

MEAN ANNUAL DIURNAL
TEMPERATURE VARIATION °C

45°C
40°C
35°C
30°C
25°C
20°C
15°C
10°C
5°C

scale 1:100 000 000

0   2000km

0   1000mi

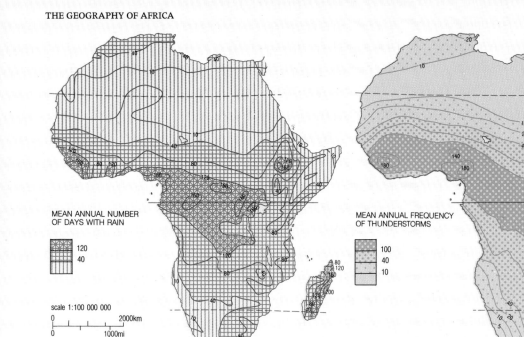

MEAN ANNUAL NUMBER
OF DAYS WITH RAIN

120
40

scale 1:100 000 000

0   2000km

0   1000mi

MEAN ANNUAL FREQUENCY
OF THUNDERSTORMS

100
40
10

Above: Annual rain days
The number of occurrences of
rainfall in areas well known for
their comparative aridity is a
reminder that total absence of
rainfall is confined to the
northeastern Sahara. On the
other hand, for almost all of the
continent, the majority of days in
the year are rainless.

**Above right: Thunderstorm
frequency**
Areas of high thunderstorm
frequency during seasons of
rainfall incidence have an
additional element of uncertainty
in their rainfall regimes, in that
thunderstorms may sometimes be
very localized in occurrence.
Marked variations in annual
totals may therefore be
experienced over very short
distances, particularly in
strongly seasonal rainfall
regimes.

**Right: National parks and
tsetse fly**
National parks are a major
component of land use of Africa,
although they are most
widespread in the areas with
seasonal wet and dry climates
where the more spectacular
fauna occur in the greatest
concentrations. In some
countries, as much as a third of
the total land area is designated
as some form of conservation
area, although the nature and
purpose of legislative protection
vary greatly and are increasingly
ineffective.
    Tsetse fly requires a very
precise set of environmental
circumstances for its survival so
that within the limits of its
distribution many local areas
may be free of the fly. However,
animals or man act as carriers to
extend the limits of occurrence,
and chemical or other control
methods are costly, so that where
environmental conditions are
appropriate there is a constant
threat of encroachment.

principal tsetse fly areas
(Glossina fusca, Glossina morsitans)

limit of Glossina palpalis (carrier of
Trypanosoma brucei, causative agent
of African sleeping sickness)

principal national parks

scale 1:40 500 000

0   1500km

0   1000mi

raw mineral soils

weakly developed soils

vertisols

sols lessivés

brown and reddish-brown soils of
arid and semi-arid regions

tropical brown soils

red and brown Mediterranean soils

ferruginous tropical soils

ferrisols

ferrallitic soils

halomorphic soils

hydromorphic soils

Soils
There is a discernible
relationship between the
distribution of soil types and
climatic conditions, but the
complexity of the soil map points
to the relevance of a range of
pedogenic factors, including the
fact that some of Africa's soils are
very old and were partly formed
in climatic conditions which no
longer prevail.

Scale 1:25 000 000

0   1500km

0   1000mi

21

Population and (inset) rate of change

Beyond the deserts of Africa, rural population densities are extremely variable, reflecting not only environmental and current economic conditions but clearly showing the impact of historical movements of people. High concentrations may occur in and around large towns as a result of recent migration, but they also occur in some of the more remote rural areas where they are frequently the product of precolonial events.

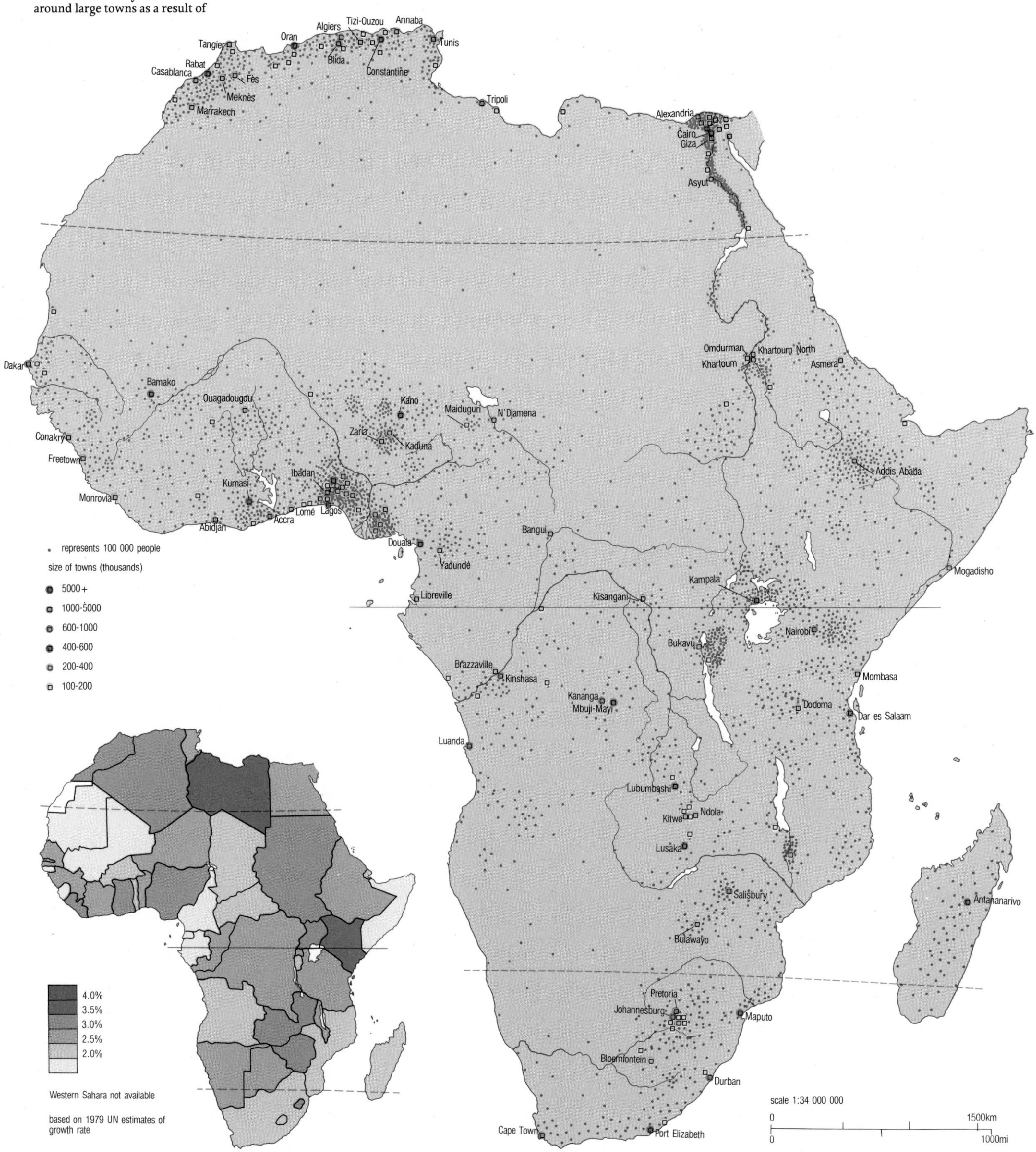

Tangier
Oran
Algiers
Tizi-Ouzou
Annaba
Tunis
Rabat
Blida
Casablanca
Fès
Constantine
Meknès
Marrakech
Tripoli
Alexandria
Cairo
Giza
Asyut

Dakar
Bamako
Omdurman
Khartoum North
Khartoum
Asmera
Ouagadougou
Kano
Maiduguri
N'Djamena
Zaria
Conakry
Kaduna
Freetown
Addis Ababa
Kumasi
Ibadan
Monrovia
Lomé
Lagos
Abidjan
Accra
Douala
Bangui
Yaoundé
Mogadisho
Libreville
Kisangani
Kampala
Brazzaville
Bukavu
Nairobi
Kinshasa
Mombasa
Kananga
Mbuji-Mayi
Dodoma
Luanda
Dar es Salaam
Lubumbashi
Kitwe
Ndola
Lusaka
Salisbury
Antananarivo
Bulawayo
Pretoria
Johannesburg
Maputo
Bloemfontein
Durban
Cape Town
Port Elizabeth

- represents 100 000 people

size of towns (thousands)

- 5000+
- 1000-5000
- 600-1000
- 400-600
- 200-400
- 100-200

4.0%
3.5%
3.0%
2.5%
2.0%

Western Sahara not available

based on 1979 UN estimates of growth rate

scale 1:34 000 000

0   1500km

0   1000mi

PART TWO
THE CULTURAL BACKGROUND

LANGUAGES AND PEOPLES

In precolonial times the peoples of Africa were divided into hundreds of different nationalities and ethnic groups, of greatly varying size and with great differences in culture and values. In some cases multi-ethnic states, such as Ethiopia in the late 19th century or the empire of Mali in the 14th century, encompassed many peoples under a single central political authority. In other cases, ethnicity was coterminous with the political unit, as in the 19th-century kingdom of the Zulu of southern Africa, while at the other extreme there were ethnic groups, such as the Chaga of Kilimanjaro, divided into many tiny independent political units, some no larger than a village. The European conquests lumped different peoples together in new ways in the colonial territories of the early 20th century, and the modern independent states of Africa, as inheritors of the colonial boundaries, today seek to blend their various peoples together into single nations. But it is safe to say that the older ethnic ties remain potent forces in African life down to the present.

Europeans have generally called African ethnic groups "tribes," but there is no need to continue to use such an ill-defined and in many cases prejudicial term. In the 19th century the Zulu nation-state, ruled by a king, was no more a tribe than England was under Henry VIII. The Igbo of Nigeria, 17 million strong, are called a tribe, while many a much smaller ethnic group in Europe has been dignified as a "nationality." Yet at the same time "tribe" could be applied to a tiny African village community of no more than a few hundred people.

The one consistently valid way of classifying African societies is by the languages they speak. People in Africa, as elsewhere, tend to identify themselves by their home language (and indeed this identification seems generally to coincide with what the Europeans thought of as "tribes"). Over 1000 languages are spoken in Africa. Some – like Mandinke, Igbo, Yoruba and Hausa in West Africa, Swahili in East Africa, Amharic and Oromo (erroneously called Galla) in the Horn of Africa, Zulu and Sotho in southern Africa and Arabic in northern Africa – have millions of speakers. Most languages have between a few hundred and a million speakers, while a few, like Kw'adza of Tanzania, are known by only a very few old people and are close to extinction.

With the exception of a few languages of relatively recent introduction to the continent, the home languages of Africa all belong to just four language families. The exceptions include: English, used by communities of settler descent in Liberia and southern Africa, and in a creole form, Krio, especially in Sierra Leone; Afrikaans, a form of Dutch used in southern Africa by people of European settler descent; Spanish, in the Canary Islands; Portuguese, by the Cape Verdians; several languages of Indian communities settled in East and South Africa, notably Urdu, Hindi and Gujarati;

and Malagasy, the language of Madagascar. Malagasy belongs to the Malayo–Polynesian family, all the others to Indo–European. Five Indo–European languages (English, French, Portuguese, Spanish and Italian) are used as second languages in various African countries, the first three being by far the most important.

The four recognized African language families, to which the rest of the continent's languages belong, are Niger–Kordofanian, Khoisan, Afroasiatic (Hamito–Semitic) and Nilo–Saharan. There remain disputes among scholars about the specific details of internal classification of each family, and also some legitimate doubts about the membership of a few particular languages in one or another of those families. A few scholars hold out against this scheme of language classification, established only during the 1950s. But the accumulation of new evidence over the subsequent two decades has progressively strengthened the case for the overall classification, so far as to put its general (though not specific) correctness beyond doubt.

Niger–Kordofanian languages fall into two primary divisions. The Kordofanian subfamily consists of about 20 languages spoken by relatively small communities in the Nuba mountains of the Republic of Sudan. In contrast, the Niger–Congo subfamily spreads across half of Africa and its several hundred languages are spoken by well over 150 million or more people. The ancient homeland of Niger–Congo was West Africa, where today a great diversity of Niger–Congo languages are spoken. At the far west along the Atlantic coast can be found peoples speaking such languages of the West Atlantic branch of Niger–Congo as Wolof in Senegal and Temne in Sierra Leone. The Fulani cattle-herders of the sahel zone of West Africa also speak a West Atlantic tongue. All across the vast interior watershed of the Niger river live speakers of languages of another branch, Mande, the best-known of these being the Mandinke or Mandingo. South of the great bend of the Niger, especially in Upper Volta, are located the poorly known languages of the Gur branch of Niger–Congo, while through southern Ghana, Togo, Benin and southern Nigeria are found the Kwa languages. The language of the Asante empire of the 18th and 19th centuries and those of the Yoruba and Igbo peoples of Nigeria all belong to the Kwa branch of the family. Still further east, in parts of eastern Nigeria and in Cameroon, southern Chad and the Central African Republic, are languages of the Adamawa–Ubangian branch. The most important language of this branch, Zande, is in fact spoken across several hundred kilometers stretching from the Central African Republic and Zaïre in the east into the far southwestern portions of the Republic of Sudan.

The most widespread and best-known subgroup of Niger–Congo is the Bantu languages, which cover most of the vast southern third of Africa, from the equatorial rain forest of Gabon and southern

Language families today (after Greenberg)
The enormous linguistic diversity of Africa poses peculiar problems for the cartographer. With very few exceptions (such as Arabic used as a lingua franca by non-Arab populations in North Africa) language and ethnic identity are the same. Most educated people are bilingual, particularly in areas where one of the colonial languages – usually French or English – still enjoys official status. The fragmented geographical distribution of some language families reflects historical upheavals and migrations which have complicated the picture presented by the language distribution of earlier periods (see maps on the next page).

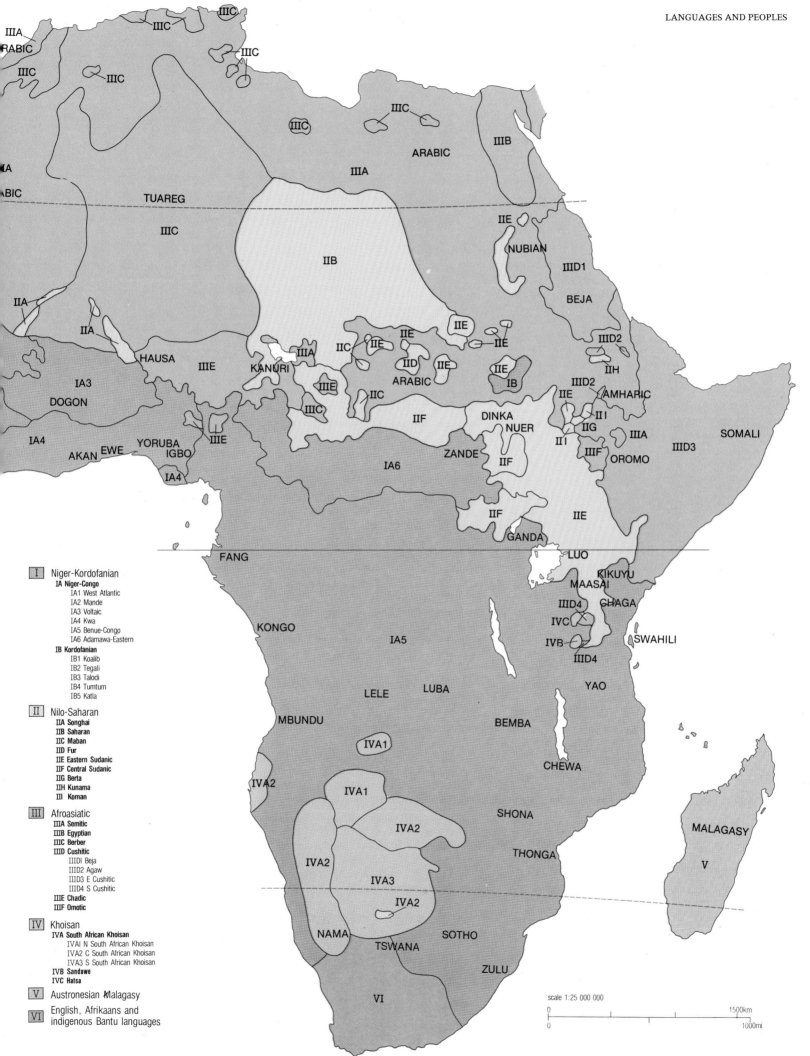

IIIA
RABIC

IIIC

IIIC

IIIC

IIIC

IIIC

IIIC

IIIC

IIIC

IIA
ABIC

TUAREG

ARABIC

IIIA

IIIB

IIIC

IIE

IIB

NUBIAN

IIID1

BEJA

IIA

IIA

HAUSA

IIIE

KANURI

IIIA

IIC

IIE

IIE

IIE

IIE

IIE

IIID2

IIH

IA3

DOGON

IIIE

IIIE

IIC

IID

IIE

ARABIC

IB

IIE

IIID2

AMHARIC

IA4

AKAN EWE

YORUBA
IGBO

IIIE

IIIC

IIF

DINKA
NUER

IIE

III

IIG

IIIA

SOMALI

IIID3

OROMO

IA4

ZANDE

IIF

IIIF

IA6

IIF

IIE

GANDA

LUO

KIKUYU

FANG

MAASAI

KONGO

IA5

IIID4

IVC

CHAGA

IVB

SWAHILI

IIID4

LELE

LUBA

YAO

MBUNDU

BEMBA

IVA1

CHEWA

IVA2

IVA1

SHONA

IVA2

MALAGASY

V

IVA2

THONGA

IVA2

IVA3

IVA2

NAMA

SOTHO

TSWANA

ZULU

VI

I	Niger-Kordofanian
	IA Niger-Congo
	IA1 West Atlantic
	IA2 Mande
	IA3 Voltaic
	IA4 Kwa
	IA5 Benue-Congo
	IA6 Adamawa-Eastern
	IB Kordofanian
	IB1 Koalib
	IB2 Tegali
	IB3 Talodi
	IB4 Tumtum
	IB5 Katla

II	Nilo-Saharan
	IIA Songhai
	IIB Saharan
	IIC Maban
	IID Fur
	IIE Eastern Sudanic
	IIF Central Sudanic
	IIG Berta
	IIH Kunama
	III Koman

III	Afroasiatic
	IIIA Semitic
	IIIB Egyptian
	IIIC Berber
	IIID Cushitic
	IIID1 Beja
	IIID2 Agaw
	IIID3 E Cushitic
	IIID4 S Cushitic
	IIIE Chadic
	IIIF Omotic

IV	Khoisan
	IVA South African Khoisan
	IVA1 N South African Khoisan
	IVA2 C South African Khoisan
	IVA3 S South African Khoisan
	IVB Sandawe
	IVC Hatsa

| V | Austronesian Malagasy |

| VI | English, Afrikaans and indigenous Bantu languages |

scale 1:25 000 000

0   1500km

0   1000mi

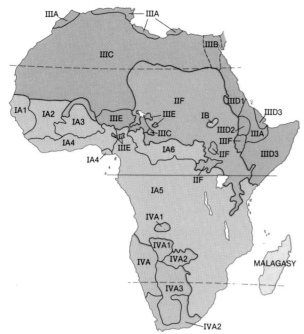

Far left: Language families c. 1000 AD (after Greenberg) In the north a major difference from the present is the wider extent of the Nilo–Saharan language family. Afroasiatic languages were confined to the shores of the Red Sea and the Horn of Africa in the east and had not penetrated far into the interior. In the south the distribution of Khoisan speakers was considerably more extensive.

Left: Language families c. 2500 BC (after Greenberg) These locations are only approximate. The comparatively confined range of the Niger–Congo languages is noticeable. Khoisan speakers are shown as ranging over the whole southern and eastern third of the continent. They were later to be pushed back by incoming Bantu speakers of the Niger–Congo language family.

Right The Nuba live in the hills of Kordofan, southwest of Khartoum, Sudan. They spoke an Eastern Sudanic language which is now being replaced by Arabic. The men are famous as wrestlers.

Cameroon to the highlands of Kenya and from the Ubangi river in the Central African Republic nearly to the Cape of Good Hope in South Africa. Swahili is a Bantu language originally spoken by people living in city-states along the Indian Ocean coasts of Africa between the 9th and 18th centuries. During the 19th century Swahili traders, opening up overland routes into the East African interior, established their tongue as the market language of a region reaching from the east coast as far west as eastern Zaïre. Now spoken by hundreds of thousands of people as a first language, Swahili has millions more who speak it as a second language, and has become the national tongue of several East African countries. Other well-known Bantu languages include Zulu; Kongo, the language of the important 15th- and 16th-century kingdom of Kongo; Lingala, a lingua franca of modern Zaïre; Shona, spoken by the majority of people in Zimbabwe; Bemba spoken by several million in Zambia; Ganda, the language of precolonial Buganda, the kingdom from which modern Uganda takes its name; and Gikuyu (Kikuyu) of the eastern Kenya highlands, the home language of the late president of Kenya, Jomo Kenyatta.

Despite their vast extent today, Bantu languages belong to just one subgroup of the Benue–Congo branch of Niger–Congo, the other languages of which are limited to parts of central and southeastern Nigeria. They only spread over the regions they now occupy during approximately the last 4000 years. The ancestral Bantu language, which we call proto-Bantu, was spoken somewhere probably in eastern Nigeria, that is, in West Africa, like the rest of Niger–Congo at that time. Then for reasons we do not yet understand, early Bantu communities began expanding into new territories, first through the equatorial rain forest belt and along its margins and then, between about 500 BC and 300 AD, eastward and southward into eastern and southern Africa. We do not know what languages preceded the Bantu in the equatorial forest and the adjoining savannas, but in eastern and southern Africa the earlier languages often belonged to the Khoisan family and, in parts of East Africa, to the Afroasiatic and Nilo–Saharan families.

Several millennia ago the Khoisan languages apparently predominated all across the lands from Somalia and Kenya clear to the Cape of Good Hope. Only relics remain today of that former distribution. Nama, a Khoikhoi language spoken by 50 000 or more people in Namibia, accounts for perhaps 40 per cent of the remaining Khoisan populations. In the 17th century there were still perhaps 200 000 speakers of the related Cape Khoikhoi (the so-called Hottentot) dialects between the Cape and the Transkei, but disease and expropriation of grazing land by European settlers destroyed the Khoikhoi economic base and with it the Cape Khoikhoi language and ethnic identity. A large number of Khoisan languages with usually a few hundred speakers each are scattered across the Kalahari region of southern Africa. These are spoken by the Bushmen or San, some of the few remaining hunter-gatherer societies of the continent. Two Khoisan languages also persist in East Africa, Sandawe with more than 25 000 speakers and Hatsa with a few hundred. The Hatsa are hunter-gatherers like the San, whereas the Sandawe are mixed agriculturists and the Khoikhoi, herders of sheep and cattle.

The Afroasiatic family, under the older name Hamito–Semitic, has long been recognized as a linguistic unit. Its best-known branch is Semitic, which includes among its languages Hebrew, Arabic, Aramaic (the language of Jesus) and ancient Akkadian. All are languages of Asia, except for Arabic which was spread across North Africa by the Muslim Arab conquests of the 7th and 8th centuries and has been spreading during the past 1000 years into parts of the eastern and central Sudan belt as well. One small subgroup of Semitic, the Ethiopic languages, is spoken entirely in Africa, but it was brought into Ethiopia and the Horn by south Arabian immigrants during the first millennium BC. Amharic, the national language of Ethiopia, belongs to the Ethiopic subgroup. The other five accepted branches of Afroasiatic are all purely African in their distributions, and it is now generally agreed by scholars of Africa that the Afroasiatic family had its distant origins in Africa, probably as much as 15 000 years ago, in or near Ethiopia.

The Chadic branch consists of about 100 languages spoken in Niger, northern Nigeria, Cameroon and Chad. The most important of these by far is Hausa, which with upwards of 23 million speakers is one of the world's most important languages.

The Berber branch is more widespread geographically but has far fewer speakers and languages than Chadic. Expanding about 2000 years ago all across North Africa and through large parts of the Sahara, the Berber languages persist today only in enclaves in the now Arabic-speaking North Africa and in the central Sahara. Most famous but not most numerous of the Berbers are the camel-owning Tuareg of the desert. The extinct Guanche language of the Canary Islands was probably related fairly closely to Berber.

The Egyptian branch of Afroasiatic, represented by ancient Egyptian and its descendant form Coptic, has now become wholly extinct, having gradually been replaced by Arabic between the 7th and 18th centuries. But the Cushitic and Omotic branches, on the other hand, each consist of large numbers of extant languages, some very important indeed. Cushitic languages extend in the north from Beja, along the Red Sea hills of the Republic of Sudan, southward more than 1500 kilometers to north central Tanzania, where the Southern Cushitic languages, are found. The most prominent of these is Iraqw. The two most important Cushitic languages today, both with several million speakers, are Somali, the national language of Somalia, and Oromo (Galla) of Ethiopia. Both belong to the Eastern sub-branch of Cushitic. The Agaw (Central Cushitic) languages of central and northern Ethiopia have largely been eclipsed by intrusive Ethiopic languages such as Amharic, even as the Southern Cushitic languages, once widespread in Kenya and Tanzania, have retreated before Bantu expansion. But the Eastern Cushitic peoples remain numerous and prominent in the affairs of Ethiopia and the Horn of Africa. The Omotic languages predominate through the southwestern portions of Ethiopia and apparently have done so for many millennia. The most notable Omotic tongue is Kafa, the language of an important kingdom from the 14th to the 19th centuries.

The languages of the fourth African family, Nilo–Saharan, are scattered across 6000 kilometers in an east–west direction, from Songhay at the bend of the Niger to the Koman languages of the western Ethiopian foothills and the Nilotic languages of East Africa. Songhay was the language of the huge Songhay empire of the late 15th and early 16th centuries, while Kanuri was the dominant tongue of the Kanem and Bornu kingdoms of Lake Chad between the 9th and 19th centuries. Important Nilo–Saharan languages in the eastern Sudan included Nile Nubian, the spoken and written language of the medieval Christian kingdoms of Nobatia and Alwa, and possibly the extinct language of ancient Meroë. A variety of Nilo–Saharan languages continue to be spoken in the Republic of Sudan and in Chad today. The best-known of these are Dinka, Shilluk and Nuer, all belonging to the Nilotic subgroup of the Eastern Sudanic branch of Nilo–Saharan. Other Nilotic peoples, the most famous of which are the Maasai, live in parts of Uganda, Kenya and Tanzania, into

which regions their ancestors spread during the past 2000 years. Along the southern edges of the Republic of Sudan, into portions of northeastern Zaïre and westward as far as central and southern Chad can be found peoples speaking languages of the Central Sudanic branch of Nilo–Saharan, among them the Mangbetu of Zaïre and the Bagirmi of Chad. Other major divisions of Nilo–Saharan are formed by the Maban languages of eastern Chad and the Fur language of Darfur in western Republic of Sudan.

The Nilo–Saharan languages apparently once extended across nearly the whole Sudan belt of Africa. In the west, between Lake Chad and the Songhay-speaking areas along the Niger, the once continuous Nilo–Saharan territories were broken by the intrusion several thousand years ago of the Chadic peoples. In the eastern and central Sudan, Bedouin Arabs have made deep inroads into formerly Nilo–Saharan speech areas during the past 1000 years.

Africa is the home of an equally diverse array of human cultures. Hardly anything can be said to be typically or universally African. Africa has patrilineal and matrilineal societies and even some in which descent is traced bilaterally. Its precolonial political systems ran the gamut from empires and sacral kingships, to age-based republics, to village democracies, and its social systems ranged from highly stratified slave-holding societies to completely classless communities. Yet there are a few sets of associated culture traits that recur very widely through the continent and what is interesting is that in a number of cases these traits seem characteristic of particular linguistic groupings of peoples.

Polyrhythmic music and dance, for which the principal accompaniment is the drum, is often thought of as quintessentially African. In fact it appears to be a feature of culture particularly associated with Niger–Congo peoples. It has spread so widely because Niger–Congo societies, especially the Bantu, have covered so much of the continent and it has come to have an enormous impact on modern Western popular music and dance because so many of the African slaves transported by Europeans were of Niger–Congo background. Outside of Niger–Congo-speaking regions in Africa other music styles, frequently based on stringed instruments, tend to prevail, along with quite different styles of dance.

Another widespread culture feature is religion based on veneration of ancestors. Again this belief system shows up among Niger–Congo speakers and those peoples influenced by them. In some cases, as among the Yoruba of Nigeria, the elevation of some royal or heroic ancestors to a special high status has added the dimension of a sort of polytheism to the basic ancestor religion. In the eastern Sudan, on the other hand, peoples such as the Nilotic Nuer and the Maasai attribute no particular role to the ancestors at all and instead focus religious observance on one God or Divinity, symbolically linked with the sky and rain. This religion seems to have spread at an early date to the adjoining Ethiopian regions, for it reappears among Omotic peoples, like the Kafa, and Cushites, like the Oromo. Still another pattern of belief occurs among some of the Omotic and Cushitic peoples of southern Ethiopia; there the focal rites of

African physical types
What do the peoples of Africa look like? Basically, people of three different physical types have lived in Africa for thousands of years. In the extreme north were brown-skinned people of similar stock to others living around the Mediterranean; in West and central Africa were people of the type we call Negroid – dark brown to black skin, tightly spiraled hair. Over much of the rest of Africa were the hunter-gatherers who have for long been known as Bushmen: smaller than the West African Negroes, and with yellowish skin, but with spiraled hair.

Over the centuries these different stocks have moved and mingled. There are certain physical types which may be thought of as typical of a given area, but there are no really abrupt divisions between one people and another. Broadly speaking, lighter people are found in the extreme north and the extreme south of Africa, and darker people in the hotter equatorial regions. In Africa may be found both the tallest people (on average) in the world – the Dinka of the southern Sudan – and the shortest – the pygmies of Zaïre. As well as the peoples of indigenous stock, there are also in Africa Arabs, whose ancestors have lived in Africa for many generations, Europeans, as in South Africa, and peoples of established mixed race, especially in the old Portuguese colonies and also in South Africa. Here we present a selection of portraits of African peoples.

Kabyle man, Algeria.

Coptic girl, Egypt.

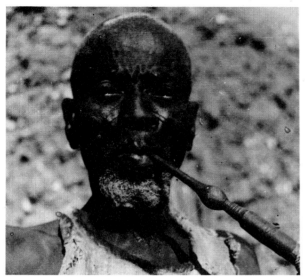

Bobo elder, Upper Volta.

Woman from Omdurman, Sudan.

Tutsi man, Rwanda.

Shilluk man, Sudan.

Turkana man, Kenya.

Karamoja woman, Uganda.

Baulé woman, Ivory Coast.

Mbuti pygmy, Zaïre.

San (Bushman) girl, Botswana.

Shangaan man, Mozambique.

Maasai girl, Tanzania.

Swazi man, Swaziland.

Alice Ndunda, a Kamba woman from Machakos District, east of Nairobi, Kenya, sits in the kitchen of her home with her small daughter.

the community were directed toward the god of the particular community. A fourth distinctive African religion turns up among Khoisan peoples, who saw the vicissitudes of life as reflecting a dualism in the supernatural realm between a good god and an evil one, or between a good god and a variety of harmful spirits.

If there is one nearly pan-African culture feature it is the circumcision of young people, especially as a sign of their graduation into adulthood. By no means universal, still it is found in one form or another in half or more of the societies of Africa and turns up in cultures as widely separated as those of the Bantu-speaking Xhosa of South Africa, the Igbo of West Africa and the Cushitic Iraqw of Tanzania. It is a very widespread feature of Niger–Congo cultures and is nearly universal among Afroasiatic peoples. It is probably because of its ancient Afroasiatic roots that the custom passed as a normative practice into the Jewish and Muslim religions. Circumcision is rarer among Nilo–Saharan speakers, except where they become Muslim, and is generally lacking in Khoisan cultures.

African peoples have also frequently been classified by physical appearance, that is, according to supposed racial types. It remains a popular approach in talking about distant peoples, both because of the 20th-century preoccupation with "race" and because, more legitimately, we all want to be able to visualize what the subjects of our interest "really" look like. It is indeed interesting, for example, that Africa contains some of both the shortest and the tallest people in the world. The pygmies of the equatorial rain forest, rarely reaching even 125 centimeters in height, appear to be distinctive in some other features than just stature, yet on the whole they fit within the broad range of African physical variation and today speak only the Bantu or Central Sudanic languages of their neighbors. In contrast, adult males among the Nuer and Dinka, Nilotes of the southern Republic of Sudan, average close to 180 centimeters in height, taller even than Americans, northwestern Euro-

peans and Polynesians. In other features of their outward appearance Africans also vary considerably across the span of the continent.

Classifications of people by physical appearance, however, turn out to be fraught with grave difficulties. The older textbooks on Africa speak of Negroid, Bushmanoid ("old yellow-skinned" or "yellow-brown-skinned") and Hamitic ("brown" or "Afro-Mediterranean") races, dividing the peoples of the continent up according to such characteristics as darkness of skin and width of nose, and even current books still use such terms. But modern physical anthropology has shown "race" in this sense to be a scientifically untenable concept. There are indeed variations in human appearance across Africa. But, leaving aside distinctively European settler populations, the variation tends to be gradual and cumulative, with the frequency of occurrence of one feature of human appearance increasing, another decreasing, as one moves progressively across the continent.

For instance, the frequency of occurrence of lighter skin tones tends to increase in Africa as one goes either northward or southward from the areas of most direct sunlight. There are undoubtedly parts of southern Africa where expansion of Bantu-speaking peoples from the equatorial regions has increased the rate of occurrence of quite dark skin, but that is not at all the same as saying, as many books on Africa do, that one "race" of people has supplanted another.

The frequency of broad noses, as another example, increases as one goes south and southwestward in Africa. But because again a gradual change in frequency of occurrence is involved, there is no basis for postulating, as earlier writers did, that the presence of narrow noses meant some sort of quasi-European or Arab-like people had once settled in a place. We may well wish to know what physical characteristics are common among this or that African people, but we will have to be specific in our description and do without the comfortable oversimplification of race.　　　C.E.

RELIGIONS

The diverse religious situation in today's Africa reflects a series of historical developments. The inhabitants of Africa north of the Sudan belt are almost all Muslims, with the exception of the minority Coptic Church in Egypt. Similarly, the Horn region and the East African coast as far south as northern Mozambique are Islamic, although in central Ethiopia there is again an ancient church which has strong links with the Egyptian Church. South and east of these almost totally Islamic zones there are regions where Muslims are a majority or a very strong minority. In western Nigeria and in Tanzania there are large Islamized rural populations, and in cities and large towns all over the continent Muslims are an important minority.

Outside the Muslim areas Africans observe traditional ethnic religious practices to a greater or lesser degree, with Christian minorities of varying sizes. Statistics are hard to come by and unreliable, but Christians are almost certainly in a majority in a number of areas, such as eastern Nigeria, Uganda, Lesotho and parts of South Africa. Some Christians may be first-generation converts, but others come from families which have been Christian for several generations, even as far back as the early 19th century.

But the religious situation is still very fluid. In one household, say in western Nigeria or the southern Sudan, may be found brothers who follow, respectively, traditional beliefs, Islam and Christianity. In very many cases the parents are still followers of traditional religion while all their children have become Christians or Muslims. Again, men and women move from one set of beliefs and practices to another and back again, as life crises occur which appear to be helped by one faith or another. There is a great deal of pragmatism in the African approach to religion.

As a generalization it may be said that Christianity and Islam are the religions of the cities, but there are many exceptions. Nevertheless, it is difficult for men and women to carry the traditional religion – so linked to a locality, to local shrines and the local community – to a distant place. One of the strengths of the two world religions has been the way in which they have been able to unite people of different cultural backgrounds. On the other hand, there are places where Christianity or Islam has become within a few generations the folk religion of a rural area.

It is only fair to say that in Africa, as in other parts of the world, are to be found an increasing number of men and women who reject all religious answers and would call themselves agnostics or atheists. Increasingly Western-educated young people fall into this category. But Africans have been, and still are, religious people and the atheists are fewer than one might expect.

Although it is true that Christianity and Islam are "traditional religions" for many Africans, it is convenient to reserve the term for the religious beliefs and practices of ethnic groups in Africa, for which no other convenient term exists. There may often be no word to translate "religion" in an African language, but religious beliefs are extremely important. Religion is linked to every part of life, not hived off as has become the case in the West, and every event in the life of an individual or a society is thought to have a supernatural cause. One acquires one's religion as a birthright; there is no conversion to it in Western terms, though there are ceremonies marking the life stages which are also connected with one's religious role in society. However, where men or women changed their social and political allegiance by accident of war, by purchase or by marriage, they would also change their religion.

It is difficult to discuss African religions historically. This is not to say that they have been totally static or that beliefs of one group may not have influenced and changed the beliefs of other groups. There is evidence to show that this has happened in some cases and it must have happened in many more. But without internal written documents, and with few shrines and temples built in long-lasting materials, it is difficult to record change over a long period. In most cases we can only discuss traditional religion from accounts written in the comparatively recent past.

Since each society differs in details of belief and practice, scholars have looked for a unifying concept that would enable them to speak of African religion rather than of African religions. For many 19th-century Europeans this concept was animism, the belief in myriad spirits inhabiting the material world. Ancestor worship was another such unifying concept. Scholars today prefer not to use either term, but both express some understanding of aspects of African belief. Some other terms – black magic, juju, fetish worship – are misleading and show no understanding of what they purport to describe.

A more recent student of African religion has written of the *force vitale* (living force) that links the animate and material worlds. This, like the rejected term animism, expresses the strong belief in a world where material objects possess, or are associated with, a living soul or spirit. This may be thought to be the spirit of a recently dead ancestor, or a nature spirit or the spirit of a long-dead ancestor who has become a deity. All have power to bring good or evil consequences to the living.

This belief, widely held across Africa, is associated with what has been called ancestor worship but which is better termed reverence for the living-dead. Those of the clan who have died are still close at hand and are remembered by name for two or three generations. Gifts are offered to them at the household shrine, which may contain their bones. A little beer is spilled for them when men are drinking together and the news of the clan is reported to them. When illnesses or misfortunes occur a

African religions

Islam is the religion of the north, including the northern section of many of the West African nations. It is the religion also of the northeast, especially Somalia and the northern Sudan. In Muslim areas neither Christianity nor traditional religions have much following. Over the rest of Africa Christians of different denominations are found in greater or smaller numbers alongside adherents of traditional practices. Roman Catholics are strongly represented everywhere, and especially in the former Belgian territories of Zaïre, Rwanda and Burundi. Anglicans are almost completely confined to the former British territories. In South Africa the Dutch Reformed Church is part of the Afrikaner tradition, and Presbyterians of reformed theology are strong in Malawi, Kenya and Ghana. Lutheran churches are strongest in the former German colonies; Methodists, Baptists and Congregationalists, Jehovah's Witnesses and Seventh Day Adventists are all to be found, following traditions taught by Western missionaries. The so-called independent churches are strongest in Ghana and Nigeria, Zaïre, Kenya, Zimbabwe and South Africa.

Right From the Kongo people in lower Zaïre come figures usually known as nail fetishes. Nails and scraps of cloth are stuck into the figure, as need arises, to deflect evil influences from the individual. A "medicine" for the same purpose may be kept in a receptacle within the figure.

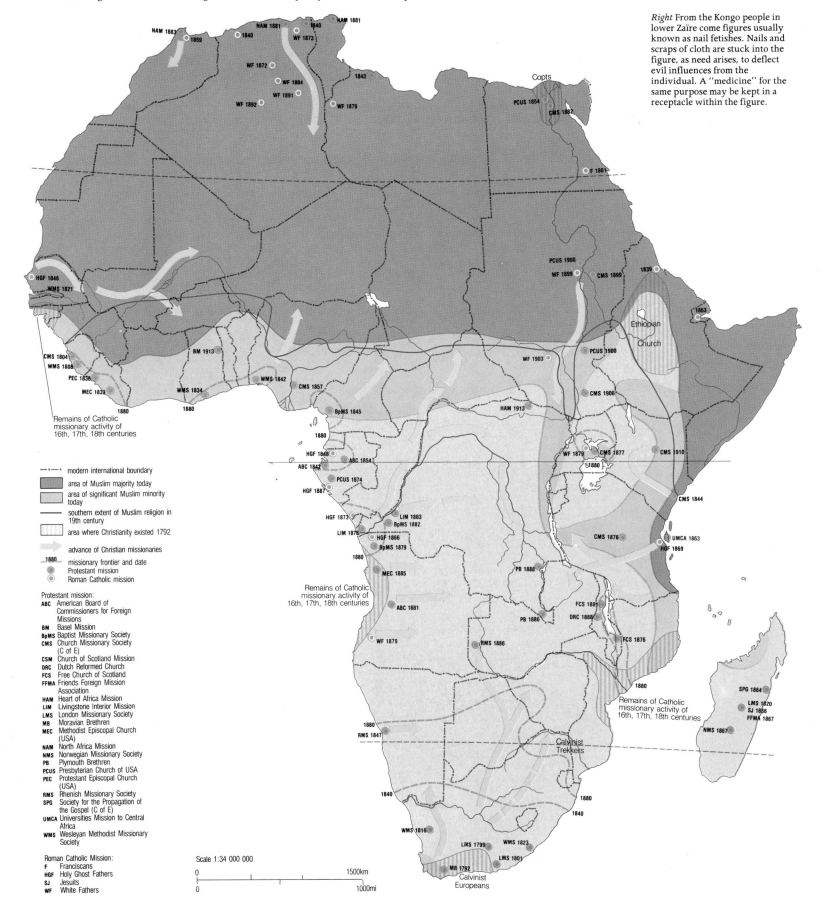

modern international boundary
area of Muslim majority today
area of significant Muslim minority today
southern extent of Muslim religion in 19th century
area where Christianity existed 1792
advance of Christian missionaries
1880 missionary frontier and date
Protestant mission
Roman Catholic mission

Protestant mission:
ABC American Board of Commissioners for Foreign Missions
BM Basel Mission
BpMS Baptist Missionary Society
CMS Church Missionary Society (C of E)
CSM Church of Scotland Mission
DRC Dutch Reformed Church
FCS Free Church of Scotland
FFMA Friends Foreign Mission Association
HAM Heart of Africa Mission
LIM Livingstone Interior Mission
LMS London Missionary Society
MB Moravian Brethren
MEC Methodist Episcopal Church (USA)
NAM North Africa Mission
NMS Norwegian Missionary Society
PB Plymouth Brethren
PCUS Presbyterian Church of USA
PEC Protestant Episcopal Church (USA)
RMS Rhenish Missionary Society
SPG Society for the Propagation of the Gospel (C of E)
UMCA Universities Mission to Central Africa
WMS Wesleyan Methodist Missionary Society

Roman Catholic Mission:
F Franciscans
HGF Holy Ghost Fathers
SJ Jesuits
WF White Fathers

Scale 1:34 000 000

Remains of Catholic missionary activity of 16th, 17th, 18th centuries

Top An Asante priest from southern Ghana. Such a personage is usually a man of prestige and influence in the local community.

Above Ancestor figures often mark burial places, where offerings are left for the departed ancestors. This remembrance pole is to appease the spirit of a young boy in southeast Angola.

Below A sacrificial ceremony in southern Ghana. Sacrifices of living animals are made to appease the living-dead or to show respect and worship to the High God. The celebrant may be the clan head or, in the ceremonies of popular cults, a professional priest who is keeper of a shrine.

religious practitioner will be consulted to find out if one of the living-dead is angry at being neglected.

The head of the family or clan usually acts as priest when offerings are made, though when there is a shrine with wider associations there may be full-time professional priests. But in almost every society there is a religious specialist often termed a witch doctor. His function is not to bewitch, but to discover the source of any form of evil and to advise how it might be got rid of. He may also be a herbalist and healer. Evil may come from neglected ancestors, from malevolent spirits or from witches. Witches are ordinary members of the community, who may inherit their power or who may become witches involuntarily, through jealousy, hatred or greed. The elimination of witchcraft is important, for the witch may not know that he or she has bewitched another person. Magic and witchcraft cannot, in the African context, be entirely separated from religion. Charms are used to protect the wearers from evil spirits and it is such charms which in parts of West Africa were called fetish or juju. These names were also given to representations of gods and spirits placed in shrines. But to call the religion fetish worship or juju worship is wrong; the African does not believe that the representation is the spirit, any more than a Roman Catholic Christian believes that the image is the saint.

Belief in a high god, creator of the universe, is almost universal in Africa. But in many traditions he is not prayed to, being seen as remote and no longer concerned with human affairs, and the spirits are the important supernatural phenomena. In a few traditions intermediary spirits are almost absent and sacrifice is made to the one high god. Are Africans then monotheists? The question is hard to answer. Are the spirits gods? But there are few societies which might be called polytheistic in the Western sense, having a pantheon of named gods. One such is the Yoruba of western Nigeria, with gods like Shango, deity of lightning and thunder.

African religion is life-affirming, and contains little of asceticism. Its paramount values are harmony and unity within the family and clan, and with the living-dead and the spirits. It is essentially communal, not individual, and Africans who become Christians or Muslims carry these values into their new faith.

Arising out of Judaism, Christianity's essential message was that Jesus of Nazareth was the Messiah or Christ and the Son of God. His followers preached his resurrection and ascension and forgiveness of sins to those who believed this gospel, throughout the Greco–Roman world of their day. This included Egypt and North Africa as part of the Mediterranean complex, so there have been Christians in the African continent since shortly after the death of Christ. There have been, broadly, three phases of Christian penetration into Africa. The first was limited to North Africa and northeast Africa, and came to an end with the rise of Islam. The second phase was from the end of the 15th century when European sailors began to travel around the coast of Africa. A new phase began at the end of the 18th century which continues to the present day.

The origins of Christianity in Egypt are lost in legend, but a strong church existed there by the 2nd century AD. It established itself also across North

Africa, and Alexandria and Carthage (near modern Tunis) became centers of Christian learning. The Church produced scholars and martyrs. Christianity also traveled south along the Nile and into the highlands of Ethiopia. Christian churches flourished in the kingdoms of Nubia and survived into the 12th century. In Egypt the Arab–Muslim invasions of the 7th century reduced the number of Christians, but the Coptic Church has continued up to the present day. In the rest of North Africa, the ancient churches have disappeared completely. The Church has also survived in Ethiopia, keeping its links with the Egyptian and Syrian Churches. It has evolved distinctive styles of art and architecture and a unique liturgy that includes dancing and drumming – sure signs of African cultural adaptation. Another feature of the Ethiopian Church is its strong tradition of monasticism; it is from the monks that its bishops are chosen.

The second phase began when Europeans began to sail around Africa, from the end of the 15th century. The first were the Portuguese, who carried priests with them, and missionary work was begun in some areas. The greatest success was in the kingdom of Kongo (present-day Zaïre) where the king and many of his court were baptized. A son of the king, educated in Portugal, was consecrated bishop. Yet this church never took deep root. The economic and territorial ambitions of the Portuguese were one handicap. Little has remained of the Christianity of the 16th and 17th centuries.

But from this time onwards there were many European coastal settlements, originally founded to provision ships. Later they developed into trading bases, forts and, tragically, depots for slave trading. At the Cape of Good Hope, a considerable number of the Dutch garrison became permanent settlers and as they flourished so did their Calvinist faith. At almost all the forts there were European chaplains who conducted schools for the settlement's children, including those of mixed race. A small number of local African children also attended the schools and received Christian teaching. But African Christians were not to be found far from the coastal settlements until the end of the 18th century.

At this time a new spirit of evangelization emerged in Europe and North America, coinciding with a reaction against the slave trade. Some former slaves were returned to form the basis of new settlements in Sierra Leone, Liberia, Libreville (Senegal) and, to a more limited extent, at Mombasa, and they came back as Christians. Such black Christians, whether returned former slaves or converts from the old coastal settlements, became the partners of the white missionaries in the pioneering ventures of the 19th century. But it was not until the partition of Africa among the Western powers, at the end of the century, that most Christian missions could really establish themselves in the interior. Now they were under the protection of colonial governments and able to use the new roads and railroads.

As the first phase of Christianity in Africa bequeathed churches linked to the eastern section of Christianity, so the second and third phases were linked to the western Church. The second phase began with Roman Catholics, with Protestants coming later to the forts; the third phase began with Protestant initiatives. But Roman Catholics soon followed, and today they outnumber Protestants in Africa. There is today a third grouping in black Africa, not linked to either Roman Catholic or Protestant, except where they have joined local councils of churches. They are sometimes termed independent or separatist churches. Some arose as schisms from mission-founded churches; others were established by leaders who had been under Christian influences of one kind or another. Since they have been less directly under the influence of western Christianity, these churches afford us valuable insights into the most Africanized forms of Christianity.

In worship they are vigorous and exuberant, using African musical instruments, dancing and drumming. Processions with banners are often seen, and many have uniforms for their members – usually white with symbolic badges and headgear. In many churches the person of the Holy Spirit is given a particularly high place, so much so that they are termed Pentecostal churches, though there is no direct connection with western Pentecostalism. A large grouping of these churches in West Africa are called *aladura* churches, and the term, meaning one who prays, indicates their particular emphasis on prayer for physical and spiritual healing. In other parts of Africa the same emphasis is found. In some churches Western and traditional medicines are totally proscribed. Whether or not this is the case, these churches place a high value on the harmony and unity of the fellowship and of the individual within himself.

Islam, like Christianity, entered Africa within a short time after its inception. Like Christianity, Islam owes much to the ancient religion of the Hebrews. Jesus is recognized as a prophet in the line of the prophet Moses, but the last and greatest prophet is Muhammad, who taught submission to the one god, Allah. As early as 640 AD, within eight years of Muhammad's death, some of his Arabic followers had begun their conquest of Egypt. These first Muslims came not as missionaries but as soldiers and settlers, and were often welcomed as saviors from the oppressive rule of Byzantium. They did not (as is sometimes believed) force their religion on the local people and were particularly tolerant of Jews and Christians, "people of the Book," who were not idolators. But over the years, as the result of intermarriage and to gain relief from taxation, many Christians became Muslims. Apostasy for Muslims was punishable by death.

The central tenet of Islam is belief in the one God, and confession of this belief is the first of the five "pillars of Islam." The others are daily prayer; giving of alms; pilgrimage to Mecca if possible; and the keeping of the fast in the month of Ramadan. The teachings of Muhammad, communicated to him by Allah, have been written down in the sacred Koran. Where Christians have stressed the necessity for the Bible to be translated into local languages so that it may be read by all believers, Muslims on the other hand emphasize the necessity for learning Arabic, so that the Koran may be read in the original. Its translation is not approved of by the most orthodox Muslims. So, as the religion spread, literacy in Arabic spread also.

Following the Arab conquest of Egypt, Islam slowly spread among the coastal and inland peoples of North Africa. Eventually, except for the Coptic

Top A Roman Catholic village church in Cameroon. Such small churches may be found over most of Africa, often built simply of local materials and identified only by their cross. The services are often led by a catechist or lay reader, for priests and ministers are too few, and consequently the sacraments are confined to special and infrequent occasions.

Above In lower Zaïre the Christian tradition goes back to the coming of Portuguese explorers and missionaries in the 15th century. This cross with an African Christ speaks of the localization of Christianity which has taken place over the centuries.

Top In All Saints Cathedral in Nairobi, Kenya, African and European Christians kneel together to take communion from African and European priests. For many years this church was attended only by Europeans; now it is a parish church for all.

Above Processions and open-air celebrations are a feature of Christian churches of all traditions, reflecting the old customs whereby ceremonies were not confined to a special building. The procession here is of a Roman Catholic sorority in Cameroon.

Overleaf The Friday Mosque at Mopti, Mali. Wherever Muslims are found, mosques are built, for though the faithful may pray anywhere, there is an obligation to pray together where possible, and especially on the holy day, Friday. The mosque has a minaret from which the prayer call goes out, and here local materials have been used and local traditions followed to create a truly African mosque.

remnant in Egypt, North Africa became and has remained deeply Muslim in religion, culture and legal systems, with Islam as the state religion.

In a second phase Islam spread across the Sahara into West Africa, and up the Nile into the Sudan. The agents of Islam at this stage were traders and clerics, who often settled on the outskirts of West African cities, establishing their own mosques and schools and remaining somewhat separate from the local population. The ruling classes tended to adopt the new religion while the people of the countryside remained wholly outside it. By the 13th century the ruler of Mali and the ruler of Kanem were Muslims, and the great Mansa Musa of Mali astounded the Muslims of Egypt with his wealth and power when he went on the pilgrimage to Mecca in the 14th century. Islam also traveled down the east coast of Africa, taken by seafaring Arabs, some of whom settled and built up coastal cities. Here also some urbanized local people became Muslims. But at this time, in both West and East Africa, Islam continued as a parallel rather than as a replacement religion for traditional beliefs.

From the mid-18th century a new phase began. One development, continuing to the present day, has been the growth of adherence to *tariqa*, religious orders or brotherhoods, founded by charismatic religious reformers. Members of *tariqa* have their own special forms of devotion which they perform in addition to the required prayers. The two most influential and largest *tariqa* are the Tijaniyya and the Qadiriyya. Another development, not unconnected to the first, was a new exclusiveness and aggressiveness. African traditions and customs were no longer to be tolerated. The leaders were in many cases clerics, who had studied and traveled widely in the Islamic world. They set out to cleanse and purify the religion of fellow Muslims and to bring others into the faith, by force if necessary, using the concept of the *jihad* (holy war). These men, starting as religious reformers, often ended as rulers of great states. Such were Usuman dan Fodio of Sokoto (northern Nigeria) and 'Umar ibn Sa'id Tall of Tukolor (western Sudan). In areas where such movements occurred the structure of society became deeply Islamized, although large numbers of people remained outside the faith, and Islam became the state religion.

The fourth phase came with the expansion of Western influence and the imposition of new colonial regimes. In cities and towns all over Africa adherence to Islam became one mode of adaptation for the migrant entering an urban trans-ethnic community. Unlike Christianity, Islam did not have the advantage of proselytization through mission schools, but again it did not usually have the disadvantage of Christianity's link with the conqueror. Some rural communities also adopted Islam in the closing years of the 19th century. In areas where Islam had spread in this fourth phase, however, it is usually in competition with Christianity and traditional religion (in the countryside) and with modern secular society, and is strictly a religion rather than a total way of life.

Islam, which appears so monolithic to the outsider, has its own internal divisions: the main one, going back to the conflict over Muhammad's successors, resulted in the Sunni and Shi'i schools. Virtually all the Muslims of Africa are Sunni; the only Shi'i Muslims are Asian migrants in East Africa. Also to be found in a number of places are missionaries of the unorthodox Ahmaddiyya sect (with headquarters in Pakistan) whose influence is perhaps greater than their number. They have been active in controversy with Christians, and have pioneered in translating the Koran into African vernaculars.

Both Islam and Christianity are vital and growing religions in Africa today. In the worldwide gatherings of both faiths, African representatives are an increasingly important section. At the same time the observance of traditional religious rituals is probably decreasing, although some young university-educated people are advocating a deliberate return to traditional culture, including its religious aspects. It is doubtful whether the majority of Africans will ever take this seriously. Even where a head of state has sought to impose such a return (as with the call for "authenticity" in Zaïre) it has not succeeded. African traditional values will certainly continue but in combination with many aspects of the modern industrialized West.

It is easy to cite political and sociological reasons for the moves to Islam and Christianity. But these are religions, and there are deep religious reasons too. Perhaps the strongest appeal of the two world religions is their emphasis on the power of God. There is a great deal of fear in traditional beliefs – fear of spirits and ancestors whose power to do evil seems to be exercised arbitrarily. This calls for a continued watch over one's actions, so that no unintended offense is committed. The high god was very remote, beyond the reach of man, for good or evil. But in Christianity and Islam the creator-god is preached as powerful and concerned with men and women: "Allah the compassionate"; "God is love." Both religions (despite sad failures) do unite their followers in a super-ethnic fellowship that seems to offer a better future for nations often torn by internal divisions.   J.M.

Yoruba Traditional Religion

Though the majority of the Yoruba in Nigeria and Benin (formerly Dahomey) are either Christian or Muslim, Yoruba traditional religion is by no means extinct. Moreover not only does it flourish among a minority of the estimated 13 million Yoruba in West Africa but it also survives in a very pure form in the West Indies and Brazil, having been implanted there during the era of the trans-Atlantic slave trade.

Yoruba traditional religion has a four-tiered system of spiritual or quasi-spiritual beings. The Supreme Being, Olodumare, also known as Olorun (owner of heaven), occupies the top tier. His ministers, the subordinate gods (*orisha*) are ranged along the second tier in some form of hierarchical order. Obatala is the most important of these lesser gods. Following on the subordinate gods, on the third tier are the deified ancestors such as Shango. Then there are the spirits associated with natural phenomena such as the earth (Ile), the rivers, mountains and trees.

The Supreme Being, Olodumare, is regarded as immortal, unique, omniscient, omnipotent and completely impartial in his judgments. The Yoruba, though they do not erect temples and shrines in his honor, do invoke, petition and praise Olodumare. By way of contrast, the subordinate gods and other spiritual beings have their own priests, temples, sanctuaries and shrines.

In addition to the more personal and private forms of worship given to Olodumare and the public cults associated with the lesser gods, respect and reverence for ancestors and divination constitute integral parts of Yoruba traditional religion. The Ifa oracle is the most widespread of the divination systems. Throughout Yorubaland there are dances and masquerades connected with the veneration of the dead and the health and general well-being of the community as a whole. The Oro and Egungun masquerades are two of the more widespread of the cults associated with the dead and the health of the community.   P.C.

Left A shrine of Obatala, who is widely acknowledged by the Yoruba to be the most important of the lesser gods. According to a number of Yoruba creation myths he played the major role as Olodumare's chief executive in the creation of the world. After Obatala himself had been taught how to mold the human form by Olodumare, he began to fashion men and women who were then infused with the principle of life by the Supreme Being.

Right The trickster god, Eshu, the harbinger of both good and evil, is the principal intermediary between heaven and earth. Eshu informs Olodumare of the activities both of the subordinate gods and of men. He has a place in every traditional household and no one fails to propitiate him.

Below There are different kinds of priests and sacred persons in Yorubaland. There are, for instance, priests attached to temples who offer sacrifices of various kinds, propitiatory, votive, thanksgiving and preventative among others. Then the different gods and deified ancestors have their own priests.

The priests of Shango are called Magba, those of Orunmila, Babalawo. After long and arduous training the priests are consecrated and invested with the power to offer sacrifice. In addition to the priests there are the sacred people, the mediums and devotees who look after the temples and shrines. Then there are the diviners. A priest may also divine, but a diviner may not offer sacrifice.

Below Some of the Yoruba divinities are worshiped on a more or less local basis, but others like Ogun are reverenced and worshiped throughout Yorubaland. Ogun, according to tradition, used his machete to clear a pathway for the gods when they first came to inhabit the earth. And on account of his skill with the machete and his strength he came to be regarded as the god of hunters, blacksmiths, butchers, barbers, soldiers and today truck and taxi drivers and all those who work with iron and steel.

It is Ogun too who witnesses pacts and convenants. When an adherent of the Yoruba traditional religion goes to a law court today he swears not on the Koran or Bible but on a piece of iron which is taken to represent and symbolize Ogun.

Above Great heroes or very gifted individuals are on occasions deified by the Yoruba. Shango, the power of the thunderstorm, the wrath of Olodumare, was, according to legend, king of Oyo. He was an autocrat and on discovering that attempts were being made to assassinate him, he fled Oyo and punished his former subjects by destroying their homes and villages by means of thunderstorms. The inhabitants of Oyo, believing that Shango had committed suicide and could not be responsible for their misfortune, consulted the oracle only to be told that Shango was in fact the author of their calamities.

The process of appeasement and propitiation began, ending in the deification of Shango. Today shrines of Shango abound everywhere in Yorubaland, and he is widely known also in North and South America and the West Indies. Only the Magba, the priests of Shango, are allowed to arrange for the burial of those killed in a thunderstorm.

Left The Yoruba use several different systems of divination. The most important objects in the Ifa system are the specially selected palm nuts, the tray which must be of a rectangular, circular or semicircular shape, the bell made of ivory or wood and used to invoke the oracular spirit, and the lots which may be animal teeth, cowrie shells or bits of broken pottery.

The Ifa priest (the Babalawo), perhaps the most highly trained of all the Yoruba priests, works from a group of 16 poems (*odus*) which are believed to contain all the experiences a human being is capable of undergoing.

Orunmila, one of the most important of the subordinate deities, is the power behind the oracle. He is imbued with Olodumare's wisdom and it is his favor that people seek.

Above left The Egungun masquerade was and still is today for some a social and religious function of great importance. The Egungun himself is regarded as the embodiment of the spirit of a deceased person believed to have returned from the spirit world to visit his "children." No part of the Egungun's body can be exposed to view for in seeing it one would cast eyes on the spirit enshrined therein and thereby break the spell and die.

Egunguns are thus robed from top to toe in costumes of cloth and fitted with a mask which is often a caricature of an animal such as a python or leopard, or a European or some other "foreigner." After a town or village has been purified with holy water and medicines, the masqueraders appear and the dancing and acrobatics begin.

Above left Some of the divinities associated with natural phenomena, the earth, rivers, mountains and trees, are male, some female, some good, some evil. Yemoja, a female deity and beneficent, is the goddess of rivers, streams, lakes and water in general : all water flows out from her body. Olokun, a male divinity, resides in the sea, controls its anger and distributes its benefits. Oya, goddess of the river Niger, is the author of heavy gales and strong winds. Oshun is the tutelary divinity of Oshogbo, and associated with a river bearing the same name. Oshun is a fertility goddess, who by means of her medicinal waters, gives the joy of childbirth to barren women.

The Ethiopian Church

The Ethiopian Church, monophysite in theology, goes back at least to the 4th century. It was once the most southern of a series of Christian churches along the Nile valley, but the Christian kingdoms of Nubia were gradually overwhelmed by Muslims from the north, and by the 15th century their Christianity had completely disappeared.

The Ethiopian Church survived. Its patriarch was an Egyptian appointed by the patriarch of Alexandria. At the capital of the kingdom, Aksum, the liturgical and literary language Ge'ez developed. As well as the connections with Egypt, there were links with Jewish religion. King Solomon was believed to have fathered the child of the Queen of Sheba, and this child, Menelik, the Lion of Judah, was the founder of the Solomonid dynasty.

Most spectacular of the monuments of the Ethiopian Church are the monolithic churches of Lalibela, a remote mountain village in Welo Province, north of Addis Ababa, but once Ethiopia's capital. King Lalibela was founder of a new dynasty which took power from the Solomonid dynasty early in the 12th century. His immense church-building project, in which he used up his wealth, probably began as an effort to legitimize his rule and enhance his capital. But according to Ethiopian legend the task conferred sainthood on the king himself, who after the work was completed abdicated his throne and became a contemplative.

J.M.

The Ethiopian Church retains many features of other Eastern churches, such as a dual clergy of village priests, who must be married, and monks, from whom alone the bishops are chosen. It has preserved also some ancient Jewish customs such as circumcision and observance of the Sabbath (as well as Sunday). But its liturgies and ceremonies, though showing borrowings, have developed a distinct indigenous flavor.

Bottom Christmas at Lalibela. White-robed monks (blowing trumpets) line the rim of one of the trenches, while priests below join in dancing the liturgy to celebrate the birth of Christ.

Below Ecclesiastical education, including the reading of Ge'ez, has traditionally taken place in monastery schools; here a deacon learns from older clergy in a monastery in Aksum, Tigre.

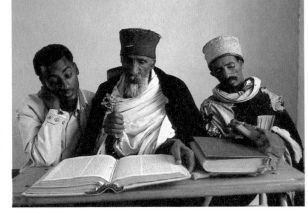

Left From above the stone church of St George at Lalibela shows as an immense cross. A square ditch was dug into the living rock, and the cruciform church was hewed out and hollowed inside. Entrance is by the sloping trench showing to the left of the church. Its roof is almost exactly level with the surrounding ground surface.

Top St George's Church rises 12 meters from a platform base which follows the cruciform shape of the church. It is only one of several similar churches at Lalibela; among others are the churches of St Mary, St Mascal and St Merkurios.

Above Murals depicting biblical scenes and incidents in the lives of saints are a feature of Ethiopian churches and monasteries. St George, slaying the dragon, with a frieze of typically Ethiopian cherubs, is shown in this mural from a church at Lake Tana, to the west of Lalibela.

EARLY MAN IN AFRICA

In his work on evolution in the 19th century, Darwin intimated that man must be of African origin, because his closest living relatives, the gorilla and the chimpanzee, are entirely African. This intuition of Darwin's has now been vindicated by the results of recent researches in a variety of natural, environmental and social sciences. Olduvai Gorge in northern Tanzania and other sites in Kenya, Ethiopia and South Africa have yielded a collection of fossil specimens from which a meaningful evolutionary sequence is becoming clear. This runs from pre-human to near-human stages and on to actual man. Several points are hotly debated and some obvious gaps remain to be filled, but the sheer wealth of available fossil evidence, with dates spaced between five million and one million years ago, demonstrates that it was in Africa, probably its eastern side, that man emerged.

This evolution was both biological and cultural.

Man is related to the apes but not descended from them, the link being that of cousinship rather than descent. We should imagine, therefore, a common ancestral group, living in the African woodland-savannas several million years ago. One division of this group (ancestors of the apes) would have begun specializing in forest dwelling and in climbing with all four limbs; the other division kept its options open with one of its variants developing bipedalism (two-footedness). Bipedalism left the hands free for holding, carrying, throwing and manipulating. Dr Mary Leakey's recognition of bipedal footprints in cemented mud in northern Tanzania shows that it was achieved at least four million years ago.

The early two-footed animals on the line to man are known generally as Australopithecines. They were small, standing about 1·25 meters, and with virtually no forehead, for their brain (measuring 500 cubic centimeters or less) was only about one-

Olduvai Gorge cuts across the middle of the Serengeti Plain, Tanzania. A hundred meters deep and several kilometers long, the eroded sides of the gorge reveal two million years of human evolution in successive geological strata. From the 1930s onwards excavations here have uncovered a unique sequence of stone tools and fossil remains, including *Zinjanthropus* and *Homo habilis*.

Early Stone Age sites

Homo habilis fossils in association with the earliest pebble tools have been found at Olduvai Gorge and Lake Turkana. *Homo erectus*, associated with the Acheulian (handax) culture, spread through most of the continent between 1 million and 100000 years ago.

Middle and Late Stone Age cultures

Coinciding with the emergence of *Homo sapiens* around 100000 years ago, the Middle Stone Age saw the beginnings of regional specializations in human culture. The map shows the three main traditions that can be discerned from the archaeological record.

The development of African agricultural systems (after Shaw, Harlan and others)

Agriculture in Africa began around 5000 BC. It was partly an indigenous development and partly due to the importation of food crops (wheat, barley) and domestic livestock from the Near East. African cereals (millet, sorghum) began to be cultivated in the area associated with the aquatic lifestyle of the Late Stone Age. Old Guinea crops (yam, oil palm, okra) were forest plants, the cultivation of which is of indeterminate antiquity. Southeast Asian crops (bananas, coconuts, etc.) were introduced from about 500 AD.

The spread of ironworking

Ironworking techniques appeared in North Africa in the middle of the last millennium BC. The general tendency of its spread from north to south supports those scholars who believe that iron technology was imported from the Near East.

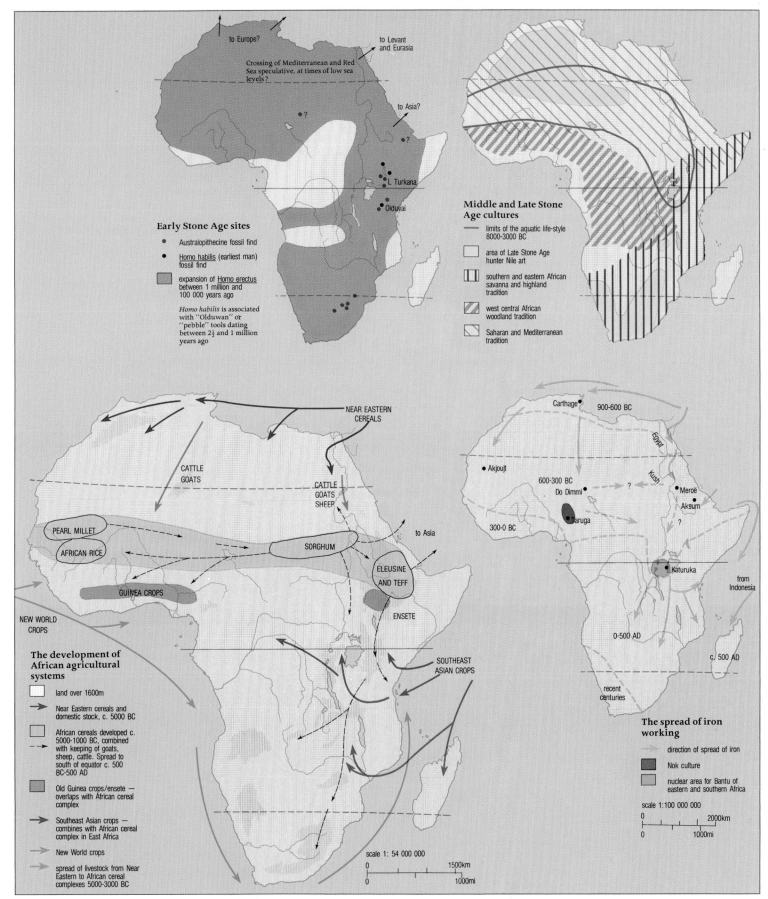

Early Stone Age sites

- • Australopithecine fossil find
- • <u>Homo habilis</u> (earliest man) fossil find
- ■ expansion of Homo erectus between 1 million and 100 000 years ago

Homo habilis is associated with "Olduwan" or "pebble" tools dating between 2½ and 1 million years ago

Middle and Late Stone Age cultures

- limits of the aquatic life-style 8000-3000 BC
- area of Late Stone Age hunter Nile art
- southern and eastern African savanna and highland tradition
- west central African woodland tradition
- Saharan and Mediterranean tradition

The development of African agricultural systems

- land over 1600m
- Near Eastern cereals and domestic stock, c. 5000 BC
- African cereals developed c. 5000-1000 BC, combined with keeping of goats, sheep, cattle. Spread to south of equator c. 500 BC-500 AD
- Old Guinea crops/ensete — overlaps with African cereal complex
- Southeast Asian crops — combines with African cereal complex in East Africa
- New World crops
- spread of livestock from Near Eastern to African cereal complexes 5000-3000 BC

scale 1: 54 000 000

The spread of iron working

- direction of spread of iron
- Nok culture
- nuclear area for Bantu of eastern and southern Africa

scale 1:100 000 000

third of the capacity of modern man's. At least two types of Australopithecines diverged in time. One was more robust, with a massive jaw and powerful molar teeth. It was probably from the other, lighter line that man arose. This type had significantly a smaller jaw, somewhat improved limbs and hands more adept for precise craftsmanship. The earliest evidence of deliberate shaping of stone into tools with a cutting edge comes from Lake Turkana (Rudolf) and dates from about 2 500 000 years ago. With tools available for cutting flesh, diet became more varied. Thus *Homo habilis*, as it is called, emerged from Australopithecine stock.

Most specimens of *Homo habilis* show a brain size slightly larger than that of the general run of Australopithecines. The stimulus for this is obvious: toolmaking, being cultural and not biological, could not be inherited, but had to be learned through demonstration and experience. Presumably the development of speech was affected. The important point is that the enlargement of the brain was late; it was not the cause of the human revolution (as was once thought) but rather a result of it. The basic cause was the earlier attainment of bipedalism.

The geographical extent of the Australopithecines and *Homo habilis* is imperfectly established. Plotting the finds, as on the map, merely records those places within the distribution area where unusually favorable conditions promoted fossilization, and where erosion, followed up by diligent scientific exploration, has revealed the bones. An alternative distribution test of earliest man may be attempted from stone tools, which preserve more readily than bones. The oldest known have been called "pebble tools" since frequently, though not invariably, they were river pebbles from which a few flakes were struck to leave a crude cutting edge. Assemblages of such tools associated with remains of *Homo habilis* or dated to that period (2 500 000–1 000 000 years ago) are known from northern Tanzania, Uganda, Kenya and Ethiopia. There are some possible examples in southern Africa and others claimed at the western and northwestern extremities of the continent. But it is not yet clear whether all these were the work of *Homo habilis* or whether the more distant examples form part of later toolkits attributable to early *Homo erectus*.

Homo erectus, which emerged a million or so years ago, was larger than *habilis*. Its brain size was bigger (about 1000 cubic centimeters), about two-thirds that of modern man's. The emergence of *erectus* from *habilis* seems to correlate roughly with the development of more advanced and distinctive stone toolkits known as Acheulian in which so-called handaxes are the most celebrated tool.

Assemblages of Acheulian tools have been found in most countries in Africa. It seems however that man continued to shun the true forests of the Guinea coast and Zaïre basin and remained a savanna hunter-gatherer. The many Saharan sites do not imply permanent occupation of the desert, but represent instead the penetration of the Saharan grasslands and exploitation of the game at certain restricted periods when the climate was wetter. In time the Acheulian tools became more refined, and altogether this technological tradition spanned a million years in Africa, eventually ending about

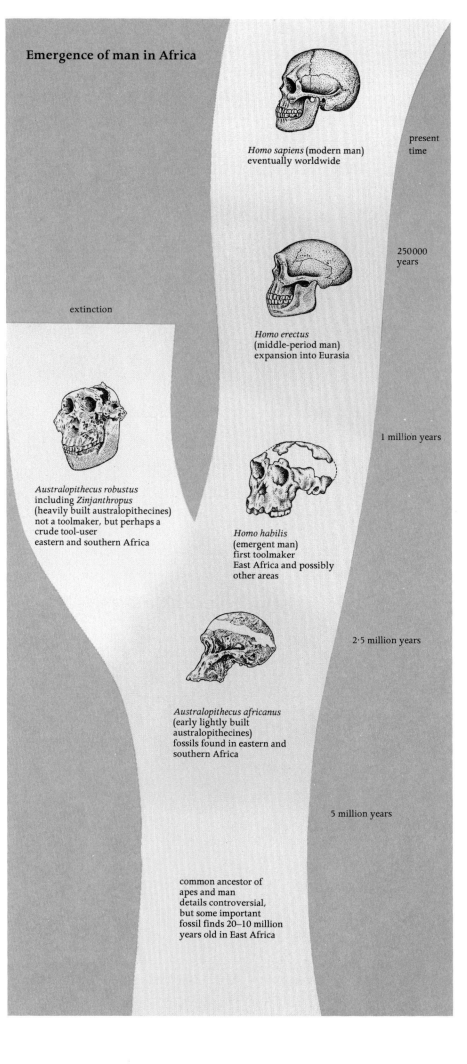

Emergence of man in Africa

Homo sapiens (modern man) eventually worldwide

present time

Homo erectus (middle-period man) expansion into Eurasia

250000 years

extinction

Australopithecus robustus including *Zinjanthropus* (heavily built australopithecines) not a toolmaker, but perhaps a crude tool-user eastern and southern Africa

1 million years

Homo habilis (emergent man) first toolmaker East Africa and possibly other areas

2·5 million years

Australopithecus africanus (early lightly built australopithecines) fossils found in eastern and southern Africa

5 million years

common ancestor of apes and man details controversial, but some important fossil finds 20–10 million years old in East Africa

The African archaeological sequence

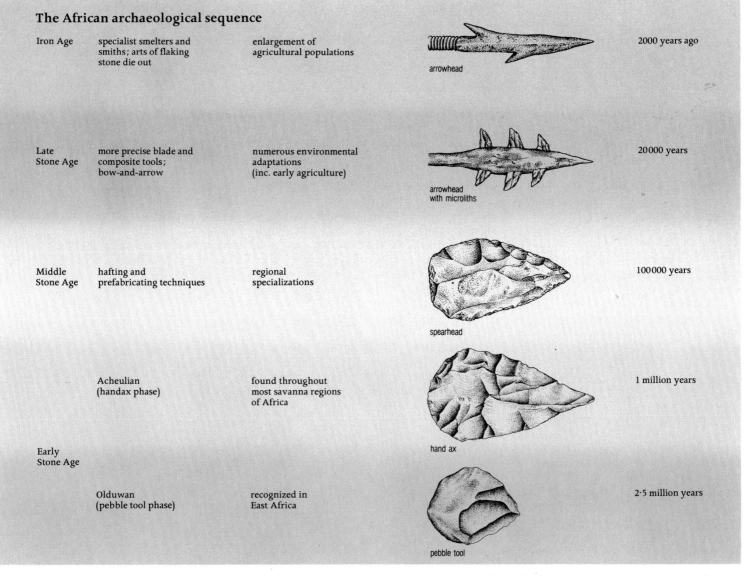

Iron Age	specialist smelters and smiths; arts of flaking stone die out	enlargement of agricultural populations		2000 years ago
Late Stone Age	more precise blade and composite tools; bow-and-arrow	numerous environmental adaptations (inc. early agriculture)		20 000 years
Middle Stone Age	hafting and prefabricating techniques	regional specializations		100 000 years
	Acheulian (handax phase)	found throughout most savanna regions of Africa		1 million years
Early Stone Age				
	Olduwan (pebble tool phase)	recognized in East Africa		2·5 million years

arrowhead

arrowhead with microliths

spearhead

hand ax

pebble tool

Above: The African archaeological sequence
The three-age system (Stone, Bronze, Iron Ages) does not apply in Africa, as, with the exception of Egypt, African cultures bypassed the Bronze Age. The dates of the different periods are very approximate and cannot be applied to the continent as a whole; for example, a Late Stone Age culture survived into the 20th century among the Bushmen of the Kalahari.

Left: The emergence of man in Africa
Available evidence suggests that the divergence of the evolutionary line leading to man (*Hominidae*) from that which led to the apes (*Pongidae*) took place in Africa. *Australopithecus africanus* is represented by skulls found at Taungs and Sterkfontein in South Africa. The "Nutcracker Man" (*Zinjanthropus*) skull, found at Olduvai in 1959 by Dr Louis Leakey, is related to the heavier *Australopithecus robustus*. This line appears to have become extinct.

100 000 years ago. The makers of the latest Acheulian may well have been no longer *Homo erectus* but essentially modern man, belonging to early or transitional forms of *Homo sapiens*.

Around 100 000 years ago – a time broadly coincidental with the emergence of the modern human type – real diversity in human ecology and behavior becomes apparent. The handaxes and other heavy equipment of the Early Stone Age were phased out. In their place were manufactured smaller, more precise and more efficient tools, the result of revolutionary techniques in working stone. These advances heralded greater ecological specialization, including penetration of the forests. Exquisite lanceheads for fishing have been found along forest rivers. In the eastern and southern grasslands there occur beautiful leaf-shaped points, doubtless used as spearheads for hunting savanna game. In the Sahara and the north, hafting was sometimes assisted by preparing a tang to the stone point. This tripartite division probably reflects reasonably fairly the three main human-ecological regions of the continent, whose distinctive cultures evolved during the Middle Stone Age and continued in a way into the Late Stone Age, which dates from about 20 000 years ago.

The transition to Late Stone Age is marked by further technological innovations. Small fine blades were used in combination, several being inserted and glued into a groove prepared in a wooden handle or shaft, to produce knives, saws, spears and barbed arrows. The invention of the bow and arrow about this time marks an important advance in hunting technique.

As the Late Stone Age proceeded towards recent times, the archaeological evidence, helped by radiocarbon dates, reveals not only marked regional diversities but also cultural developments, some of them clearly reacting to environmental changes. These traditions and differences relate (though not always simply) to the cultural and population patterns of recent and present times.

The first part of the Late Stone Age corresponded with a dry period between the tropics. But around 9000 BC a marked wet trend set in and lasted, with some oscillations, till 3000 BC. This promoted an extension of the savanna grasslands (and savanna animals) into the southern Sahara and its central highlands. It also meant longer and more permanent rivers, and the enlargement of lakes and the creation of new ones. Various fishes were thus able to extend impressively their ranges; hippos and crocodiles moved into the central Sahara.

Human populations likewise adapted to these new conditions and increased their numbers and their range. From around 7000 BC there radiated across the continent, from the western Sahara to the Nile and upriver to the East African rift valleys, a distinctive water-oriented way of life. These communities hunted aquatic animals and fished intensively, using nets, bone-pointed spears and harpoons, later supplemented by hook and line. With a reliable and concentrated food supply (even, it seems, without any formal cultivation) some communities became relatively settled and developed new crafts. Boating is an obvious one; but there is also evidence of matting, basketry and, most interesting of all, pottery.

This aquatic lifestyle began to break up regionally after 5000 BC, once the wet peak had passed. By 2000 BC it survived in only a few, rather secluded localities by shrunken lakes and rivers. This retreat coincided approximately with the advance of pastoralism and cultivation. Maybe some of the waterside people were assimilated piecemeal into the new food-producing communities: indeed much of the process of ennobling certain nutritious wild plants and grasses of the African savanna may have been pioneered by these settled and skilled waterfolk.

Although this last point remains speculative, what is now clear is that African agriculture was historically an indigenous development, and not something introduced from outside. This is especially true of West Africa where almost all the food crops of historical significance, in the forest and savanna zones alike, have been developed from wild African plants. In the savanna belt south of the Sahara several grasses were transformed into important and productive grain crops in the last five millennia BC. Most important of these cereals is sorghum (guinea-corn), whose region of origin is between Lake Chad and the upper Nile. Of the true millets, eleusine (or finger) millet is native to the eastern African highlands, pearl (or bullrush) millet to the West African savanna and sahel. And around the swamps of the upper Niger an indigenous rice was exploited and developed. While cereals are not naturally suited to wet forest regions, there is archaeological evidence for the early use of oil palm, and it is likely that this was accompanied by suitable tuberous starches. The yam which is now and has for a long time been the staple of southern Nigeria and Ghana is a seedless crop and as such leaves no obvious archaeological trace, so its real antiquity remains unknown.

Some crops have been introduced to sub-Saharan Africa in later times. Especially important for the wetter regions of eastern and equatorial Africa is the banana, which was carried around the Indian Ocean in the first millennium AD. Once adopted in Africa it has been enormously diversified to suit a variety of soils, climates, purposes and tastes. In very recent centuries several New World crops have been added, notably maize and cassava. The temperate cereals of Near Eastern origin, wheat and barley, have of course been very important for North Africa, and were cultivated in Egypt from about 5000 BC. Further south their relevance has been extremely marginal.

Cattle, goats and sheep penetrated from northern Africa to become the important domestic animals of the African savannas (with goats being kept by cultivators in the forest clearings too). They were kept in North Africa as early as 5000 BC and in the favorable conditions then prevailing their range was soon extended up the Nile and into the central Saharan highlands (where cattle are attested by rock art). This brought pastoralists into contact with the earlier established aquatic people. Drier conditions affected both economies; they forced Saharan cattle southward no later than 3000 BC. By 1000 BC cattle and goats were being kept by the forest edge in West Africa and also over much of the East African highlands. This is attested by the archaeological recognition of their bones at dated occupation sites.

Thus, from about 7000 BC onwards, productive economies based on fishing, livestock and various types of agriculture were pioneered, with success leading to cultural and population expansion. We are not yet able to assign these various developments to particular ethnic or language groups, but the combined efforts of linguists, anthropologists and archaeologists are making some progress here. What is clear is that these various economic and cultural developments were formative in the dominance of the modern Negroid type in sub-Saharan Africa.

From much earlier, probably Middle Stone Age times, a general distinction was emerging between the African peoples south of the Sahara and the Caucasoid type of the Mediterranean, including North Africa. For the Sahara in its more arid periods constituted a barrier, at least relatively. Within the African stock subdivisions naturally developed. The pygmy subtype adapted to a specialized hunting-gathering life in the thick forests of the Zaïre basin; in southern Africa and in eastern Africa as far north as Tanzania, the type known as "Bushmanoid" was dominant until the early centuries AD.

In these southerly savanna regions agriculture and domestic livestock penetrated late, only during the Iron Age. Here a hunting and gathering culture persisted and is well attested at numerous campsites. Many of these are natural rock-shelters, where the hunters frequently painted the animals which they loved to chase: eland, giraffe, elephant and other animals, often realistically and beautifully executed. Thousands of such paintings are known in southern Africa; there is a smaller group, probably related, in central Tanzania. (But the hunter rock art of the Sahara, generally older than the cattle paintings there, is probably unrelated to that of the south.) The tradition is clearly many thousands of years old. The so-called Bushmen, now confined to semidesert areas of the Kalahari, are essentially descendants of this once successful and widespread hunting population in eastern and southern Africa. Studies of surviving Bushmen communities and of their Khoisan languages are therefore important in assisting an understanding of the Late Stone Age way of life and in particular of the beliefs behind the rock art. But the comparison is not a perfect one, for the present Bushmen are confined to semidesert areas, having over 2000 years lost the best savanna lands to the southward-expanding agricultural and iron-using Bantu.

The expansion of people with early Bantu languages through the southern third of Africa during the first five centuries AD showed agricultural economy and iron technology extending their ranges together where neither had been known previously. Archaeologically this Early Iron Age settlement across the savannas of eastern and southern Africa is documented by numerous sites of

Top Tuareg relax in front of prehistoric paintings in a rock shelter at Sefar in the Tassili-n-Ajjer, southern Algeria. The monstrous human figure, 3·25 meters tall, forms the centerpiece of a scene with suppliant women. Several distinct styles appear in Saharan rock art but they are difficult to date precisely.

Above Masked hunters attack an eland in this scene from the Kamberg rock shelter in the Drakensberg mountains of Natal, eastern South Africa. Eland, often depicted with meticulous realism, were a favorite subject of Bushman art.

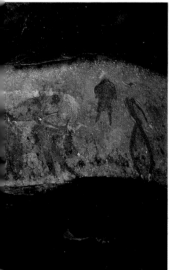

A smith at Uvinza, western [Tanza]nia, uses skin-covered [bellow]s with wooden nozzles. [These] are connected through a [pi]pe to the charcoal fire to [give s]ufficient heat for the iron [to be m]ade workable. Similar [techni]ques are used all over

agricultural homesteads with distinctive related pottery styles. By contrast, in most regions north of the equator, agriculture and pastoralism were considerably older, so that iron when it first appeared did not promote such spectacular population movements. It did however improve agricultural efficiency. There were moreover all sorts of minor adjustments within an already very complicated situation – as the linguistic map for the whole region between the Sahara and the equator shows.

Recent archaeological research indicates that as early as 600 to 300 BC iron was being mined, smelted and forged by a number of widely separated communities in the savannas and woodlands as far south as Lake Victoria Nyanza. Three regions in particular stand out: central Nigeria, the interlacustrine region (notably northwestern Tanzania) and the middle Nile. It is now clear that there was a rapid radiation of the knowledge of iron between the Sahara and the equator (and even slightly beyond) around the middle of the first millennium BC.

Some scholars argue that ironworking may have been invented south of the Sahara, independent of outside stimulus. However, as new discoveries push the dates back closer to those for the Mediterranean, it becomes more likely that developments in the two regions were connected, especially in view of the basic similarity of techniques. A central Saharan link looks likely from comparison of early smelting furnaces in Nigeria with those of northwestern Africa. From the beginning, however, iron technology south of the Sahara and the toolkits produced for domestic, agricultural and military purposes began developing along lines distinct from those of the Mediterranean.

In this period it is possible to discern some of the broader ethnic, linguistic and cultural groupings of African peoples that still persist – the Bantu, for instance. But the individual peoples of recent centuries had not then emerged, nor on the whole had the famous kingdoms of later Africa. A few examples belong to this Early Iron Age period; especially celebrated is the kingdom of Cush along the middle Nile which flourished during the last centuries BC and the earliest AD.

Despite instances of contact with the wider world in Early Iron Age times, either across the Sahara or through the Red Sea and Indian Ocean sailing routes, the fuller development of such commercial and cultural contact has happened during the last millennium. But it should not be inferred from this that trade was previously unknown in Africa: local and regional trade in essential commodites was definitely ancient (and was a prerequisite for the evolution of long-distance traffic in precious goods). Grains and other cultivated foods, livestock and skins would have been traded within African communities and between neighboring ones, especially along the borders of contrasting ecological zones. Crafts moreover imply specialization and trade; of these, pottery and more particularly ironworking tended to be concentrated in suitable localities. Pure and productive sources of salt are rare in the interior and were therefore prized and influenced the siting of markets, whether formal or informal, and the directions of trade in general.

J.E.G.S.

KINGDOMS AND EMPIRES

In Africa as everywhere else in the world, people organized themselves for countless millennia into small, more or less self-sufficient political communities. From about the fourth millennium BC they began forming more centralized units, owing allegiance to a king. By the middle of the 19th century the majority of Africans were under some kind of monarchical rule. But one must beware of seeing the establishment of royal government as inevitable progress or an inner teleological necessity. Many rejected it. Well into the 20th century millions remained for choice within loosely organized political structures, without kings or apparatus of continuous government, including large populations like the Igbo and Tiv of modern Nigeria.

If people reorganize themselves politically with a new form of government there must first be some organizing stimulus. The earliest African kingdom, Egypt, grew up through control of the flood waters of the Nile delta. Predicting and controlling annual floods demanded rigorous organization of land and people – under control of one ruler. From towards the end of the fourth millennium BC Egypt was united under a succession of kings who ruled, with interregna, until the conquest by the Greeks in 332 BC, leaving for posterity a wonderful legacy of building, painting and sculpture, much of it designed to glorify the monarchy.

Higher up the Nile arose the kingdom of Cush. A province of Egypt at some periods, it developed as a separate entity with its own distinctive culture. During the 8th century BC Cushite kings conquered Egypt and ruled it for about 80 years. Subsequently it survived as a separate kingdom, wealthy from trade in tropical produce, and exploiting its iron resources, with its capital eventually at Meroë. Temples, burial pyramids and palaces were built, deriving stylistically from Egypt but executed in a distinctively Meroïtic style. A Meroïtic script evolved, quite different from the Egyptian hieroglyphs. In the 4th century AD it was destroyed, probably by neighboring Nubian peoples who founded their own kingdoms which were converted to Christianity by missionaries from Constantinople.

In the rest of Mediterranean Africa the organizing stimulus came from outside. Phoenicians founded the Carthaginian republic, stimulating their African neighbors to form rival inland kingdoms, Numidia (roughly modern Algeria) and Mauretania (roughly modern Morocco). The Numidians allied with the Romans to destroy Carthage. Ultimately both kingdoms were annexed to the Roman empire. The Romans also annexed coastal Tripolitania and Cyrenaica, Greek settlements, but not their hinterland where, in country now desert, the African kingdom of Garama maintained its independence.

During the 7th century the whole of Mediterranean Africa was conquered by Muslim Arabs. The Berbers, lineage-based desert peoples like the Arabs, adopted Islam, but grew restive under Arab rule. In the 9th century the Berber Fatimid family asserted political independence and conquered a state which extended over Egypt to Syria and Arabia. During this period of African empire Cairo, the Fatimid capital, was built up with beautiful palaces and mosques, including the great center of higher Muslim learning, the Al-Azhar mosque, founded about 970. In the 12th century Turkish rulers drove the Fatimids from Egypt. Thenceforth Turkish governments (after 1453 centered on Constantinople) held sovereignty over Egypt until the 20th century.

In the Maghreb Berber rule continued. Two successive Muslim reform movements (known to Europeans as Almoravid and Almohad) extended it north over Spain. But by the 13th century the empire had broken down into small rival states. During the 16th century most of the Mediterranean shore became part of the Turkish empire. Morocco however remained independent under its own Muslim rulers.

Trade sometimes provided the stimulus towards the institution of monarchical government. The kingdom of Aksum, on the northeastern edge of the Ethiopian plateau, grew wealthy through control of the neighboring Red Sea port of Adulis, trading

African kingdoms
At successive periods kingdoms and empires covered much of Africa, though there were always peoples who for choice retained loosely structured political organizations. Almost all were of African origin. Only along the Mediterranean shore, where Romans and then Arabs invaded, and in the East African city-states were outside political influences significant. Elsewhere indigenous political systems developed, reflecting the socioeconomic organization of the different peoples. The early 19th century in particular was a period of widespread state building, with powerful rulers creating nation-states all over the continent – a process thwarted in the last decades of the century by European conquest.

scale 1:54 000 000

0   1500km

0   1000mi

By the beginning of the 1st century AD Aksum, from which the kingdom of Ethiopia was to emerge, was a powerful trading state. Its kings caused tall, flat-sided monoliths (stelae) to be raised, some over 30 meters high. Originally there were more than a hundred at Aksum. Now only one remains standing.

with the Indian Ocean countries and dominating the peoples of southern Arabia. Its kings commemorated their glories with stone stelae, up to 30 meters high, surmounting subterranean royal tombs. In the mid-4th century King Ezana adopted Christianity. But with the rise of Islam, Aksum lost control of the seaboard to Muslim rulers. It developed inland as the mountain kingdom of Ethiopia, with its heartland in Amhara on the northwestern plateau. The Ethiopian Church followed the monophysite belief of the Coptic Church of Alexandria, but with its own liturgical language, Ge'ez, and distinctive rites. It was closely linked with the monarchy and used as an instrument of government, particularly after the accession of the Solomonian dynasty in the 13th century. The kings enriched it with landed estates. Churches and monasteries proliferated.

Trade also provided an organizing stimulus in West Africa: kingdoms grew out of markets. Trade across the Sahara was immensely stimulated when camels were introduced in about the 3rd century AD. Gold mined in the forest country around the sources of the Niger, Senegal and Volta was taken north to market centers on the grassland edge of the desert (the sahel) and thence by camel to North Africa. Much of it was ultimately exported to Europe, which relied on West African gold until American resources became available. Those who

gained control of an urban market center could levy customs duties and taxes on the traders and brokers, and extract the surplus product from the surrounding lineage-organized farmers and pastoralists, thus turning themselves into kings.

Some of the sahel kingdoms were founded by Berber or other desert peoples who moved south to dominate the trading cities, others by indigenous individuals or groups who gained power by force or persuasion. Ghana, the largest of the early kingdoms of the western Sudan, was already flourishing by the 8th century. Its Soninke king and his opulent court were supported by control of the export trade in gold, copper and salt, and of the subject rural population.

North African traders brought Islam to the western Sudan. Most traders adopted it, but the mass of the people retained their own religions. Indeed until the 20th century Muslims were a small minority in West Africa. Hence any king who adopted Islam had to go on performing indigenous rituals to keep his people's allegiance. The king of Takrur in the far west is believed to have been the first to adopt Islam, in the 11th century. In the kingdom of Mali, which succeeded Ghana during the 13th century as the predominant state in the western Sudan, the kings became Muslims. Some undertook the pilgrimage to Mecca, including

Great Zimbabwe

In the gold-mining country around the Zambezi, kingdoms grew up from about the 7th century AD, evidenced by the discovery of royal burial sites. In the eastern part (modern Zimbabwe and Mozambique) walled stone enclosures, *zimbabwes*, were built for the kings. The ruins of several hundred survive. The most spectacular is the palace known as Great Zimbabwe, built by the Shona people. Construction was spread over about 400 years. Work began in the early 11th century and reached its peak in the early 15th. Then the king moved away. It is not altogether clear why the site was abandoned, but it seems likely that the soil around it had become exhausted and could no longer maintain a royal court. Pastoralism was the dominant method of subsistence, and the land may have been overgrazed. Though no longer a royal residence, it remained an important religious shrine until the 19th century. Despite legends put about by Europeans prospecting for gold that Great Zimbabwe was built by mysterious Asian or European immigrants, archaeologists have conclusively shown that it and the other *zimbabwes* were of African construction.   C.F.

Left The elliptical building is bounded by an outer wall over 250 meters long. It rises tapering from a base which is 5 meters thick at its widest to a height of 9·75 meters. Parallel with it, separated by the narrow paved passage shown here, runs a smaller, earlier wall of less skilled workmanship.

Below The architectural focus of Great Zimbabwe is the conical tower which, with the outer wall, represents the last phase of building. It was constructed by setting back successive courses of stones as the tower rose. Decorated monoliths, some of them surmounted by sculptured birds, once stood in the forecourt.

Far left The vast elliptical construction dominating the site of Great Zimbabwe is the royal palace. It contains the most spectacular buildings, dating from the 15th century, the towering outer wall and the conical tower. In the foreground are the ruins of buildings dating from earlier periods.

Left The site of Great Zimbabwe was originally covered with large granite boulders. Some were incorporated into the buildings. Some were used for quarrying. Slabs were hacked off, or fires were lighted to heat the boulders, which were then cooled with water to split them into building blocks.

Mansa Musa, whose spectacular munificence, lavishing presents of gold as he went, caused the price of gold in Egypt to fall. In the late 15th century the Mali hegemony was replaced by that of Songhay, which survived until 1591 when it was overthrown by invasion from Morocco.

Trade from the central Sudan went northeastward to Tripoli and Egypt. South of Lake Chad the kingdom of Kanem (later Bornu) was founded in the 8th or 9th century by the Saifawa dynasty which ruled until 1846. Eastwards the Keira dynasty founded the kingdom of Darfur. Further east, in the Nile valley, Muslim rulers supplanted the Christian kings of Nubia during the 14th century. Later they were conquered by the Funj people who moved up the Nile, adopted Islam and established the kingdom of Sinnar. Thus right across the Sudan, from Nile to Atlantic, stretched a series of kingdoms in which Muslim rulers controlled non-Muslim, lineage-organized peoples.

In the grasslands and forests of the lower Niger too, kingdoms grew up from market centers. The Hausa kingdoms developed through trade, Katsina and Kano growing into large cities through industry (textile-weaving and leather-working for export) as well as commerce. Further south were the Yoruba kingdoms, of which Oyo in the northern grasslands grew to dominate the rest; near the coast was Benin. The forest kingdoms carried on the fine sculpture tradition already evolved among the so-called Nok people further north, and created new and rich styles of court art, particularly in Ife and Benin. Across the Niger a royal burial containing elaborate sculpture has been found at Igbo-Ukwu.

From about the end of the first millennium BC, iron-using peoples who spoke some kind of Bantu language began moving out from a homeland in the grasslands between Lake Chad and the Benue river. They moved gradually, in small communities, not as an invading horde, among the indigenous hunter–gatherer and pastoral peoples. Eventually they peopled most of subequatorial Africa. Those who settled in the mineral-rich country around the upper reaches of the Zaïre and Zambezi exploited the gold, copper and iron resources. Gold was exported overseas (as from West Africa), carried down the Zambezi to Sofala and thence to the Indian Ocean trading sphere. Chinese porcelain and other Oriental wares were imported in exchange. Here, too, kingdoms grew up, through control of trade and of natural resources, particularly cattle. In the kingdoms of the lower Zambezi the Shona people constructed large stone buildings for their kings, the most famous being Great Zimbabwe. Further inland the Lunda, Luba and Bemba also organized kingdoms.

Along the East African coast Arabs and other Asians came to trade with the Bantu population. Their market centers developed into 30 city-states, including Mogadisho, Malindi, Mombasa and Kilwa, each under its own ruler, competing for control of the gold trade from the south. Politically disunited, they shared a common religion, Islam, and the Swahili language and culture that grew up among the Afro–Arab inhabitants – a fusion of Bantu and Arabic elements. Handsome mosques and palaces were built in a distinctive style out of locally cut coral.

It is not clear what stimulated the organization of kingdoms around the great lakes. State building seems to have begun at a period when immigrant pastoralists combined with indigenous cultivators; mixed farming gave rise to a better diet, and hence larger populations. Some kingdoms were founded by immigrants from the upper Nile valley, like the Luo. An earlier generation of historians assumed that they all derived from conquest by pastoralist Nilotes. But though in all the kingdoms (which included Bunyoro, Buganda, Nkore, Rwanda and Burundi) ruling clans claiming alien origin maintained an ascendancy, sometimes based on control of cattle, over subordinate clans, there is no evidence that they had a common origin or formed a cohesive conquest group. East of the great lakes the peoples retained their loosely structured political organizations.

Forms of government varied greatly, but it seems safe to say that these African kingdoms, excepting ancient Egypt, were usually constitutional monarchies. Though in any society where sacred and secular are not strictly differentiated – which they were not in these kingdoms – a ruler will tend to claim divine authority, divinity was hedged. Royal power was limited by recognized political controls – often relics of the non-hierarchical forms they had superseded. Succession disputes, when a king died, prevented the accumulation of hereditary powers that automatic primogeniture may bring. Wealth was customarily redistributed, preventing capital formation by kings or subjects. Usually men ruled, but in some kingdoms queen mothers had recognized powers.

Direct European trading contacts, beginning in the 15th century, gradually drew coastal West Africa into the orbit of expanding European capitalism. Africa became a market for the growing manufactures of Europe and a supplier of raw materials and labor – the slaves shipped across the Atlantic. But in most places the political structures were unaffected. Europeans came as traders, not invaders, paying customs duties and rents to African rulers who retained sovereignty over the European trading posts. Some kingdoms grew more powerful through the slave trade, particularly Asante and Dahomey.

Only in southern Africa did the Portuguese establish a small colonial presence, in coastal Angola (where, after a century of warfare, they destroyed the Mbundu kingdom and seriously weakened the inland kingdom of Kongo) and to a much lesser extent in coastal Mozambique. They also dominated the East African Swahili city-states until supplanted there in the 17th century by the sultans of Oman.

In the extreme south, around the Cape of Good Hope, the rainfall pattern did not fit the Bantu-speaking peoples' agriculture. The land was inhabited by small, loosely organized chiefdoms of cattle-herding Khoikhoi (Hottentots). In 1652 the Dutch East India Company established a trading post among them. Eventually, by persuasion and then force, the European settlers (who came to call themselves Afrikaners) reduced the Khoikhoi to subjection.

The 18th and 19th centuries saw a political transformation of the western Sudan. Many strict Muslims resented having to obey nominally Muslim governments which tolerated and practiced non-Muslim rites. About 1725 a full-scale *jihad* started in

the upland kingdom of Fouta Djallon where a group of Muslim scholars and traders, supported by discontented non-Muslims with political grievances, overthrew the government and established a Muslim state. Their success set off a series of *jihads* throughout the western Sudan, the most famous being those of Usuman dan Fodio in Hausaland, which began in 1804, and of al-Haj 'Umar in Segu (Upper Niger) in the early 1860s. The old kingdoms were replaced by new Muslim states, governed ostensibly by the *shari'a* (Muslim law), though it could not always be strictly enforced.

Among the Yoruba, the kingdom of Oyo broke down, and from the early 1820s the Yoruba states began fighting one another, each trying to gain supremacy. *Jihad* leaders from Hausaland, called in to help, ended by taking over northern Yorubaland themselves. Their advance southwards, ''to dip the Koran into the sea,'' as they put it, was checked at the edge of the forest country. Meanwhile the Yoruba civil wars continued intermittently, almost until the end of the century.

Some Muslim leaders used the rhetoric of *jihad* to create personal empires. Such were Samori Touré, who conquered a large area around the upper Niger in the 1870s and 1880s, and Rabih who, having established himself in the central Sudan, southwest of Darfur, advanced westwards and in 1893 conquered Bornu, where in 1846 a Muslim leader had supplanted the ancient Saifawa dynasty. In the eastern Sudan another Muslim leader, Muhammad Ahmad, proclaimed himself the *Mahdi* in 1881, and conquered a large state which was taken over at his death by his successor the *Khalifa* Abdallahi. So by the last decades of the 19th century nearly the whole Sudan, from Nile almost to Atlantic, was ruled by recently installed, dynamic Muslim governments.

In Egypt, nominally part of the Turkish empire,

during the early 19th century an Albanian officer, Muhammad Ali, became hereditary ruler of what was virtually an independent state, modeled on the secular states of Europe, and expanding up the Nile. In Ethiopia, where feuds among the nobility during the 17th and 18th centuries almost dissipated central authority, the power of the monarchy was revived in the early 19th century by a usurping king, Tewodros. Under the rule of his successors, notably Menelik, Ethiopia became a powerful, aggressive state, whose boundaries by 1902 stretched far beyond the area of the historic kingdom over the whole plateau and down on to the coastal plains.

In southern Africa radical political changes were stimulated early in the 19th century by the transformation of the Nguni peoples of the southeast coast from a lineage-based society into a militarized nation-state, the Zulu kingdom. Under their ruthless king Chaka, the Zulu conquered their neighbors and set off a series of bitter wars (the *Mfecane*) which depopulated large parts of the interior, leaving them vulnerable to Afrikaner expansion. Sotho refugees from these wars were organized by a skillful leader, Moshoeshoe, into the mountain kingdom of Lesotho. Near the Indian Ocean coast others, under Sobhuza, founded the Swazi kingdom. To the west Tswana kingdoms developed. Thus the political pattern changed, states based on national allegiance replacing the former lineage-based systems.

Aggressive migrant armies from Chaka's kingdom moved north. The Ndebele, under Mzilikazi, established themselves among the Shona beyond the Limpopo. The Ngoni, under Zwangendaba, brought under their rule peoples in the modern Tanzania, Malawi and Zambia, over 1600 kilometers away from their homeland. Such large-scale militarized invasions were something new — very

Above left The kingdom of Bunyoro, in what is today Uganda, was probably founded in the 15th century, one of the largest of the great lakes kingdoms. Here the Mukama (king of Bunyoro) appears with his royal retinue and regalia. The monarchy was abolished in 1966.

Above A ceremonial procession in Niger. The military strength of the kingdoms of the western Sudan, which flourished from about the 8th to the 19th century, was based partly on cavalry. Horses had to be imported from North Africa across the Sahara to Bornu and the other kingdoms, as they do not breed easily in central Africa.

Above right Muhammad Ali (1769–1849), a Turkish officer of Albanian origin, seized power in Egypt in 1805 with the help of the Cairo population, and founded a dynasty that ruled until 1952. He sent military expeditions up the Nile and established Egyptian claims over what is today the Republic of the Sudan.

different from the small-scale movements hitherto usual.

The Omani Sultan Seyyid Said, who controlled the East African coastal cities, made Zanzibar his capital in 1840. Trading networks were established inland along routes already opened up by Nyamwezi ivory traders. As well as ivory, the Zanzibari traders obtained slaves which were in demand on Zanzibar Island, where a plantation economy developed, growing cloves for export. Small communities of Zanzibari traders settled themselves along the inland trade routes, trading with African suppliers.

Enterprising African traders took advantage of the expanding economy to gain political power – for example, Msiri, who won himself a kingdom in the Lunda country of the eastern Zaïre basin, ruling his subjects autocratically. A few Zanzibari traders, notably Tipu Tib, also turned themselves into rulers. The new trading networks opened up the lakes kingdoms, till then unconnected to the coast by trade, particularly Buganda, where the kings began seeking to break down existing constitutional checks and introduce absolute rule. The disturbances caused by the Ngoni invasions also stimulated political change. The Fipa and Hehe peoples of present-day southern Tanzania seem to have reorganized themselves into more centralized monarchies. Thus from the upper waters of the Zaïre, eastwards to the coast, political allegiances and structures were changing.

By the last decades of the 19th century the older kingdoms and clan-based communities were disappearing. States of new types, organized on their own indigenous lines, were dividing up the continent, an internally generated political process that owed little to European pressure. This already partially completed African partition of Africa was however forestalled by the European partition.   C.F.

Asante Ceremonial Regalia

The kingdom of Asante, in the modern state of Ghana, rose to power in the early 18th century under *Asantahene* (king) Osei Tutu. To strengthen the power of Asante he and his chief priest revised the constitution, deliberately using regalia as constitutional symbols. Until his time the royal throne (a stool) had symbolized the individual ruler. Osei Tutu substituted for it a special Golden Stool, said to have descended from heaven into his lap, symbolizing the Asante nation. Thus the ruler would die, but the nation live on in the stool. Every year the people assembled after the yam harvest for a national festival, the *Odwira* (misleadingly called by Europeans the Yam Custom), where the nation was glorified, and the national identity of its people reinforced, by purificatory ceremonies linking together the living and the dead. The Golden Stool,

hung with the golden death masks of generals defeated by Asante armies, was carried in procession and placed on a throne without ever touching the ground. Royal power was further manifested in the proliferation of regalia worn and used by the *Asantahene* and his subordinate chiefs, devised as symbols of their political status. Shielded from the sun by vast umbrellas, which were topped by gold-plated insignia with symbolic meanings, they were loaded with ornaments, usually of gold or gold-plated, since Asante lies in a gold-mining region. Their golden crowns, breastplates, bracelets, rings, even sandals, were worked with elaborate designs of symbolic significance, conveying an overwhelming sense of opulence, dignity and supernatural authority.

C.F.

Above A chief wears a distinctive *kente* cloth, woven on a narrow loom. The narrow strips are sewn together into a cloth, worn thrown over one shoulder. There are special types of patterned silk cloths worn only by royalty and chiefs.

Top right Asante thrones take the form of backless stools. Some chiefs also have *asipim* chairs with backs, as depicted here, probably copied from chairs used by early European traders. The wooden frame is studded with brass nails.

Right Elderly chiefs, holding gold-hilted state swords and protected by umbrellas, mourn the death of *Asantahene* Sir Agyeman Prempeh II in 1970. Installed in 1935, Prempeh II revived the monarchy, suppressed during the first decades of British rule, and restored its ceremonies to something of their former splendor.

Far right Musicians with drums and wooden gongs at the *Asantahene*'s funeral. The royal funeral ceremonies are spread out over a whole year after an *Asantahene*'s death and involve all the people.

Far left Chiefs with their retinue of wives and attendants waiting on the *Asantahene*, protected by ceremonial umbrellas and attended by a musician with a side-blown horn. The chief in the foreground wears a distinctive *kente* cloth, a gold-hilted state sword, a gold bracelet and an elaborate gold ring.

Left Chiefs attending on the *Asantahene* wearing ceremonial gold-plated headdresses.

Below Musicians blowing side-blown ivory horns at an Asante state ceremony. Each chief has his own horn-blower who carries out special duties. He sounds on his horn the distinctive notes which identify the chief and warn people of his presence. Each type of horn has its own name.

EUROPE IN AFRICA

In the last two decades of the 19th century almost the whole of Africa was rapidly taken under European political control; the colonies and protectorates which were then established are substantially the states of modern independent Africa. Yet the interaction between Europe and Africa has a history going back much further and modern Africa is as much the creation of this earlier series of contacts as of the colonial period itself. Of course, neither the story of European contacts nor that of the creation of states tells the whole story of modern Africa; even at the height of colonial rule, Africans maintained their own ways of organizing their social lives, worshiping God and expressing their cultural values. Nor were they wholly without the ability to take initiatives in the political and economic fields.

Certainly the voyages promoted by Prince Henry the Navigator in the 15th century resulted in contacts on a basis of equality with societies on the western side of Africa. Along the West African coast as far as the Bight of Benin, the Portuguese and other European traders accepted a role as tenants of African rulers. Further south and on the east, however, by about 1600, when the great military fortress of Fort Jesus had been built at Mombasa, the Portuguese were attempting to dominate – for several reasons. In the first place Islam had to be made to yield to Christianity. Hence the attempt to take the ancient Christian kingdom of Ethiopia into the Catholic fold involved a bitter war with the surrounding Muslims in the 1540s. The Muslims were defending not only Islam but also the Arab domination of the Indian Ocean network of trade. Military overlordship seemed to be the prerequisite for any economic benefits. The major prize was the gold trade of Sofala and Kilwa but the Portuguese soon found that control of the coastal outlets would not secure the supply; expeditions were therefore sent inland to gain control of the Zambezi valley and the gold-producing empire of Monomotapa.

In western Africa the principal economic prize was slaves. Portuguese demands soon outran what was offered by the Africans with whom they traded; this was the principal reason for the breakdown, for example, of the initially good relations between the Europeans and the Kongo kingdom. The Portuguese, though few in number and weak in real resources, had a margin of technological and organizational superiority over Africans, but this was outweighed by difficulties of disease and communications. Already by the mid-17th century their position along the Guinea coast had been overtaken by more active Dutch, French and British competitors who had built up a formidable collection of trading posts and castles along the coast. In East Africa a resurgence of Arab power, led by adventurous traders from Oman, resulted in the fall of Mombasa in 1699. Africans themselves in the Angola and Mozambique regions coped with the Portuguese as just one group who had to be

Above African artistic traditions were often adapted to provide comments on the new colonial situation. Here a carver from the Congo (Zaïre) has amusingly characterized the Belgian official of the 1920s in his chauffeur-driven car.

Left One item among grafitti by 17th-century Portuguese soldiers on the gun platform of the S. Mateus bastion of Fort Jesus. Perhaps the artist was hoping for relief from the sea during the long siege by the Omanis in 1698–99.

Right An example of the latest in European fortification science, Fort Jesus at Mombasa was built in 1593–96 to enable the Portuguese to dominate the East African coast. Though impregnable, it could be starved into submission, as in 1699.

managed in the ever-changing political struggle. Much as one might emphasize the independence and enterprise of rulers like Queen Nzinga of Matamba in dealing with the Europeans, perhaps a disturbing pattern had been set: one of the principal prizes of political success in tropical Africa was access to European goods. The prices were high but did not seem high, for all that was demanded were things that could be extracted from, rather than produced by, the African environment – slaves, ivory and some gold.

By 1800 the slave trade had become very big business indeed. The greater volume of all trade between Europe and Africa was now in the hands of much more resourceful and powerful groups than the Portuguese. The pattern, however, remained the same: Europeans stayed on the fringes of the continent and the political initiatives in the interior undoubtedly lay with Africans. Yet they and large numbers of their fellows, whether they realized it or not, were having their lives affected by the demands of the European capitalist-organized trade centered on an Atlantic region or the European/Oriental capitalist nexus of the Indian Ocean.

From about 1800, there were signs that Europeans would intervene more. These signs included geographical exploration, missionary endeavor, mercantile activity, mineral prospecting, European settlement and increasing governmental interference. In crude terms, these developments might be explained by alterations in the nature of world market demands on Africa which were themselves a product of Europe's industrial revolution and the political and ideological changes that accompanied it. Equally crudely, it might be said that the effects of the new developments were to be largely disruptive. The disruption was sufficient by the end of the century, in the judgment of some historians, to cause Africans to lose control of their environment as well as their political destiny. Europeans themselves saw Africa as disordered and needing firm government; this was more than just an excuse for their ambitions. Indeed the image of Africa in European eyes as backward and disorderly may be one of the most important legacies of the 19th century for it underlies 20th-century racial attitudes.

The most dramatic manifestation of new European activity in North Africa was Napoleon's invasion of Egypt in 1798. Although the French forces were ousted by Britain and Turkey, the invasion marks the beginning of attempts to modernize Egypt with the aid of European advisers and entrepreneurs who also took part in the campaigns to bring more of the Nile valley into the Egyptian orbit. The French also undertook the other major European initiative in North Africa when Algeria was invaded in 1830 after a minor trading dispute. As more of the territory was captured during the next 40 years, settlers moved in to become wheat and vine growers.

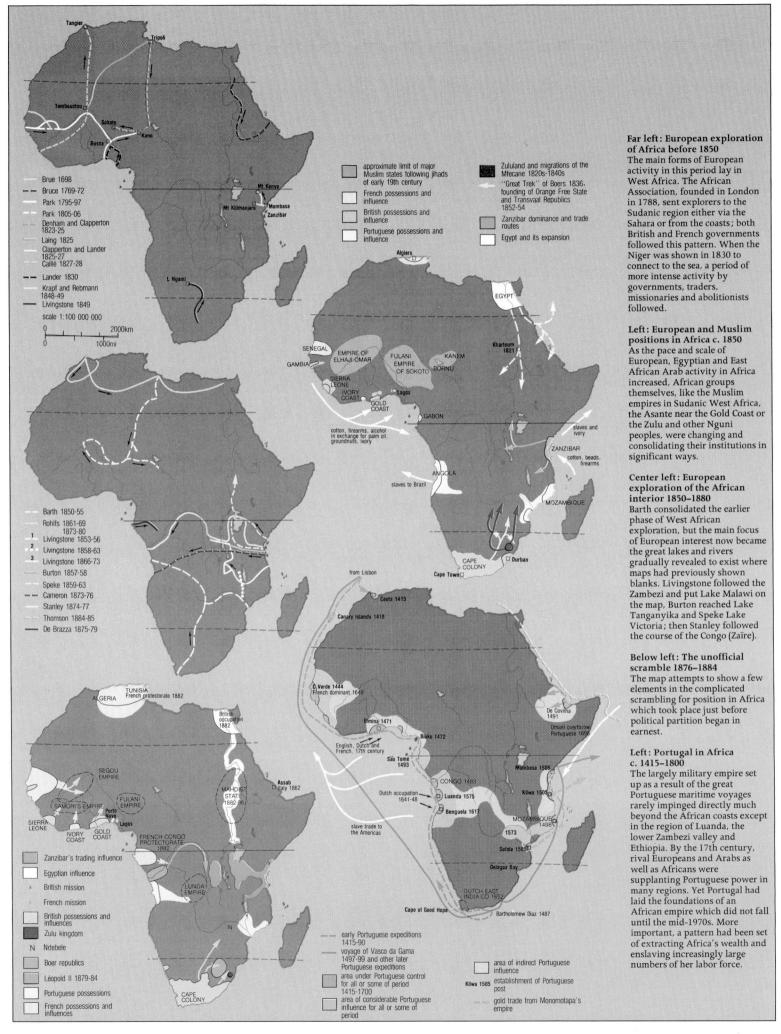

Brue 1698
Bruce 1769-72
Park 1795-97
Park 1805-06
Denham and Clapperton 1823-25
Laing 1825
Clapperton and Lander 1825-27
Caillé 1827-28
Lander 1830
Krapf and Rebmann 1848-49
Livingstone 1849

scale 1:100 000 000

0   2000km
0   1000mi

Tangier
Tripoli
Tombouctou
Sokoto
Kano
Bussa
Mt Kenya
Mt Kilimanjaro
Mombasa
Zanzibar
L Ngami

Barth 1850-55
Rohlfs 1861-69 1873-80
1 Livingstone 1853-56
2 Livingstone 1858-63
3 Livingstone 1866-73
Burton 1857-58
Speke 1859-63
Cameron 1873-76
Stanley 1874-77
Thomson 1884-85
De Brazza 1875-79

approximate limit of major Muslim states following jihads of early 19th century
French possessions and influence
British possessions and influence
Portuguese possessions and influence
Zululand and migrations of the Mfecane 1820s-1840s
"Great Trek" of Boers 1836, founding of Orange Free State and Transvaal Republics 1852-54
Zanzibar dominance and trade routes
Egypt and its expansion

Algiers
EGYPT
SENEGAL
GAMBIA
EMPIRE OF ELHAJI-OMAR
SIERRA LEONE
IVORY COAST
GOLD COAST
Lagos
FULANI EMPIRE OF SOKOTO
KANEM
BORNU
Khartoum 1821
GABON
ANGOLA
ZANZIBAR
cotton, beads, firearms
MOZAMBIQUE
cotton, firearms, alcohol in exchange for palm oil, groundnuts, ivory
slaves and ivory
slaves to Brazil
CAPE COLONY
Cape Town
Durban

from Lisbon
Ceuta 1415
Canary Islands 1418
C. Verde 1444 French dominant 1640
Elmina 1471
Bioko 1472
English, Dutch and French, 17th century
São Tomé 1493
CONGO 1483
Dutch occupation 1641-48
Luanda 1575
Benguela 1617
slave trade to the Americas
De Covilha 1491
Omani overthrow Portuguese 1698
Mombasa 1505
Kilwa 1505
MOZAMBIQUE 1498
1573
Sofala 1505
Delagoa Bay
DUTCH EAST INDIA CO 1652
Cape of Good Hope
Bartholomew Diaz 1487

TUNISIA French protectorate 1882
ALGERIA
British occupation 1882
SEGOU EMPIRE
SAMORI'S EMPIRE
FULANI EMPIRE
MAHDIST STATE 1882-96
Assab Italy 1862
SIERRA LEONE
IVORY COAST
GOLD COAST
Porto Novo
Lagos
FRENCH CONGO PROTECTORATE 1882
LUNDA EMPIRE
N
CAPE COLONY

Zanzibar's trading influence
Egyptian influence
x British mission
x French mission
British possessions and influences
Zulu kingdom
N Ndebele
Boer republics
Léopold II 1879-84
Portuguese possessions
French possessions and influences

early Portuguese expeditions 1415-90
voyage of Vasco da Gama 1497-99 and other later Portuguese expeditions
area under Portuguese control for all or some of period 1415-1700
area of considerable Portuguese influence for all or some of period
area of indirect Portuguese influence
Kilwa 1505 establishment of Portuguese post
gold trade from Monomotapa's empire

Far left: European exploration of Africa before 1850
The main forms of European activity in this period lay in West Africa. The African Association, founded in London in 1788, sent explorers to the Sudanic region either via the Sahara or from the coasts; both British and French governments followed this pattern. When the Niger was shown in 1830 to connect to the sea, a period of more intense activity by governments, traders, missionaries and abolitionists followed.

Left: European and Muslim positions in Africa c. 1850
As the pace and scale of European, Egyptian and East African Arab activity in Africa increased, African groups themselves, like the Muslim empires in Sudanic West Africa, the Asante near the Gold Coast or the Zulu and other Nguni peoples, were changing and consolidating their institutions in significant ways.

Center left: European exploration of the African interior 1850–1880
Barth consolidated the earlier phase of West African exploration, but the main focus of European interest now became the great lakes and rivers gradually revealed to exist where maps had previously shown blanks. Livingstone followed the Zambezi and put Lake Malawi on the map, Burton reached Lake Tanganyika and Speke Lake Victoria; then Stanley followed the course of the Congo (Zaïre).

Below left: The unofficial scramble 1876–1884
The map attempts to show a few elements in the complicated scrambling for position in Africa which took place just before political partition began in earnest.

Left: Portugal in Africa c. 1415–1800
The largely military empire set up as a result of the great Portuguese maritime voyages rarely impinged directly much beyond the African coasts except in the region of Luanda, the lower Zambezi valley and Ethiopia. By the 17th century, rival Europeans and Arabs as well as Africans were supplanting Portuguese power in many regions. Yet Portugal had laid the foundations of an African empire which did not fall until the mid-1970s. More important, a pattern had been set of extracting Africa's wealth and enslaving increasingly large numbers of her labor force.

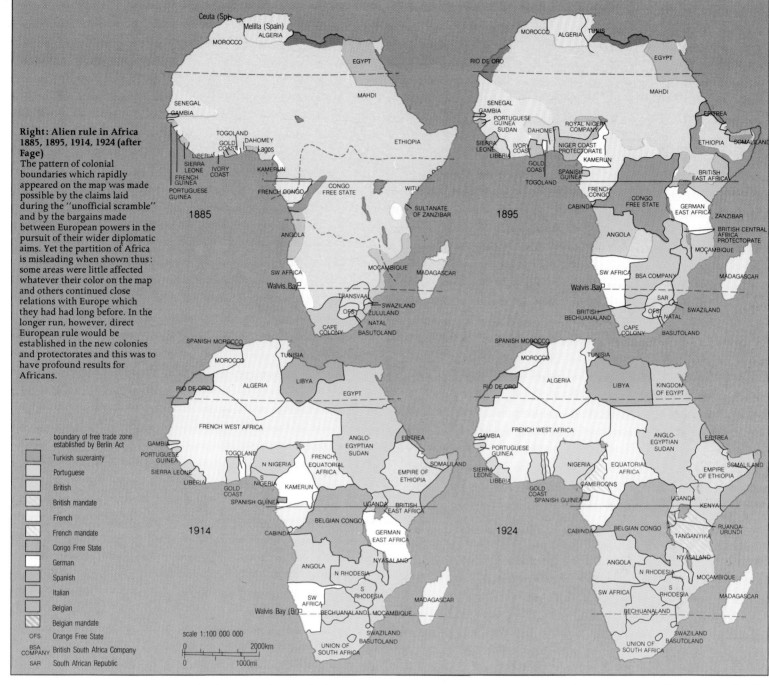

Right: Alien rule in Africa 1885, 1895, 1914, 1924 (after Fage)
The pattern of colonial boundaries which rapidly appeared on the map was made possible by the claims laid during the "unofficial scramble" and by the bargains made between European powers in the pursuit of their wider diplomatic aims. Yet the partition of Africa is misleading when shown thus: some areas were little affected whatever their color on the map and others continued close relations with Europe which they had had long before. In the longer run, however, direct European rule would be established in the new colonies and protectorates and this was to have profound results for Africans.

- - - - boundary of free trade zone established by Berlin Act
Turkish suzerainty
Portuguese
British
British mandate
French
French mandate
Congo Free State
German
Spanish
Italian
Belgian
Belgian mandate
OFS   Orange Free State
BSA COMPANY   British South Africa Company
SAR   South African Republic

scale 1:100 000 000

Less dramatic but in the long run more important were European moves in West Africa. Although James Bruce who explored Ethiopia in the 1760s may be an early example of the phenomenon, scientific exploration properly began with the foundation of the African Association in London in 1788. The Association believed that Europe's ignorance of Africa was "a reproach upon the present age." Later bodies like the Paris Geographical Society of 1821 and the Royal Geographical Society of 1830 were to continue to try to remove that reproach. Of course the desire to have accurate maps and accurate botanical and ethnographic information was itself a characteristic of the revolutionary and industrial age. At the more practical level, Europe's increasing wealth made it feasible to finance scientific expeditions which, in the long run, might lead to a pay-off of some kind. For example, the course and termination of the Niger became the great geographical question of the age and when Richard Lander demonstrated in 1830 that the river debouched into the Gulf of Guinea,

attempts to use it as a means of access to the far interior by steamboat soon followed.

If scientific inquiry was one sign of new European interests, determined attempts to promote the Gospel overseas were another. This characteristic of the evangelical revival was seen most clearly in West Africa in the work of the (Anglican) Church Missionary Society from 1806, the Methodists and the German Basel and Bremen societies. The story of these Protestant missions is part of the larger story of the revolution in moral attitudes which led to the growth of the anti-slave-trade movement. British abolitionists set up Sierra Leone in 1787 for freed slaves and, when the British government abolished the slave trade in 1807 and began to try to persuade other countries to do the same, a new era dawned. Missionary work was part of the larger philanthropic campaign to repair the ravages of the slave trade by introducing "legitimate commerce," education and Christian civilization. No doubt there was an element of hypocrisy here; if industrial Europe wanted palm oil rather than slaves it was as much a reflection of changing industrial needs as of changing morality. Nevertheless, the fervor of the Christian and humanitarian campaigns in West Africa was to help to change the face of the region.

Whatever the precise mixture of economic interest and humanitarian pressure which accomplished it, governments, especially the British and French, became increasingly involved in West African affairs. Officials on the spot gradually began to see the need to interfere in the interior and often did so even when the home governments maintained a cautious attitude. As the British took a firmer hold on the Gold Coast, for example, they found themselves in conflict with Asante power inland. French initiatives in the Senegal valley region led to the beginnings in the 1850s of a series of conflicts with Islamic kingdoms of the interior. In fact the early 19th century had seen the political transformation of the Islamic region as the result of a series of reforming *jihads*; empires such as that of al-Haj 'Umar or Muhammad Bello were certainly now strong enough to resist any European encroachments.

In eastern Africa there was a comparative dearth of European activity in this period. Although more European and American merchants arrived, the impact of Europe's economic revolution was mostly felt indirectly via India and Arabia. Thus Zanzibari traders began to wrest control of the slave and ivory trades between the interior and the coast from Africans. Yet the economic and strategic interests of France and Britain in the Indian Ocean made them take some note of what was going on and Zanzibar itself increasingly became a client state of the British.

In South Africa, British government involvement was much more direct. Although Cape Town was captured in 1795 and retained in 1815 for strategic reasons, the British soon found themselves beset with problems in the hinterland. The original Dutch settlers, reinforced later by French Huguenots, considered themselves as Afrikaners. Many of them, the so-called Boers, had become pastoralists, constantly seeking new areas outside the Cape Colony itself where the British provided some measure of protection for the Khoikhoi people whom Afrikaners had previously dominated or enslaved. The Great Trek of the late 1830s was partly a response to the abolition of slavery in the British empire in 1833. But by this period the trekkers had encountered Bantu peoples much more formidable than the Khoikhoi. The Bantu east of the Drakensberg range also needed more land, a desire seen most clearly in the rise of Chaka's Zulu state in the 1820s. Out of the consequent *Mfecane* (scattering of peoples), the Boer treks which eventually created the republics of the Orange Free State and Transvaal in the 1850s, the contests between the Africans and the Boers and the often unavailing attempts of the British to exert control were founded the roots of modern South Africa. The Boers, pious but narrow Calvinists, were determined to preserve their identity against British officials, soldiers and missionaries and even more against the black peoples around them.

The third quarter of the century was a classic age of scientific exploration in Africa with the focus now on the question of the Nile source and great lakes of East and central Africa. Although the

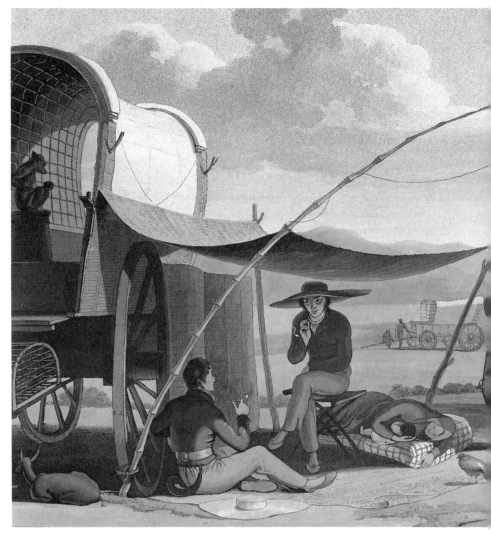

motives were broadly similar to those which had taken explorers into West Africa 50 years before, one great difference lay in the amount of public interest created in Europe. Indeed one of the most famous episodes, the meeting of Stanley and Livingstone, was a newspaper "scoop." Nor was interest confined to the adventure story element in the explorers' work: their verdicts on the condition of Africa nearly all suggested that increased European intervention was necessary. Great economic opportunities existed in the shape of mineral resources or supposedly fertile agricultural areas which Africans, either through inherent inabilities or restraints placed upon them by the slave trade, were incapable of developing. Great evangelical and educational opportunities existed for the missionary and both he and the trader could overcome problems of transport by using steamboats on the rivers and lakes discovered by the explorers. There were other signs of impending change. Diamonds were discovered at Kimberley in 1869 and gold was to be found in the Witwatersrand area of Transvaal in 1885; the Suez Canal was opened in 1869; Egypt established a claim to control of the upper Nile valley in the mid 1870s; in West Africa, the French began a project to develop rail and river traffic between their Senegal colony and the interior.

In 1876 Léopold II, King of the Belgians, called a conference of African explorers at Brussels which set up the International Association to continue the scientific exploration of Africa and begin the process of developing it. Under both the direct and

Above Many descendants of the 17th-century Dutch and French Huguenot settlers at the Cape moved northeastwards in the 1770–1870 period to become pastoral farmers, the "Boers." Their treks in search of the promised land free of British control led to serious clashes with the Bantu.

Below Human porterage was the only practicable transportation in most of interior tropical Africa. As international demand for ivory increased, long "caravans" of carriers marched hundreds of kilometers each with burdens of 35 kg or more. This porter's own meager supplies and possessions are tied to the tusk.

Below The *Ma Robert* on the Shire river, 1859. Livingstone experimented with river and lake steamboats as one means of replacing slave porterage in Africa during his Zambezi expedition of 1858–64.

Bottom A meeting of cultures. The Scottish explorer J. A. Grant's own sketch of his attempt to join in a dance in 1861 at Ukulima's village in what is now northern Tanzania.

Above If European and African interests clashed seriously enough, Europeans might bring the weight of their technological superiority to bear as Britain did in 1873 to subdue the Asante who threatened the political and economic interests of Britain and her African allies on the Gold Coast in West Africa.

Below Henry Morton Stanley (1841–1904), most effective – and ruthless – of explorers, "found"

Livingstone in 1871, solved the problems of the Nile and Congo in 1874–77, and helped create Léopold's Congo Free State and British possessions on the upper Nile in the 1880s. The ex-slave boy Kalulu, acquired in 1871, visited the US and Britain but was drowned on Stanley's next expedition.

Below right The German Dr Heinrich Barth (1821–65) led a British-sponsored expedition to

West Africa in the 1850s.

Bottom The greatest European explorer, David Livingstone (1813–73) worked almost continuously in Africa from 1841 to 1873. He evolved from conventional missionary to scientific explorer and advocate of "Christianity, Commerce and Civilization" to heal the "open sore of the world" – the African slave trade.

The Source of the Nile Debate

The quest for the source of the Nile excited 19th-century Europe because it involved adventurous exploration, intellectual controversy and individual rivalries. There was also interest in the political and economic implications of the discoveries. The Nile problem was only part of the larger task of delineating east central Africa's great lakes, rumored to exist on the basis of Classical sources like Herodotus and Ptolemy, 17th-century Portuguese accounts and confused reports by Arab ivory traders. As "armchair" scholarship and practical exploration revealed the existence of the lakes, the possibility of steamboats on them carrying commerce and the Gospel became attractive. In the 1880s this happened and the area of the source of the Nile itself in Uganda became a key strategic objective of rival imperialists.

R.C.B.

Right John Hanning Speke who reached the source of the White Nile in July 1862.

Below right James Bruce at the source of the Blue Nile drinking the health of George III, 1770. Although Pedro Paez and other Portuguese had visited the Blue Nile's source in Ethiopia, their reports remained little known. When therefore the eccentric Scottish laird James Bruce (1730–94) reached the spot on 4 November 1770, he claimed "a trophy in which I can have no competitor." This romanticized engraving well reflects his boast. Yet the major puzzle of the White Nile source remained.

Below left Grant's drawing of the source of the White Nile at the Ripon Falls, Uganda, shows the point where the river flows out of Lake Victoria. The falls are now submerged by the effects of a hydroelectric dam downstream.

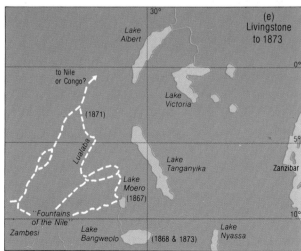

Left and below right The White Nile and the great lakes, 1845–1873. The theoretical geographer Cooley argued that there was only one lake in East Africa even after explorers found more (map a). Erhardt heard on the coast of all three lakes but ran them into one (map b). The Royal Geographical Society then sent Burton and Speke to find the truth. They reached Lake Tanganyika, and Speke alone the southern end of Lake Victoria, immediately claiming it as the Nile source (map c). On a second expedition, now with Grant, Speke reached the Ripon Falls in July 1862 where the Nile flows out of Victoria. Baker came up the Nile to find Lake Albert as part of the Nile system, whereupon Burton and his allies, jealous of Speke, ingeniously showed that Lake Tanganyika could be the source of the Nile (map d). Speke accidentally shot himself dead and could not dispute this. The doubts encouraged Livingstone to believe the "fountains" even further south and he died trying to prove this (map e). In 1875–76 Stanley finally vindicated Speke and ended the vitriolic arguments about who deserved the palm Bruce had claimed in 1770.

Maps:

(a) Cooley 1845 — Lake Nyassi, Zanzibar, Zambesi; 30°, 5°, 10°

(b) Erhardt 1856 — Mt Kenia, Mt Kilimandjaro, Ujiji, Zanzibar; 30°, 5°, 10°

(c) Burton & Speke 1858 — source of Nile?, Lake Rusizi, Lake Victoria, SPEKE, Ujiji, BURTON, Lake Tanganyika; 30°, 0°, 5°

(d) Speke & Grant 1862, Baker 1864 — Nile, Lake Albert, BAKER, Lake Victoria, Lake Rusizi, SPEKE & GRANT, Lake Tanganyika; 30°, 0°, 5°

(e) Livingstone to 1873 — Lake Albert, to Nile or Congo?, (1871), Lualaba, Lake Victoria, Lake Tanganyika, Zanzibar, Lake Moero (1867), "Fountains of the Nile", Zambesi, Lake Bangweolo (1868 & 1873), Lake Nyassa; 30°, 0°, 5°, 10°

Sir Richard Burton (1821–90). Arabist, linguist, explorer, not wholly respectable Victorian, Burton questioned Speke's 1858 and 1862 discoveries, refused to communicate with his ex-companion and generally injected controversy into the Nile source issue.

James A. Grant (1827–92). During their 1859–63 expedition, Speke denied Grant the chance to visit the actual source of the Nile. Yet Grant loyally supported Speke's geographical claims and was to become an acknowledged expert on African affairs.

Sir Samuel Baker (1821–93) traveled up the Nile valley to reach Lake Albert in March 1864, so supplementing yet complicating Speke's discovery. Baker later returned to the upper Nile to claim the area for the Khedive of Egypt – and to make a fortune for himself.

indirect influence of Léopold's initiative, a multitude of projects for Africa emerged. Few involved European governments which, for the most part, were still cautious about responsibilities in Africa. Yet this unofficial scramble of miners, merchants and missionaries was to create conditions which seemed to oblige official intervention.

When the major powers met at the Berlin Conference in 1884–85, their object was not to partition Africa but to try to limit the international friction beginning to be caused by the unofficial scramble. The ground rules of international conduct in Africa which they laid down did not, however, prevent the rapid assumption of European overlordship in the next ten years or so. Inevitably there were clashes of interest between unofficial agencies from different countries. Brazza, working for a French committee, and Stanley, working for the Belgian branch of the International Association, clashed over control of the access route to the interior via the lower Zaïre river. As thousands of British flocked into Transvaal in the wake of the mineral discoveries, bitter disputes broke out between these *Uitlanders* and the resident Boers. Europeans might also clash or cooperate uneasily with non-European agencies like Egypt or the Zanzibar sultanate as white men sought more direct influence on events. More significantly still, Africans were involved in a scramble for position and influence. Some might be detribalized Christian converts like the creoles of Sierra Leone, but most Africans remained subjects of African leaders who had modified old political structures or created new ones to meet 19th-century conditions. The states which men like Samori in West Africa or Mirambo in the east had built up now struggled to withstand the more determined initiatives from Europe. In some cases, Islam constituted a counterforce to the Europeans; such was the case with the Mahdists who took over the Sudan from Egypt in the 1880s or the Sokoto empire of the middle Niger.

If the situation in Africa itself seemed to cry out for the imposition of a European civil order, there were, too, European reasons for official annexations. First, in the conditions of the great depression of 1876–93 it seemed important to secure sources of raw materials and markets for the present or the future against possible rivals. Moreover, European traders in many regions no longer considered it possible to expand their activities within a context of African political control; they felt they needed a modern infrastructure of railroads, telegraphs and political control by European governments or, at least, chartered companies. Secondly, domestic difficulties in European states could to some extent be alleviated by expansionist policies. Thirdly, the general problems of international rivalries, particularly the rise of Germany after 1871, had implications for Africa.

The details of the process by which Africa was partitioned can be understood only by reference to the complex interweaving of all these African and European factors. Broadly speaking, however, it may be said that Léopold's ambition to create his own Congo Free State brought into question ill-defined rights of Britain, France and Portugal. Germany exploited the incipient rivalries in 1884–85 and annexations to establish claims rapidly

proceeded in West and East Africa. Most of the resulting conflicts were resolved in treaties of 1890–91. Meanwhile, in North Africa, local authorities found themselves unable to cope with the consequences of modernization; the classic case was Egypt where a proto-nationalist revolt in 1882 against the European-influenced Khedive's regime could be put down only by British occupation. This not only upset France but gave Britain a reason for wishing to protect the whole Nile valley. In South Africa, British attempts to impose some sort of overall control of both the Boers and the Bantu resulted in wars like the Zulu War of 1879 and the first Boer War of 1882. More successful were international arrangements with Germany and Portugal in 1890 and 1891 which kept them out of these southern African preserves of the British, which had by this time extended to the Zambezi and beyond with the energetic activities of the followers of Cecil Rhodes. The real crisis in South Africa, however, came in 1899–1901, when the British government, now fully associated with local British mining interests, fought the Boer War to bring the Afrikaners once more fully into the British empire. In 1910 a political compromise was reached and South Africa was given independence as a mixed Boer–British state. By the time the Boer War started, Britain had, fortunately for it, resolved most of its remaining difficulties with France over West Africa in 1898, though both powers were to find it difficult to overcome African resistance to overlordship. The sharpest clash came also in 1898 when, as Britain reconquered the Sudan from the Mahdists, a French expedition moved in to question Britain's right to control the whole of the Nile valley. A little earlier, in 1896, the only major and permanent repulse of an attempted European annexation occurred when Italy was defeated by Ethiopia at the battle of Adowa.

The rest of Africa was taken over and only relatively minor border readjustments occurred after 1900, although it was not until 1911 that Libya was taken over by Italy and Morocco by France. The bitter dispute with Germany on the latter occasion showed that African bargains could no longer be used as international safety valves. Indeed, Africa became heavily involved in World War I. Not only were campaigns fought on its soil as Germany's colonies were wrested from it, but thousands of Africans fought for their colonial overlords. The question of what to do with German territories provoked a new mini-scramble in 1919. The League of Nations B mandates given to Britain, France and Belgium in practice, if not theory, simply added to their possessions and South Africa with a C mandate over South West Africa began to incorporate the ex-German territory.

Colonial control for most Africans, then, began at the end of the 19th century. Obviously it brought tremendous changes, most notably by providing the basic political framework for the Africa of today. Yet in many ways what happened was only a speeding-up of processes of European–African interaction which had begun earlier. Perhaps the main effect was to set limits on the extent to which Africans could choose how far to allow their ways of life to be modified and on how far they could resist the peripherization of their economies. With political independence in the 1960s the process continues under slightly different rules.   R.C.B.

The Mapping of Africa

Very few maps were published in inter-tropical Africa prior to this century, so that it is tempting to suppose that the early printed maps of Africa are a chronicle of external penetration. This is not the case. External contact with sub-Saharan Africa by Arab travelers predates printing by many centuries, and the European map-publishing houses of the 15th century and later made use of Arab sources if they were available; but much was not available. Early maps of Africa printed in Europe are a very incomplete record of Arab knowledge. Furthermore, the content of early maps of Africa is not only a reflection of the number of accurate geographical facts known to the cartographer. It also reflects the demands of the readership which may have been happy to see maps used as frameworks for expressing myths, tradition or geographical speculation in what were otherwise blank areas. Such maps depict more of what was believed than what was known of Africa.

By the 19th century, a more scientific attitude prevailed. Great blank areas on maps of Africa suggest that the inclusion of unsubstantiated myth was no longer acceptable but it does not follow that what the cartographer shows is accurate. He was still dependent on travelers' reports of what they had seen and what they believed lay beyond their personal experience.

J.C.S.

Right John Senex's map of 1720 represents a transition in that an increasing amount of detailed information is now coming to hand but fables remain acceptable. Hence there is much detail along the coast and some firmly depicted features inland, although rivers tend to stop short through lack of knowledge, which is openly admitted in inscriptions. The state of Monomotapa had been contacted by the Portuguese and was known to exist, by contrast with other more ill-founded inscriptions in the interior and with the little tent symbols which are no more than embellishment. There are traits in this map of both a much earlier and a much later period.

Below The Catalan Atlas of 1375, a series of manuscript maps drawn on parchment. The radiating rhumb lines show that maritime charts were important sources of this document. The detail along the North African coast derives from charts and contrasts with the embellishment in the interior, although Moroccan merchants were the source of information about the Guinea coast.

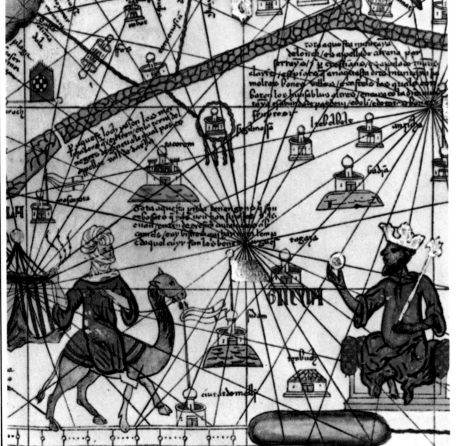

64

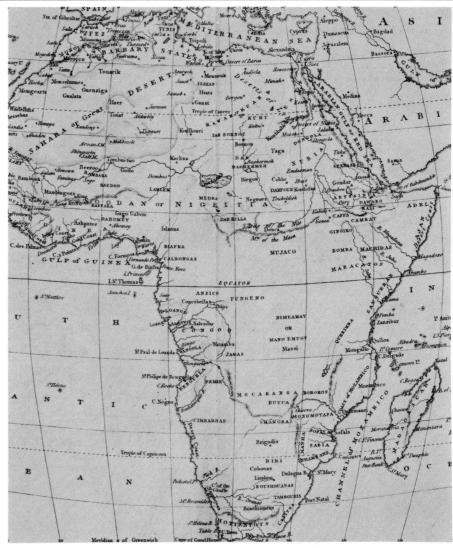

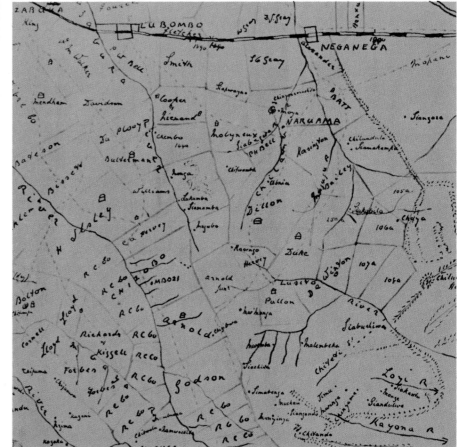

Left Münster's woodcut map of Africa, printed in 1540, derives in part from the work of Claudius Ptolemy, almost 1400 years earlier, but it also draws on Arab and Portuguese sources. The chain of mountains aligned east-west across North Africa was a Ptolemaic feature which also occurs on the Catalan Atlas. The Nile is shown rising in the Mountains of the Moon far to the south and the upper Niger is shown flowing in the wrong direction. These were features carried forward on maps for several centuries.

Above right A map published in London in 1822 contains less information about Africa south of the equator than the relatively accurate parts of the Senex map which was published 100 years previously. Little more had become known of the interior but attitudes towards maps had changed. The cartographer was more reluctant to include uncertain information. This did not mean that what he included was correct. The Niger now becomes a possible tributary of the Nile and the Ptolemaic Mountains of the Moon remain one of the Nile sources.

Right During the early colonial period in British Africa, a great number of little-known but often very detailed manuscript maps were prepared by District Officers. The information on these maps was sometimes used in the first published large-scale maps of the territory. This section of a map of Magoye Subdistrict, Northern Rhodesia, was drawn in 1921 and shows both land alienated for commercial farming and adjacent African villages.

Communication by Rail

Africa's rail network is still in a very rudimentary stage of development, except in South Africa. Most lines run from the interior to the coast. There are few transcontinental links and existing lines are often not integrated with the growing network of all-weather highways. However, unlike elsewhere in the world, more lines are being built than are being taken up. The African network is expanding and there are a number of projected new lines undergoing feasibility studies. There is now an international body, the Union of African Railways, to foster pan-African integration, the main problem being the five different gauges which exist. Training programs have been established to overcome the shortage of skilled personnel and priorities worked out for the construction of international links and feeder lines.   J.C.S.

Right Two large 25NC 4–8–4 engines meet on the line from Bloemfontein to Bethlehem in South Africa, whose advanced rail network is being further expanded for strategic and economic reasons.

Below One of tropical Africa's earliest lines was constructed to run inland from the Kenya coast just before the turn of the century. It hastened the coming of the European settlers in Kenya, who proved it commercially viable.

Bottom The trans-Gabon railroad is one of Africa's new lines, although the incentive for its construction is the traditional reason of extraction of primary products, in this case timber and minerals.

Top The line from Mombasa was built largely by manual labor, not by Africans but by indentured laborers from India, most of whom returned home after completion of their contract.

Above Great distances and the low purchasing power of the potential passengers mean that most of the cheaper forms of public transport in Africa tend to be infrequent and overcrowded. Many lines are single track, necessitating stops for passing traffic, as here in Sudan.

Left A Sierra Leone station, a scene that is familiar elsewhere in Africa. Stations are simply constructed, without platforms, but may occur at short intervals along the line so that stops are frequent. There is usually ample time to purchase food and drink from numerous vendors.

THE AFRICAN DIASPORA

The word diaspora has traditionally been used to describe the experience of the Jews, scattered from their historical homeland in Israel. More recently, by analogy, the same word has been applied to the dispersal of peoples of African descent outside the African continent. The analogy is not entirely accurate: in contrast to the Jews, diaspora Africans came from a wide range of distinct cultures and they have been able to look back not only to a physical point of origin, but also to African societies which had not shared the experience of dispersal. Again, though the African diaspora communities, like the Jews, have succeeded in defining and maintaining their own cultures in foreign lands, they have been much more successful than the Jews in influencing the cultures of the societies in which they lived. In modern Brazil, for instance, the black presence has had a deep impact on the national culture and in most societies of the Caribbean the cultures of the diaspora communities have become the dominant ones. However, it is more important for African history that the diaspora has had an impact in the opposite direction. Here there is a striking parallel with the way Jewish communities throughout the world have affected the evolution of modern Israel. Pan-Africanism, and indeed modern African nationalism, would have developed along different lines without the interaction between African intellectuals and the diaspora communities of Britain, France and the Americas.

The African diaspora is still one of the most dramatic population movements in modern history, as emigration from the Caribbean continues to build new communities of African descent in France, Britain and the USA. Its origins go back at least to Classical antiquity, when small numbers of Africans were sold northwards down the Nile or across the Sahara. Throughout the European Middle Ages, and indeed until the late 19th century, these routes provided much greater numbers of black slaves for entrepôts on the Mediterranean, particularly Tripoli, Benghazi and Alexandria. Thence they were distributed throughout the Islamic world, from the Iberian peninsula to India. Though no scholar has gone beyond guessing at the numbers involved, it is clear that they were huge, perhaps as many as the victims of the Atlantic traffic. The mainland trade only began to slacken in the 19th century, when the European powers expanded their influence in the Mediterranean simultaneously with becoming committed to abolition.

It was easy to find alternative sources of supply. The Islamic world had always bought black slaves from fellow Muslims trading by sea south of the Horn of Africa. In the late 18th century the bulk of this trade fell into the hands of the Omani Arab sultans who conquered and settled Zanzibar. They developed new trade routes into the interior, to the great lakes and the Congo. Though they retained some slaves to staff their expanding clove plantations in Zanzibar and neighboring Pemba, they greatly increased the volume of the trade to the ports of the Red Sea and the Persian Gulf. From there African men and women continued to be dispersed throughout Islam. It is quite impossible to estimate the volume of the East African trade, which only slackened after the British–Zanzibari treaty of 1873 and was not fully eradicated until the present century. One educated guess is that by 1870 60 000 slaves were being exported from East Africa each year.

We know too little about the history of African expatriates in Islamic societies. Most of them were bought as domestic servants, some as concubines and many as eunuchs. At first they were also used extensively for military purposes. By the mid-11th century 30 000 out of the 100 000 troops in the Egyptian army were black, but this became much less acceptable after the "War of the Blacks" in 1169, when 50 000 African mutineers almost overthrew Saladin in Cairo. In North Africa many blacks became galley slaves, and in the city-states of the Persian Gulf they were used in date farming, as pearl divers, as port laborers and as sailors. A very few rose to political prominence, whether through domestic or military service: the 10th-century Nubian eunuch, Abu'l-Misk Kafur, became regent of Egypt; Sidi Badr briefly seized the throne of Bengal in the 1490s; Malik Ambar, the great 17th-century general, led the resistance of the Deccan against the Mughals. In Indian political history, groups of "Habshis" or "Siddis" have sometimes taken an important role. Those on Janjira Island, for instance, were in effect naval mercenaries whose friendship became crucial to the East India

Above The massive slave trade across the Sahara and the Indian Ocean had a less obvious demographic impact than the Atlantic traffic. But diaspora Africans played a range of roles in the societies of Islam and throughout Asia. Malik Ambar was an important figure in the history of 17th-century India.

Below Nothing about slavery horrified its critics more than the slave auction. The sentimental paternalism of American slaveholders could not get over the inconsistency of treating human beings as a form of real property. And it could not protect black children from being torn from their families under the auctioneer's hammer.

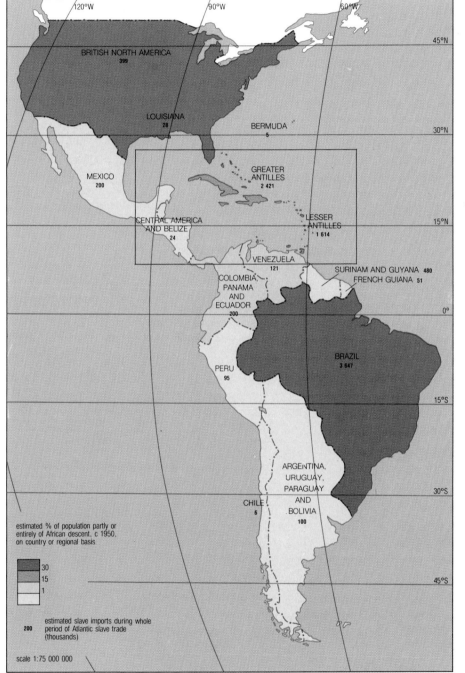

estimated % of population partly or
entirely of African descent, c 1950,
on country or regional basis

▓	30
▒	15
░	1

200 estimated slave imports during whole
period of Atlantic slave trade
(thousands)

scale 1:75 000 000

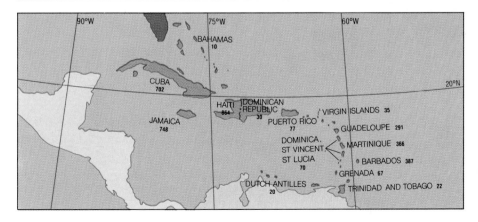

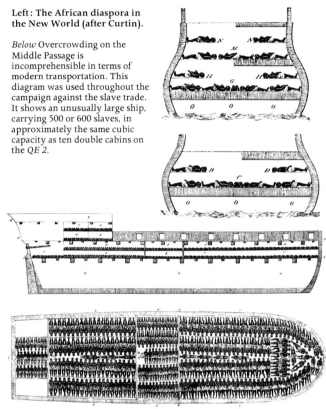

**Left: The African diaspora in
the New World (after Curtin).**

Below Overcrowding on the
Middle Passage is
incomprehensible in terms of
modern transportation. This
diagram was used throughout the
campaign against the slave trade.
It shows an unusually large ship,
carrying 500 or 600 slaves, in
approximately the same cubic
capacity as ten double cabins on
the *QE 2*.

Company's 18th-century strategy for defending
Bombay from the Dutch. The descendants of the
Janjira Siddis, now politically weak, are still a
recognizably distinct group. The same is true of the
Nizam of Hyderabad's African Cavalry Guard, only
disbanded in 1951. Siddi Risala, the neighborhood
in which Hyderabadis of African descent live, still
shows cultural survivals in music and dance and
some local usage of Swahili words. In Iran, too, there
is still a distinctive black community at Jiruft. In
general, however, the descendants of diaspora
Africans in Islam have tended to become absorbed
into the wider culture. Except in special cases, the
low proportion of blacks available for liaisons with
other blacks, the relative cultural and racial
receptivity of Islamic culture and the sheer lack of
concentrated demographic mass have prevented the
development of diaspora cultures similar to those of
the Americas.

The diaspora entered a new phase in the 15th
century, when the Portuguese broke the Islamic
monopoly of trade with Africa and Asia by pushing
down the Guinea coast and ultimately rounding the
Cape to India. They quickly began to carry black
people back to Europe and thence to the settlements
in the New World. Before this, the few African
slaves who reached Europe through capture, or
through the Venetian and Genoan trade with the
Levant and North Africa, had been mere exotics.
Such individuals still appear in the modern period –
like the Scottish "ladye with the meckle lippis" in
Dunbar's poem, for whose favors James IV's knights
jousted; like Ibrahim Hannibal, Peter the Great's

black general, who provided the germ of the novelette by another figure of the diaspora, Alexander Pushkin; or like the black pages who remained fashionable among the European aristocracy until the 18th century. However, the new Portuguese trade, and the Dutch, British and French initiatives which followed, deposited Africans in Europe and its possessions in numbers which make it possible to speak of genuine diaspora communities. By 1551 a tenth of Lisbon's population of 100 000 was black, and by the 1590s it had its own annual African festival. However, Portuguese blacks were in the long run unable to remain culturally and racially distinct from the general population. The same was true of the smaller black groups in Spain and other European countries. The only real exception was Britain. After it acquired colonies in North America and the West Indies, and became heavily involved in the slave trade, it developed small but distinct communities of African descent in port towns like Bristol, Liverpool and London. Their total numbers may have been as high as 15 000 by the 1780s.

The African presence in Europe was never as significant as the great diaspora communities which emerged in the New World as a consequence of the Atlantic slave trade. The numbers carried to the Americas will never be known precisely. The most probable figure is between 10 and 11 million between Columbus's discovery of Hispaniola and the effective ending of the Cuban trade in 1868. Though lower than earlier estimates, this is still an enormous number, roughly equal to the whole population of the USA in 1825. Although different national systems of ethnic classification make computation difficult, there are at least 60 million people of African descent in the Americas today. However, because different agricultural staples created different labor needs and because each produced its own demographic conditions, slave importations were unevenly distributed throughout the Americas. Moreover, they bear little relationship to modern population. The horrifying fact is that the slave population was able to maintain its numbers by natural reproduction only in the USA. Under half a million Africans were brought to North America, but they had produced a population of four and a half million, four million enslaved, by the Civil War. Elsewhere, masters relied on the slave trade to replace the blacks who fell victim to the demands of the plantation. The British, French and Dutch West Indies had to carry close to four million into slavery. Almost as many went to Brazil alone – close to two million in the 18th century and over a million in the 19th. The Spanish possessions absorbed at least a million and a half new slaves, over a third of them going to Cuba during the 19th-century sugar boom.

It is difficult to be precise about the African origins of the slave trade's victims. Each of the trading nations relied on different parts of the continent in different political conditions and at different times. A majority of North American blacks came from the coastal societies of West Africa and the states of the western Sudan, although over a quarter probably originated in Angola and other parts of central Africa. The same areas provided the slaves for the British and French Caribbean. As the 18th century went on, they drew

an increasing proportion of new blacks from Congo and Angola. These were a particularly strong element in the population of Saint Domingue at the time of the Haitian revolution. Brazil and the Spanish colonies also took slaves from the Guinea coast, but they relied more consistently than their neighbors on central African blacks shipped from ports like Luanda and Benguela. The trade from East Africa to the Americas was negligible until the mid-17th century, when the French began to carry slaves from Mozambique and other entrepôts. By the late 18th century these sources were being more energetically tapped by the Portuguese, particularly to provide slave labor for the Spanish settlements on the Plate. This trade was relatively unimportant for the British possessions, but it came to be even more significant to Brazil and Cuba in the 19th century, when the ports of West and central Africa came under increasing pressure from British naval patrols.

The black slaves of the Americas represented almost the whole range of African cultures. Even their masters were aware of the diversity of the civilizations from which they came. Though white perceptions were imprecise and inconsistent, they ascribed different values and characteristics to people of different origins – Asantes were quarrelsome, Congos stupid, Yorubas faithful, Bantus physically strong and so on. More important, different mixes of African nationalities meant that the complex diaspora cultures which developed during and after the slave period varied widely in different parts of the Americas.

Simpler demographic forces also had their impact. In areas like Chile, where black population was tiny, or like New England, where blacks were characteristically used side by side with servants of other races, the chances of maintaining a distinct culture during slavery or surviving as a viable community after it were slight. Even in Mexico, which absorbed an estimated 200 000 slaves, and where there are still over 300 000 citizens of identifiable African origin, diaspora Mexicans have tended ethnically and culturally to merge into the general population. Other environments were more favorable. Where large black populations lived close to an inaccessible hinterland, they usually produced communities of escapees who were quite independent of white society. Where the proportion of recent arrivals among escapees was high, which it commonly was, such groups evolved cultures which, though inevitably composite and adaptive, may be called genuinely African. The classic case is that of the Bush Negroes of French and Dutch Guiana, whose religious and political systems were almost wholly African. Today 25 000 of them maintain their distinctive ways in communities of their own. The most famous was the republic of Palmares, which used recognizably African forms of government and flourished for almost a century until it was crushed by Portuguese troops in 1695. The limitations of North American terrain prevented major communities of this sort developing, but stable maroon societies became a factor in most areas where slave population was dense enough.

No maroon community, however, became as threatening as the slaves of Haiti, the old colony of Saint Domingue, who rose en masse against their masters in the great revolution of 1791. The slaves in

Right The black religions of the New World are richly influenced by African traditions. Some forms, like those of the Bush Negroes, borrow minimally from Christianity. The black churches of the United States are among the most vigorous branches of modern protestantism. Haiti, the home of this priest, is the most complex religious melting pot in the Americas.

Below right In the 17th and 18th centuries runaway slaves of Angolan origin founded settlements in remote areas of the Brazilian forest, many of which survive today with a high degree of cultural and social independence. In this community near Diamantina a Negro woman perpetuates the African tradition of pounding foodstuffs with a pestle. However, the substance in the mortar is not millet or maize, but coffee beans.

Haiti heavily outnumbered the whites and they included an unusually high proportion of first-generation African arrivals. Voodoo was a major theme in resistance to the French. With the masters gone, Haitian culture retained an extraordinarily rich range of African adaptations in social structure, language, folklore, art, music and religion. However, only a minority of blacks in the Americas were able to evolve genuinely African cultures like that of the Bush Negroes; even Haiti absorbed much that was French or Christian. Other Caribbean islands are more Europeanized – but they too, particularly in Jamaica and Cuba, have drawn on their African background to mold their different varieties of creole language, their syncretistic forms of religion, their conceptions of magic and the supernatural, certain aspects of their kinship structure and their corpus of folklore.

Brazil is an entirely different case, where a predominantly European culture has been deeply influenced by the diaspora. Slavery was not abolished there until 1888. By then a richly diversified Afro–Brazilian culture had developed, both on rural plantations and among the urban slaves and free blacks of coast cities like Bahia. Its religious components are particularly interesting. Brazil, for instance, is the only American country with an Islamic tradition which is rooted in black Africa. However, the Brazilian slaves and their descendants also managed to preserve Africanisms in language, music and dance, and to inject them into the mainstream of their country's extraordinary polyglot culture.

Though it has not always been their own choice, North American blacks have also managed to survive as distinct communities. However, their distinctiveness has depended on a culture which has incorporated fewer African survivals than that of any other large group of African descent in the New World. Though the slave population of the South was colossal, the trade ended in 1807, and the vast majority of them were born into families already acculturated in America. This militated against extensive continuities with Africa. Even here, however, it is a myth that the black heritage was wiped out by the Middle Passage. Southern slaveholders were only too well aware of the connection between resistance and their slaves' alarmingly distinctive usages in religion, magic and music. Their Christianity took, and still takes, syncretistic forms, their folklore, games and humor have clear African antecedents, and their speech has developed along distinctive lines – not only in special cases like the Gullah dialect of the Sea Islands of South Carolina, but in the speech patterns and inflections which distinguish modern black English. Some black family structures and naming patterns may also be adaptations of African usages. Above all, the descendants of the slaves have adapted Africa's musical legacy to give America and the Western world the unique musical gift of jazz, one of the most powerful cultural forces in modern history. Even in the United States the diaspora carried a great deal of cultural baggage with it. Many younger American blacks have tended increasingly to try to fit their historical experience into a larger African framework – not only through adopting their own versions of African styles in dress and appearance, but through an intense interest in their African origins. The furore over the television serial *Roots* in the late 1970s would have been unthinkable 20 years before.

Nevertheless, the tendency to look back to Africa is not new, and for modern African history it is the most important aspect of the diaspora. At the simplest level, it has brought many expatriates back to Africa. Some have traveled as individuals, like the missionaries from the Watchtower movement who deeply influenced the development of central African nationalism in the interwar years. Others have formed recognizable groups, like the Brazilians of Nigeria, Portuguese-speaking Fon, Ewe, and Yoruba who returned to Africa at the end of the slave-trade period and took a major role in the commercial life of Lagos. There were 3000 of them there by the 1880s, and they extended their operations throughout West Africa. Even in East Africa 150 Bombay Africans managed to return in 1875 to a settlement at Freretown, outside Mombasa. The most outstanding of all these group ventures was the colony of Sierra Leone, founded by British abolitionists in 1787. Although the bulk of its 19th-century immigrants were Africans of different cultures freed from captured slave ships, its first settlers were drawn successively from the diaspora community in England, from American blacks temporarily settled in Nova Scotia as a consequence of the American Revolution, and from the maroon Negroes of Jamaica.

Settlement in Africa has been particularly attractive to a series of groups from the USA. The most successful of such ventures is the black republic of Liberia. Though many blacks resented its white supporters' assumption that they had no place in America, it was founded by ex-slaves and governed by their descendants. Liberia's whole history has been strongly influenced by its economic and political ties with the USA. At the end of the 19th century, when Bishop Henry Turner of the African Methodist Episcopal Church revived the interest of poor American blacks in emigration, it was still Liberia which was the focus of their plans. In the 1920s the flamboyant nationalist leader Marcus Garvey was still interested in colonizing some of his American followers there.

For African history itself, however, the real importance of the diaspora is its influence on modern nationalism and pan-Africanism. A period of residence or study abroad has had an effect on almost every modern African leader by bringing him into contact with intellectuals from other black communities. The concept of *négritude*, which has been crucial to the ideologies of French-speaking Africa, would never have developed as it did if Paris had not provided a forum for interaction between men like Léopold Sédar Senghor of Senegal and Caribbean intellectuals like Aimé Césaire of Martinique and Jean Price-Mars of Haiti. The nationalism of anglophone Africa has also had its foreign debts. As early as 1915 the great revolt in the Shiré highlands of Nyasaland was led by John Chilembwe, who had been a student in Virginia. Hastings Banda and Kwame Nkrumah are better-known leaders who spent part of their student days in America. Other Africans were influenced by a period of military service outside their own country. Between the World Wars, another major factor was the influence of Marcus Garvey, the

Left The example of the new African nations overseas increased the cultural and political self-confidence of black communities in the United States, just as American society was entering a period of anxiety over pluralism and its own mainstream values. Alex Haley's *Roots*, which glued every black and many white Americans to the television, was itself part of a revolution in attitudes to Africa.

Below The 20th century has seen new bonds grow up between diaspora Africans throughout the world. One of the pioneers of the pan-African ideal was the Jamaican Marcus Garvey (1887–1940). His work in America had deep symbolic importance for several of the young men who became leaders in the new African nations.

Jamaican whose Universal Negro Improvement Association was the focus of American working-class black protest. Nkrumah once noted that he had been a more important influence than Lenin or Marx.

Modern African leaders have also been subtly influenced by the American and European contacts they have made through the pan-African movement. Its pioneers already worked in a web of influence stretching between Africa, Europe, the Caribbean and North America. Africanus Horton of Sierra Leone was educated in London and Edinburgh. Edward Wilmot Blyden lived in Liberia, but was born in St Thomas, and visited the USA 11 times between 1872 and 1888. In the 20th century a series of pan-African conferences gave young intellectuals a golden opportunity to make contacts in other diaspora communities. With the exception of Blaise Diagne, the deputy from French Senegal, the towering figures at the earlier conferences were all diaspora blacks: Duse Mohammed Effendi from Egypt, George Padmore from Trinidad, and above all W. E. B. Du Bois, the father of modern black consciousness in the USA. Duse Mohammed and Padmore, like the Guyanan leader Ras Makonnen, had prolonged spells of residence in Britain, where they had an incalculable influence on the way in which young Africans studying there perceived the common cause of colonial and particularly African peoples.

By the time of the Fifth Pan-African Congress, held in Manchester in 1945, the situation had changed. Du Bois was there as usual, Padmore was still joint secretary, but the main leaders were men from emerging Africa, like Nkrumah, Kenyatta, and I. T. A. Wallace-Johnson of Sierra Leone. Their future triumphs in forging nations would soon give a new source of pride to the tens of millions of diaspora Africans who had been born into alien societies far from the mother continent.   C.D.R.

THE GROWTH OF CITIES

The city is probably the last idea one would associate with Africa. Africa is certainly the least urbanized of all the continents and many of its cities are very new. But it also has a great diversity of regions: it can be claimed that one region, Egypt, gave birth to the oldest cities of all, and its northern fringe has for millennia shared in the urban civilization of the Mediterranean. We cannot generalize for the continent as a whole. But before looking at distinctive regions, different cultures and epochs, it is useful to examine the extent of urbanization today in purely arithmetic terms. This alone will indicate why Africa has experienced the sudden rise of urban problems on a massive scale.

In 1920 about 6·9 million (5 per cent of the population) lived in towns of more than 20 000; in 1930 the figure was 9·7 million (6 per cent); in 1940 13·8 million (7 per cent); in 1950 21·5 million (10 per cent); in 1960 36·4 million (13 per cent); and by the 1970s probably well over 50 million (16 per cent) would be urbanized.

Enclosed by the Sahel hills and a fortified city wall, the pirate stronghold of Algiers appears on a 17th-century map by the English cartographer John Speed. Despite the impression of compactness, Algiers at this period had a population of 100 000. From here Barbary pirates sailed out to prey on Mediterranean shipping.

Thus although the urban proportion of the population is still small, the ten-year increases have been progressively greater and the total number living in towns is now quite considerable. The jump between 1950 and 1960 was 69 per cent, the most rapid rate of increase in the world.

The percentage of town dwellers who live in cities of over 500 000 is also increasing: 13 per cent in 1920 and 30 per cent in 1960. The trend in Africa, as in many developing countries, is towards comparatively few very large cities rather than a great increase in the number of towns. Cities of over 100 000 flourish and attract the great majority of rural migrants.

Differences between African states are still very considerable. The most urbanized are South Africa, Egypt, Morocco and Algeria. On the other hand, populous states such as Ethiopia and Tanzania have little urbanization. Gabon and Namibia have small populations but a high degree of urbanization. Lastly, there are some very large cities: Cairo with five million people, Alexandria with two million, Lagos with one and a half, Addis Ababa, Johannesburg and Cape Town all with over a million and Algiers with just under a million.

Rapid growth and the attraction of the large metropolis are the two things that underlie the major problems of urbanization in Africa. In the smaller countries with very meager resources problems are no less acute because they are on a smaller scale. Before looking at these problems we should consider briefly the development of urbanization in the different regions of Africa as a necessary background to understanding their modern context.

Historically, three core areas of urbanization can be distinguished, separated greatly in space, time and in complexity of culture: the Mediterranean, Nigeria and South Africa. The Mediterranean fringe has shared in a series of urban periods. The great urban civilization of the Nile came and went; its impetus passed to Greece, but returned again to Egypt with Alexander. He built Alexandria, which by the beginning of the Christian era was a great trading center at the crossroads of Africa, Asia and Europe and may have had three-quarters of a million people. Here Greek, Jewish and Egyptian cultures blended and gave the city its renown as the scientific center of the world with one of the greatest libraries ever known. It declined with the 7th-century Muslim conquest, a decline which accelerated after the diversion of eastern trade routes via the Cape.

It was Muslim Arabs also who established a city just north of the ruins of Memphis in the year 641. In the 10th century it became a new capital, Al-Qahirah; by the 14th century Cairo was the biggest metropolis in Europe and the Middle East, with half a million people and a famous university. Although, like Alexandria, it lost its trade and declined in population after the 16th century, it remained a large city and grew dramatically in the 20th century, due to westernization. Meanwhile, Islam had spread throughout the whole of North Africa, and coastal cities flourished. Tunis was established in the late 17th century, near the site of Carthage. Further west a former Phoenician settlement gave way in the 10th century to the Muslim city of Algiers, dominated by the Turks in the 17th century, when it was a town of a 100 000 people. Muslim influence also extended up the Nile and beyond the Sahara. A great network of trade routes crossed the Sahara, linking east with west and the Mediterranean coast with the savanna forest lands bordering equatorial Africa.

This last domain was under Muslim control until the middle of the last century and its influence remains in the northern parts of the second core region of urbanization, in what we now know as Nigeria. Early 19th-century travelers have given us graphic accounts of the contemporary towns of Nigeria. In the northern grassland area, relatively rich in resources and well peopled, the towns were the centers of Saharan trade and owed much to Muslim influence. Now much declined, Tombouctou is a fabled example. Kano is no less famous. Many of these towns had populations of 20 000 or 30 000, and the chief city, Sokoto, may have had

100000 when Europeans first reached the scene. They were mud-built walled towns, centering on market place, palace and mosque.

Between grassland and coast is a wide belt of forest land, and most of its towns reflect the Yoruba culture. The Yoruba, immigrants from the northeast, used towns, as did the Muslims, as a means of dominating and organizing the people they

conquered. They were bases of administration and power and formed a network within southern Nigeria. Each town center was dominated by the chief's compound set in a ceremonial space; trade was also important and the central market a major feature of the town. The first Europeans estimated their size; of the 34 they described, 24 probably had more than 10000 people; 18 of these were over

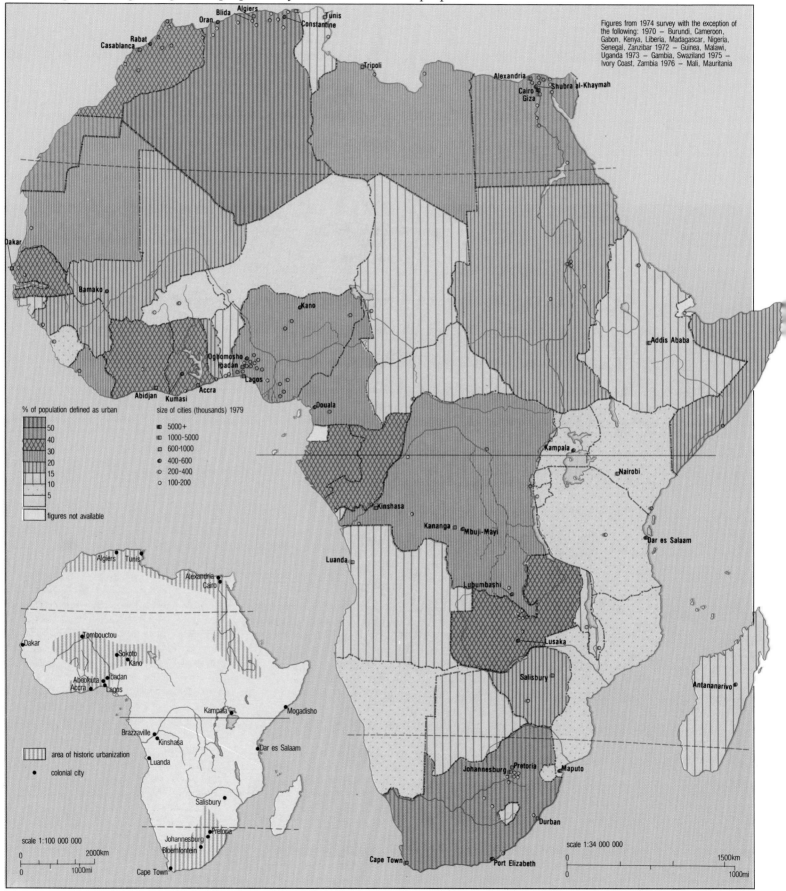

Figures from 1974 survey with the exception of the following: 1970 – Burundi, Cameroon, Gabon, Kenya, Liberia, Madagascar, Nigeria, Senegal, Zanzibar 1972 – Guinea, Malawi, Uganda 1973 – Gambia, Swaziland 1975 – Ivory Coast, Zambia 1976 – Mali, Mauritania

% of population defined as urban

50
40
30
20
15
10
5

figures not available

size of cities (thousands) 1979

5000+
1000-5000
600-1000
400-600
200-400
100-200

area of historic urbanization

colonial city

scale 1:100 000 000

0   1000mi   2000km

scale 1:34 000 000

0   1000mi   1500km

The panoramic view of Ibadan in western Nigeria exhibits the contrast between old and new seen in many African cities. Modern skyscrapers in the city center tower above the corrugated iron roofs of a rundown residential suburb. A thriving Yoruba town in the 19th century, Ibadan maintained its economic importance under British colonial rule. Its significance as a market was enhanced by the construction of the Lagos–Kano railroad in the early 1900s.

The degree of urbanization of the African population
Rapid urbanization is a characteristic of many parts of Africa as the drive towards industrialization gathers momentum. Within the countries where such a process is taking place there is generally a pattern of explosive expansion of one or two urban centers into vast sprawling cities while the remainder of the country remains almost totally rural. Medium-sized industrial towns are rare. Clusters of places in this category often denote the presence of extractive industries based on mineral deposits. Most people still live in villages or in towns that have thrived by virtue of being traditional market or administrative centers.

20 000, 8 were over 40 000; Abeokuta may have been between 60 000 and 100 000 and Ibadan was probably more than 100 000. Although the majority of their people were farmers, these walled towns presented an impressive and distinctly urban scene and give this region of West Africa an important role in the urban story.

The third core region is southern Africa, where a transplantation of western European culture took place late in African history. Although the indigenous people now form the major part of this urban population, it has no local roots. The cultural gap between indigenous and European peoples was so great that the former have had no impact on either the system of cities or their form.

The earliest European city was Cape Town, which began as a supply station on the sea route between Europe and the East. It became a town under the Dutch, came under British rule in 1806, and became legislative capital of the Republic of South Africa in 1910. It is now a metropolis of 1·5 million; only a third of its population is white. Pretoria (500 000) and Bloemfontein (180 000), mid-19th-century Dutch foundations and formerly the capitals of independent states, are the administrative and judicial capitals respectively of the republic. Durban (one million), founded by the British in 1835, is one of the world's major commercial ports. Johannesburg (1·5 million) was an outcome of the gold rush of 1886 and Salisbury (500 000), the capital of Zimbabwe, was established in 1890 and grew rapidly after rail links were established with Beira. The urban populations of the South African cities, comprising whites, blacks, Asians and Coloreds, constitute a problem which is highlighted by racial segregation.

Outside the three major regions we can distinguish the colonial cities and recent administrative capitals, in which Europeans form a very small class of administrators and managers in an overwhelmingly indigenous urban population. For example, Dakar (500 000) has about 7 per cent white population; Accra (750 000) about 5 per cent; and Lagos (1·6 million) less than 1 per cent. The main characteristics of these cities are their newness, the size and Western appearance of the business and

administration centers and the contrasting shanty towns which extend for miles beyond. Some have long antecedents: Accra was established in 1482 and Luanda in 1576, both by the Portuguese; Dakar in 1670 by the Dutch. But many of them date from the 1880s when the continent was carved up between European powers; Dar-es-Salaam (German) in 1885, Mogadisho (Italian) in 1892, Kampala (Imperial British East African Company) in 1890. Kinshasa (1881) and Brazzaville (1883) grew up as river ports. All these cities owe their size to a great postwar boom.

The movement of tribal folk to the growing cities of Africa has had dramatic effects on their size and also on their nature. These cities have none of the resources which would enable them to absorb immigrants at the normal standard of housing and services. Outside the modern core of offices and administration buildings which most African cities have acquired, and the restricted areas which once housed colonial whites and which now house the native elite, most cities lack water, roads, sewerage and electricity, and the houses appear to be little better than crude shelters.

Shanty towns of this kind account for a very large proportion of the urban growth: 180 000 people in Casablanca live in *bidonvilles*, and a third of the population of Algiers and Oran. Hastily erected shelters of beaten tin cans, cardboard, odd bits of timber and corrugated iron, are typical of vast areas around the cities. Many squatters start life in slum property in the center of cities and their move to the periphery indicates their need to do something for themselves. Ramshackle though much of it appears, the resulting shanty town is often better than rural housing, and its nearness to possible work is a great advantage to the migrant.

In addition to such spontaneous or unauthorized squatters on land not legally acquired, many cities have sectors in which they try to regulate migrant housing. In South Africa the rigid segregation of black and white is reflected in the strict control of black settlements. One of the largest of these, Soweto, is on the outskirts of Johannesburg. Here some 35 000 sites were prepared before occupation, and the migrants were allowed to construct a temporary shack at the back of each site, to be replaced subsequently by a more permanent house at the front. The result is a mechanically organized and uniformly stereotyped city of half a million people, but one in which the physical standards of the houses are better than they would be in uncontrolled settlements.

Outside South Africa it is more usual to find a mixture of controlled and uncontrolled growth. For example, in Nairobi a valley to the east of the city has a settlement of more than 50 000; 20 000 of these are squatters and the remainder live on plots rented from landlords. Control, in private hands, means houses of slightly higher standards – timber with corrugated roofs, compared with mud and wattle – though amenities are minimal. About half the population of Lusaka lives in shanty towns and an increasing proportion are now engaged in a site-and-service scheme. Sites available for renting are prepared, provided with some amenities (such as water and sanitation, to be shared by several plots) and served by roads capable of taking buses. The occupier is helped to buy material to build his own house of brick and corrugated iron on a concrete floor. The minimal cost is still too great for most immigrants, who resort to illegal squatting. The Lusaka squatters, as in many cities, are not amorphous, haphazard groups, but are often highly organized, and able to look after communal needs, even sometimes trying to replicate their former village lives. This kind of settlement may well represent a traditional way of urban growth, but it is on a scale which is frightening. Experiments in providing infrastructure to encourage self-help are a way of ensuring some improvement.

Urbanization is very much more than a shift of population, the growth of cities and the pro-liferation of shanty towns. It implies radical change of life and conditions for those who have migrated there. Only in some of the older cities does the excess of births over deaths produce a natural growth: almost universally, a rapid rural popu-lation growth is sending its surplus to the cities. The attraction is almost wholly economic, but although work is the main lure of the city, we should not underestimate the non-economic motive. In some cultures the city confers status on those who live or have lived there. It also offers freedom from the restraints of the social group and the excitement of a more sophisticated way of life. Labor movements in Africa are of long standing and the attractions of the city are well publicized.

Severance from tribal life and commitment to the city may be neither complete nor final. Ties with villages are often maintained, for the insurance of the home agricultural plot sustains many, and a great number look upon the experience as tran-sitory. Nevertheless, the social changes are per-manent for many millions and this trend will accelerate as education and the media make information about cities more accessible and help to tie rural life to the city in a multitude of ways.

The migrant often pays dearly for his move. Attractive wages do not always compensate for exacting urban conditions and overcrowding. Density of population may be very high; in Accra in 1960 the density was 18·4 persons to the house; in Dar-es-Salaam, eight persons to a room of 30 square meters; and in many cities street sleepers are a

Above A township near Johannesburg houses African laborers who are prohibited by South Africa's apartheid laws from living in the predominantly white urban areas where they work. This housing is healthier than shantytown shacks but lack of medical, recreational and transportation facilities makes such townships unattractive places to live.

Left Kairouan in Tunisia is one of the holy cities of Islam and a pilgrimage center. Founded in 670, it served as a base for the Muslim subjugation of northwest Africa. Traditional courtyard houses cluster together along narrow streets. A minaret breaks the skyline.

reminder that some have no shelter at all. Because the majority of immigrants are young men (in Lagos 70 per cent are between the ages of 20 and 29), the population is unbalanced. Hopes for jobs are often illusory, for population growth far outstrips increase in employment. Malnutrition is rife, infant mortality is very high and life expectancy still hovers between 34 and 40. Although there are indications of some of the characteristics of Western cities – such as the substitution of impersonal relations for family networks and of secondary contacts for primary, the growth of anonymity and of antisocial behavior – this should not hide the degree to which traditional ways of life survive in the city. Tribal social relationships are maintained and links with rural life replenish older values; these factors make for stability and easier adaptation. Reasserting rural patterns cushions the impact of the city and makes the transition easier.

This also means that the influence of the city on the countryside may be less than one thinks. In any case it varies a great deal as the pattern of urban life varies in the many kinds of cities. The older native towns are much more homogeneous and socially balanced. Based on a traditional economy dependent on the land, they have always produced an entrepreneural class, and with education this has turned into an indigenous elite. Towns based on extractive industries, like Johannesburg, merely emphasize the cultural gap between exploiter and exploited. Between the tight administrative control of the latter and gradual emerging indigenous control of the former, are states like Zaïre, where the control is more theoretical than real. In between too are the older cities in the north, where multi-ethnic populations have for centuries played complementary roles in the economic and social life of the city.

In many ways cities are a link between tribal Africa and an emerging "political" continent. They are agents of change, but so far their effects have been modified by the weight of traditional culture, which is so often a feature of much of the life of the cities themselves.

E.J.

VERNACULAR ARCHITECTURE

The wealth and beauty of African architecture have for too long been sadly neglected and misunderstood. Despite its relatively low population density, much of the continent has a greater architectural complexity than any other continent. Over 1500 peoples live in Africa and it can be broadly stated that each one of these has a unique material culture, not in every detail but certainly in aggregate. To understand African houses it is important not just to look at the way they were built and what they were built of but to consider as well how they relate to the landscape around them and to the needs and beliefs of the people who built them. The enormous diversity of beliefs and practices in Africa, however, makes it very difficult to write about African architecture as a whole. Nevertheless, certain common characteristics do make it possible to offer a few generalizations about the attitudes that produced this architecture.

The ideal of perpetuating a lifestyle through the generations was fundamental to many African societies and total cultural heritages were handed down orally from one generation to the next. That is not to say that there was never any change, but that any change, social or economic, was subtly absorbed into a system that was fundamentally conservative in nature. Under such circumstances architecture became a group solution to habitation problems, communally worked out and reaffirmed by each generation. The houses fitted precisely the social and economic lifestyle of those who lived in them. They were purpose built and were built on the whole by those who lived in them.

House building was one of the main regular family tasks and a great deal of effort was devoted to the construction and finish. Indeed one can say without exaggeration that housing in traditional Africa was accorded a high political priority. Everyone had a house and no one went without and the people were proud to live in their houses because they were an outward symbol or manifestation of their community identity. In many African societies stress was laid on conformity rather than innovation, with unduly successful people being suspect. Often what was valued was congeniality and equality rather than aspirations to wealth in the form of cattle or crops. In many societies threats of witchcraft were used to safeguard these ideals. There was therefore no great incentive to use houses to absorb money or for a conspicuous display of wealth. As a result most houses were equal, or rather some were quantitatively rather than qualitatively grander than others. Villages became therefore a collection of similar houses which in themselves were a collection of similar buildings. It is very often difficult to tell where one house ends and another begins.

In Europe and North America it is common for a house to be under one roof. In Africa this was hardly ever the case. Houses were usually a collection of similar buildings linked together or surrounded by a wall or fence, each building becoming in effect one room of the homestead, with one specific purpose such as a kitchen, a bedroom, store etc. Physically, little distinction was made between one building and another in a homestead and the sleeping room and the storage hut would look identical from the outside. The buildings used by the head of the household were often not especially elaborate or larger than the rest, and sometimes the granary or the cattle house would be the largest building in the compound. In many parts of the Western world people believe in the idea of building for posterity and go to great length to preserve buildings for several generations. Most African villages eschewed this particular idea of permanence. There was no question of people adapting themselves to houses which may have been unsuitable or inadequate. There was always a quick response in buildings to changed family requirements, such as marriage, divorce or adoption of children. Buildings were put where people needed them and they were tailored to their needs.

Vernacular architecture generally is founded on an appreciation of environmental factors. Traditional communities have to take a long-term view of their habitat; the materials needed could not simply be plundered from the land but had to be utilized only in such quantities and at such times as to cause minimum harm to the surroundings. In Africa houses were often rebuilt at least every generation to reflect changed social groupings. This fact, taken together with the ideals of equality and universal housing already mentioned, had a profound influence on the sort of building that could be put up in any location. For there had to be sufficient materials for everybody all the time. It is perhaps not surprising that a significant proportion of African houses were built of vegetable materials which grow and are continually replaced and are therefore always ready when needed.

The temporary nature of many houses did not therefore reflect unstable or unsure societies. On the contrary the continual renewal of short-lived buildings bred feelings of permanence and security. Nor did it reflect a temporary solution to housing problems. House designs were very long-term solutions to the needs and constraints of any particular society and its environment. Indeed there is archaeological evidence from some areas to show that buildings built until recently were in a style that had remained basically unchanged for more than a millennium.

Pictures of traditional African villages taken over the last 50 years can give us a glimpse into the past, not because the buildings themselves are of any great age but because the way they are arranged and built has often persisted through many centuries. Actual family relationships vary from year to year as people are born, are married or die, yet the overall social structure and the physical manifestation of it – the houses and villages – remain unchanged. The traditional Dogon village is a good

Below The Mousgoum live on the flat flood plains between the Logon and Shari rivers in Cameroon. Their houses were built like pots of mud, sometimes using small stones. The striking relief decoration may have prevented rain eroding the buildings. This is an old photograph taken in about 1900.

Below Bamileke houses were built in dense clusters on the slopes of the lush grassland valleys of western Cameroon. Six to eight of these tall, square-plan buildings with conical roofs together formed a homestead.

Right This aerial view of Labbe Zanga village, Mali, expresses beautifully the relationship of individual buildings to homesteads and to the whole village. Many of the buildings shown are granaries. Here there is a short growing season and much food has to be stored.

example. The Dogon appear to have lived on the Bandiagara escarpment for at least 500 years and to be the direct descendants of the Tellem peoples whose buildings, carvings and textiles have been preserved, some from the 14th century, in the dry caves of the escarpment and show a remarkable continuity of material culture.

Although conservative in essence, African architecture did nevertheless have the capacity to adapt to ecological and social changes. But the changes facing it in the 20th century are probably more cataclysmic and irreversible than any before. In many areas tin roofs and cement blocks have all but swept away any traces of the local architecture. Paradoxically it survives best in the richer states of West Africa where mud was used as the building material and is relatively fireproof. Its continued survival will depend now not so much on the rate of economic growth as in a shift of attitude back towards a respect for and knowledge of local crafts and traditions. For the rest of the world, traditional African architecture shows signs of becoming the focus of much interest because of its human scale and elegant functional simplicity.

S.D.

Traditional House Types

Traditional African houses rarely consisted of one single building subdivided into rooms. The more usual arrangement was for each building of the homestead to be in effect a "room," the complete homestead being made up of a collection of buildings or "rooms," perhaps surrounded by a fence or wall.

The shape of these buildings varied enormously across the continent. At least 20 different major categories can be identified and each of these displayed numerous variations, not only in size and form but also in building materials.

The examples illustrated here have been chosen to represent some of the more common individual unit types as well as a few of the ways in which these were assembled to form homesteads.

S.D.

The Nuba peoples live in the hills of southern Kordofan. Many of their homesteads are built on the ring pattern with individual buildings linked by walls or fences. House walls are of red gravelly clay, sometimes mixed with stones and often built on a foundation of large boulders. Each house consisted usually of several bedrooms, a grinding room/store with grindstones set into a raised bench and sometimes a pig- or goat-house which had a bedroom above for young children.

Below Zulu homesteads, scattered across the undulating plains of the southeastern tip of Africa, were symmetrical arrangements of buildings within two concentric hedges or stockades.

The inner circle surrounded the cattle kraal, underneath which storage pits were often dug, and the outer circle protected the homestead. Each homestead was usually made up of a room for each wife, arranged around the chief wife's room which normally faced the entrance gate, together with rooms for the unmarried sons and extra granaries.

The framework of Zulu houses was an arrangement of two sets of semicircular hoops, arranged at right angles to one another and tied where they intersected. This framework was covered first with matting and then with thick layers of grass thatch.

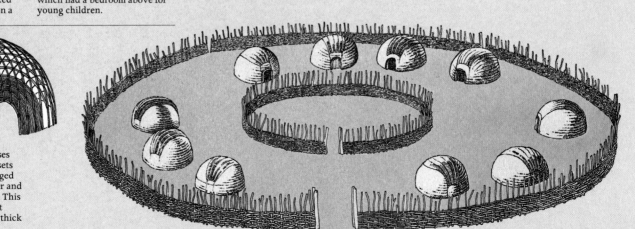

The Yoruba live in densely populated villages and towns in the forest areas of western Nigeria. Their houses were built around one large courtyard and sometimes also around subsidiary courtyards and impluvia – tiny courtyards often no more than 3 meters in diameter used not only to let in light and air to the surrounding rooms but also to collect rainwater in pots or tanks. The outside walls of the houses were built of puddled mud laid in courses, while the sides of the rooms facing the courtyards were often open between elaborately carved roof posts. Each house consisted of rooms for wives and children, a kitchen and a store as well as rooms for craftwork in the urban areas.

The Somolo live in southern Upper Volta. Their multistory houses, with walls of puddled mud and ceilings and roofs of palm fronds supported on posts, can be seen to be a coalescence of several circular buildings. In the center of each house there is a tiny courtyard. The thatched roof covers a granary. Houses sometimes consist of as many as 20 rooms, one for each wife, as well as kitchens, stores, children's rooms, granaries and grinding rooms.

Above The Nupe live in densely populated settlements in central Nigeria along the fertile alluvial valleys of the river Niger and its tributaries. Their villages are scattered in irregular patterns over the flat plains, while their houses are collections of round-plan mud buildings within enclosing mud walls breached by a *kitamba* or entrance room. Inside the walls houses normally contained a room for each wife, a room for unmarried daughters, one for unmarried sons, an inner entrance room for visitors, a man's room, a stable and granaries – the small buildings raised up on staddle stones in the drawing.

Right The Asante live in the forest areas of southern Ghana. Their houses were traditionally built around one or more courtyards, and around each were four rooms joined at their corners with a short length of wall. Puddled mud was used for the walls, reinforced with a wooden framework. The sides of rooms facing the courtyard were often left open or partly enclosed with pillars of palm fronds covered with mud plaster. Many of the walls and pillars were ornamented with complex relief patterns. A detail from one such wall is shown here.

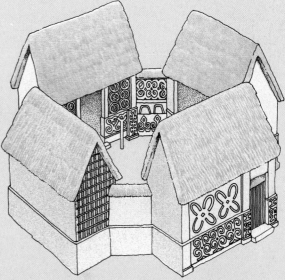

AFRICAN ARTS

Despite the numerous books on African art and the familiarity of many of its pieces, now prominently displayed in museums, much remains to be discovered about its creation and use. The only common characteristic of what is usually discussed under the term African sculpture is its non-abstract form. As well as wood, sculptures were made from iron, brass, terracotta, stone, basketry covered with clay or skin, ivory and even cloth and encompassed such varied forms as figures, dolls, masks, stools, headrests, staffs, bowls and so on.

The impulse behind the creation of traditional African art can only be understood with reference to the community that produced it. Indeed, African figurative sculpture can almost be thought of as the private face of the community in which it originated. Some of the sculpture was made to be seen only by the spirit world, some was never seen by women, and much, when not in use, was hidden away in rafters between ceremonial occasions or was housed in shrines to which noninitiates and strangers were not admitted. Many dancing masks were made to be seen in motion, swirling in semidarkness, lit up intermittently by the low flickering light of a fire, with deep recesses and strong contrasting planes catching the low light. Brightly lit and static in museums, wrenched from their contexts, they have lost half their power.

Since African art is essentially a community art, the form that sculptures took was on the whole very specific to the peoples who produced them. They used a language of shapes that was known and understood by both the artists and their patrons. The carver, for instance, was not an individual expressing his own personal feelings and taking inspiration at random; rather the art was produced to satisfy the needs of a community by someone who was closely integrated into that community. Nevertheless this did not mean that an artist's work was merely repetitive; on the contrary, an artist was free to evolve his own personal adaptations within a framework accepted by the community and his work might be either acclaimed or rejected.

This framework of forms often only had significance for the originating community and sometimes meant very little to even neighboring communities. Thus art was a unifying force within each community; it reasserted community identity by using a unique language. Misunderstandings, therefore, arise when norms from other cultures are used to assess African sculpture. Chokwe sculptures, for example, with half-open mouths and pointed teeth, are sometimes said by Western observers to look "fierce" or "cruel," although nicely pointed teeth are a mark of beauty among the Chokwe. Similarly vitality or movement is considered by many African carvers to exist only in works which are balanced, that is exactly symmetrical about a central axis, whereas Western observers consider those were the very sculptures which were most static.

In Africa all art is in some sense functional,

although without adequate documentation it is often impossible to tell, just by looking at it, what a piece of sculpture was originally intended to be used for, whether to amuse the living or pacify the dead or both. Among the Yoruba similar carvings found in shrines and in palaces had very different functions, the first to honor the spirits and the second to honor the Oba or king. In all cases the importance of a piece of sculpture lay not just within itself but depended on where it was, who owned it and how it was used. In some societies once a carver had finished a mask, it was then given its life-giving force through paint or continuous offerings of food or oil by its owner or guardian without which things it would have been worthless. Elsewhere the significance of a mask could be altered by it being bequeathed from one man to another.

Most of the vast amount of sculpture now housed in museums comes from western and central Africa with comparatively little from eastern and southern Africa. The exact reasons for this distribution are not yet quite clear. It is often stated that the settled agriculturalists of the rain forests and the savanna woodlands on the forest margins had the right materials (large enough pieces of wood) and the right political institutions to encourage the development and preservation of major works of sculpture, in contrast to the pastoralists and mixed farmers elsewhere. Nevertheless, in other parts of the world pastoralists have been very prolific producers of carvings. Another factor must be the high population density of parts of West and central Africa, which means that any carving tradition will produce many more pieces than in an area of low population density. A third important point is that eastern and southern African may not have produced as little as has been imagined. Recent research in Malawi has produced some interesting masks from an area formerly thought to be devoid of all figurative work.

In general, however, the finest works have come from areas where political institutions, settlement patterns and social organization made it possible for several carvers to thrive and to compete for patrons within a small area. The Yoruba kingdoms in western Nigeria, the Kuba of Zaïre and the Bamoun in southern Cameroon are good examples. Each carver evolved his own personal adaptation of the accepted community style; the most successful ones gained more commissions and perfected their techniques still further. In several areas the names of the carvers from 50 years back are still known and their skills remembered. Carving was not in all instances a professional affair; among the Dogon and the Tiv, for example, carving was done by nonspecialists. In some instances a particular carver's success extended far beyond the boundaries of his own community, and masks, for example, would be bought from him to be used in ceremonies for which they were not specifically

Above Much of Ivory Coast Baulé sculpture is gentle and humanistic, and was among the earliest African art to be admired by European collectors. This seated, bearded figure of an ancestor demonstrates the care typically taken by Baulé carvers to represent exact details of the hair and face.

Right This selection of baskets comes from Tanzania and Nigeria but is representative of baskets sold in markets all over Africa.
Center column, from the top
Large plaited basket, Adamawa, Nigeria. This basket was used for head carrying and its base is padded.
Wickerwork food basket, Kafanchan, Nigeria.
Coiled threshing basket, Nyamwezi, Tanzania.
Wickerwork sieve for straining grated coconut, Swahili, Tanzania.
Right hand column
Twined food cover, Bornu, Nigeria.
Twined basket, Pogoro, Tanzania.
Plaited and twined storage basket, Nyakusa, Tanzania.

designed. Trading of castings and carvings was certainly not unknown, too, and gifts of items of regalia were quite common from one ruler to another. Many of the African empires were organized around vassal chiefs who espoused the culture as well as the political institutions of the central rulers. The cultural influence of the Asante of Ghana over their hinterland is a good example; gold jewelry, silk *kente* cloth and gold-handled swords spread to the chiefs of surrounding peoples.

To give the study of African art a historical dimension is very difficult. Very little wood carving survives for more than 100 years. What historical

Below Decorated calabashes from Nigeria. Calabashes or gourds grow on creeping plants over fences and roofs or in between crops. When cut and dried they are used as rafts, food containers or as sound boxes for musical instruments and decorated in a variety of ways as illustrated here.

Above White Hunter in the Pygmies' Jungle, painted in gouache on board, is by Twins Seven-Seven, one of the best-known Nigerian Oshogbo artists who came to prominence in the 1960s interpreting traditional legends with new techniques.

Left This font was carved by Bandele, one of several Yoruba carvers recently encouraged to use their skills to interpret Christian themes. He seems to have conceived it as a large drum.

material we do have is of metal, terracotta, ivory and stone. Nevertheless the terracotta sculptures from Nigeria span two and a half millennia and so give a very good picture of stylistic development over a very long period of time. Much of the figurative sculpture is magnificent – the Nok and Ife terracotta heads and figures, the Benin, Ife and Igbo-Ukwu bronzes, the Benin and Afro–Portuguese ivories – but it is necessarily an arbitrary and unrepresentative part of the total production. The first Nok terracottas and some of the bronzes from Ife and Igbo-Ukwu were found by accident. Many pieces have been found above ground but obviously far from where they were made. Much of the early material is still unrelated to centers of production or to the societies that produced it and so its original purpose remains obscure.

Sculpture is only marginally important economically. By contrast pots, jewelry, textiles, baskets and ironwork are often very important and are traded in markets, either because they are surplus to requirements or because they have been produced for sale by specialist craftsmen. Pottery produced by specialist potters can sometimes be sold over very large areas. Kisi pots are famous all over southwest Tanzania: very thinly walled and a reddish color, they are carried by their makers in boats up and down Lake Malawi. The Bamessi women potters of the southern Cameroon have a virtual monopoly there, while the Degha of the Black Volta control the finest beds of clay and trade their wares to large areas of Ghana and the Ivory Coast.

Large bundles of calabashes on the backs of lorries or on boats on the Niger on the way to markets are a familiar sight; unfinished calabashes (dried but not decorated) are widely traded. Baskets for storage, carrying, threshing and straining are sold in markets all over Africa and all the various techniques of twining, plaiting, coiling and wickerwork are found. In West and central Africa cloth merchants crisscross the area carrying, for example, Yoruba narrow-strip cloths north and Hausa tie-dyed cloth south. Trans-Saharan trade may have atrophied, but elsewhere improved roads have speeded up the existing trade in locally produced craft goods. Handwoven and dyed cloths, for example, still manage to compete successfully with machine-made goods.

The individual artist is now becoming a part of the 20th-century African scene. In Nigeria the Oshogbo group of artists, who came to prominence in the 1960s, experiment with adaptations of traditional techniques, such as repoussé aluminum work with subjects often based on traditional folk tales. Elsewhere in Nigeria woodcarvers have been encouraged to produce plaques, doors and carvings for churches and secular buildings. In Tanzania the delicate lino prints of Francis Msangi contrast with the forceful sculptures now produced by Makonde artists to sell to visitors. Everywhere artists are emerging to supply patrons both in the urban areas of Africa and overseas with the kind of portable self-contained art they require. But this is very definitely an African art, linked with the sculpture of the traditional artist through shared techniques, background and motifs, the last often representations of folk tales now being written down by African writers.   S.D.

Nigerian Bronzes

The history of Nigerian bronze casting cannot yet be written with completeness or certainty. Much of the corpus of works now known has been found accidentally – like the hoard dug up at Igbo-Ukwu in 1939, or the Ife bronzes excavated near the palace of Ife in 1937 – and so must represent only a fragment of the total production. At any time another chance find could completely alter the picture.

Most Nigerian bronzes were produced by the lost-wax process. A model of wax or latex was sandwiched between two layers of sun-baked clay held in place with iron pins. The wax or latex was melted out and replaced by molten bronze.

Bronze casting appears to have had many centers of production, the most prolific being the court of Benin where casting was a royal prerogative and persisted from the 16th to the 19th century. Further north, at Ife, the fine naturalistic bronze heads and figures were probably produced as early as the 12th century to commemorate Onis (chiefs) and, together with their terracotta counterparts, show a distinct feeling of continuity with the Nok terracotta sculptures of 1000 years earlier.

Elsewhere, centers of production probably existed in the lower Niger area around Ijebu, at Owo, as well as among the Tiv and Jukun and latterly around Adamawa. S.D.

Below This bronze snufftaker was probably made earlier this century. It would have been worn on the little finger and snuff taken from the round top disk. The Tiv still have a lively casting industry but usually only produce small bronzes.

Below Ogboni Edan staffs were usually made in pairs representing the earth spirit in two forms, one male and one female, attached by a chain secured at the top of each head. They were used by the Oshugbo Ogboni cult which flourished around Ijebu.

Below Benin city was by the 15th century the center of a powerful state in the forest area west of the Niger delta. The 17th-century Dutch geographer Olfert Dapper described its palace as having "wooden pillars encased in copper, where their victories are depicted." Here is a plaque from

such a pillar showing hunters and leopards intertwined with stylized leaves and flowers.

Right Also from Benin is this superb bronze ram's head ornament worn on a belt by a chief, probably in the 17th century.

Right Bronze casting in Benin was the prerogative of the Oba and a court style evolved which over the centuries seems to have become almost stultified through lack of outside contact. This rather stiff horseman belongs to the middle period around the 17th century. The rider is shown wearing an elaborate headdress modeled to represent tiers of feathers.

Above Small masks, such as this one, representing grotesque faces with snakes curling out of the nostrils, were used as hip pendants hanging from a girdle and worn with court dress in Benin.

Below About 27 bronzes are known from Ife – all found near the royal palace. It seems the art of Ife evolved in terracotta and was only later translated into bronze, perhaps in the 13th century. This figure probably represents an Oni bedecked in royal regalia. Ife sculpture in both bronze and terracotta is the most famous manifestation of naturalism in African art.

Above right This dwarf, one of the most naturalistic pieces to have been found at Benin, belongs to the earliest period, around the 16th century. It is close in style to the Ife tradition from which it is thought the technique of bronze casting may have been derived.

Right This is one of a group of bronzes in fluid style thought to have perhaps been made in the lower Niger area. It shows a hunter returning home with an antelope slung across his shoulders and a dog by his right foot.

Masterpieces of Wood Carving

Since African wood carving burst on the Western art scene in the early years of this century, "discovered" and patronized by Picasso, Matisse and their contemporaries, it has been collected avidly by museums and private collectors and much misunderstood. It has been valued for its so-called "brutalism," "cubism," "primitiveness" and so on without an understanding of the societies and attitudes that produced it. Over the last decade, however, meticulous research into the names and styles of individual artists in many areas as well as into the uses and provenance of sculptures has done a lot to change this attitude. It is also beginning to show that African art is susceptible to the same techniques of analysis as Western art. It is hoped that over the next decade much more information will be collected which will lead to a better understanding of the historical perspective of African wood carving.   S.D.

Above The Yoruba were among the most prolific producers of sculpture. Much was made for cults of major deities as furniture for shrines in the form of carved devotees, such as this piece.

Above Dogon wood carvings preserved in the dry caves on the Bandiagra escarpment in Mali are the oldest woodcarvings known to have survived in Africa. Some have been carbon dated to around 1400 AD.

Left These small figures made by an Ekoi carver are covered in skin. The practice of making skin-covered wooden masks, sometimes topped by small figures like these, was concentrated around the Cross river on the border of Nigeria and Cameroon. The masks belonged to associations which performed various rites and celebrations for members. Before use, a mask would usually be dressed up – polished with oil and decorated with feathers or quills.

Right Chokwe art has flourished in the large chiefdoms in the heart of Angola since they grew up in the 16th century. This statue, collected in 1878, was an effigy of the chief Chibinda. The large upturned hairstyle and exaggerated hands and feet, which apparently reflect their power and strength, are characteristic of much Chokwe sculpture.

Below The figures of the Bena Lulua of Zaïre are very distinctive, with their heads and bodies covered in elaborate scarification marks and the navel always emphasized. All Bena Lulua carvings are thought to have been made before 1880 when religious pressures seem to have stopped production.

Left Headrests were used principally to preserve the elaborate, much-prized coiffure worn by Luba women of the Congo. They were also sometimes used in conjunction with small rectangular frames for divination. The hairstyles shown on this piece – a series of wavelike crests – are characteristic of the Luba Shankadi style.

Above This imposing couple from Ivory Coast are Senufo ancestor figures – both male and female. Characteristic of the genre are their large size – up to 1 meter tall in some cases – and their rugged quality, accentuated in early examples by the weathering of the surface of the wood.

Left This Dan mask from Liberia may have been used for teaching initiates, although among the Dan the appearance of a mask is not always a reliable guide to its use, for masks were sometimes "promoted" from one activity to another. Masks such as these were also sometimes used by members of the *Poro* men's society.

Right Compared with the wealth and volume of sculpture produced in West and central Africa, very little appears to have been made in southern Africa. This piece is one of the few examples of work by Sotho carvers and is the head of a staff.

Above Headrests were designed to be used as pillows, thereby protecting elaborate hair decorations. This example from southwest Tanzania has unusual carved decoration.

Below A detail of the face of a female caryatid on a Baluba chief's stool from Zaïre said to have been carved by a "master of the long-faced style of the Buli." The female figures, whose

hairstyles and cicatrization were carved with complete accuracy, seem to have been symbolic ancestor figures, supporting the chiefs both physically and metaphorically, and may also have alluded to a Baluba practice of a member of the ruling family using a slave as a seat.

Above This Senufo equestrian figure from Ivory Coast represents the *bandeguele,* a divinity used by divination experts as a messenger to the spirit world.

MUSIC AND DANCE

In a strict sense the term African music/dance applies today exclusively to the musical cultures of African peoples south of the Sahara, including the Khoisan peoples in the extreme southwest. In ancient time the black African cultural region extended much further north, as is evident, for instance, from rock paintings in the Sahara. The musical cultures of present-day North Africa are fundamentally different from those of black Africa, belonging to an Afro–Asian rather than an African stylistic area. Similarly the music and folk dances of European settler communities in southern Africa are not included under the term African music and dance.

Africa, so defined, contains the following song-style divisions according to Alan Lomax: Western Sudan, Equatorial Bantu, African Hunters, South African Bantu, Central Bantu, Northeast Bantu, Eastern Sudan, Guinea Coast, Afro–American, Muslim Sudan, Ethiopia, Upper Nile and Madagascar. The inclusion of an Afro–American region indicates that black Africa has been considered as culturally extending to include the African diaspora. The musical cultures of the Guinea coast (for instance, Yoruba and Fon), of the Congo/Angola region and to a lesser extent of southeast Africa have extensions in various parts of the New World. But only recently has it been possible to link precisely some stylistic elements in the various types of Afro–American music to local style areas in black Africa. Paul Oliver, for instance, has linked the roots of Blues with the large region of western Sudan, the hinterland of the West African coast.

In spite of the distinct musical traditions of North Africa and black Africa, there has been considerable historical interaction and cross-cultural contact between these two areas. Trade, slavery and Islamic colonization have resulted in the Islamization of African music in vast areas of black Africa, and also in the strong impact of black African musical traits in some areas of North Africa, as in southern Morocco. Muslim Sudan is one of the Islamized musical regions. In East Africa musical forms showing Arab or Islamic influence are found even far inland, for instance in southern Uganda, not only along the Indian Ocean coast. Several musical instruments of Arab introduction can be seen in these parts, the one-string fiddle being the most visible example. On the other hand, vast areas of black Africa are virtually free from Arab or Islamic influence. The traditional circumcision schools for boys found in west central Africa, with their associated dances and music, are an independent black African development and in no way to be related to Muslim practices.

It is now widely acknowledged that African music/dance in various parts of the continent has constantly undergone decisive changes in history. What is termed traditional music today is probably very different from what African music sounded like some centuries ago. Nor is African music always ethnic in the sense ethnomusicology would have it. Music forms and traits are not rigidly linked to ethnic groups; in addition the individual musician, with his individual style and creativity, is very important.

Ethnic groupings have themselves been in a state of continuous flux and musical traits and fashions have been exchanged across ethnic and linguistic boundaries. When the *likembe*, a small box-resonated lamellophone invented in the lower Zaïre region, began to spread upriver in the late 19th century, carried by Lingala-speaking porters and colonial servants, it was soon adopted by non-Bantu speakers such as the Ngbandi, Gbaya and Azande. The music of the *likembe*, which shows marked stylistic traits from western Bantu-speaking central Africa, was only gradually modified to suit local musical styles. At the beginning of the 20th century the *likembe* distribution area extended further northeast into Uganda, where it was adopted by the Nilotic Alur, Acholi and Langi. Later, workers from northern Uganda introduced the instrument to southern Uganda, where Bantu-speaking Soga and Gwere adopted it and have since produced outstanding composers and performers. In west central Africa the *likembe* gradually spread southwards from the Kasai (Zaïre) to eastern Angola and was adopted in the 1950s as far south as the Khoisan-speaking !Kung' of southeastern Angola. This example shows that distribution may change quite rapidly; distribution maps, therefore, are valid only if based on material collected within a relatively narrow time span and even so may present a fragmented and perplexing picture.

Extremely distant areas often show similar, even identical, traits, while adjacent areas may at the same time be set apart stylistically. The multi-part singing style in triads within an *equiheptatonic* tone system of the Baulé in the Ivory Coast is so close, if not identical, to the part-singing style of Ngangela-, Chokwe- and Luvale-speaking peoples in eastern Angola, that this is immediately recognized by informants from both cultures. Why this is so, is a riddle. The two areas are separated by several countries with different approaches to multi-part singing. Another historical riddle is the presence of practically identical xylophone playing styles and instruments in northern Mozambique (among Makonde- and Makua-speaking peoples) and certain peoples of the Ivory Coast and Liberia (especially the Baulé and Kru). The *jomolo* of the Baulé and *dimbila* of the Makonde are virtually identical instruments.

Diffusionist theories of different kinds have been offered to resolve such riddles. One explanation, by Arthur M. Jones, has been the suggested presence of Indonesian settlers in certain areas of East, central and West Africa during the early centuries AD, who would have been responsible for the introduction of xylophones and certain tonal-harmonic systems

Opposite Ensembles of composite gourd horns are a prominent feature of Nilotic musical cultures in the Sudan. In this picture, taken in the late 1950s, hunters are being called to assemble at a place known as Loitanit Rock in northern Karamoja, in the Uganda/Sudan border area.

Above African music is now becoming increasingly available to international audiences and to tourists in the form of public performances and concerts, outside its original social context. This performance by a Ghanaian player of the one-string fiddle demonstrates the presence of musical instruments of Arabic background in West Africa, as a result of the historical trans-Sahara trade routes. It is now found in many parts of the West African savanna belt, for instance among the Wolof of Senegal, the Hausa of Nigeria, the Songhay and Djerma of Niger and the Dagomba of Ghana.

Above At the climax of the *Nkili* dance a young man leaps high into the air, caught and steadied by a young woman. This little-known dance style is cultivated by the Humbi and Handa of southwestern Angola. It demands great precision from both dancers as well as strength on the woman's part.

(equipentatonic, equiheptatonic and Pelog scales). Ethnohistorians on the other hand have tended to stress the importance of coastal navigation, with Africans as hired or forced labor on European ships, as an agent of cultural contact.

Attempts at reconstructing African musical history are highly speculative without the evidence of historical sources. Such sources are, in fact, more abundant than might be expected, but should be distinguished as to whether they are internal or external, that is, whether they come from black Africans themselves or from outside observers. The most important ancient black African sources are archaeological (iron objects, such as bells or lamellophone notes), rock paintings (such as occur abundantly in the Sahara), and later art objects collected by contemporary observers. Equally important is the evidence from oral traditions.

Among the most important external sources are written and pictorial documents by visitors and travelers. Arab travelers visited the East African coast from the 10th century onwards. Early European records still await detailed evaluation by Afro-musicologists who are familiar with the musical areas concerned. A specific class of sources is musical notations from earlier centuries by Europeans. There are some 18th-century notations, but the 19th century is particularly rich. However, the notations by musically trained Westerners

rarely do justice to the intrinsic qualities of African music, and give a distorted picture depending on the specific musical background of each observer, and also because of the inherent cultural bias of the Western staff notation system itself. Nonetheless, these notations are not completely worthless. Though the music cannot be produced from them in a straightforward manner, it is possible after careful analysis to reconstruct at least approximately what the traveler may have heard. It has been possible, for instance, to interpret the notation by Carl Mauch (1872) of a *mbira dze midzimu* lamellophone tuning, which he observed in a village near the ruins of Great Zimbabwe, by comparison with present-day measurements of *mbira* tunings from the same area.

Sometimes historical data on African music/dance can be obtained indirectly from Latin American sources. Peoples deported from Africa to the New World most typically came from the hinterland and African trading groups acted as intermediaries for the European slave traders on the coast. The Ovimbundu of Angola, for example, filled such a role, selling war prisoners from eastern Angola to the Portuguese. As a result, music and dance of peoples from the interior of Mozambique and Angola became accessible indirectly from 18th- and 19th-century Brazil, at a time when European observers had not penetrated to such inland areas of Africa.

The shape of current African music and dance in sub-Saharan Africa results from a variety of historical changes: ecological, cultural, social, religious, political and so on. Change in the ecology was a long-term factor affecting population movement which in turn provoked changes in the expressive culture, including music and dance. Since the drying-out of the Sahara, populations have tended to shift southwards. In Tanzania within the last 20 years the Maasai have been grazing their cattle increasingly further south and in 1977 they were a common sight in Sangu country (east of Mbeya). When settled populations accepted the newcomers, they often adopted musical styles from them or new dance types. Thus, the choral singing style of the Maasai has had a fundamental influence on the vocal music of the Gogo of central Tanzania, as can be seen in their *nindo* and *msunyunho* chants.

If there is any trait in the black African music/dance cultures of nearly pan-African validity, it is the distinctive black African concepts about and attitudes towards motion. Movement style is what sets black Africa apart from the rest of the world. Unfortunately, this is an area where research is still in the initial stages. Dance research has been mostly descriptive and from a Western viewpoint as far as black Africa is concerned, and current systems of dance notation claiming universal applicability – Laban, Benesch and others – are even less adequate tools for capturing the structure and feel of African motional systems than is Western staff notation for African music.

One basic difference between European and black African dance cultures is that in the former the body tends to be used in a single block, while in black African dance movement it seems to be split into several seemingly independent body areas. Helmut Günther has characterized African and Afro–American dances with the term "polycentric" and has also pointed to a prevailing body attitude, the "collapse." Olly Wilson has pointed out that the most important trait which links black music in America with African music is motional behavior. Indeed, motional style, at least in its basic principles, has been among the most persistent traits in African cultures. In black Africa identical motional patterns and concepts embrace music and dance. An eminent guitarist from Malawi, Daniel Kachamba, once expressed it like this: "My fingers dance on the strings of my guitar."

As there is always more than one motional center in a given black African dance, so there is also in the playing of musical instruments. The musician does not only produce sounds but moves his hands, fingers, and even head, shoulders, or legs, in certain coordinated patterns during the process of musical production. The music is really the whole of the motional organization and this is one of the reasons why African music is not notated traditionally, in contrast to Western music. The lack of notation systems in black African music is not a deficiency; on the contrary, the idea of writing down music and "playing it from paper" (the expression of a traditional musician) would be utterly perverse in musical cultures where the motional aspect of musical production is so intimately linked with the auditory one.

Analysis of films has been crucial in the study of dance movement in black Africa, and many scholars are now using this method. Dauer proposed a geographical division of black Africa into several dance-style areas, for example Western Sudan, Sahara, West African Coast, Central African Bantu and Southern Bantu; these coincide to a great extent with the song-style regions of Lomax. Acknowledging that black African dances are "polycentric," these dance-style areas are based on the observation that in different areas different parts of the human body tend to be emphasized in dance practice. For instance, motional prominence of the pelvis is considered a diagnostic trait of the movement style of the southern Zaïre/Angola region. There is, however, a good deal of stylistic spill-over across the presumed dance-style areas. In masked dancing of the large Ngangela group of peoples in eastern Angola, for example, many different movement patterns are used by the same community, and each is identified with a local name. Which pattern is used depends on the type of masks.

In solo dancing, especially masked dancing, there are also movements aimed at communicating with the audience or submitting certain coded messages. A masked dancer is an actor who has to play out the character his mask represents. This includes not only dancing, but pantomimic action, gestures and certain styles of walking.

Masked dancing has an interesting distribution area in black Africa. It occurs in a variety of social contexts and often with different functions. It is widely found in West Africa and west central Africa, while it is rare in East Africa and absent in southern Africa. The Makonde, Makua, Ndonde and Chewa are the principal East African peoples with masked societies. One of the richest areas in masks is the culturally rather homogeneous territory comprising almost all of eastern Angola, northwestern Zambia and some southern parts of Zaïre. Among the Chokwe, Luvale, Luchazi, Mbunda, Nkangala, Lwimbi and others there is an abundance of mask types, each specific in appearance and meaning, with a well-defined place in a hierarchic order, specific movement reportories, gestures and pantomime. Most masks of these eastern Angolan peoples represent ancestral members of an ancient court hierarchy. Kings and members of the royal families, their officials and retinue, including servants and slaves, resurrect in the masked theater.

Movement organization in black African music/dance follows rigidly certain principles of timing. These cannot be compared with Western metrical systems. Black African systems of timing are based on at least four to five fundamental concepts:

1. The overall presence of a mental background pulsation consisting of equal-spaced pulse units elapsing ad infinitum and often at enormous speed. These so-called elementary pulses function as a basic orientation screen. They are two or three times faster than the beat or gross-pulse.

2. Musical form is organized so that patterns and themes cover recurring entities of a regular number of these elementary pulses, usually 8, 12, 16, 24 or their multiples, more rarely 9, 18 or 27 units. These are the so-called cycles; the numbers are referred to as form numbers.

3. Many of the form numbers can be divided and split in more than one way, thus allowing the

Top Nuba girls in Kordofan, Sudan, wearing decorative belts, perform a traditional dance with highly individualistic movements. Their bodies are smeared with sim-sim oil and ocher.

Center By striking the water surface, girls from southern Cameroon produce rhythmic combinations and sounds very close to those of a drum.

Above African music/dance is often linked stylistically with work movement. Here, three Chamba women ease their work of pounding grain by dropping their pestles in a rhythmic sequence.

Left This player of panpipes, accompanying himself with a rattle, is from Zimbabwe.

simultaneous combination of contradictory metrical units. For instance, the number 12, which is the most important one in African music, can be divided by 2, 3, 4 and 6.

4. Patterns of the same form number can be shifted against each other in combinations so that their starting points cross ("cross rhythms"). In certain instances they cross so completely that they fall between themselves (interlock) with no two notes sounding together ("interlocking combination").

In some areas there is a further principle of timing: the so-called time-line patterns. Broadly speaking, it is found in the areas covered by the Kwa and Benue–Congo subgroups of the Niger–Congo group of languages. Here we encounter time-line patterns in many (though not all) kinds of music to be danced to. These are short, usually single-note, rhythmic patterns, often of asymmetric structure, struck on a bell, a bottle, a high-pitched drum, the rim of a drum, or clapped with hands. A time-line pattern represents the *structural core* of a musical piece, something like a condensed and extremely concentrated representation of the rhythmic-motional possibilities open to the participants (musicians and dancers). Singers, drummers and dancers in the group find their bearings by listening to the strokes of the time-line pattern, which is repeated at a steady tempo throughout the performance. Time-line patterns are transmitted from teacher to learner by means of mnemonic syllables or mnemonic verbal patterns.

Musical patterns are often conceived as verbalized in black African cultures. The same applies to dance patterns. For example rattle playing is often taught with syllables such as *cha-cha-cha-cha* or *ka-cha-ka-cha-ka-cha*, depending on which pattern the student is expected to play. An important time-line pattern for the accompaniment of *likembe* music in eastern Angola is taught with the mnemonic formula *Mu chana cha Kapekula* (in the river grassland of Kapekula). The phonetic structure of such mnemonic patterns reflects the timbre, rhythmic and accental structure of the pattern to be played.   G.K.

Musical Instruments

There is an abundant variety of musical instruments in Africa, some of which, such as lamellophones, are specific to this continent. Contrary to common Western belief, drums are not necessarily the "most typical" African musical instruments. Drums with a wooden body, for instance, are absent in areas lacking large trees; lamellophones with metal notes are traditionally found in places where a blacksmith is available; the hunting bow is used as a musical instrument (mouth bow) in Namibia and southern Angola, where the hunting-and-gathering background is strong. Some instruments may be in common use, others reserved for either men or women; some may belong to religious groups, others to traditional educational institutions; others may be associated with traditional political organizations, such as royal courts. G.K.

Right A rare type of musical bow called *sagaya* is found among the Humbi of southwestern Angola. Musician Pequenino uses an ordinary hunting bow with a brace added to transform it into a musical instrument. The brace divides the bow near the middle, giving two fundamental notes from the two unequal lengths of string; these are about a whole tone apart. For playing, the bow is held in the lips. The right hand holds a leather wand. The left hand supports the bow in the way shown in the photograph. The musician strikes one or other segment of the string, continually altering the shape and size of his mouth cavity. The melody formed implies a text, although the musician does not sing.

Right Some traditional African musical instruments are becoming increasingly rare. Madame Nke is one of the remaining players in southern Cameroon of the transversal flute called *oding*. This instrument is reserved for women. The playing style combines vocal sounds (often indistinguishable from those of the flute) with blown instrumental tones. Before playing, water is put into the flute. The plant, similar to a liana, from which this flute is made is not found in southern Cameroon which suggests that this flute was originally not indigenous to the area. Madame Nke's mother-in-law brought it from near Ngaoundere in the north.

Above The playing of so-called time-line patterns is a prominent feature in much music of the West African coast. The 12-pulse standard pattern, struck as 12 (x . x . xx . x . xx .), is the musical backbone of many performances in the area of the former kingdom of Dahomey. An eminent Fon singer, Soso Njako, uses a time-line pattern to accompany his songs. Holding a nail in his right hand he taps out the pattern on a bottle, while the left index finger silently taps a complementary pattern on the bottle's neck. Other instruments in this group include *ogo* (a large calabash struck with a leather flap) and *ogan* (a double bell on a stem grip). In the Fon language this kind of music is called *Toba*.

Above right A court musician of the Timi of Ede announces a visitor. He uses one of the most prominent musical instruments in Yorubaland: the *iya-ilu* (mother drum) of a *dundun* set of hourglass-shaped tension drums. The *iya-ilu* is a "talking drum" designed for performing recitals, announcements and praise poetry (*oriki*) for important persons. The principle of "talking" on a drum relies on the

fact that Yoruba is a tone language in which the meaning of a word depends partly on speech tones. The pitch-lines produced by the talking drum follow as closely as possible the tonal and rhythmic patterns of spoken texts. The drums of the *dundun* set have two membranes connected by leather thongs. By pressing the thongs with his left hand or arm the musician can change the pitch of the drum. A hooked stick is used for striking. Small bells, jingling during play, are attached to the drum.

Right Part of a percussion group from Togo. The *ogo* is a big calabash struck with a leather flap (*afafa*) made from antelope skin. The *Tochng* is a remarkable instrument consisting of two pails filled with water in which two calabashes of different size are floated. The player strikes them lightly with wooden sticks.

Below Court musicians of the emir of Zaria perform in front of his palace. Hausa music of northern Nigeria is characterized by strong Arabic, specifically Islamic, influences. Several instruments were imported from North Africa. The ensemble in this picture uses the following instruments: several double-skin cylinder drums with vibration string attached; double bells; and the *kakaki* metal horns. The court music ensemble of some 10 to 15 performers consists of men of a respectable age. Children of the large family of the emir and his retinue stand behind and watch the performance. One of the drummers sings praise songs and recitals in honor of the emir.

Below right A musician from northwestern Zambia plays the *likembe*. Of Zaïrian origin, the *likembe* (pl. *makembe*) is a distinctive kind of lamellophone, characterized by a box-resonator with a cut-out section on top projecting from one end of the hollowed-out box. Two sound-holes are burned into the body of the *likembe*, one in the end closest to the player's body, the other at the back of the instrument. The *likembe* is played with the thumbs, and by alternately opening and closing the back hole with the middle finger of his left hand the musician produces timbre modifications.

Above At a village near Atakpamé in Togo, two men play the *ogan*. The instrument comprises a double bell with a stem grip, one bell short and the other long, representing a mother with a child on her back. The bells are struck with sticks made of light wood. The *ogan* is one of the percussion instruments commonly used to accompany the *achya*, a very popular and highly acrobatic dance among the Fon people.

Above Xylophone player Jean Numbikamba represents an important central African instrumental tradition. This type of portable xylophone, with a rail to hold it away from the player's body and with gourd resonators equipped with mirliton buzzers, came to Cameroon from the south. Its most likely center of dispersal was the old kingdom of Kongo, where comparable instruments were seen by 17th-century missionaries. In Cameroon present-day oral tradition among the southern peoples confirms that when a chief intended to undertake a journey and visit neighboring areas, his xylophone band, which usually consisted of four musicians, went ahead walking and playing the processional music. This is why this particular variety of xylophone is designed to be portable. With the xylophone music spreading north into the interior of what is now Congo-Brazzaville and beyond, the possession of a band playing portable xylophones became a symbol of authority and status among many of the small chieftainships.

Above Uzavela walks with his *chihumba* through the plantation of a Portuguese farmer, where he was employed. The playing attitude is characteristic: the *chihumba* is carried on a string around the neck and held with the arcs pointing away from the player's body. The *chihumba* pluriarc or ''bow lute'' is an instrument very popular among the people of southwestern Angola. It is often played walking, during a long journey. Many songs refer to the long march with goods from the rural areas to the port of Benguela. Benguela was also an important center for the deportation of Angolans as slave workers to the New World, especially to Brazil. The pluriarc is one of the instruments which had already reached Brazil with the slave trade in the 18th century. The instrument seen in the present picture is practically identical in construction and playing technique with that reported from 18th-century Brazil.

Masks and the Dance

Traditionally in black Africa masks are an expressive aspect of exclusive associations (normally for men). Membership can only be achieved by submission to graded instruction and an often horrific initiation process. There are also in some societies women's associations with "masks." In local languages the same term is often used as for the masks of men, while Western observers would describe the women's "masks" as body paint.

Masked dancing provides a link between the secluded "masked society" and society at large. Access to the place where the masks are made and where the dancers dress is restricted, but the dance theater of the various masked characters takes place in public. A mask in black Africa is to be appreciated as a character in motion; it is the whole — face-cover and costume. Though "masked societies" have religious aspects, they should not be misconstrued as religious cult groups; masked dancers do not fall into "trance," nor are they possessed by spirits. Nor do the owners of masks practice "magic," though fanciful and misleading stories are often deliberately circulated.   G.K.

Above These masked dancers from southern Zaïre belong to the Pende people. The Pende have much in common with the northeastern Angolan peoples in their traditional institutions and in the technology of making masked costumes in the form of an interlaced network.

Left Young girls of Bigene village, CAR, perform the *Akulavye* dance. During the dance the girls sit on chairs and move legs, arms, shoulders and breasts. They imitate the *siu*, an animal "with a white face, which often comes to the village to kill chickens."

Below left The head of this bird mask from southeastern Angola is painted with white clay to resemble the white head of the fish eagle. The beak, in which a fish is grasped, is genuine. When dancing, the mask is made to imitate the yelping cries of the fish eagle.

Below This mask was photographed during the Ogun festival of the Yoruba in Nigeria. Ogun is the god of iron and war in Yoruba religion.

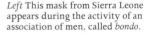

Left This mask from Sierra Leone appears during the activity of an association of men, called *bondo*.

Right Another mask from Sierra Leone demonstrates the great variety of theatrical characters, including modern ideas, which appear in the traditional dance dramas.

Below The masked society (*awa*) of the Dogon plays a vital role in preserving their elaborate mythology. Funeral rites are occasions for elaborate public dances, accompanied by chants in a secret language. Dancers wear vegetable fiber skirts stained red with a dye obtained from hibiscus leaves. Red costumes are particularly associated with the dancers who drive out the spirit of the dead person from its house. Another part of the rite recalls the Dogon myth of how death entered the world through the disobedience of young men. The dancers lash the ground around the corpse, seeking its forgiveness.

Below right Among the Luchazi, Mbwela and related peoples in eastern Angola and northwestern Zambia the local name referring to the masked characters is *makisi* (singular *likisi*). Among the Mbwela two categories of *makisi* are recognized. One is called *makisi avamala* (the "masks" of men), the other *makisi avampwevo* (the "masks" of women). A Western observer would not consider the latter to be "masks" at all, but rather women with body paint on. In the Mbwela conceptualization the "masks" of the women, as seen in this picture, are the equivalents of the masks in which men are hidden. The names of the individual "masks" of the women are exactly the same as those for the masks of the men, and the women also perform identical dance movements, as they are ascribed to the individual masked characters.

Above right and *right* One of the most spectacular masks of the Mbwela people in southeastern Angola is *ndzingi*. He is an anthropomorphic creature representing a giant living far away in the forest. He has a very large round head made from a scaffolding of twigs covered with barkcloth. The uninitiated are told that the impressive red mouth can swallow a dog. *Ndzingi* appears during the large masked festivals held to coincide with the *mukanda* circumcision school. In these festivals many individual masks appear in succession. Those performing well are usually rewarded with gifts, including money. Such earnings are used by the guardians of the boys' circumcision school to support the teaching activities. *Ndzingi* runs through the dancing square, threatening to beat anyone he meets with the twigs held in his hand. Then he begins to dance, stamping on the ground and shoveling up clouds of dust. But suddenly he staggers, the head wobbles as if it were dangerously loose, and finally he collapses, falling down "dead" on the ground, "because the head is too heavy." Young boys, laughing and cheerful, run to "help him up." This episode is repeated every few minutes until the dancer returns to the *mukanda*, to be replaced by another character.

EDUCATION AND LITERACY

The political changes that have altered the face of Africa have been accompanied by educational controversy. In all African countries the role of education is a debated subject, and discussion is sharpened by awareness that the education sector often consumes a quarter of governmental budgets and one-twentieth of gross national product. Education is widely hailed as a tool for liberation and a solution to economic problems, but it simultaneously causes many other difficulties.

Despite many changes in curriculum, goals and structure, there remains a discouraging, almost desperate continuity between much current debate and that which preoccupied colonial administrations. The links between education and the labor market, for example, and its effects on social stratification have been a focus of discussion for many decades.

A review of the role of education must begin with its classification. Educationists frequently remark that learning is a lifelong process extending far beyond the formal classroom and pervading every activity. Though the boundaries between each sector are not clear, it is common to describe education as formal, informal or nonformal. The formal sector refers to the highly structured, chronologically graded system running from primary school through university, and embraces the common conception of schools with desks and blackboards. Informal education is the truly lifelong process whereby every individual acquires attitudes, values, skills and knowledge from daily experience and the environment. Mother tongues, for example, are informally acquired, as is information gathered from the media and family. Nonformal education refers to organized activities outside the formal system intended to serve identifiable clienteles and learning objectives. It ranges from adult literacy classes to driving instruction and the Boy Scouts.

In part because of the cost of formal education, and in part because of its ineffective and sometimes counterproductive nature, attention in the mid-1970s focused on the potential of nonformal education. Programs in this sector also experienced drawbacks, however, so that towards the end of the decade attention was redirected towards basic formal learning. Strategies for eradication of illiteracy have also been reassessed, for in recent years governments have fought a losing battle. According to UNESCO, so fast has been the rate of population growth that, although the proportion of illiterates in Africa was reduced from 81 to 74 per cent between 1960 and 1970, the absolute number increased from 124 million to 143 million. Between 1974 and 1977 the estimated global number of illiterates increased by some 24 million, and in 1977 UNESCO decided not to award its two customary annual prizes for outstanding contributions to literacy.

A large number of African societies have specific traditional education systems. In many cases these include circumcision and other initiation ceremonies into adult life, and though their place is being usurped in the modern world, their continued existence remains important. Almost without exception, indigenous education has been non-literate, since only the Ge'ez speakers of Ethiopia, the Vai of Liberia and the Mum of Cameroon invented their own systems of writing. In some cases apprenticeship schemes are incorporated, and the system is structured according to age grades.

In the past, many Christian missionaries and other visitors to Africa classed indigenous education with the whole of traditional African life as primitive or barbaric, though the work of anthropologists has helped to rationalize views. Indigenous education must not be considered homogeneous throughout the continent; a child in a hunting band of Mbuti pygmies learns a different body of knowledge from one in the agricultural and politically centralized Hausa societies. Certain peoples, such as the Yoruba of Nigeria, also exhibit considerable internal social differentiation in education.

Formal systems have tended to take little account of traditional ones, though, while attempting to avoid a romantic view, the 1970s witnessed a growth of so-called community schools, which aimed to improve the relevance of education. Like every other aspect of African life, indigenous education responds to changing circumstances; instead of making hoes and cutlasses, apprentice blacksmiths increasingly weld burglar bars and repair motors. Yet modern skills are still widely acquired in the traditional way, through years of progressively more difficult work supervised by a master. And while the formal system remains limited in coverage, especially for girls, indigenous African education will continue an important role.

Particularly in North and West Africa, Islamic education systems also operated many centuries before the advent of colonial rule. The Al-Azhar University in Cairo was founded in the 10th century and is said to be the oldest in the world. Also prominent were the ancient universities of Fès and Tombouctou. In each case, learning took place in the mosque and was closely related to the Islamic religion.

In contrast to both indigenous and Western systems, Islamic education displays a remarkable homogeneity. At the lowest level is the *khalwa*, at which memorization of the Koran and accompanying rituals is taught, and at the secondary level is the *madrasa* at which a pupil deepens his Koranic knowledge and learns philosophy, jurisprudence and often some science. The time devoted to each unit varies widely, depending on the inclinations and abilities of both students and teachers, but an average pupil may spend four years at the basic level and a little longer in the *madrasa*. The highest level of learning often necessitates some travel in search of a particularly learned teacher for each subject.

There is no compulsion at a Koranic school, nor are there fixed periods of attendance. The schools operate from Saturdays to Wednesdays, and the year is divided into two terms separated by approximately three weeks' holiday after each major religious festival. Lessons are generally held twice or three times a day, in the early morning, the late afternoon and in the evening around a bonfire. This arrangement permits attendance at Western-type schools in the day and Koranic schools in the evening. The curricula of Islamic schools have been criticized for their inflexibility. In countries where Arabic is not the mother tongue, pupils are taught solely to recite the Koran, not to understand it. Similarly, at the secondary level, learning proceeds by listening to exposition rather than argument or discussion. However, the schools do provide valuable training in discipline and respect.

Attempts to integrate formal Western-type schools with Islamic institutions have met with varying degrees of success. Whereas in northern Nigeria, for example, the two systems broadly coexist side by side and attempts at integration have borne little fruit, in northern Sudan, partly because Arabic is a widespread mother tongue, integration is almost complete. This has the benefit of promoting the impact of schooling as well as maximizing use of resources. In parts of West Africa, members of the Ahmadiyya group have established formal schools. Many of them are staffed by missionaries from the Indian subcontinent and are thus parallel to the Christian missionary activities. However, more orthodox Muslims consider the Ahmadiyya heretics, and the latter's interest in Western-type schooling has become an additional reason why the orthodox often reject attempts at integration.

In the majority of African countries, the formal school systems were established by Christian

Below right: Adult literacy. Because of rapid population growth, in recent years most governments have been fighting a losing battle against illiteracy. Although the proportion of illiterates in most countries has been reduced, the absolute number has increased. One major problem, especially in rural areas, is that reading materials are in short supply, and because adults do not practice their skills, acquisition of literacy is not permanent. Nevertheless much has been achieved, and the proportion of literates will grow as primary schooling approaches universality and as many specific programs take effect.

Below National enrollment rates in primary schools. After UNESCO 1978.

		age group	gross			net		
			MF	M	F	MF	M	F
Algeria	1975	(6–11)	89	105	72	73	85	61
Angola	1972	(6–9)	79	101	57	—	—	—
Benin	1975	(5–10)	53	73	33	—	—	—
Botswana	1976	(6–12)	92	84	99	—	—	—
Burundi	1976	(6–11)	22	27	17	—	—	—
Cameroon	1975	(6–11)	119	133	106	85	93	77
CAR	1975	(6–11)	79	102	56	—	—	—
Chad	1976	(6–11)	41	61	21	30	44	16
Comoro Islands	1973	(6–11)	51	71	32	—	—	—
Congo	1975	(6–11)	155	166	143	100	100	100
Egypt	1975	(6–11)	72	88	56	—	—	—
Equatorial Guinea	1973	(6–12)	72	80	65	—	—	—
Ethiopia	1974	(7–12)	23	31	14	—	—	—
Gabon	1976	(6–11)	202	208	197	100	100	100
Gambia	1976	(6–11)	32	44	21	27	37	18
Ghana	1976	(6–15)	44	50	38	—	—	—
Guinea	1971	(7–12)	28	39	18	—	—	—
Guinea-Bissau	1976	(6–11)	123	175	72	—	—	—
Ivory Coast	1975	(6–11)	87	109	66	—	—	—
Kenya	1976	(5–11)	105	112	98	79	82	76
Lesotho	1976	(6–12)	119	98	139	80	65	95
Liberia	1975	(6–11)	62	79	44	—	—	—
Libya	1976	(6–11)	155	163	147	—	—	—
Madagascar	1976	(6–11)	88	94	82	—	—	—
Malawi	1976	(5–12)	63	76	50	—	—	—
Mali	1975	(6–11)	28	36	20	—	—	—
Mauritania	1971	(6–12)	17	24	9	—	—	—
Mauritius	1976	(5–10)	103	106	101	—	—	—
Morocco	1975	(7–11)	61	77	44	42	54	30
Mozambique	1972	(6–10)	52	69	35	41	53	28
Niger	1976	(7–12)	21	28	15	—	—	—
Nigeria	1973	(6–11)	48	58	58	—	—	—
Réunion	1976	(6–10)	122	124	119	—	—	—
Rwanda	1976	(7–12)	61	66	57	56	59	52
Senegal	1975	(6–11)	45	55	35	—	—	—
Sierra Leone	1975	(5–11)	37	45	29	—	—	—
Somalia	1976	(6–11)	45	58	32	24	28	19
South Africa	1972	(6–12)	107	107	107	—	—	—
Sudan	1976	(7–12)	39	49	30	—	—	—
Swaziland	1976	(6–12)	103	105	101	78	76	79
Tanzania	1975	(7–13)	70	79	60	—	—	—
Togo	1976	(6–11)	103	133	73	—	—	—
Tunisia	1977	(6–11)	100	118	81	—	—	—
Uganda	1976	(6–12)	51	61	42	—	—	—
Upper Volta	1976	(7–12)	16	20	12	—	—	—
Zaïre	1970	(6–11)	90	114	66	65	79	51
Zambia	1975	(7–13)	95	103	86	—	—	—
Zimbabwe	1976	(7–11)	98	106	90	—	—	—

gross = total number of children attending primary school expressed as a percentage of the estimated number of children in the official age group. Percentages over 100 are due to the inclusion of pupils outside the official age group.

net = estimated percentage of children actually attending primary school who are within the official age group.

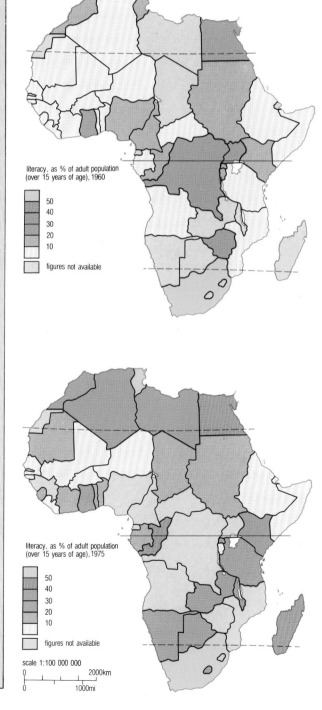

literacy, as % of adult population (over 15 years of age), 1960

50
40
30
20
10

figures not available

literacy, as % of adult population (over 15 years of age), 1975

50
40
30
20
10

figures not available

scale 1:100 000 000

0 ——— 2000km
0 ——— 1000mi

missionaries. Christianity was considered a religion of the book. It was not sufficient for a preacher merely to proclaim the Gospel; his congregation must literally see the Word as well as hear it. Missionaries therefore strongly emphasized the establishment of schools, sometimes according them precedence over more direct evangelism. "Where it is impossible for you to carry on both the immediate task of evangelism and your educational work," enjoined the Apostolic Visitor in Dar es Salaam in 1929, "neglect your churches in order to perfect your schools." Since work among the young was often more fruitful, and, it may be added, since the young had a greater life expectancy and were therefore a better investment, education of adults was often relegated to second place.

Several consequences arose from this pattern. The first was that territories frequently displayed as wide a range of systems and curricula as there were missionary groups in operation. This caused divisions in society, and some systems were barely relevant to their recipients' needs. For many years in Mozambique, for example, Anglican missionaries taught not in local languages, nor in Portuguese, but in English. Even where the missionaries employed more appropriate languages, they usually took limited account of the nature of the societies in which they worked, transplanting instead what they saw as the values of their own home countries. The practices of drinking and dancing, for example, were widely condemned, and the doctrine of celibacy of Roman Catholic priests often led to conflict because in almost all African societies the deliberate rejection of parenthood is anathema.

A second consequence was a tendency for the interests of missionaries, governments and various African groups to conflict. In the early years the governments' role in education was usually restricted to provision of grants in return for fulfillment of certain minimum requirements. Their main concern was a supply of clerks for the administration and generally they were content to leave missionaries to their self-appointed tasks. The first government school in Lagos, for example, was opened only in 1896, 50 years after the first mission school, in response to an appeal from the Muslim community, which felt neglected. However, some colonial officers disliked the effect and type of education provided, and in northern Nigeria, for instance, missionary activities were tightly controlled to prevent interference with the existing social order and thus the institution of indirect rule.

In the period following World War II, it became clear to British, Belgian and French governments that the advent of independence was less distant than had hitherto been assumed and that increased educational provision at all levels was a necessity. Expansion of higher education was particularly notable. Between 1947 and 1950 institutes or university colleges were opened at Bukavu (Belgian Congo), Brazzaville (French Congo), Accra (Gold Coast), Ibadan (Nigeria), Makerere (Uganda) and Dakar (French West Africa). During the 1950s and 1960s this trend continued until almost every country had a university.

The rise of African nationalism owed much to the missionaries, for while the latter were often employed as a vanguard of imperialism, equally,

Above Children play outside a school in Tanzania. During the 1970s illiteracy was considerably reduced, but only a very small percentage of pupils progress beyond primary education.

Left A crowded classroom in Nigeria indicates the strain upon educational resources. Since 1976 primary education has been free, but lack of books and other educational aids retards progress.

Right A white-clad Muslim teacher instructs his class in a street in Kano, northern Nigeria. The pupils use wooden writing boards. Instruction in the Koran is the basic object of these Muslim schools which supplement more formal institutions run by government or missionary agencies.

through education, they helped lay nationalist foundations. It is perhaps ironic that in some ways missionaries played a greater role in the 1960s in newly independent countries, for in many cases they expanded their work and bridged the gap between the departing colonial and the new indigenous administrations. The 20th century has witnessed increasing control of missionary educational activities, however, and in some territories all voluntary agency schools have been taken over by the government. The transition has not always been smooth and in Zaïre, for example, financial and administrative difficulties forced the government in the mid-1970s to return proprietorship of many missionary institutions. This reflects the role that missionaries will continue to play for some time.

Frequently it is incorrectly asserted that colonial regimes provided only academic education and had no interest in technical training. On the contrary, several missions held in high regard what they called "the dignity of labor" and made considerable efforts to train artisans. Similarly, colonial reports continually stressed the dangers of an over-academic framework. The 1920s witnessed the establishment of Jeanes Training Colleges in East and central Africa, which introduced peripatetic teachers and emphasized agriculture and other practical subjects. Likewise, the Malangali School in Tanganyika sought relevance through use of traditional clothing instead of uniforms, twice weekly spear throwing and tribal dancing. These examples are by no means unique.

It is true, however, that school systems were based on those of the colonial powers. Pupils sat the baccalaureat, school certificate, or other metropolitan examinations, and studied the history, geography, flora and fauna of Britain, France, Portugal, Spain and Belgium rather than their own regions. The worst excesses have now been rectified, though curricula are still influenced by European developments and by desires to adhere to external standards.

Similarly, although the need to provide agricultural and technical training is frequently restated, generally the same obstacles to its development remain. Missionary and colonial efforts were widely perceived by Africans as attempts to maintain European ascendancy by diverting scholars from "real" education into the more limited sphere of technical training. It was no coincidence that so large a proportion of nationalist leaders were lawyers, for it was through this type of training, not agricultural or technical, that they could attain an equal footing with the colonialists. In this sense, academic education was more vocational, because it led further. It may be added that the situation has not greatly changed today, and technical training will continue to be considered inferior so long as the economic structure awards preferable employment opportunities to those with academic backgrounds.

In the 1960s a large number of African nations attained independence. In these years of optimism, entitled "The First Development Decade" by UNO, education was widely seen as the means through which this development would be achieved and independence made real. The optimism was reflected in the targets set by the 1961 Conference of African Ministers of Education in Addis Ababa. By 1980 they aimed to have achieved universal, compulsory and free primary schooling; 30 per cent enrolment rates at the secondary level; and higher education for 20 per cent of those completing secondary. As many resources as possible were devoted to education, for it was considered an investment in human capital which would enable the new nations to catch up with the developed world. The 1960 Nigerian Ashby Report was not atypical with its suggestion that the people "will have to forgo other things they want so that every available penny is invested in education," continuing, "Even this will not be enough. . ."

As the decade progressed, however, increasing disparities in wealth made it clear that growth was not the same as development and that investments in education were not yielding their anticipated fruits. During the colonial era, policies had often deliberately aimed at creation of elites. These elites were widely applauded when the nations achieved independence, for they replaced the departing colonialists. But by the late 1960s the undesirable aspects of social stratification derived from education had become more serious. Unemployment, especially of primary leavers, but also of secondary and then university graduates, became an increasing problem It added emphasis to charges that schooling was irrelevant and that educational expenditures were excessive. Since most school leavers sought employment in towns, debilitation of rural areas was added to the undesirable effects of the system.

The rapid educational expansion of the 1960s, and thus the rapid escalation of many problems as well as solutions, was brought not only by increased government and mission activity but also by a surge of self-help projects, of which Kenya's village polytechnics and Harambee schools provide good examples. Although the spirit of self-help was applauded, the uncontrolled nature of these projects accelerated qualitative decline and exacerbated the unemployment situation.

Though many countries have condemned the colonial mold, few have attempted fundamental reform. Tanzania stands out as the most ambitious. Its conscious change of direction was part of the 1967 Arusha Declaration in which the government recognized that for the majority of citizens, for some time to come, primary education would be a misnomer disguising its terminal nature. The Tanzanian government realizes that agriculture will remain the national mainstay for the foreseeable future, and is trying to implement an Education for Self Reliance policy which among other things hopes to reduce costs and promote relevance by requiring institutions to be self-sufficient. This is a brave experiment which is not being accomplished with ease and which, while other nations watch with interest, few have attempted to emulate. The majority have found it easier to retain the basic features of the existing model and make minor modifications to alleviate pressing crises.

As previously mentioned, the mid-1970s witnessed a major display of interest in nonformal education. This was partly because the international aid agencies were prepared to give it financial backing, and further illustrates the continued links between Africa and the developed world. The wide scope of nonformal education was seen as an advantage, for it hoped to promote both impact and cost effectiveness by avoiding compartmentalization. Whereas in the past many nonformal schemes had been designed to give a second chance to those who had missed or never been offered an earlier opportunity, educationists with renewed vigor asserted that nonformal learning could also complement the formal system. They further pointed out that too often literacy was seen as an end rather than a means, and that increased use of radios could fulfill some of the same functions.

Many nonformal programs, however, suffered the same fate as earlier technical schemes. They were sometimes implemented solely as a cosmetic, obscuring rather than removing the need for fundamental reform. The breadth of certain projects was also more of a problem than an advantage since the required cooperation of ministries and other agencies was not always forthcoming. The best avenues to advancement usually remained in the formal system and nonformal schemes therefore had limited appeal. This situation was linked to the structure of the economy and heavy emphasis on certification rather than possession of skills. Thus, while the nonformal fashion did much to widen perspectives and stimulate thinking, attention in the late 1970s reverted to the formal system and attempts to provide universal basic education.

At the beginning of the 1980s education remains a controversial subject. Even Nigeria with its petroleum revenues has found no easy answers to development issues, so that by contrast the prospects of poorer countries like Upper Volta and Mali appear all the bleaker. Yet the importance of education in development is undeniable. Perhaps the brightest and most promising aspect of the current picture is the ever-increasing body of research and the broader and more realistic perception of education that has evolved over the last two decades.

M.B.

Health and Healing

Health and wholeness – harmony of body and mind, and harmony within the community – are valued highly in Africa, perhaps the more because of the menace of tropical diseases. Illness and death, except in the very old, have been seen as evidence of ill will from humans or from the spirit world. Witchcraft, bringing misfortune, springs from envy and hatred. In every community specialist practitioners existed, to identify witches, to divine causes of illness and misfortune, and to prescribe treatment, sometimes magical, sometimes medicinal. Western forms of medical treatment have alleviated many diseases, but Western physicians have sometimes neglected the spiritual causes of illness and disharmony. Some of the African independent churches refuse all medical treatment, traditional or Western, relying on healing through prayer and the laying on of hands. In some Christian and mission hospitals, doctors are acknowledging the need to treat the whole person – body and spirit as well.

J.M.

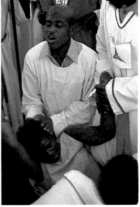

Above A prophet of the Vapostori – an independent Christian sect of Zimbabwe – lays hands on a young woman to cast out the evil spirit which possesses her and causes her illness.

Above left In northern Cameroon a sick woman lies on a mat in her compound with her family around her, as a traditional healer performs a ritual for her recovery.

Left Diseases spread through various types of mosquito – malaria, yellow fever, sleeping sickness – have been major killers in Africa. In Senegal health workers spray swampy ground to destroy the mosquitoes which spread malaria.

Above A trained African medical assistant takes a blood sample from a child, at a village clinic in Togo. Through such work research on the extent of diseases is accomplished, while treatment is given to the sick who attend the clinics.

Right Infant mortality is still high in Africa, and since the bearing of live children is of supreme importance to all African women, the work of Western hospitals in preserving the lives of newborn babies is highly valued. In a large hospital in Senegal a nursery for premature babies gives them a chance of life they would not have received otherwise.

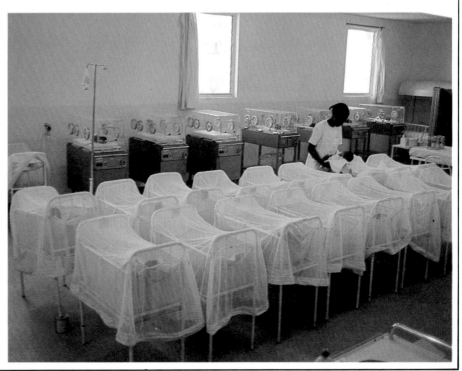

Game Parks and Conservation

The wildlife of Africa is now severely restricted by comparison with only a century ago, but Africa remains the last great home of much of the world's more spectacular wildlife. This is largely due to the great parks of Africa which have a history going back almost one hundred years, although their function has changed greatly in recent years. Initially, they were established to shelter and protect wildlife from the onslaught of man, although the removal of man the predator, far from restoring a balanced and natural state, sometimes meant a deleterious faunal population explosion. Increasingly, parks are seen not as sanctuaries and wilderness areas to be sealed off, but as areas to be utilized and managed like any other part of the country. It is now appreciated that a mixed faunal population more efficiently uses a much wider range of floral species and habitats than a corresponding cattle population. The conversion rate from vegetable to animal protein may therefore be much greater with a wildlife population, a very significant fact for a protein-deficient human population. This raises the possibility of game culling or game ranching for human consumption. Parks may serve other useful purposes, however. Not only do they form the bases of tourist industries. The well-being of the wildlife is not incompatible with controlled fishing, grazing and afforestation.   J.C.S.

Below Tourist lodges, particularly in parts of East Africa, combine luxurious accommodation with splendid opportunities for game viewing. However, it is debatable whether tourism does much to enhance the material well-being of the very low income earners, since much of the economic returns go to airlines, hotels, car hire firms etc., and many of the tourists' needs may have to be imported.

Below Photo safaris meet with the conservationists' approval, but tourists in the more easily accessible parks of East Africa have so grown in numbers that the more popular animals may scarcely ever be left unattended during daylight hours.

Opposite above The professional hunter of the turn of the century, who shot for the commercial value of the kill, was replaced by the safari hunter who was licenced, for a fee, to shoot a stipulated number and variety of species and hired the professional to guide him. The local inhabitants were often excluded, but professional guides had a vested interest in preventing extermination.

Opposite below Availability of modern firearms, the very high commercial value of wildlife products and the inability of parks authorities to patrol their extensive areas are severely reducing wildlife stocks in some parks, but the temptation of quick reward to people without employment or on very low incomes is great.

Right The impounding of Lake Kariba in the late 1950s led to "Operation Noah," one of the best-known game-rescue operations of recent times. As the waters rose, animals were stranded on diminishing islands. Tranquilizers and all sorts of makeshift devices were employed to transport the animals to the new shoreline, but the great extent of the lake and the increased human usage of the remaining land in the Zambezi valley, at least on the north shore, were in themselves disruptions to the habitat of the low-lying valley floor.

The Copper Industry

Open-cast mining at Likasi, Zaïre. After independence, both Zambia and Zaïre assumed increased control of the mining industry, upon which the modern sectors of their economies were highly dependent. In Zaïre, Gecamines, a state-owned organization, was created to control both mining and refining, although there is continuing dependence on expatriate expertise and personnel.

The discovery of copper deposits in Africa in the past was usually made by prospectors seeking more exotic minerals, but more recently they have been systematically sought in their own right. Copper is typical of many of the mineral deposits of Africa in that in total the continent is a major producer, but within the continent there is extreme maldistribution. Zambia and Zaïre dominate the continent's league table of copper producers, since their common international boundary bisects the continent's largest deposit. South Africa, Namibia, Zimbabwe and Botswana are also major producers.

Great fluctuations in the price of copper on world markets have given rise to grave problems for the major producers who plan to finance development elsewhere in their country by means of copper revenues. The establishment of an international copper agreement by the world's producers has proved illusory, particularly by comparison with the success of the OPEC nations in the 1970s. Demand for copper is much more elastic than for oil. Economic recession among the industrialized consumers results in significant decline in demand, as do high prices which make substitute metals attractive. Political conditions or a mining disaster may lead to a sudden decline in output by a major producer, while profitable extraction is not solely the result of efficiency through economies of scale since some 40 per cent of world capacity is in the hands of a large number of small producer countries.   J.C.S.

Above left Electrolytic processes are used to produce a highly refined product with a high value/bulk ratio. This is advantageous in view of the long haul to the seaports serving the Copperbelt.

Above The shallow oxide ores of Zambia are underlain by deeper sulfide deposits which are extracted by underground mining. Both open-cast and underground methods are employed in Zambia and Zaïre.

Left Mufulira is a mining township making extensive use of low-value land, and one of a cluster of eight towns all in close proximity on the Zambian Copperbelt.

Above The ore is processed locally by the major producer countries, reducing costly haulage of bulky ores. The smelter at Mufulira, Zambia, is well served by the coal deposits and hydroelectricity production of the Zambezi basin.

PART THREE
THE NATIONS OF AFRICA

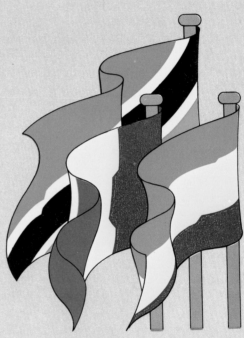

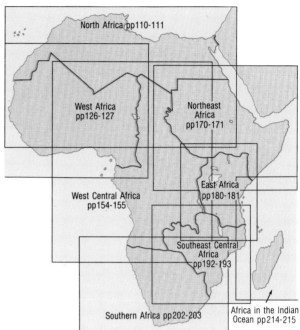

This section contains an account of each independent nation and territory in Africa, including the islands of the western Indian Ocean, with a map indicating mineral, agricultural and industrial resources for each country, and a regional map emphasizing physical features. The 55 nations have been divided into eight regions, and the basic category of division is purely physical propinquity. Some of the regions are generally accepted as such; this is especially true of North Africa. The physical description limits the region in cases like the islands; but in most other regions the allocation has of necessity to be arbitrary. Cameroon is here included in West Africa; many divisions would place that nation in West Central Africa. The totally arbitrary boundaries of the colonial period still prevail in Africa. In a matter of two or three generations new alignments and unions may have taken place, and an atlas of Africa in the year 2050 may show different and more rational regional and national divisions.

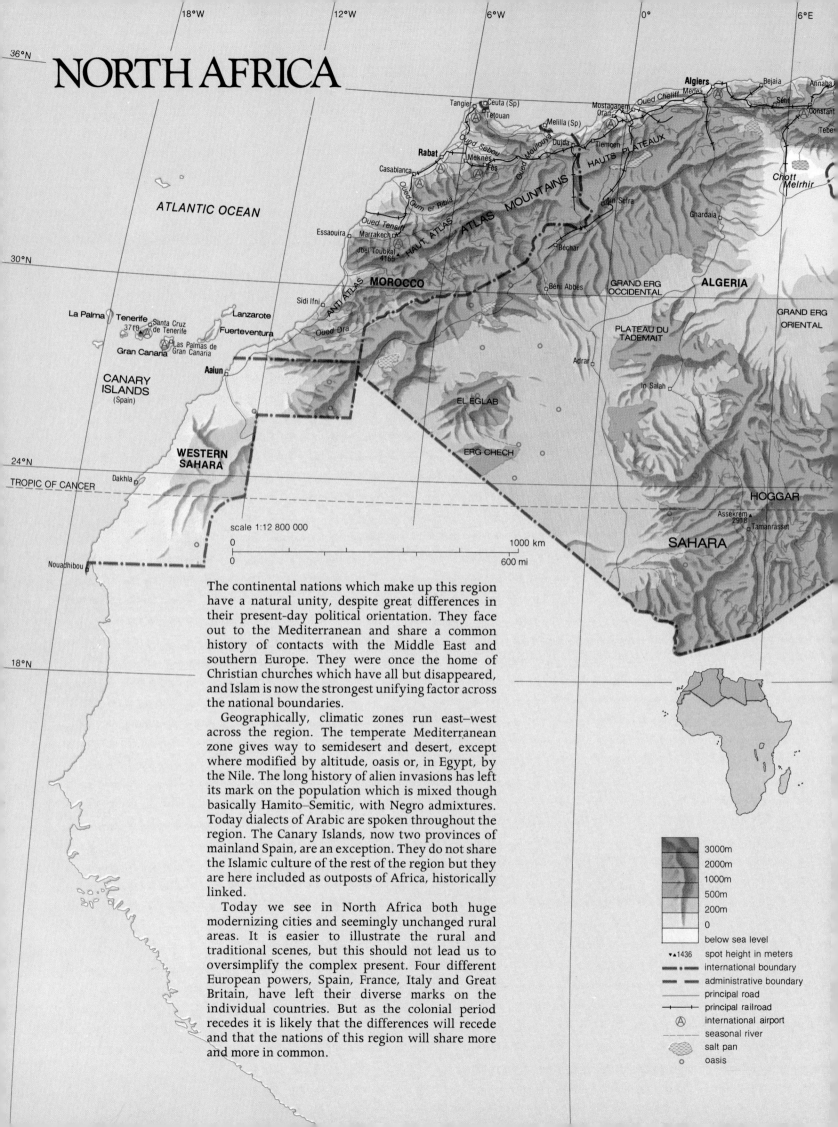

NORTH AFRICA

ATLANTIC OCEAN

CANARY
ISLANDS
(Spain)

La Palma   Tenerife
   3710
   Santa Cruz
   de Tenerife
Gran Canaria   Las Palmas de
   Gran Canaria

Lanzarote
Fuerteventura

Dakhla

WESTERN
SAHARA

Aaiun

Nouadhibou

Sidi Ifni

ANTI-ATLAS

Oued Dra

MOROCCO

Essaouira   Marrakech

Jbel Toubkal
4165

HAUT ATLAS

Casablanca

Rabat

Meknès

Fès

Tangier   Ceuta (Sp)
Tetouan

Melilla (Sp)

Oued Sebou

Oued Oum er Rbia

Oued Tensift

Oued Moulouya

Oujda

Tlemcen

Aïn Sefra

Béchar

Béni Abbès

ATLAS MOUNTAINS

HAUTS PLATEAUX

Mostaganem

Oran

Oued Cheliff

Algiers   Bejaia   Annaba
Medea   Sétif
   Constant
   Tebes

Chott
Melrhir

Ghardaïa

GRAND ERG
OCCIDENTAL

PLATEAU DU
TADEMAIT

Adrar

In Salah

ALGERIA

GRAND ERG
ORIENTAL

EL EGLAB

ERG CHECH

HOGGAR

Assekrem ▲
2918 ▲ Tamanrasset

SAHARA

scale 1:12 800 000

0   1000 km

0   600 mi

The continental nations which make up this region have a natural unity, despite great differences in their present-day political orientation. They face out to the Mediterranean and share a common history of contacts with the Middle East and southern Europe. They were once the home of Christian churches which have all but disappeared, and Islam is now the strongest unifying factor across the national boundaries.

Geographically, climatic zones run east–west across the region. The temperate Mediterranean zone gives way to semidesert and desert, except where modified by altitude, oasis or, in Egypt, by the Nile. The long history of alien invasions has left its mark on the population which is mixed though basically Hamito–Semitic, with Negro admixtures. Today dialects of Arabic are spoken throughout the region. The Canary Islands, now two provinces of mainland Spain, are an exception. They do not share the Islamic culture of the rest of the region but they are here included as outposts of Africa, historically linked.

Today we see in North Africa both huge modernizing cities and seemingly unchanged rural areas. It is easier to illustrate the rural and traditional scenes, but this should not lead us to oversimplify the complex present. Four different European powers, Spain, France, Italy and Great Britain, have left their diverse marks on the individual countries. But as the colonial period recedes it is likely that the differences will recede and that the nations of this region will share more and more in common.

3000m
2000m
1000m
500m
200m
0
below sea level

▼▲1436   spot height in meters
      international boundary
      administrative boundary
      principal road
      principal railroad
Ⓐ   international airport
      seasonal river
      salt pan
○   oasis

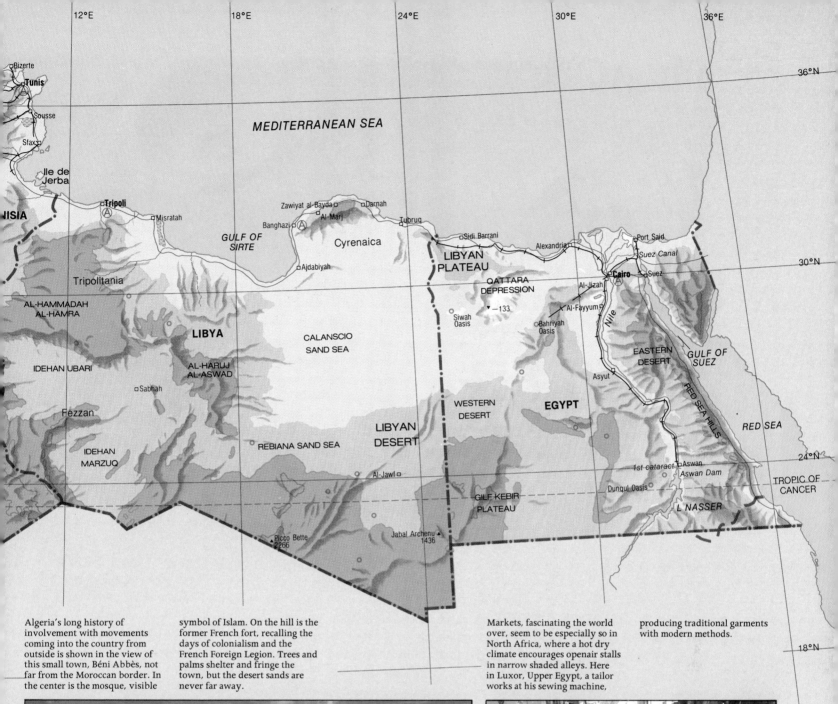

MEDITERRANEAN SEA

GULF OF SIRTE

Cyrenaica

LIBYAN PLATEAU

QATTARA DEPRESSION

−133

Tripolitania

AL-HAMMADAH AL-HAMRA

LIBYA

IDEHAN UBARI

AL-HARUJ AL-ASWAD

Fezzan

CALANSCIO SAND SEA

Siwah Oasis

Bahriyah Oasis

EASTERN DESERT

GULF OF SUEZ

IDEHAN MARZUQ

REBIANA SAND SEA

WESTERN DESERT

EGYPT

RED SEA HILLS

RED SEA

LIBYAN DESERT

Al-Jawl

1st cataract Aswan
Aswan Dam

Dunqul Oasis

TROPIC OF CANCER

GILF KEBIR PLATEAU

L. NASSER

Picco Bette 2266

Jabal Archenu 1436

Bizerte
Tunis
Sousse
Sfax
Ile de Jerba
TUNISIA
Tripoli
Misratah
Zawiyat al-Bayda
Darnah
Banghazi
Al-Marj
Tubruq
Ajdabiyah
Sidi Barrani
Alexandria
Port Said
Suez Canal
Cairo
Al-Jizah
Al-Fayyum
Suez
Nile
Asyut
Sabhah

Algeria's long history of involvement with movements coming into the country from outside is shown in the view of this small town, Béni Abbès, not far from the Moroccan border. In the center is the mosque, visible symbol of Islam. On the hill is the former French fort, recalling the days of colonialism and the French Foreign Legion. Trees and palms shelter and fringe the town, but the desert sands are never far away.

Markets, fascinating the world over, seem to be especially so in North Africa, where a hot dry climate encourages openair stalls in narrow shaded alleys. Here in Luxor, Upper Egypt, a tailor works at his sewing machine, producing traditional garments with modern methods.

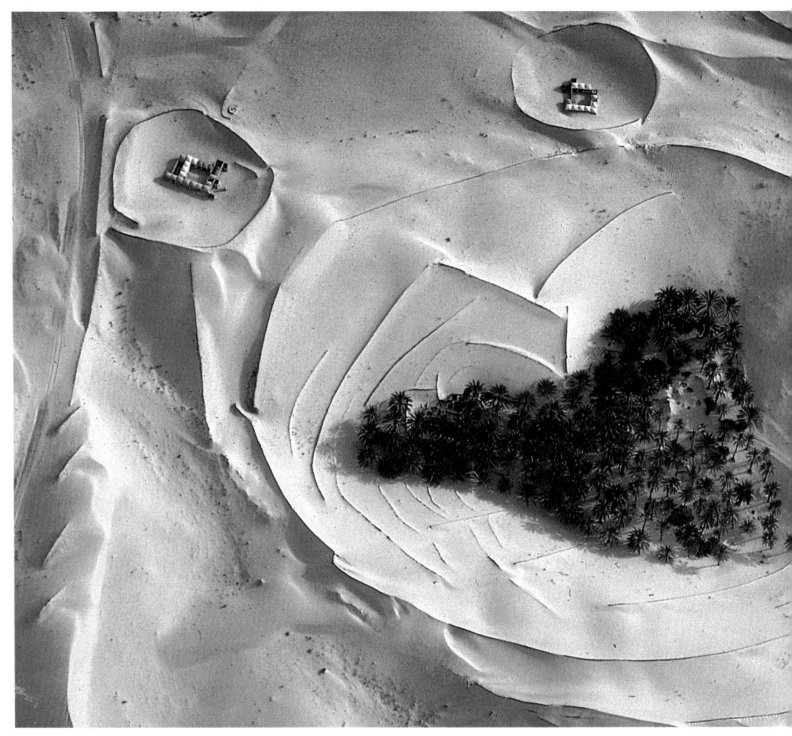

Above An aerial photograph of Souf, an oasis in the Algerian Sahara, shows clearly the tiny limit of cultivation and date palms, and the threat of the encroaching desert all around.

Right The discovery and utilization of oil in North Africa have brought great wealth, great power, and attendant problems. Oil wealth is greatest in Libya, once an extremely poor country and now one of the richest; this illustration shows an oil installation in Algeria.

Far right This view of the west coast of Gran Canaria shows well the rugged nature of the landscape on the islands, formed by volcanic peaks rising direct from the Atlantic seabed.

Left At Hergla, on the east coast of Tunisia, a village woman carries water back from the well. Traditional dress is still often seen in the rural areas, and the village women are not veiled.

Overleaf In November 1975 about 350000 unarmed civilians, led by the king of Morocco, took part in the so-called ''Green March'' to assert Morocco's claims to the former Spanish Sahara, granted independence by Spain and still, as the Western Sahara, the scene of conflict between Morocco, Algeria, Mauritania and the internal Polisario movement.

Above right City life is the norm rather than the exception in North Africa, but the nomadic life continues for some at least. Here, in Morocco, a nomad family sit at the door of their tent as a new day dawns.

Right In the villages of Egypt pigeon houses are a universal feature with their nesting recesses and roosting perches. Pigeons form an important supplement to the simple vegetable diet of the farming population.

MEDITERRANEAN SEA

Marsah Matruh

Alexandria Industry: textile, chemical, paper, food

Al-Mahallah al-Kubra Industry: textile, food

Dumyat

El Dikheila Industry: iron and steel complex planned

Abu-Qir
Alexandria
Port Said

nuclear-powered generating station planned

Ad-Dab'ah

El Dikheila
Mex
Damanhur
Al-Mahallah al-Kubra
Mansurah
Al Mansurah Industry: textile, food
Al Qantarah

Al-Amiriyah
Tanta
Az-Zaqaziq
Al-Isma'iliyah
new city planned 5kms east

Razzaq
Yidma

Suez Canal

Tanta Industry: textile, food

Great Bitter Lake

Abu Gharadiq

Musturud

Qattara Depression

Cairo Industry: textile, food, iron and steel

Giza **Cairo**

Suez

Hulwan

Suez Industry: petrochemical, harbor project planned

Siwa Oasis

Hulwan Industry: iron and steel complex, cement, chemical

Ain Sukhna

major reclamation project underway — completion c. 2000

Birkat Qarun

Tanakah Mt

Siwa

Al-Fayyum

GULF OF SUEZ

Sitrah

Bani Suwayf

Wadi Arabah

Jebel al Wasit

Sinai

Bawiti MANGANESE

Bahariya Oasis

Al-Minya

Ras Gharib

Morgan

El Heiz IRON ORE

EGYPT

Mallawi

Eastern Desert

Ras Muhammad

Dayrut

Qasr Farafra
Farafra Oasis

Asyut

Wadi al-Asyuti

Nile

Western Desert

Asyut Industry: chemical, textile, food

Sawhaj

Bur Safajah
PHOSPHATES

URANIUM

RED S

Naj Hammadi

Qina

Quesir
PHOSPHATES

Dakhla Oasis

Naj Hammadi Industry: aluminum complex

El Qasr

Luxor

Mut
PHOSPHATES

Abu Tartur

El Kharga

The Great Oasis

Isna
PHOSPHATES

Wadi al-Miyah

Idfu

Baris

Aswan Industry: chemical

Wadi Natash

Aswan High Dam
HEP source

Aswan
IRON ORE

TROPIC OF CANCER

Dunqul Oasis

L NASSER

Wadi al-Allaqi

desert	mineral resource site
irrigated zone of intense crop cultivation (cereals, olives, figs, rice, sugar cane)	oil refinery
fertile zone around oasis	oil pipeline
oasis	oil field
principal cash crops:	gas field
cotton	oil/gas prospecting
rice	Alexandria major industrial port
sugar cane	Alexandria major oil port
	tourist center

scale 1:5 000 000

0   300km

0   200mi

116

Egypt

Egypt lies on the northeastern limit of Africa with its territory stretching to the Sinai region across the Gulf of Suez. The Nile, which flows from the south to the Mediterranean in the north, provides an irrigated agricultural area, but only 3·5 per cent of the whole country is cultivable. The Eastern Highlands and the

Egypt

Official Name
Arab Republic of Egypt

Area
997 667 sq km

Date of Independence
1937 (Convention of Montreux)

Status and Name in Colonial Times
A long history of occupations and foreign-controlled monarchies: Egypt

Population
38 228 180 (1976); 41 000 000 (est 1979)

Annual Growth Rate
2·7%

Capital City
Cairo (Al-Qahirah)

Population of Capital
5 715 000 (est 1974)

National Language(s)
Arabic; English, French

Gross National Product (US dollars)
12 230 million; 310 per capita (est 1977)

Local Currency
1 Egyptian pound = 100 piastres = 1000 millièmes

Western Desert are barren regions. The climate is arid with an average rainfall of 80 millimeters per annum in the south. Near Alexandria rainfall rises to an average of 220 millimeters per annum. The population is a mixed one, though basically of Mediterranean stock.

The fertile valley of the Nile produced one of the earliest known civilizations. The dynasties of native Egyptian kings began in the third millennium BC and only ended with the conquest of Alexander the Great in the 4th century BC. The Ptolemaic Greek rulers were succeeded by the Romans who in their turn were overthrown by the Muslim invaders of the 7th century. Medieval Egypt retained its own identity under a succession of Muslim dynasties whose prosperity was ensured by the trade routes from the east which converged on the entrepôt port of Alexandria. In 1517 the Ottomans took Egypt and the country remained in Turkish hands until the 19th century.

The modern history of Egypt began with Napoleon's expedition to the country in 1798. The conquest was not successful, but it opened the way for an army officer, Muhammad Ali, to break with the Ottoman empire. He handed the state on to successors who attempted to develop the economy with cotton as the cash crop. Egypt's strategic importance grew with a project for a canal through the Suez peninsula. France and Britain invested in the Suez Canal Company, and in 1875 Britain gained a commanding control because of the financial difficulties of the Egyptian ruler, the Khedive Ismail. In the 1880s the country was torn by nationalist conflict which drew Britain more closely into its administration under the Consul General Evelyn Baring, later Lord Cromer. The British conquest of the Sudan at the end of the century and France's growing involvement in North Africa, led to Britain's exclusive control of Egypt.

When World War I broke out Britain declared a protectorate over Egypt which played a notable part in the defense of the eastern Mediterranean and of the route to India. Egypt's role enabled it to demand some measure of independence in 1922. Its ruler was given the title of king and a constitution was granted. The interwar years saw a political struggle among the British, the king and the Wafd, or Constitutional Party. Political unrest and anxiety over the future of the canal made Britain reluctant to grant concessions to Egypt, but in 1936 the threat of Italy's ambitions in the Mediterranean forced her to grant a 20-year agreement which ended the British occupation of Egypt but secured Britain's right to bases in the Canal Zone.

Egypt also played an important part in World War II and the Wafd party maintained loyalty to Allied interests although the king favored the German cause. After the danger of invasion was over, political discontent increased. Communists and the radical Muslim Brotherhood vied to fill the vacuum created by the decline of the Wafd party, but it was the Free Officers of the Army who carried out a coup against the shaky regime of King Farouk in 1952. The monarchy was abolished and a program of land reform was begun. In 1954 Colonel Gamal Abdel Nasser became head of state. His position was firmly consolidated at home and abroad after the abortive Suez

invasion by Britain, France and Israel in 1956. Egypt, in these years, was a leading advocate of Arab unity, and attempted a union with Syria. President Nasser played an eminent role in Arab summit conferences. In the mid-1960s he sent troops to assist the republican cause in Yemen. In 1967, after skirmishes on the Syrian frontier, President Nasser ordered the withdrawal from the Canal Zone of United Nations troops and on 5 June Israel invaded the Gaza strip. After six days the war was over and Egypt accepted a ceasefire. In November 1967 the United Nations Security Council passed a resolution (242) stating the requirements for a peace settlement in the Middle East.

In Egypt itself President Nasser faced great difficulties. The country possessed no oil nor other natural mineral resources, and a rapidly growing population outpaced the cultivable land. Attempts were made to redistribute large estates and to increase agricultural productivity and hydroelectric power by schemes such as the Aswan High Dam project. In 1960 the first national plan was introduced to double the real national income within ten years. This and subsequent plans have had to be modified, but there has been an effort to diversify the economy and to increase industrial production. The plans have demanded great capital investment. In the mid-1960s increasing financial and technical assistance was accepted from the USSR, but disillusionment with the pressures exerted by the Russians led to a break in 1972. Loss of revenue after the closing of the Suez Canal in 1967 emphasized the economic difficulties.

President Nasser died in 1970. His successor, Colonel Anwar Sadat, almost immediately faced internal difficulties after a proposed Egyptian merger with Libya. Economic problems caused open Left-wing violence. In October 1973 Egypt made a surprise attack on Israel and was defeated. Nevertheless President Sadat's personal prestige increased and he was able to lift press censorship and to release political prisoners. Egypt moved towards closer relations with the USA. Henry Kissinger, the US envoy, conducted "shuttle diplomacy" to try to ensure a peace settlement in the Middle East. In the years 1975–77 poor performance of the Egyptian economy led to a great increase in the cost of living and to food riots. Some attempts to liberalize the constitution by allowing the Wafd party to take part in politics were soon reversed.

In November 1977 President Sadat visited Israel and spoke in the Knesset. This personal peace initiative increased his popularity inside Egypt, but made his position precarious in the Arab world, and particularly threatened his relations with Saudi Arabia on whom he was dependent for economic aid. Negotiations between Egypt and Israel continued at Camp David in September 1978 under the chairmanship of President Carter. It was declared that a peace treaty would be signed within three months, but the question of the Palestinians and of the West Bank settlements delayed its completion. However, President Sadat shared the 1978 Nobel Peace Prize with the Israeli prime minister. In March 1979 a peace treaty was signed by the two parties, and a national referendum in Egypt endorsed President Sadat's policy. Ambassadors were exchanged by Israel and Egypt in 1980.   A.W.

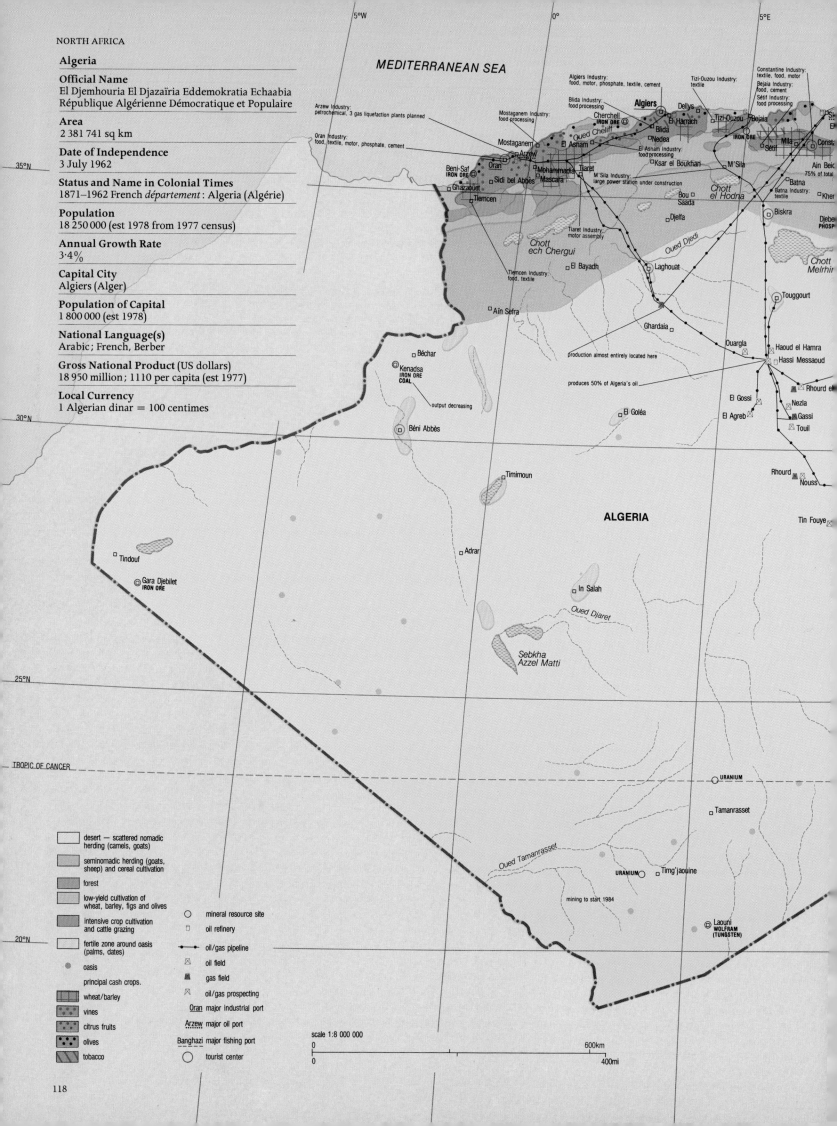

NORTH AFRICA

Algeria

Official Name
El Djemhouria El Djazaïria Eddemokratia Echaabia
République Algérienne Démocratique et Populaire

Area
2 381 741 sq km

Date of Independence
3 July 1962

Status and Name in Colonial Times
1871–1962 French *département*: Algeria (Algérie)

Population
18 250 000 (est 1978 from 1977 census)

Annual Growth Rate
3·4%

Capital City
Algiers (Alger)

Population of Capital
1 800 000 (est 1978)

National Language(s)
Arabic; French, Berber

Gross National Product (US dollars)
18 950 million; 1110 per capita (est 1977)

Local Currency
1 Algerian dinar = 100 centimes

MEDITERRANEAN SEA

Arzew Industry:
petrochemical, 3 gas liquefaction plants planned

Oran Industry:
food, textile, motor, phosphate, cement

Algiers Industry:
food, motor, phosphate, textile, cement

Mostaganem Industry:
food processing

Blida Industry:
food processing

Constantine Industry:
textile, food, motor

Tizi-Ouzou Industry:
textile

Bejaia Industry:
food, cement

Sétif Industry:
food processing

El Asnam Industry:
food processing

Batna Industry:
textile

Tiaret Industry:
motor assembly

Tiemcen Industry:
food, textile

M'Sila Industry:
large power station under construction

Algiers
Cherchell
IRON ORE
Dellys
Tizi-Ouzou
Bejaia
Mostaganem
Arzew
El Asnam
Blida
Nedea
El Harrach
IRON ORE
Mila
Constant
Oued Cheliff
Oran
Mohammadia
Tiaret
Ksar el Boukhari
M'Sila
Ain Beic
75% of total
Beni-Saf
IRON ORE
Sidi bel Abbès
Mascara
Bou
Saada
Chott
el Hodna
Batna
Ghazaouet
Tlemcen
Chott
ech Chergui
Djelfa
Biskra
Djebe
PHOSP
El Bayadh
Laghouat
Oued Djedi
Chott
Melrhir
Aïn Sefra
Ghardaia
Touggourt
Béchar
Ouargla
Haoud el Hamra
Kenadsa
IRON ORE
COAL
production almost entirely located here
Hassi Messaoud
Rhourd el
output decreasing
produces 50% of Algeria's oil
El Gossi
Nezla
Béni Abbès
El Goléa
El Agreb
Gassi
Touil
Timimoun
Rhourd
Nouss
ALGERIA
Tin Fouye
Adrar
In Salah
Tindouf
Oued Djaret
Gara Djebilet
IRON ORE
Sebkha
Azzel Matti

TROPIC OF CANCER

URANIUM

Tamanrasset

Oued Tamanrasset

URANIUM
Timg'jaouine

mining to start 1984

Laouni
WOLFRAM
(TUNGSTEN)

desert — scattered nomadic herding (camels, goats)	
seminomadic herding (goats, sheep) and cereal cultivation	
forest	
low-yield cultivation of wheat, barley, figs and olives	
intensive crop cultivation and cattle grazing	mineral resource site
fertile zone around oasis (palms, dates)	oil refinery
oasis	oil/gas pipeline
principal cash crops.	oil field
wheat/barley	gas field
vines	oil/gas prospecting
citrus fruits	Oran major industrial port
olives	Arzew major oil port
tobacco	Banghazi major fishing port
	tourist center

scale 1:8 000 000

0   600km

0   400mi

118

Libya

The state of Libya (the Popular Socialist Libyan Arab Jamahariya) consists of three provinces linked by historical accident rather than geographical unity. These provinces are Tripolitania (now Western Province), Cyrenaica (Eastern Province) and Fezzan (Southern Province). The country stretches from the Mediterranean in the north to Chad and Niger in the south. The whole area is part of the North African plateau, varied slightly by hills behind the Mediterranean coastal region and high mountains in the south. The rest of the country is either desert or semidesert with a rainfall of less than 200 millimeters per annum. The small population has only just passed the two million mark. Most Libyans live in Tripoli and its hinterland. Two ethnic groups predominate, the Mediterranean people in the north and the African Negroid people in the Fezzan.

Historically the three provinces developed differently, Cyrenaica under Greek influence, Tripolitania under Roman. Islam spread over the whole area in the 7th century, providing one unifying element. In the 19th century

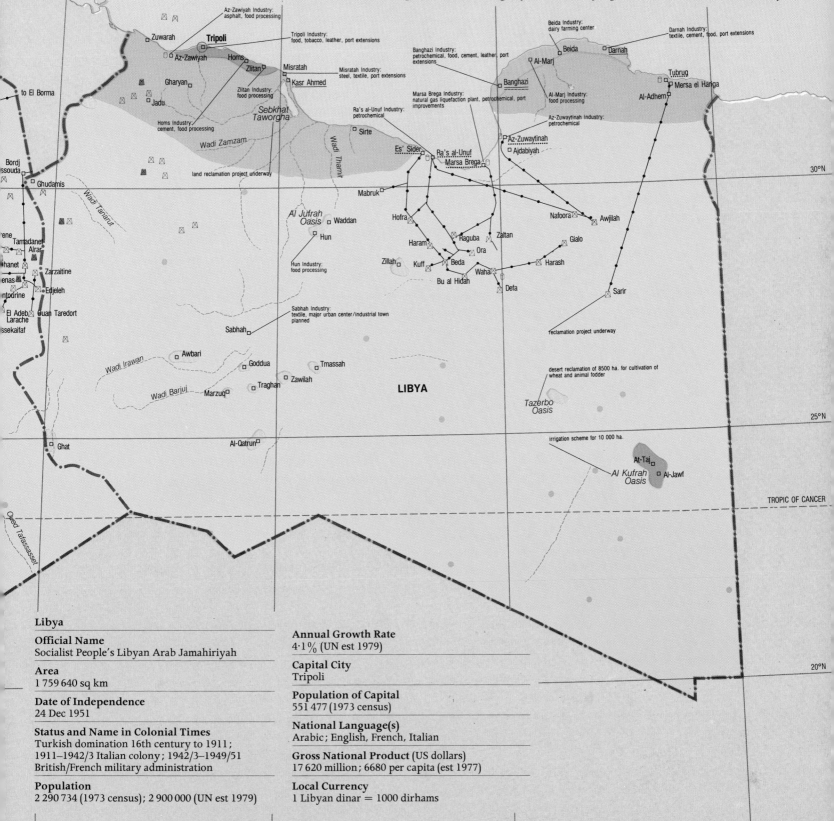

Skikda Industry:
petrochemical, 2nd gas liquefaction plant planned

Annaba Industry:
chemical, motor, food, textile

Tebessa Industry:
cement, chemical

10°E

35°N

Az-Zawiyah Industry:
asphalt, food processing

Zuwarah
Tripoli
Az-Zawiyah Homs
Zliten
Gharyan
Jadu
Misratah

Tripoli Industry:
food, tobacco, leather, port extensions

Misratah Industry:
steel, textile, port extensions

Kasr Ahmed

Banghazi Industry:
petrochemical, food, cement, leather, port extensions

Beida Industry:
dairy farming center

Beida
Al-Marj
Darnah

Darnah Industry:
textile, cement, food, port extensions

Banghazi
Al-Marj Industry:
food processing

Tubruq
Mersa el Hariga
Al-Adhem

Homs Industry:
cement, food processing

Zliten Industry:
food processing

Sebkhat
Taworgha

Marsa Brega Industry:
natural gas liquefaction plant, petrochemical, port improvements

Ra's al-Unuf Industry:
petrochemical

Az-Zuwaytinah Industry:
petrochemical

Wadi Zamzam
Wadi Thamit
Sirte

land reclamation project underway

to El Borma

Es' Sider Ra's al-Unuf
Marsa Brega

Az-Zuwaytinah
Ajdabiyah

30°N

Bordj
ssouda

Ghudamis

Wadi Tanarut

Mabruk

Al Jufrah
Oasis Waddan

Hun

Hofra

Nafoora Awjilah

Raguba
Haram Zaltan
Ora
Zillah Kuff Beda
Bu al Hidah Waha Harash
Defa

Gialo
Harash

Hun Industry:
food processing

Sabhah Industry:
textile, major urban center/industrial town planned

Tamadanet
Alrar
Zarzaitine
Edjeleh
Ouan Taredort
El Adeb
Larache
ssekaifaf

Wadi Irawan

Sabhah

Awbari
Goddua Tmassah
Zawilah
Traghan
Wadi Barjuj Marzuq

Sarir

reclamation project underway

desert reclamation of 8500 ha. for cultivation of wheat and animal fodder

Tazerbo
Oasis

LIBYA

25°N

Ghat Al-Qatrun

irrigation scheme for 10 000 ha.

At-Taj
Al Kufrah Al-Jawf
Oasis

TROPIC OF CANCER

Oued Tafassasset

20°N

Libya

Official Name
Socialist People's Libyan Arab Jamahiriyah

Area
1 759 640 sq km

Date of Independence
24 Dec 1951

Status and Name in Colonial Times
Turkish domination 16th century to 1911; 1911–1942/3 Italian colony; 1942/3–1949/51 British/French military administration

Population
2 290 734 (1973 census); 2 900 000 (UN est 1979)

Annual Growth Rate
4·1% (UN est 1979)

Capital City
Tripoli

Population of Capital
551 477 (1973 census)

National Language(s)
Arabic; English, French, Italian

Gross National Product (US dollars)
17 620 million; 6680 per capita (est 1977)

Local Currency
1 Libyan dinar = 1000 dirhams

Ottoman rule linked the area in a loose political union. This was threatened by the strong Muslim revival movement in Cyrenaica led by a Muslim brotherhood under the leadership of the Sanusi family whose *zawiyas* (or settlements) spread throughout the province.

In the early 20th century Libya became the object of Italy's colonial ambitions. The Sanusi order united with the Ottomans against the Christian threat, but the defeat of the Ottoman empire in World War I and the exile of the Sanusi leader, Muhammad Idris, in 1922 opened the country to the Italians. The succeeding settlement was bitterly fought and costly to the Italian government. Libya became Italy's "Fourth Shore," and "demographic colonization" began in 1934 with Mussolini's accession to power. Landless peasants, particularly from Sicily and southern Italy, were settled on lands either taken from Muslim owners or hitherto unclaimed. By 1938 10 per cent of the population of just over 880 000 were Italian settlers. Fascism took a strong hold on the colonial government.

World War II had a profound effect in Libya. The Italian, German and Allied armies fought backwards and forwards over the terrain for control of the strategically valuable points of Egypt and the Suez Canal. Italy's ultimate defeat meant that the area would not be returned to her direct rule but France and Britain, still the most important powers in the Mediterranean, disagreed about Libya's future. The USA had also developed strategic interests in the cold-war period and had built up the Wheelus Air Base near Tripoli. Finally the matter was settled in the United Nations and independence was granted in December 1951.

Libya emerged as a federated state under the Sanusi ruler, Idris. The solution was not welcomed by nationalist groups in Tripolitania but they were not united. In the 1950s King Idris attempted to keep a balance among the provinces and their interests. Libya joined the Arab League in 1953 and in the same year made a 20-year treaty with Britain for the right to maintain bases in return for aid. In September 1954 a similar agreement was made with the USA. Libya also made a rapprochement with Egypt. Internally its miserably poor economy was boosted by the discovery of oil in 1953. Concessions granted to the US oil companies and to British Petroleum became productive in the 1960s when exports rose from eight million tons in 1962 to more than 70 million in 1966.

On 1 September 1969 a group of young army officers under the leadership of Colonel Muammar Gaddafi carried out a coup. A Revolutionary Council was set up and the new regime was based on Islam and "freedom, socialism and unity." In May 1973 President Gaddafi promulgated his "Third Theory" which rejected both communism and capitalism. In 1977 the Revolutionary Council was replaced by the General People's Congress with a secretariat and in March 1979 Colonel Gaddafi gave up executive power "to devote himself to revolutionary action."

Economically Libya has prospered with the discovery of oil, but attempts to diversify the economy by agricultural schemes such as the Kufra Oasis project have not been notably successful. In foreign policy Colonel Gaddafi has followed an idiosyncratic line. Suggestions of union with Egypt and Syria (1969 and 1972) and Tunisia (1972) came to nothing. Relations with Egypt have deteriorated in the past years, particularly since President Sadat's 1977 peace initiatives. President Gaddafi has rejected links with both Russia and the West. He has consistently supported dissident groups like the Palestine Liberation Organization and the African liberation movements, such as FROLINAT in Chad. His support of Tunisian malcontents led to assistance for a raid on Gafsa in January 1980.   A.W.

Algeria

Algeria is the largest country of the Maghreb, stretching far into the Sahara in the south. The northern region comprises the mountainous area of the Atlas and the Mediterranean coastal strip on which the capital, Algiers, and the larger towns lie. The climate varies from Mediterranean (mild wet winters and hot summers) in the north to semi-arid steppe conditions in the south.

The modern territory of Algeria did not constitute a political entity in the Middle Ages. The region was converted to Islam and later came under the nominal overlordship of the Ottoman empire. The coastal towns under a bey provided shelter for the Barbary corsairs. In the early 19th century western reaction against the slave trade and increasing strategic interests in the Mediterranean led to French interest in Algeria. On the specious excuse of an insult offered to the French consul the country was invaded by the French in 1830. The next 70 years were spent in bringing the country under French control by a harsh military policy. Land was confiscated and *colons* from France settled and took over political control. In 1871 the major part of Algeria became a French *département*, part of the mother country.

The indigenous Arab and Berber population had been reduced in numbers by the bitter wars and was left in economic and cultural poverty. Algerian troops fought for France in World War I and came into contact with nationalist ideas, but Algerian nationalism was slow in growing. In 1923 Messali Hadj started the first nationalist newspaper which a decade later was demanding complete independence for Algeria. More moderate nationalists like Ferhat Abbas were less sure that there was an Algerian nation to promote. The late 1930s and the World War II period, illustrating as they did the political and military weakness of France, encouraged more radical ideas among the Muslim population. Algeria, like Tunisia, had a Vichy government, but later in the war the Free French government set up its headquarters in Algiers. In 1943 Ferhat Abbas presented the "Manifesto of the Algerian people" asking for reforms and a constitution. This was rejected but it formed the basis of the nationalist movement in the immediate post-war years.

The period of violence began with the French suppression of riots at Sétif in May 1945 and the arrest of Ferhat Abbas. By 1947 numbers of Algerian Muslims were joining the Secret Organization (OS) and collecting arms and money. Attempts by the French to offer a limited constitution were no longer possible. In 1956 the various national groups joined with Abbas's National Liberation Front (FLN). The bitterly fought war of independence lasted until 1962. The success of the FLN caused a backlash from the French settlers in 1958. Supported by the army they caused the fall of the Fourth French Republic and the return to power of General de Gaulle. His cautious steps towards granting independence were countered in 1961 by the colonialist Secret Army Organization (OAS) which carried out terrorist attacks. In 1962 agreements were signed at Évian granting Algerian independence.

The new government led by Ahmed Ben Bella, who became president in 1963, faced formidable economic problems. The devastation of the war years and the loss of French professional and skilled workers increased the difficulties of building the new state. Both industry and agriculture were organized under a system of workers' management called *autogestion*. In 1965 Ben Bella was overthrown in a bloodless coup. His personal style of ruling had proved unpalatable to his colleagues.

A Council of Revolution was set up under Colonel Houari Boumédienne. He proposed the creation of "an authentic socialist society" by building up the national economy. Government administration was overhauled and nationalized groups of companies, like Sonatrach for hydrocarbons, were created. A rapidly growing population (in 1977 54 per cent of the population was under 18) called for an extensive program of education and technical training at all levels. In 1976 in response to demands for more representation, a National Charter was put forward restoring a constitution, and at the beginning of 1977 a popular National Assembly was set up. Two plans, 1970–73 and 1974–77, have been completed and Algeria appears to have put its economy on a satisfactory footing, although problems in the agricultural sector remain.

In foreign policy President Boumédienne moved cautiously. In 1966 an agreement was made with France for financial aid and technical assistance, and although relations between the two countries went through a period of tension in the early 1970s, the link has remained. Algeria also accepted aid and expertise from Western and Eastern countries. It has consistently supported the Palestine Liberation Organization and revolutionary movements in Africa. Relations with Morocco were strained in the 1970s because of conflicting interests in the Spanish Sahara. Algeria has maintained a strong line on Arab policies and in the Organization for African Unity. President Boumédienne, an austere and dedicated man, led his country in a difficult period, and his death in December 1978 left the country with no obvious successor. Colonel Benjedid Chadli, a compromise candidate, was chosen in February 1979. His policy has been one of compromise at home and abroad. He released a number of political prisoners, including Ben Bella, and lowered tension with Morocco over the question of Mauritania.   A.W.

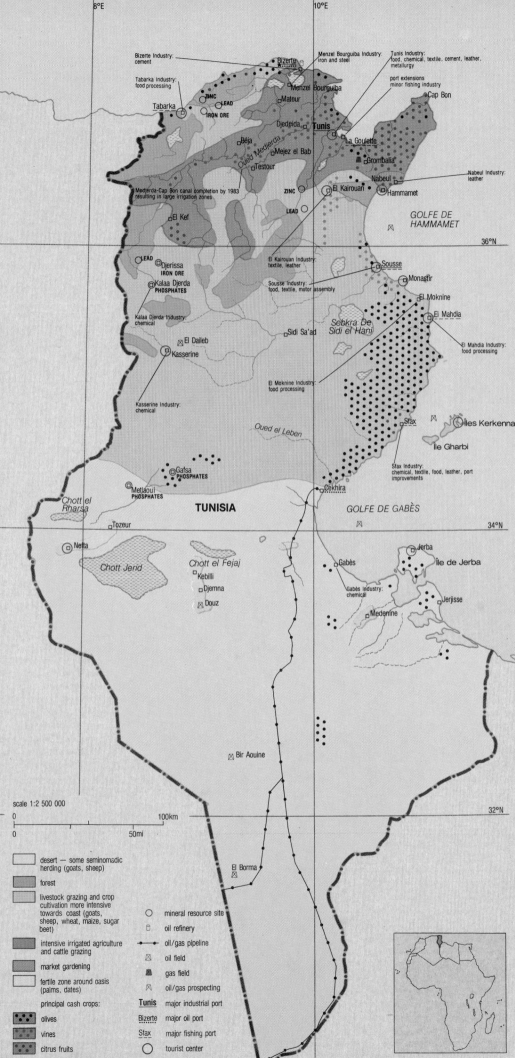

Map labels (clockwise/by region):

8°E · 10°E

Bizerte Industry: cement
Tabarka Industry: food processing
Menzel Bourguiba Industry: iron and steel
Tunis Industry: food, chemical, textile, cement, leather, metallurgy
port extensions minor fishing industry

Bizerte
Menzel Bourguiba
Mateur
Tabarka
ZINC
LEAD
IRON ORE
Djedeida
Tunis
Cap Bon
Béja
La Goulette
Mejez el Bab
Oued Medjerda
Testour
Grombalia
Medjerda-Cap Bon canal completion by 1983 resulting in large irrigation zones
Nabeul
Nabeul Industry: leather
ZINC
El Kairouan
Hammamet
El Kef
LEAD
GOLFE DE HAMMAMET
36°N

LEAD
Djerissa
IRON ORE
Kalaa Djerda
PHOSPHATES
El Kairouan Industry: textile, leather
Sousse
Monastir
Sousse Industry: food, textile, motor assembly
El Moknine
El Mahdia
Kalaa Djerda Industry: chemical
Sebkra De Sidi el Hani
El Mahdia Industry: food processing
El Daileb
Kasserine
Sidi Sa'ad
El Moknine Industry: food processing
Kasserine Industry: chemical
Oued el Leben
Sfax
Iles Kerkenna
Île Gharbi
Gafsa
PHOSPHATES
Sfax Industry: chemical, textile, food, leather, port improvements
Metlaoui
PHOSPHATES
Cekhira
Chott el Rharsa
TUNISIA
GOLFE DE GABÈS
34°N
Tozeur
Netta
Jerba
Chott Jerid
Chott el Fejaj
Gabès
Île de Jerba
Kebilli
Djemna
Gabès Industry: chemical
Jerjisse
Douz
Medenine
Bir Aouine
32°N
El Borma

scale 1:2 500 000

0 — 100km
0 — 50mi

Legend:

- desert — some seminomadic herding (goats, sheep)
- forest
- livestock grazing and crop cultivation more intensive towards coast (goats, sheep, wheat, maize, sugar beet)
- intensive irrigated agriculture and cattle grazing
- market gardening
- fertile zone around oasis (palms, dates)

principal cash crops:
- olives
- vines
- citrus fruits

- ○ mineral resource site
- oil refinery
- •─• oil/gas pipeline
- ⋈ oil field
- gas field
- oil/gas prospecting
- **Tunis** major industrial port
- Bizerte major oil port
- Sfax major fishing port
- ○ tourist center

Tunisia

Tunisia is the smallest state of the Maghreb, bounded on the north by the Mediterranean, on the west by Algeria and on the east by Libya. The country has a rich fertile area, comprising the Medjerda valley, the Mateur plain and the steppe from Hammamet to Gabès. There are some minerals, including phosphate, iron ore and lead. Petroleum and natural gas are now exported.

Tunisia was the center of the Carthaginian trading empire from the 6th century BC until its overthrow by the Romans in the 2nd century BC. Tunisia enjoyed prosperity under a succession of Muslim dynasties in the Middle Ages. Spanish and Ottoman ambitions in North Africa led to the overthrow of the last member of the Hafsid dynasty in 1574 and the establishment of Ottoman rule. In a few years Tunis regained independence under a bey who accepted the nominal overlordship of the Ottoman empire. The 19th century saw growing European interests in Tunisia as in Algeria. By the second half of the century the country was deeply in debt to foreigners and in 1869 France, Britain and Italy took over financial control. In 1881 France invaded the country and imposed the treaty of Kassar Said (or Bardo) on the bey, leaving him as nominal ruler with the French in charge of foreign, military and financial policy. Two years later a French protectorate was established and a French Resident General imposed. The office of bey was not abolished but he had little power.

Although Tunisia was deeply affected by French culture and education, it nevertheless kept its contacts with the Islamic world and its aspirations. In 1888 a Young Tunisian movement coupled demands for reform with a

Tunisia

Official Name
Tunisia
Al-Djoumhouria Attunisia

Area
164 150 sq km

Date of Independence
20 Mar 1956

Status and Name in Colonial Times
1883–1956 French protectorate: Tunisia

Population
5 588 209 (1975 census); 6 400 000 (UN est 1979)

Annual Growth Rate
2·7% (UN est 1979)

Capital City
Tunis

Population of Capital
944 000 (1975 census)

National Language(s)
Arabic; French

Gross National Product (US dollars)
5070 million; 860 per capita (est 1977)

Local Currency
1 Tunisian dinar = 1000 millièmes

request for the restoration of the bey's authority. This achieved no success but one of its leaders launched the Destour or Constitution Party in 1920. France conceded a few administrative reforms but no political representation. In 1934 a new generation of Destourians emerged under the leadership of a Tunisian lawyer, Habib Bourguiba. His organization of the party in the late 1930s built up a considerable opposition to the French administration.

During World War II Tunisia was placed under a Vichy government after the fall of France and became the supply base for Germany's campaigns in Libya. The nationalist leaders were imprisoned in France for the duration of the war. On his release Bourguiba traveled widely to explain the Tunisian point of view and in 1946 he spoke to the United Nations. Three years later he returned to Tunisia and began to work for the nonviolent achievement of political rights.

The early hope that France might accept his proposals was dashed by the reaction of the European settlers. Demonstrations against the regime began in 1952 and Bourguiba and the other nationalist leaders were imprisoned. Violence increased and in 1954 France agreed to grant internal self-rule to a country on the verge of civil war. Independence was eventually granted in 1956 and a year later Tunisia was declared a republic with Bourguiba as its head.

The new president steered a careful course between his need for aid from the West and the concern to associate Tunisia with the Arab world. Relations with France went through a period of stress after the bombing of the town of Sakiet Sidi Youssef during the Algerian war, and later conflict arose over the French base at Bizerte. In 1961 Tunisia received aid from France and also from West Germany and the USA. Within the Arab sphere of influence Bourguiba had a dispute with Algeria over the latter's support for a group opposing the Tunisian president in 1963 and in 1965 he opposed the Arab League's policy in Israel. Tunisia sent troops to support Egypt in the Six Days' War in 1967.

Internally Bourguiba set his country on a path of "Tunisian Socialism." It began with the appropriation of French lands in 1963 and the attempt to collectivize agriculture. Associated with the Minister of Finance and Planning, Ahmed Ben Salah, the movement came to an end with the imprisonment of the minister in 1964 after conviction on a number of charges. In 1974 Bourguiba was elected president for life, but opposition was not stilled. From 1974 to 1976 hundreds were imprisoned for opposition to the state.

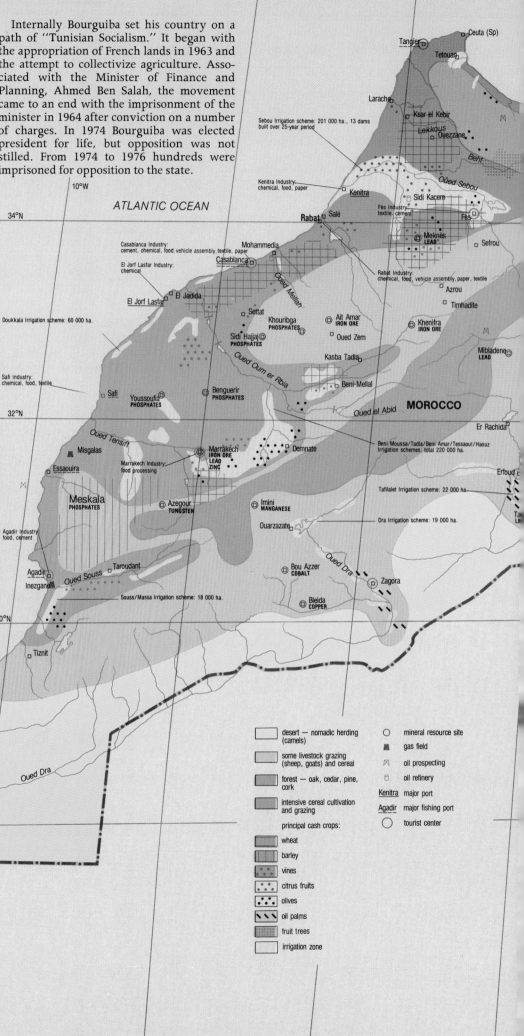

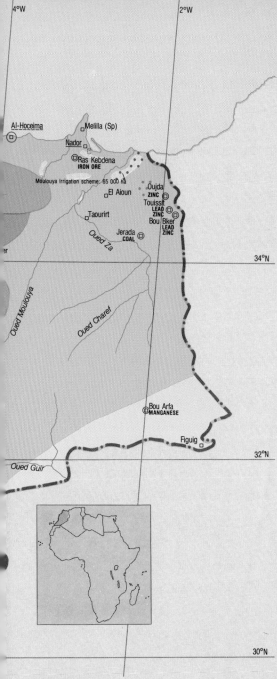

At the beginning of 1974 a merger was proposed between Tunisia and Libya. The affair dragged on for three years but was rejected. Tunisia turned to the USA and France for renewed aid. President Bourguiba's advancing age and bad health led to anxiety over the future of the state. Ahmed Ben Salah in exile and Mahmoud Mestiri, leader of a Social Democrat group, made demands for a multi-party democracy. The government also came into conflict with Habib Achour, leader of the General Union of Tunisian Workers. In January 1980 a raid on Gafsa took place, probably organized by dissident Tunisians with Libyan support. The government's request for help from France led to the country's increased isolation in the Maghreb.

A.W.

Morocco

Morocco is a land of contrasts: geographical, historical and human. Within its borders are desert sands and thick forests; the rocky Atlas Mountains and fertile plains; sparsely populated desert and mountain areas and teeming cities like Casablanca, Rabat, Fès and Marrakech. It has known periods of chaotic anarchy and internal strife and periods of highly centralized control; periods of intellectual and artistic glory and periods of decline; periods of conquest and empire and a period of foreign rule. Its people range from the traditional Berber-speaking mountain peasant tribesmen to the urbane, European-educated, French-speaking upper crust of Casablanca and Rabat. Even within the elite there are the traditional, old, wealthy families of Fès, many of whom cling to traditional Islamic values, the nouveaux riches who look to Europe and the USA, and the increasingly wealthy merchants from the Sous valley now established in Casablanca.

Morocco is a country demarcated by geographical features and molded by its people. Occupying the northwest corner of Africa, it has long Atlantic and Mediterranean coasts. The Rif and Atlas mountains form the backbone of the country and, together with its new and historic cities, give Morocco a unique character – a blend of the urbane life of the traditional Islamic city, the traditionalism of the mountain tribes and the hustle and bustle of growing modern urban centers.

As Mauretania Tingitana, Morocco made its first appearance in recorded history as a Roman province. Relics of the Roman presence can still be seen at Volubilis (near Meknès) and Lixus (near Larache). After the Romans left the area, local Berber tribes controlled the area until the Arab conquest in the 7th century. Morocco, or *al-Maghrib al-Aqsa* (the furthest west) as it is known to the Arabs, became the jumping-off point for the Muslim conquest of Spain in 711. However, Morocco soon reasserted its distinctive identity in the 8th century under Mulay Idris I and Mulay Idris II, who founded the first of a series of Moroccan dynasties. From the rise of the Idrissids until the Franco–Spanish partition

into a dual protectorate in 1912, these dynasties ruled Morocco and surrounding areas from capitals in Fès, Marrakech, Meknès and occasionally Rabat. The Almoravids (11th–12th centuries) also ruled much of Islamic Spain, as did the Almohads (12th–13th centuries) who extended their control over present-day Algeria and Tunisia as well. The Merinid (13th–15th centuries) successors to the Almohads in Morocco were replaced by the Sa'adis (16th–17th centuries) who restored Moroccan control of extensive areas in the western Sudan and conquered Tombouctou in 1590. Following an extended period of political turmoil the 'Alawis replaced the Sa'adis in the 1660s and still rule Morocco today.

After the Franco–Spanish protectorate divided the country into two zones in 1912, a nationalist movement came in being. In the late 1940s and early 1950s King Muhammad V emerged as the spiritual leader of the independence struggle and he and the 'Alawi dynasty retained control of the country once the French and Spanish restored Morocco's independence in 1956. Both Muhammad V (d. 1961) and his son, King Hasan II, have ruled as well as reigned ever since. Opposition parties are permitted to function in a constitutional parliamentary system. The two largest organized groups are the Istiqlal (Independence) party, first organized in 1944, and the Union Socialiste des Forces Populaires (USFP), previously known as the Union Nationale des Forces Populaires (UNFP), formed as a result of a schism in the Istiqlal in 1958. Opposition members sit in the Chamber of Deputies elected in March 1977, but it is controlled by a loose coalition of the king's supporters. The monarch selects the cabinet himself. Press freedom has fluctuated over the years. Opposition dailies have consistently been published, but frequently under the careful eye of government censors. Since the March 1977 elections the number of dailies and weeklies has increased substantially at all points on the political spectrum.

Recurrent droughts and a burgeoning population have forced Morocco to import sizable quantities of foodstuffs in recent years, despite vast fertile areas and a number of irrigation projects aimed at bringing more land under cultivation. Until 1975 the government concentrated its development efforts in the agricultural sector, building dams, reforesting and irrigating large areas. Since then there has been more emphasis on industrial development, particularly in phosphates and agro-industry. With nearly half the world's known reserves, Morocco relies on phosphates as its principal economic resource and largest export. But the economy is more diversified than the oil-based economies of Saudi Arabia and the United Arab Emirates. Other important sources of foreign exchange are tourists (more than 1·5 million annually), citrus fruits, canned fish, vegetables and various minerals, especially cobalt, lead, iron and manganese.

More than 300 000 Moroccans work in European countries, especially France and Belgium, and send remittances back to their families. They are representative of the bipolar pull on Moroccan society – modernity and traditional values.

J.W.

Morocco

Official Name
Kingdom of Morocco
Al-Mamlaka al-Maghrebia

Area
659 970 sq km (458 730 sq km excluding annexed portion of Western Sahara)

Date of Independence
18 Nov 1956

Status and Name in Colonial Times
1912–56 divided into French protectorate, Spanish protectorate and international zone of Tangier

Population
16 309 000 (1971 census); 19 800 000 (UN est 1979)

Annual Growth Rate
2·4% (1965–73); 3·2% (est 1979)

Capital City
Rabat

Population of Capital
367 620 (1971 census)

National Language(s)
Arabic, French, Spanish, English

Gross National Product (US dollars)
10 100 million; 570 per capita (est 1977)

Local Currency
1 Moroccan dirham = 100 Moroccan francs

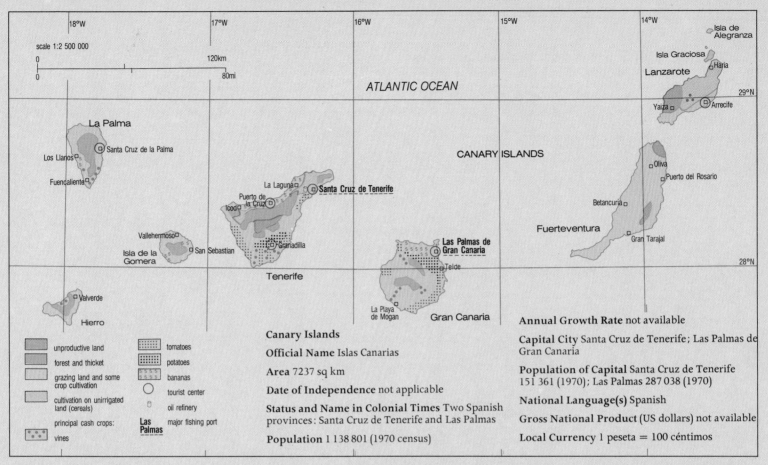

Canary Islands

Official Name Islas Canarias

Area 7237 sq km

Date of Independence not applicable

Status and Name in Colonial Times Two Spanish provinces: Santa Cruz de Tenerife and Las Palmas

Population 1 138 801 (1970 census)

Annual Growth Rate not available

Capital City Santa Cruz de Tenerife; Las Palmas de Gran Canaria

Population of Capital Santa Cruz de Tenerife 151 361 (1970); Las Palmas 287 038 (1970)

National Language(s) Spanish

Gross National Product (US dollars) not available

Local Currency 1 peseta = 100 céntimos

Canary Islands

The Canary Islands are not a nation-state but comprise two provinces of the Spanish state on an equal basis with the mainland provinces. Independence has some support, particularly among political parties of the Left, but is an unlikely prospect in the near future owing to the high degree of cultural and political integration with the mainland. The archipelago consists of seven islands: La Palma, Gomera, Hierro, Tenerife (which comprise the province of Santa Cruz de Tenerife), Lanzarote, Fuerteventura and Gran Canaria (province of Las Palmas). Geomorphologically the islands have been seen as an extension of the Saharan platform, but recent research considers only Lanzarote and Fuerteventura as extensions of the continental crust, with a non-continental origin for Gran Canaria and the others.

The hydrology of the archipelago presents stark contrasts. Fuerteventura and Lanzarote are desert islands, with virtually no surface water and a maximum of 30 rain days per year. Gran Canaria, Tenerife and La Palma are miniature continents, each divisible into three climatic zones: a coastal zone (below 300 meters altitude) characterized by high mean temperature and low mean precipitation, where irrigation agriculture is practiced; a temperate zone whose upper limit varies from 600 to 900 meters; and a subalpine region with low temperatures and high precipitation. At 3718 meters above sea level, Pico de Teide on Tenerife is the highest peak on Spanish territory.

Before the European conquest, the Canaries were inhabited by the Guanches, whose culture was related to that of North African Berbers. In 1402 Norman French knights conquered Lanzarote, Fuerteventura, Hierro and Gomera in the name of the king of Castile. The islands with denser native populations were conquered directly by Castile: Gran Canaria in 1478–83; La Palma in 1491; and Tenerife in 1493–96. Unlike the Norman islands, which were ruled as feudal fiefs, the latter three were controlled directly by the crown, and their administration anticipated the organization of the future American colonies. The three islands were organized together with a common *audiencia*, or appeals court, in 1526, although each was considered a municipality, administered by a city council, or *cabildo*. The surviving natives were converted to Christianity and quickly assimilated into the Spanish population. The islands early became a point of transit between Spain and her American colonies and have steadily provided migrants to Spanish America.

Development of irrigation in Gran Canaria, Tenerife and La Palma permitted the installation of sugar plantations in the 16th century. Sugar technicians were recruited from Madeira, and Canarians later manned the sugar mills of Mexico and the Caribbean. Unable to meet the competition of British West Indian sugar, agriculture shifted to grapevines. A dominant trade pattern of the 17th century was the exchange of wine with British New England in return for dried fish and oak staves for wine pipes. Wine gave way between 1825 and 1885 to another monoculture, the *Opuntia* cactus on which the dye-yielding cochineal insect feeds.

The current economy of the Canaries is dominated by tourism and agriculture, with some incipient industrial development. The number of tourists, principally from northern Europe, rose dramatically from 23 000 in 1958 to 484 000 in 1967.

Bananas have been the monoculture of the 20th century, with more than 12 500 hectares planted, yielding 3 600 000 quintals in 1975. The next most important crops are tomatoes (6000 hectares; 1 900 000 quintals) and potatoes (14 000 hectares; 13 000 000 quintals). In Lanzarote, a curious system of constructing microcatchments (*gavias*) of rocks and volcanic ash has accounted for the displacement of sheep and camel herding by agriculture over the past two centuries.

Industrial development has been minimal, limited by lack of water and local energy sources. The establishment of free ports in 1852 failed to stimulate the economy, owing to the smallness of the local market. Until the 1950s the only large industry was a petroleum refinery established in 1927. The industrial sector of the 1970s is dominated by food processing, the production of cigars and cigarettes from imported tobacco and chemicals. T.G.

Western Sahara

Western Sahara is a geographical area rather than a discrete nation-state. It lies between Morocco and Mauritania along Africa's Atlantic coast. The desert territory is divided into two regions, Saguia el Hamra in the north and Wadi adh-Dhahab (Rio de Oro) in the south. Both are sparsely populated. Nocturnal dew and infrequent rains allow some agriculture along a 10-kilometer-wide coastal strip, and there is a small fishing industry. However the major economic resource is the huge phosphate deposit at Bu Cra'a, about 160 kilometers inland from the capital Aaiun. Proven reserves total more than 2000 million tons, most of it accessible to open-pit mining. The population is about 75 000, many of them desert nomads. For the most part Saharans are members of major Arab tribal groups – Reguibat, Ould Delim, Tekna – or a number of smaller tribes. Even those who live in the principal towns – Aaiun, Smara and Dakhla – are, for the most part, only a few years, or at most a generation, away from the tribal encampment.

Western Sahara's juridical status is at present in limbo. From the 1880s until February 1976 it was ruled by Spain, most recently as a province. After years of Moroccan and Mauritanian pressure in the United Nations, Spain announced its intention to withdraw in 1974. Moroccan politicians had long claimed that historically, religiously and legally the territory formed part of Morocco. They pointed to the Saharan connections of Moroccan dynasties dating back to the 11th century and continued political ties under the Sa'adis in the 16th and 17th centuries as well as in the 19th century under the 'Alawis. Together with Mauritania, Morocco asked the International Court of Justice for an advisory opinion on the status of the territory before Spain's colonization, which was delivered in October 1975. It acknowledged Moroccan and Mauritanian ties but not their sovereignty. The opinion was quickly followed by the "Green March," a dramatic government-organized assertion of the Moroccan claim by 350 000 unarmed civilians in November 1975. This led to negotiation of a tripartite agreement signed on 28 November 1975 by Morocco, Mauritania and Spain. It divided the territory on a line running southeast from the coast north of Dakhla. However, when Spain withdrew its military forces on 28 February 1976, the Popular Front for the Liberation of Saguia el Hamra and Rio de Oro (Polisario Front), an Algerian-backed Saharan independence movement which had opposed Spanish rule, proclaimed the Saharan Arab Democratic Republic, with a government-in-exile based in Algeria. At first Morocco and Mauritania exercised *de facto* control over much of the territory, but Polisario contested this and a guerrilla war ensued. In 1979 Mauritania renounced its claims.

For centuries Saharan tribesmen have lived a simple nomadic life in close communion with nature. In the latter years of Spanish rule there were some government-sponsored efforts at settling them. With the opening of the 158-kilometer-long conveyer belt from Bu Cra'a's phosphates to the port at Aaiun in 1972, migratory routes were cut for some and jobs created for others. More than a quarter of the territory's populace is now employed in some phase of the phosphates industry. Together with the political upheavals accompanying Spain's decolonization, these economic forces are leading Saharans into uncharted areas of social change   J.W.

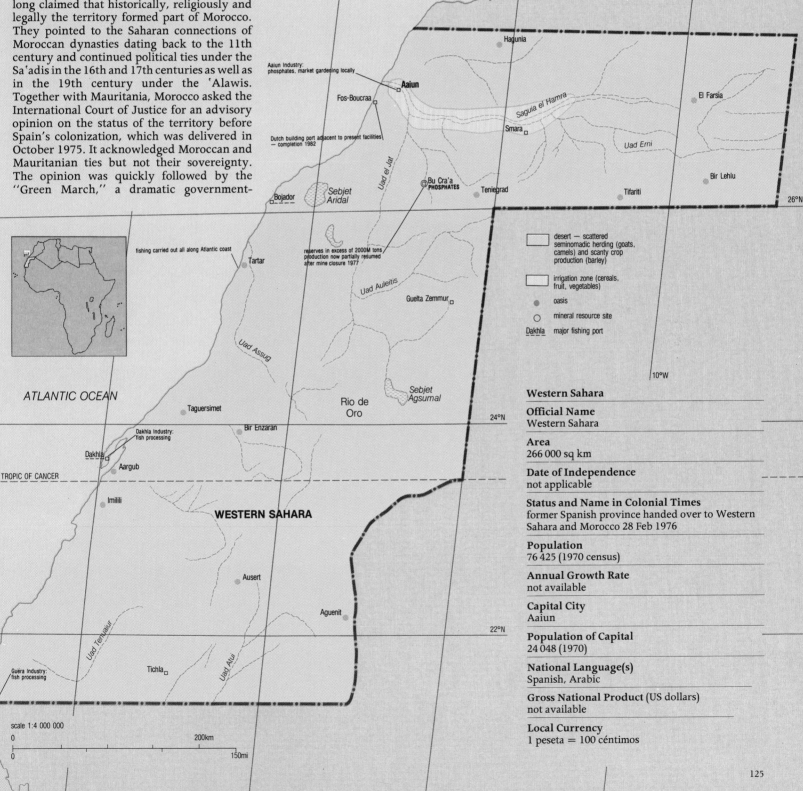

Western Sahara

Official Name
Western Sahara

Area
266 000 sq km

Date of Independence
not applicable

Status and Name in Colonial Times
former Spanish province handed over to Western Sahara and Morocco 28 Feb 1976

Population
76 425 (1970 census)

Annual Growth Rate
not available

Capital City
Aaiun

Population of Capital
24 048 (1970)

National Language(s)
Spanish, Arabic

Gross National Product (US dollars)
not available

Local Currency
1 peseta = 100 céntimos

WEST AFRICA

This region's greatest claim to unity may be the fact that much of it constituted the French West African Federation during the colonial period, from the late 19th century up to 1960. But there are also the former British colonies, from tiny Gambia to gigantic Nigeria, the Portuguese possessions of Guinea-Bissau and Cape Verde, and independent but deeply Americanized Liberia. There were also the German colonies of Togo and Cameroon.

Historically some peoples lived in very small-scale, simply organized communities. But many lived in highly structured and widely flung chiefdoms and kingdoms. Indeed, one of the distinctive marks of this region of Africa may be its kingdoms and empires – Ghana, Mali, Benin. The earliest and greatest kingdoms arose in the northern grasslands, but others later grew up among the agricultural and fishing people of the southern forests. Crafts and the arts flourished in these kingdoms – delicate metalwork, carvings in wood and stone, weaving and dyeing, elaborate palaces.

The various independent nations which now make up West Africa have not thrown off completely the traces of their colonial past. The English/French divide still separates. Islamic nations like Mauritania and Niger provide a bridge between north and south. The presence of oil and minerals, only recently exploited, is opening a door to new economic opportunities, while subsistence agriculture, herding and cash crops still provide a living for the majority of West Africa's peoples.

Below left The Atlantic and the Guinea coasts of West Africa have been visited by Western sailors and merchants since the 15th century. Fortified trading posts, such as Cape Coast Castle in Ghana, illustrated here, were established by European merchants under the protection of local rulers. In the absence of deep-water harbors, canoes were used to transport people and goods from shipping standing off shore.

Below Lagos harbor. West Africa has few good natural harbors, and the building of modern ports has not kept pace with modern demands. In many cases ships must still stand off shore for loading and unloading from lighters.

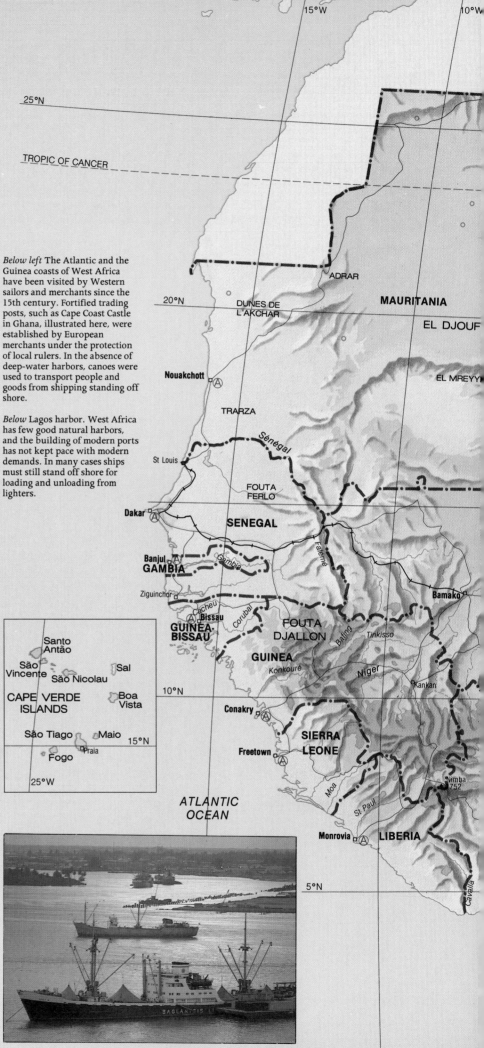

EL HANK

25°N

TROPIC OF CANCER

3000m
2000m
1000m
500m
200m
0

▲1752   spot height in meters
━━•━•   international boundary
━━━━   principal road
━┿━┿━   principal railroad
Ⓐ   international airport
⋯⋯   seasonal river
   marsh
○   oasis

SAHARA

SAHARA

PLATEAU DE
MANGUENI

TÉNÉRÉ DU
TAFASSASSET

20°N

ADRAR DES
IFORAS

MALI

AÏR
(AZBINE)

Ténéré

GRAND ERG
DE BILMA

▲Baguezane
1900

Agadez

NIGER

Tombouctou

Niger

Gao

15°N

L Débo

Mopti

Birni Nkonni

Zinder

Komadougou Yobé

L CHAD

gou   Bani

UPPER VOLTA

Niamey

Sokoto

Zamfara

Kano   Hadejia

Maiduguri

Ouagadougou

Volta Blanche

Kano

Komadougou Gana

Volta Rouge

Zaria

Bobo Dioulasso

CHAÎNE DE
L'ATACORA

Kaduna

Gongola

10°N

BENIN

Kainji
Reservoir

Kaduna

JOS
PLATEAU

Komoé

Black Volta

Tamale

Oti

TOGO

Kainji Dam

NIGERIA

Benue

Vogel
2040

Béroué

RY COAST

Bui
Dam

GHANA

Mono

Parakou

MASSIF
DE L'ADAMOUA

Bouaké

L VOLTA

Ogbomosho

Benue

Ngaoundéré

Oyo
Iwo

Oshogbo

Bouaké

Bandama

Kumasi

Akosombo
Dam

Ibadan

Abeokuta

Porto
Novo

Benin City

Onitsha

CAMEROON

5°N

Abidjan

Lomé

Cotonou

Lagos

Niger

oum

Accra

Bight of Benin

Port
Harcourt

Cameroon
4070

Douala   Sanaga

Yaoundé

GULF OF GUINEA

Nyong

Dja

Bight of
Biafra

Ngoko

scale 1:11 000 000

0   600 km

0   400 mi

Top In Upper Volta a village elder stands by one of the grain stores which hold his family's provisions through the dry months between harvests.

Above left The Creoles of Sierra Leone and the Americo–Liberians of Liberia are descendants of freed slaves who migrated to or were returned to West Africa. They have tended to adopt Western styles of building and dress; this is an old corrugated-iron house at Lower Buchanan, Liberia.

Left At Oulata, in the dry semidesert of western Mauritania, mudbrick mud-plastered houses are painted and decorated with murals.

Above In Ganvie, southern Benin, houses raised on stilts are built in the lagoon, and canoes transport the inhabitants across the water.

Above right At markets all over Africa – this picture shows one in Dakar, Senegal – various types of baskets and woven goods for carriage, storage and furniture are made and sold.

Top right The Dogon people of Mali, from the area south of the Niger bend, live in villages, often built on steep hillsides, in rectangular walled compounds.

Right Groundnuts (peanuts) are an important cash crop, as well as a food, across the dry north of West Africa. At Kano, in northern Nigeria, pyramids made up of sacks of groundnuts are being demolished for export.

Far right Here in Kano, as in other parts of Nigeria, great earth vats are used for the indigo dyeing of locally woven cloth.

Cape Verde Islands

Located in the Atlantic Ocean about 600 kilometers west of Senegal, between 14° 48′ and 17° 12′ N, and between 22° 40′ and 25° 22′ W, the Cape Verde Islands comprise ten islands and five islets in two groups. To the north are the Barlavento or Windward islands of Santo Antão, São Vicente, Santa Luzia, São Nicolau, Boa Vista and Sal, with the islets of Raso and Branco, and to the south the Sotavento or Leeward islands of Maio, São Tiago, Fogo and Brava, with the islets of Grande, Luís Carneiro and Cima. More than a third of the entire population lives on São Tiago, while Santa Luzia is uninhabited. Because many males have emigrated to Europe and North America in search of work, there are many more females than males in the population. Volcanic in origin (Pico do Cano on Fogo was active as recently as 1951), they present a jagged appearance with high coastal cliffs and are vulnerable to erosion. Only four of the islands, São Tiago, Santo Antão, São Nicolau and Brava, have year-round running streams, and aridity is characteristic despite the presence of an estimated two million hectares of as yet untapped water underground. The climate is warm, with the temperature varying from a mean high of 27° to a mean low of slightly above 21°.

Uninhabited at the time of their discovery in the 15th century, the islands became the possessions of Portugal which sent among its settlers a high proportion of convicts. After the discovery of America, the islands achieved importance as an entrepôt for the slave trade, and blacks were imported to work the harbors

and plantations. The breakdown of African tribal structures and widespread racial intermarriage in time evolved a multinational, nonracist culture leavened constantly by new arrivals from passing ships of many nations. Today the population mix is about 2 per cent white, 70 per cent mixed, the remainder black. This creole culture has a developed literature in Portuguese–African *crioulo* and is strongly Roman Catholic. The decline of the slave trade in the 18th century meant declining prosperity. After 1747 cycles of drought and famine racked the islands, the impact growing more devastating with the end of the slave trade in 1876. In the decade following 1968 drought caused an almost complete cessation of agricultural production and required massive aid from other nations. Dissatisfaction with the Portuguese regime's failure to cope with the crisis contributed to the breakaway of the islands from the mother country in 1974.

The African Party for the Independence of Guinea-Bissau and Cape Verde (PAIGC) has erected a one-party state and is seeking to guarantee its political hegemony in the islands and lay the groundwork for union with the Republic of Guinea-Bissau. The government is republican, with a popularly elected People's Assembly which elects the president and premier. The republic has joined the ACP–EEC group of nations and is seeking closer ties with the West. Cape Verde's chief economic importance is as a refueling station for ships and aircraft. By reason of its poor soil and frequent droughts, it must import food. Chief among its exports are bananas, salt, physic nuts, coffee, fish, pozzolana, hides and potatoes. The government is pursuing a conservative agrarian policy, ending sharecropping but stopping short of redistributing land.
J.M.M.

Mauritania

The Islamic Republic of Mauritania came into existence in 1960, when France granted independence to most of its former African colonies. It had previously been a part of French West Africa. One of Africa's largest countries, with a population that is small in proportion, Mauritania lies with two-thirds of its area in the Saharan zone. Most of the country is a series of vast plateaus, consisting of sand over the western Saharan shield of crystalline rocks. Rainfall is minimal – always less than 100 millimeters annually. To the south the Saharan zone merges gradually into the sahel, with slightly higher rainfall and more abundant vegetation. While parts of the north cannot support even the camel, cattle as well as sheep and goats are grazed in the sahel. In the extreme south, along the Senegal river, is a narrow zone where fruit, vegetables and grains are grown. Along the Atlantic coast is a 30-kilometer strip where the hot dry climate is modified by oceanic trade winds.

Population densities and ways of life have been controlled by climatic factors. In the Saharan and sahelian zones, nomadism has been the only life possible outside towns and oases. Towards the Senegal border the people have been sedentary cultivators, and fishing was important along the Atlantic coast. Three-quarters of the population are Moors. Originally nomads and for centuries Muslim, they are of mixed Arab–Berber stock and speak dialects of Hassaniyya (Arabic modified by Berber vernaculars). A minority of Mauritanians, mainly in the extreme south, are black Africans – Fulani, Soninke, Bambara – speaking Nigritic languages.

Gradual contact with the West came through Portuguese, Dutch and French merchants venturing inland for trade, especially in gum arabic. It was not until 1899 that the French announced their intention of establishing rule over the territory "from the right bank of the Senegal" up to the borders of Algeria and Morocco, to which they gave the name of Western Mauritania. It became a protectorate in 1903–04 and a separate colony in 1920. Western education was accepted more readily by the Negro agriculturalists of the south, thus laying the grounds for future conflict. Political movements arose only in the late 1940s, and the first president, Moktar Ould Daddah, was a protégé of the French. Independence was granted in 1960 and an Islamic Republic proclaimed.

Factions soon became apparent. Was alignment to be with the Arab north or the African south? Initially Daddah saw Mauritania as a bridge between the two, but gradually moved to the north. Arabic was made an official language in 1968, angering black Africans who did not speak it as a first language. Increasing wealth derived from extensive mineral deposits (iron near Zouérate, and copper near Akjoujt). When Spain decided to grant independence to the Spanish Sahara (rich in phosphates) the territory was claimed by Mauritania and Morocco. A division of the territory between the two was not accepted by the Algerian-backed Polisario movement within Western Sahara. The resulting guer-

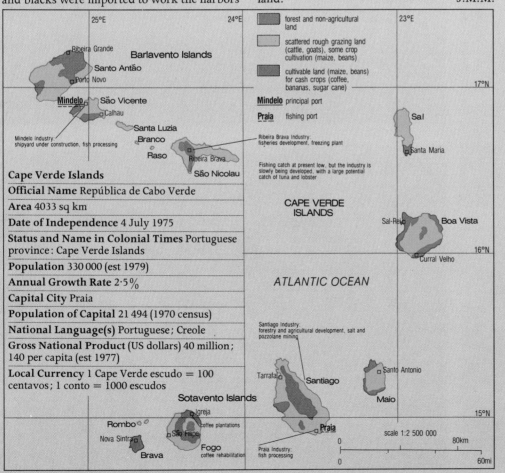

Barlavento Islands

Ribeira Grande
Santo Antão
Porto Novo
Mindelo
São Vicente
Calhau
Mindelo industry:
shipyard under construction, fish processing
Santa Luzia
Branco
Raso
Ribeira Brava
São Nicolau

forest and non-agricultural land

scattered rough grazing land (cattle, goats), some crop cultivation (maize, beans)

cultivable land (maize, beans) for cash crops (coffee, bananas, sugar cane)

Mindelo principal port
Praia fishing port

Ribeira Brava industry:
fisheries development, freezing plant

Fishing catch at present low, but the industry is slowly being developed, with a large potential catch of tuna and lobster

CAPE VERDE ISLANDS

Sal
Santa Maria
Sal-Rei
Boa Vista
Curral Velho

ATLANTIC OCEAN

Santiago Industry:
forestry and agricultural development, salt and pozzolane mining

Tarrafal
Santiago
Santo Antonio
Maio

Sotavento Islands

Rombo
Nova Sintra
São Filipe
Igreja
coffee plantations
Praia
Praia Industry:
fish processing

Fogo
coffee rehabilitation
Brava

scale 1:2 500 000
0   80km
0   60mi

Cape Verde Islands

Official Name	República de Cabo Verde
Area	4033 sq km
Date of Independence	4 July 1975
Status and Name in Colonial Times	Portuguese province: Cape Verde Islands
Population	330 000 (est 1979)
Annual Growth Rate	2·5%
Capital City	Praia
Population of Capital	21 494 (1970 census)
National Language(s)	Portuguese; Creole
Gross National Product	(US dollars) 40 million; 140 per capita (est 1977)
Local Currency	1 Cape Verde escudo = 100 centavos; 1 conto = 1000 escudos

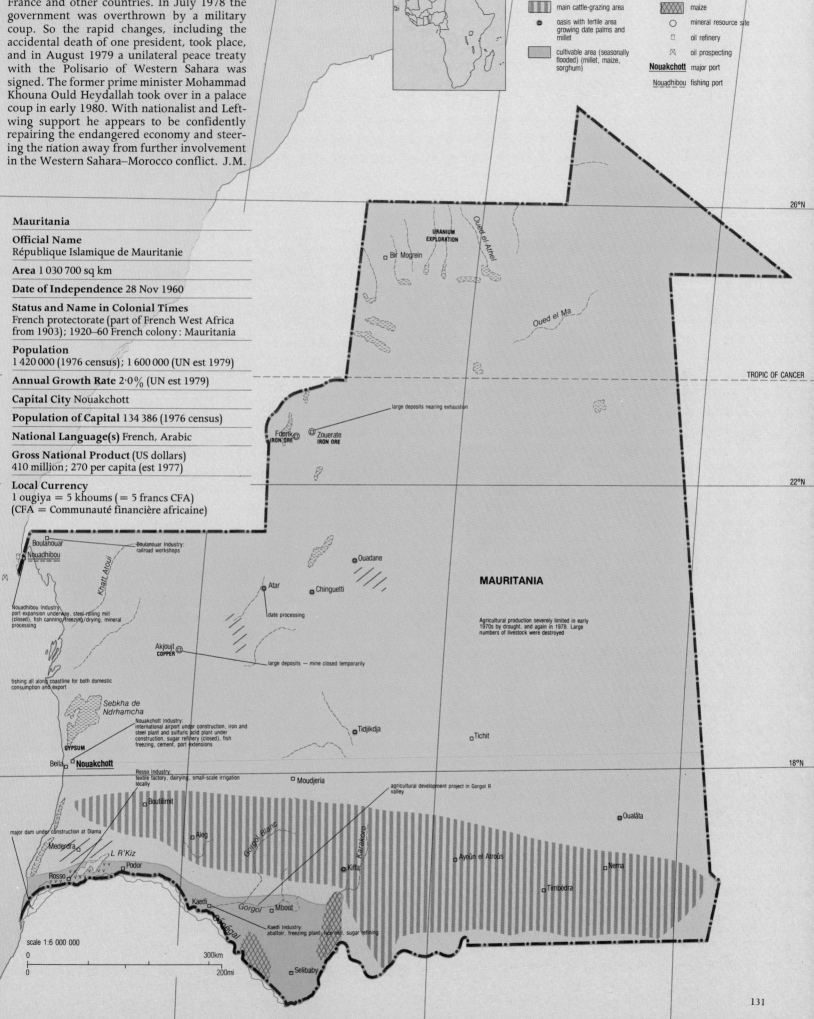

rilla war was a severe strain and Mauritania carried on only through support from Morocco, France and other countries. In July 1978 the government was overthrown by a military coup. So the rapid changes, including the accidental death of one president, took place, and in August 1979 a unilateral peace treaty with the Polisario of Western Sahara was signed. The former prime minister Mohammad Khouna Ould Heydallah took over in a palace coup in early 1980. With nationalist and Left-wing support he appears to be confidently repairing the endangered economy and steering the nation away from further involvement in the Western Sahara–Morocco conflict. J.M.

Mauritania

Official Name
République Islamique de Mauritanie

Area 1 030 700 sq km

Date of Independence 28 Nov 1960

Status and Name in Colonial Times
French protectorate (part of French West Africa from 1903); 1920–60 French colony: Mauritania

Population
1 420 000 (1976 census); 1 600 000 (UN est 1979)

Annual Growth Rate 2·0% (UN est 1979)

Capital City Nouakchott

Population of Capital 134 386 (1976 census)

National Language(s) French, Arabic

Gross National Product (US dollars)
410 million; 270 per capita (est 1977)

Local Currency
1 ougiya = 5 khoums (= 5 francs CFA)
(CFA = Communauté financière africaine)

Legend:
- desert — nomadic herding (camels, goats in north, sheep, cattle further south)
- main cattle-grazing area
- oasis with fertile area growing date palms and millet
- cultivable area (seasonally flooded) (millet, maize, sorghum)
- gum arabic
- rice
- maize
- mineral resource site
- oil refinery
- oil prospecting
- **Nouakchott** major port
- Nouadhibou fishing port

URANIUM EXPLORATION

Bir Mogrein

Oued el-Athel

Oued el Ma

TROPIC OF CANCER

large deposits nearing exhaustion

Fderik IRON ORE
Zouerate IRON ORE

Boulanour
Boulanour Industry: railroad workshops

Nouadhibou

Nouadhibou Industry: port expansion underway, steel rolling mill (closed), fish canning/freezing/drying, mineral processing

Krett Atoui

Ouadane

Atar
Chinguetti

date processing

Akjoujt COPPER

large deposits — mine closed temporarily

MAURITANIA

Agricultural production severely limited in early 1970s by drought, and again in 1978. Large numbers of livestock were destroyed

fishing all along coastline for both domestic consumption and export

Sebkha de Ndrhamcha

Nouakchott Industry: international airport under construction, iron and steel plant and sulfuric acid plant under construction, sugar refinery (closed), fish freezing, cement, port extensions

Tidjikdja

Tichit

GYPSUM
Beila **Nouakchott**

Rosso Industry: textile factory, dairying, small-scale irrigation locally

Moudjeria

agricultural development project in Gorgol R valley

Oualâta

major dam under construction at Diama

Mederdra

Boutilimit

Aleg

Gorgol Blanc

Kalakoro

Nema

L R'Kiz
Podor

Ayoûn el Atroûs

Kiffa

Rosso

Gorgol
Kaedi
Mbout

Timbédra

Kaedi Industry: abattoir, freezing plant, rice mill, sugar refining

Senegal

Selibaby

scale 1:6 000 000

0   300km

0   200mi

131

Senegal

Senegal is situated at the western extreme of the African continent, bounded by Mauritania to the north and northeast, Mali to the east and Guinea and Guinea-Bissau to the south. To the west is the Atlantic Ocean. From the Atlantic the Republic of the Gambia protrudes into the Senegalese interior like a finger – the bizarre outcome of 19th-century European rivalries in the colonization of Africa. Senegal is drained by the Senegal, Gambia and Casamance rivers. The Senegal, the only navigable river, is no longer important as a waterway.

The transitional climate is reflected in the landscape: the north is semidesert, the middle belt is savanna and the south is given to rain forest. Rainfall varies from about 280 millimeters in the north, to about 1650 millimeters in the south.

Senegal's principal ethno-linguistic groups include Wolof (about 25 per cent of the population), Serer, Fulani, Tukolor, Dyola and Malinke (Mandingo). Except for the largely nomadic Fulani, the rural populations are settled agriculturists. Senegal has five urban centers: Dakar (the capital), Saint-Louis, Rufisque, Thiès and Kaolack. The population is predominantly Muslim.

Early Arabic geographers refer to the 9th-century kingdom of Takrur on the Senegal river, one of the first Sudanese kingdoms to embrace Islam. From the 13th century, the Wolof empire dominated Senegal; in about 1488 a claimant to the empire visited Portugal. Senegal was an early participant in the Atlantic slave trade, but most slaves appear to have been transported from the Sudanic interior.

Senegal has strong historical ties with France. In 1638 French traders established a station, which later became the city of Saint-Louis, at the mouth of the Senegal river. The French were primarily interested in the gum arabic trade until the 1850s, after which the cultivation of peanuts began. The sale of peanut products to France has been the principal source of export revenue for Senegal ever since.

During the 19th century a series of Muslim *jihads* (wars of conversion) shook West Africa. The leader of one of the largest of these, al-Haj 'Umar, was born near Podor. 'Umar hoped to extend his conquests to the Senegalese coast, but was thwarted by the forces of the French general Faidherbe and forced to turn eastward. Faidherbe and his successors established military control over the Senegalese interior, putting down a number of resistance leaders.

Senegal was to have been the showpiece for France's official policy of *assimilation*, the making of Africans into black Frenchmen. Senegalese in four cities had full French citizenship and considerable access to education. In the 20th century a number of Senegalese were elected to the French National Assembly, including the man who was to become Senegal's first president, Léopold Sédar Senghor. The assimilation policy could not work in the hinterland, however, and the French had to rule through local authorities.

During World War II France's African holdings became particularly important, sup-

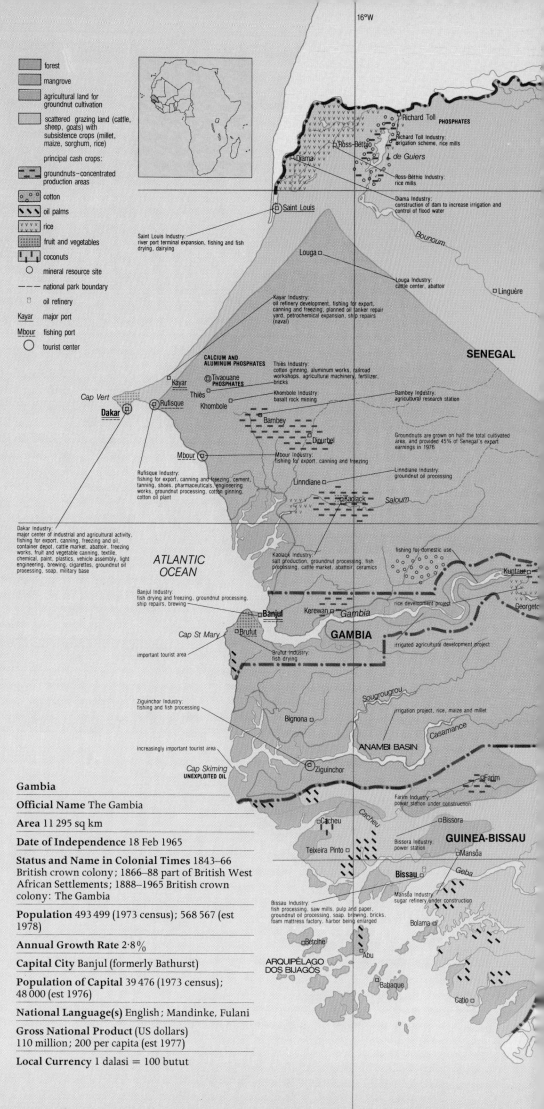

Gambia

Official Name The Gambia

Area 11 295 sq km

Date of Independence 18 Feb 1965

Status and Name in Colonial Times 1843–66 British crown colony; 1866–88 part of British West African Settlements; 1888–1965 British crown colony: The Gambia

Population 493 499 (1973 census); 568 567 (est 1978)

Annual Growth Rate 2·8%

Capital City Banjul (formerly Bathurst)

Population of Capital 39 476 (1973 census); 48 000 (est 1976)

National Language(s) English; Mandinke, Fulani

Gross National Product (US dollars) 110 million; 200 per capita (est 1977)

Local Currency 1 dalasi = 100 butut

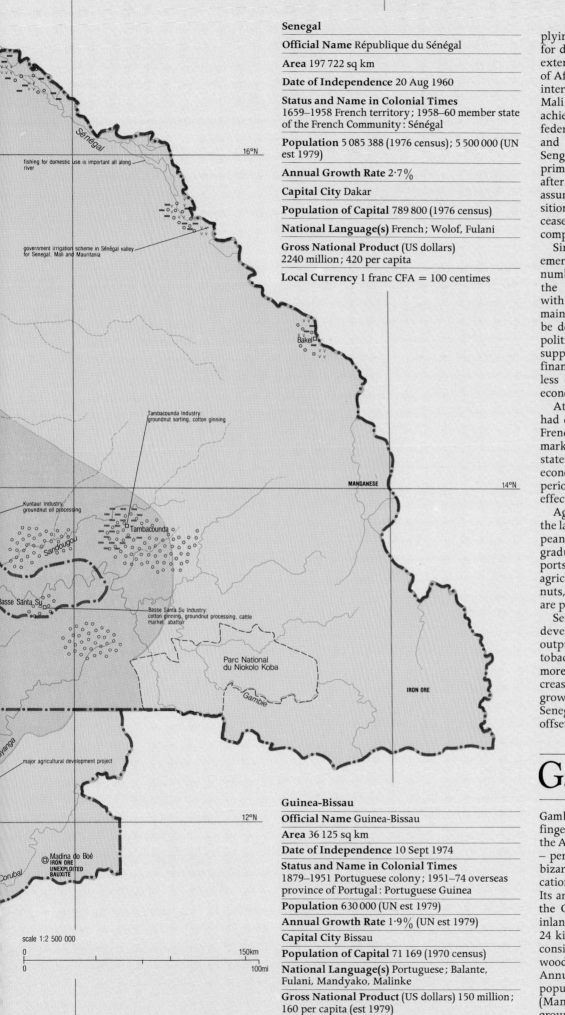

fishing for domestic use is important all along river

government irrigation scheme in Sénégal valley for Senegal, Mali and Mauritania

Sénégal

16°N

Bakel

Tambacounda Industry: groundnut sorting, cotton ginning

MANGANESE

14°N

Kuntaur Industry: groundnut oil processing

Tambacounda

Sandougou

Basse Santa Su

Basse Santa Su Industry: cotton ginning, groundnut processing, cattle market, abattoir

Parc National du Niokolo Koba

IRON ORE

Gambie

12°N

major agricultural development project

Madina do Boé
IRON ORE
UNEXPLOITED
BAUXITE

Corubal

scale 1:2 500 000

0 — 150km
0 — 100mi

Senegal

Official Name	République du Sénégal
Area	197 722 sq km
Date of Independence	20 Aug 1960
Status and Name in Colonial Times	1659–1958 French territory; 1958–60 member state of the French Community: Sénégal
Population	5 085 388 (1976 census); 5 500 000 (UN est 1979)
Annual Growth Rate	2·7%
Capital City	Dakar
Population of Capital	789 800 (1976 census)
National Language(s)	French; Wolof, Fulani
Gross National Product (US dollars)	2240 million; 420 per capita
Local Currency	1 franc CFA = 100 centimes

Guinea-Bissau

Official Name	Guinea-Bissau
Area	36 125 sq km
Date of Independence	10 Sept 1974
Status and Name in Colonial Times	1879–1951 Portuguese colony; 1951–74 overseas province of Portugal: Portuguese Guinea
Population	630 000 (UN est 1979)
Annual Growth Rate	1·9% (UN est 1979)
Capital City	Bissau
Population of Capital	71 169 (1970 census)
National Language(s)	Portuguese; Balante, Fulani, Mandyako, Malinke
Gross National Product (US dollars) 150 million;	160 per capita (est 1979)
Local Currency	1 Guinea peso = 100 centavos

plying soldiers as well as a base of operations for de Gaulle. In 1946 French citizenship was extended to all Senegalese. In 1956, on the eve of African independence, Senegal was granted internal self-government. In 1959 Senegal and Mali joined in the Mali Federation, which achieved independence the next year. The federation collapsed a few months afterward, and independent Senegal was born, with Senghor as president and Mamadou Dia as prime minister. Dia was imprisoned in 1962 after an alleged coup attempt and Senghor assumed increased powers. After 1963 opposition to Senghor's ruling party gradually ceased, although a great deal of political competition existed within the party.

Since 1974 new opposition parties have emerged, although their organization and number are regulated by the constitution. In the 1978 elections, Senghor was reelected with 82 per cent of the vote. Senegal has maintained its close ties with France; these may be deteriorating with the passing of Gaullist political leaders. Senegal has been a staunch supporter of African independence, although financial dependence on France has made it less outspoken on the question of Western economic domination.

At the time of Senegal's independence, it had one of the most developed economies in French West Africa. However, the loss of markets due to independence of its sister states, combined with France's decreased economic and physical presence and long periods of bad weather, has had disturbing effects on the economy.

Agriculture employs about 75 per cent of the labor force, with half the cultivated land in peanut production. In the 1960s France gradually discontinued its peanut price supports. Government policy aims to diversify agriculture, thus ending dependence on peanuts, and cotton, rice, sugar and vegetables are planted in increasing quantities.

Senegal has Francophone Africa's most developed manufacturing sector. Much of the output is concentrated in food, beverages and tobacco. The mining of phosphate has become more and more important as prices have increased on the world market. Tourism has grown substantially in the 1970s. However, Senegal depends on foreign assistance to help offset a chronic balance-of-trade problem.

M.L.

Gambia

Gambia, one of Africa's smallest states, forms a finger-like protrusion jutting eastward from the Atlantic Ocean into the Republic of Senegal – perhaps the best example of the sometimes bizarre geographical and political ramifications of the European colonization of Africa. Its area is confined to the navigable valley of the Gambia river, extending 470 kilometers inland from the sea and measuring only about 24 kilometers across in most places. The land consists of mangrove swamps, marshes and woodland areas largely cleared for cultivation. Annual rainfall is 1150 millimeters. Gambia's population is over 40 per cent Malinke (Mandingo); other major ethno-linguistic groups include Fulani, Wolof, Dyola, Serer and Soninke. About 90 per cent of the people

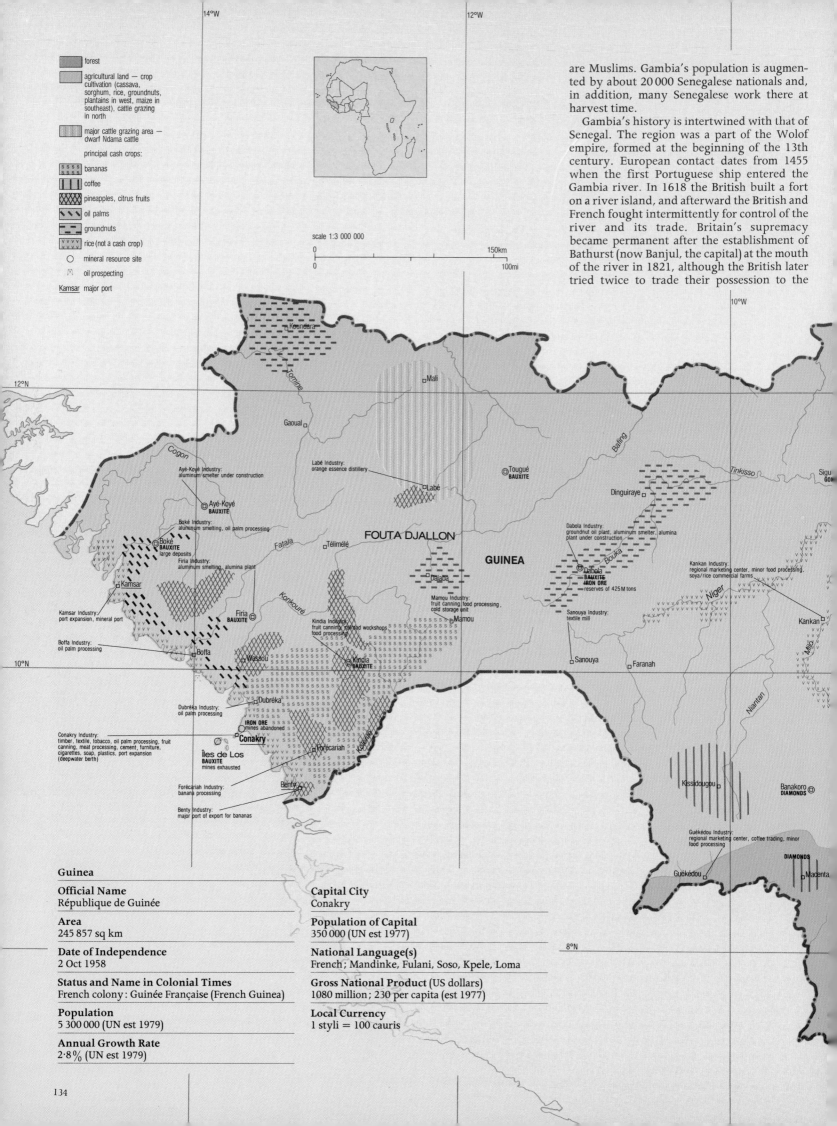

Legend

forest

agricultural land — crop cultivation (cassava, sorghum, rice, groundnuts, plantains in west, maize in southeast), cattle grazing in north

major cattle grazing area — dwarf Ndama cattle

principal cash crops:

SSSS bananas

coffee

pineapples, citrus fruits

oil palms

groundnuts

rice (not a cash crop)

○ mineral resource site

⊠ oil prospecting

Kamsar major port

scale 1:3 000 000

0   150km
0   100mi

are Muslims. Gambia's population is augmented by about 20 000 Senegalese nationals and, in addition, many Senegalese work there at harvest time.

Gambia's history is intertwined with that of Senegal. The region was a part of the Wolof empire, formed at the beginning of the 13th century. European contact dates from 1455 when the first Portuguese ship entered the Gambia river. In 1618 the British built a fort on a river island, and afterward the British and French fought intermittently for control of the river and its trade. Britain's supremacy became permanent after the establishment of Bathurst (now Banjul, the capital) at the mouth of the river in 1821, although the British later tried twice to trade their possession to the

Map labels

Koundara

Mali

Gaoual

Tominé

Cogon

Balin g

Tinkisso

Sigu GO

Ayé-Koyé Industry: aluminum smelter under construction

Labé Industry: orange essence distillery

Tougué BAUXITE

Dinguiraye

Ayé-Koyé BAUXITE

Labé

Boké Industry: aluminum smelting, oil palm processing

Boké BAUXITE large deposits

Fatala

Télimélé

FOUTA DJALLON

GUINEA

Bouka

Dabola Industry: groundnut oil plant, aluminum smelter, alumina plant under construction

Kankan Industry: regional marketing center, minor food processing, soya/rice commercial farms

Firia Industry: aluminum smelting, alumina plant

Kamsar

Dalaba

Dabola BAUXITE IRON ORE reserves of 425 M tons

Niger

Kamsar Industry: port expansion, mineral port

Firia BAUXITE

Konkouré

Kindia Industry: fruit canning, railroad workshops, food processing

Mamou Industry: fruit canning, food processing, cold storage unit

Mamou

Sanouya Industry: textile mill

Kankan

Milo

Boffa Industry: oil palm processing

Boffa

Wassou

Kindia BAUXITE

Sanouya

Faranah

Niantan

Dubréka Industry: oil palm processing

Dubréka

IRON ORE mines abandoned

Conakry Industry: timber, textile, tobacco, oil palm processing, fruit canning, meat processing, cement, furniture, cigarettes, soap, plastics, port expansion (deepwater berth)

Conakry

Forécariah

Koba

Îles de Los BAUXITE mines exhausted

Kissidougou

Banakoro DIAMONDS

Forécariah Industry: banana processing

Benty

Benty Industry: major port of export for bananas

Guékédou Industry: regional marketing center, coffee trading, minor food processing

DIAMONDS

Guékédou

Macenta

Guinea

Official Name
République de Guinée

Area
245 857 sq km

Date of Independence
2 Oct 1958

Status and Name in Colonial Times
French colony: Guinée Française (French Guinea)

Population
5 300 000 (UN est 1979)

Annual Growth Rate
2·8% (UN est 1979)

Capital City
Conakry

Population of Capital
350 000 (UN est 1977)

National Language(s)
French; Mandinke, Fulani, Soso, Kpele, Loma

Gross National Product (US dollars)
1080 million; 230 per capita (est 1977)

Local Currency
1 styli = 100 cauris

French, whose holdings in Senegal surrounded the tiny colony.

The people of the interior had for centuries resisted Islamic influences, but after 1850 a number of powerful Islamic leaders declared war on the local political leadership, and rapid conversion of the population ensued. In 1894 Britain declared a protectorate over the interior. The British governed through traditional rulers, giving little attention or money to Gambia until after World War II.

The independence movement in Gambia lagged behind that in other African countries. Political parties did not develop until the 1950s and the earliest of these were based in the urban coastal area. However, David (later Sir Dawda) Jawara formed the People's Progressive Party to represent the interior, and was named prime minister after the elections of 1962, the time at which internal self-government was achieved. Full independence came in 1965. In 1970 Gambia became a republic, with Jawara as president.

Politically Gambia has been one of the most stable countries in Africa. Opposition groups have made little headway against Jawara's party, which has retained power and popularity since independence. Of key importance to Gambia are relations with Senegal, which have improved over the years, though smuggling is a major point of contention. Jawara has said that he sees a union with Senegal as an eventual inevitability.

The Gambian economy is dependent on the peanut, the price of which is wholly controlled by external factors. Nevertheless, Gambia has been relatively prosperous in recent years, and, due to sound fiscal policies and government thrift (for instance, the country has no standing army), it has one of the strongest currencies in West Africa. Finance for development comes largely through foreign aid. Gambia is working toward self-sufficiency in the production of rice, the staple crop, and toward continued expansion of the developing tourist industry.

M.L.

Guinea-Bissau

Bounded by Senegal on the north, the Republic of Guinea on the east and south and the Atlantic Ocean on the west, the Republic of Guinea-Bissau includes, in addition to its mainland territory, the Bijagós archipelago and a string of coastal islands. The country is low, rarely rising to more than a few hundred meters above sea level, and is crisscrossed by a large number of rivers which are used for transportation. From the coastal swamps and rain forests, which are gouged with numerous inlets, the land slopes upward to a heavily forested interior plain, then to characteristic African savanna. The climate is hot, ranging from a mean high of 29° to a mean low of 25°. The country receives all its annual rainfall between December and May, an average of 2413 millimeters along the coast and 1397 millimeters inland. Apart from about 3000 Portuguese and Lebanese and a relatively small percentage of mestizos, the population is black African and represents some 30 identifiable tribes speaking a variety of tribal languages and dialects, in addition to a Portuguese–African *crioulo* quite similar to that spoken in the Cape Verde Islands. About 60 per cent of the population, mainly coast dwellers, are animists and about 35 per cent are Muslims.

Prior to European exploration, the area was occupied by coastal farmers. The Portuguese first came to the Guinea coast in the middle of the 15th century and maintained settlements there for centuries because of the slave trade. The Colony of Portuguese Guinea was established in 1879, its borders finally demarcated in 1905. The Portuguese waged almost constant campaigns of pacification against the inhabitants from 1884 to 1917 and again in 1925 and 1936. In 1958 the massacre of 50 striking dockworkers at Pijiguiti inaugurated the liberation struggle which ended with the establishment of the Republic of Guinea-Bissau in 1974.

During the liberation struggle, the already precarious economy was all but destroyed, but the coming of independence found the African Party for the Independence of Guinea-Bissau and Cape Verde (PAIGC) well prepared for power by reason of its prior administration of huge tracts of liberated territory. The PAIGC has erected a one-party state and seeks to advance rural development, rural electrification, mass literacy and agricultural development as well as unification with the Republic of Cape Verde. The government is republican, with popularly elected regional councils selecting delegates to the National Popular Assembly, which in turn selects the State Council, whose president is the nation's president.

The economy is almost entirely agricultural, with rice, maize, cotton and sugar cane being produced for domestic use, and peanuts, copra, palm kernels and vegetable oils for export. Some rubber, livestock and lumber are also exported. The government has been establishing experimental farms and centers to spearhead agricultural reform. Large plantations have been nationalized. Deposits of phosphates in the north and bauxite in the east and south remain largely unexploited. What little industrialization Guinea-Bissau has is concentrated in processing agricultural products and in construction. The government plans a number of dams and power plants to foster electrification and industrialization.

J.M.M.

Guinea

The People's Revolutionary Republic of Guinea is bordered by the Atlantic Ocean to the west, by Guinea-Bissau, Senegal and Mali to the north and east, by the Ivory Coast to the southeast and by Liberia and Sierra Leone to the south. The country's four natural geographic regions are the mangrove swamps and marshy lands along the coast (Lower Guinea), the extensive Fouta Djallon highlands which rise sharply from the coastal plain (Middle Guinea), the highlands in the southeast corner (the Forest Region) and the Niger plain in the northeast part of the country (Upper Guinea). The Fouta Djallon is the source of three major West African rivers: the Niger, Senegal and Gambia. The climate consists of two alternating seasons, a dry season from November to March and a wet season from April to October. The average annual temperature is over 20° but it is usually cooler inland on the Fouta Djallon plateau. Vegetation ranges from mangrove swamps along the coast to rain forest in the southeast and savanna grassland in the northeast.

Human settlement in the area of present-day Guinea predates the western Sudanic empires that emerged from the 10th century onwards. The next major influence on the population was the advent of Islam marked by the Muslim Fulani conquest of the Fouta Djallon during the second half of the 19th century. By the time of the French conquest in the 1890s Guinea's population consisted of the Susu along the coast, the Fulani on the Fouta Djallon, the Malinke in Upper Guinea and the Kissi, the Loma and the Kpelle, among others, in the forest region.

In September 1958, after about 60 years under French rule, Guinea became the first of the French colonies to achieve independence and was admitted to the UN in the same year. Since independence, Guinea has developed as

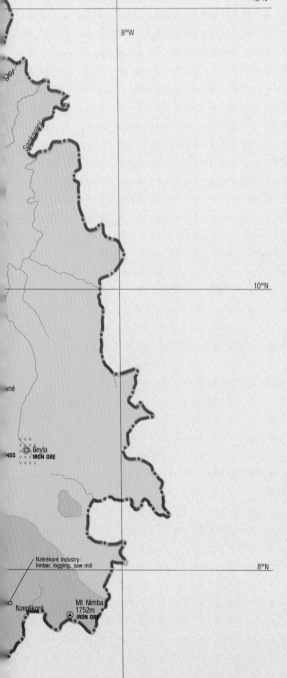

12°N
8°W
10°N

Beyla
IRON ORE

Nzérékoré Industry:
timber, logging, saw mill

8°N

Mt Nimba
1752m
IRON ORE

Nzérékoré

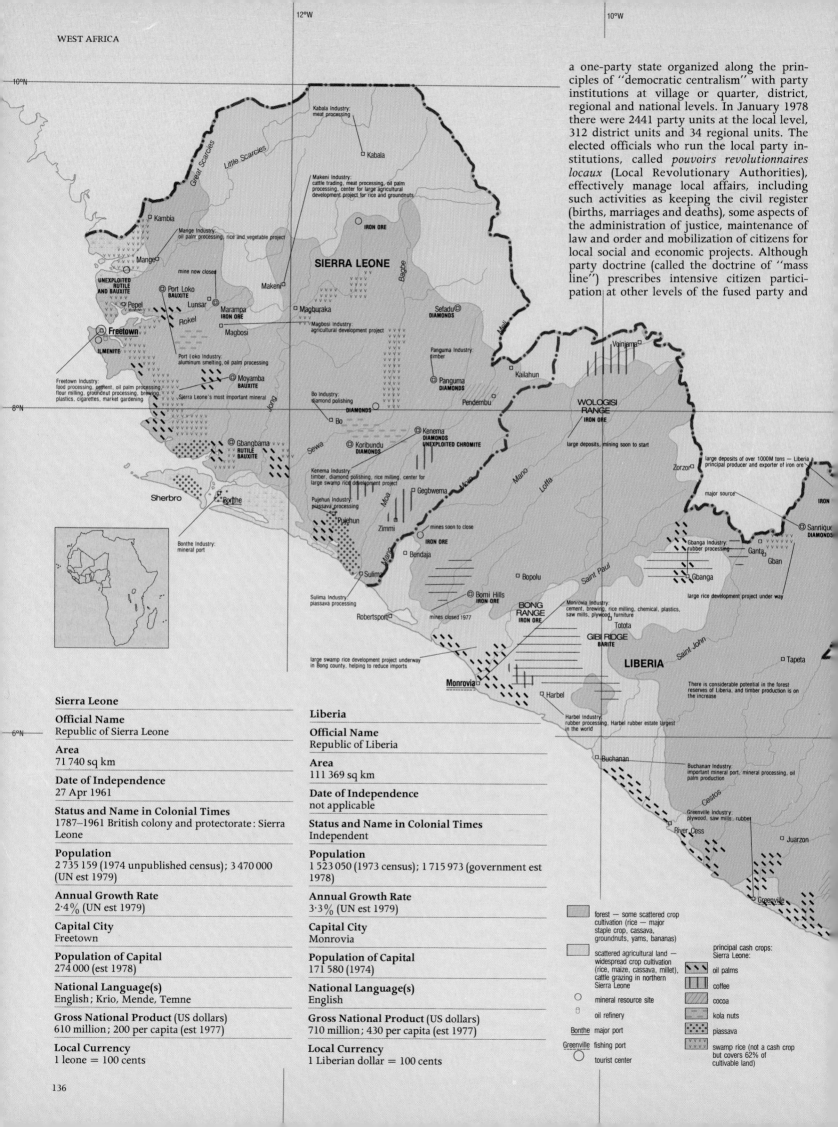

a one-party state organized along the principles of "democratic centralism" with party institutions at village or quarter, district, regional and national levels. In January 1978 there were 2441 party units at the local level, 312 district units and 34 regional units. The elected officials who run the local party institutions, called *pouvoirs revolutionnaires locaux* (Local Revolutionary Authorities), effectively manage local affairs, including such activities as keeping the civil register (births, marriages and deaths), some aspects of the administration of justice, maintenance of law and order and mobilization of citizens for local social and economic projects. Although party doctrine (called the doctrine of "mass line") prescribes intensive citizen participation at other levels of the fused party and

Kabala Industry: meat processing

Makeni Industry: cattle trading, meat processing, oil palm processing, center for large agricultural development project for rice and groundnuts

Mange Industry: oil palm processing, rice and vegetable project

Magbosi Industry: agricultural development project

Port Loko Industry: aluminum smelting, oil palm processing

Freetown Industry: food processing, cement, oil palm processing, flour milling, groundnut processing, brewing, plastics, cigarettes, market gardening

Sierra Leone's most important mineral

Bo Industry: diamond polishing

Panguma Industry: timber

Kenema Industry: timber, diamond polishing, rice milling, center for large swamp rice development project

Pujehun Industry: piassava processing

Bonthe Industry: mineral port

Sulima Industry: piassava processing

large swamp rice development project underway in Bong county, helping to reduce imports

large deposits, mining soon to start

large deposits of over 1000M tons — Liberia a principal producer and exporter of iron ore

major source

mines soon to close

mines closed 1977

Gbanga Industry: rubber processing

large rice development project under way

Monrovia Industry: cement, brewing, rice milling, chemical, plastics, saw mills, plywood, furniture

There is considerable potential in the forest reserves of Liberia, and timber production is on the increase

Harbel Industry: rubber processing, Harbel rubber estate largest in the world

Buchanan Industry: important mineral port, mineral processing, oil palm production

Greenville Industry: plywood, saw mills, rubber

mine now closed

Sierra Leone

Official Name
Republic of Sierra Leone

Area
71 740 sq km

Date of Independence
27 Apr 1961

Status and Name in Colonial Times
1787–1961 British colony and protectorate: Sierra Leone

Population
2 735 159 (1974 unpublished census); 3 470 000 (UN est 1979)

Annual Growth Rate
2·4% (UN est 1979)

Capital City
Freetown

Population of Capital
274 000 (est 1978)

National Language(s)
English; Krio, Mende, Temne

Gross National Product (US dollars)
610 million; 200 per capita (est 1977)

Local Currency
1 leone = 100 cents

Liberia

Official Name
Republic of Liberia

Area
111 369 sq km

Date of Independence
not applicable

Status and Name in Colonial Times
Independent

Population
1 523 050 (1973 census); 1 715 973 (government est 1978)

Annual Growth Rate
3·3% (UN est 1979)

Capital City
Monrovia

Population of Capital
171 580 (1974)

National Language(s)
English

Gross National Product (US dollars)
710 million; 430 per capita (est 1977)

Local Currency
1 Liberian dollar = 100 cents

forest — some scattered crop cultivation (rice — major staple crop, cassava, groundnuts, yams, bananas)

scattered agricultural land — widespread crop cultivation (rice, maize, cassava, millet), cattle grazing in northern Sierra Leone

principal cash crops: Sierra Leone:
oil palms
coffee
cocoa
kola nuts
piassava
swamp rice (not a cash crop but covers 62% of cultivable land)

○ mineral resource site
◻ oil refinery
Bonthe major port
Greenville fishing port
○ tourist center

state organization, administration at the district, regional and national levels is left to professional civil servants. These officials are expected to be committed party members.

Guinea's monolithic political institutional arrangements prohibit the existence of a formally organized opposition. Every Guinean is automatically a member of the Parti démocratique de Guinée (PDG), each adult paying his party dues with his tax until the latter was abolished in 1977. This monopolization of political power by the PDG has alienated many Guineans who are either in prison or have fled into voluntary exile in France or neighboring African states. By December 1978 the number of exiles was estimated at about 800000.

The regime's opponents claim that Guinea's economic potential has not been sufficiently realized and, in the opinion of some, Guinea has actually experienced economic regression since independence. The national developmental strategy attaches great importance to a planned state-controlled economy and some form of collectivist organization in the rural areas. About 70 state enterprises had been established by the early 1970s, but several mixed-enterprise companies have also been formed in partnership with investors from Western capitalist countries, Eastern socialist states and Third World states. It is largely through the latter enterprises that the country's rich mineral resources, especially bauxite and iron ore, are being exploited. In contrast to the relative progress in the industrial sector, the agricultural sector's performance has been rather poor. This is particularly true of food production where Guinea has remained a net importer of rice, the staple food.

In socio-cultural development, state monopoly appears to have produced impressive results, especially in education and health care. A national health service system covers both the urban and the rural areas. Great importance is attached to culture, which is considered an excellent means of preaching mass commitment to socialist ideology. Above all, the leaders display a conscious and systematic determination to promote inter-ethnic harmony and to contain all possible sources of conflict that could have adverse effects on social relations.

L.A.

Sierra Leone

Sierra Leone is bounded by Guinea to the north and east, Liberia to the southeast and the Atlantic Ocean to the west and southwest. From the ocean, mangrove swamps extend about 100 kilometers inland. An upland plateau covers the north and east, where there are also mountain ranges with some peaks exceeding 1800 meters. The country is mostly rain forest, although primary growth has been cleared for agriculture. Rainfall is heavy, particularly between June and September, and averages about 5000 millimeters in Freetown, the capital, and about 3500 millimeters in the north. None of the country's rivers is navigable.

The Mende people in the south and the Temne in the north together make up about three-fifths of the population. There are about nine smaller ethno-linguistic groups. The most prominent of these are the Creoles, citizens of Afro–European descent who live almost exclusively in the Freetown area and who comprise a western-educated elite. Krio, a language based on English but incorporating African and other European languages, is the tongue of the Creole people and is widely spoken throughout the country. About 30 per cent of the people are Muslims, Islam being most widely practiced in the north.

The origins of Sierra Leone's present ethnic composition are in the 15th and 16th centuries when the "Manes" – probably refugees from the break-up of the great Sudanic empires – invaded the area and integrated with local peoples. The primary societal unit was the small chiefdom rather than the tribe.

The colony of Sierra Leone was founded in 1787 as part of a scheme to find a home for unwanted free blacks and whites living in England and North America. In 1808 it became a British Crown Colony, growing as the British captured slave ships and released their cargoes at Freetown. The descendants of these groups became the present-day Creoles. Western missionary education and religion were firmly rooted among Sierra Leonean Creoles, and throughout the 19th century they were prominent in politics and trade in all of England's West African colonies. The colony prospered from the second half of the 19th century, largely from the export of palm-kernel products.

The British annexed the interior in stages, and in 1896 declared a protectorate over what is present-day Sierra Leone. The Temne and Mende chiefdoms unsuccessfully resisted this loss of sovereignty in the 1898 Hut Tax War. The colony declined economically after the turn of the century. Creole merchants could not compete with expatriate traders and confined their activities to the Freetown area. At the same time, Creoles lost much of their influence in government.

The independence movement was initially dominated by the Creoles. However, the interior peoples became politicized after World War II, and in 1951, when the British granted a new constitution, an interior-based political party led by Sir Milton Margai won the national elections. Supported by the Mende people in the south, Margai became prime minister when Sierra Leone achieved independence in 1961; however, divided ethnic loyalties and uneven economic development caused continued instability.

Margai died in 1964 and was succeeded by his brother, Albert. The winner of the 1967 elections appeared to be Margai's challenger, trade unionist Siaka Stevens, a northerner. The elections triggered three military coups, the last of which handed over power to Stevens. In 1971, after an abortive coup, Sierra Leone became a republic, with Stevens as president. Stevens signed a defense agreement with Guinea, and Guinean troops arrived to support the government. Rival political parties were ultimately suppressed. In 1978 a new constitution established one-party rule.

Economic imbalances account for much of Sierra Leone's political turmoil. Beginning in the 1950s, people flooded to the east to prospect for diamonds, resulting in a surge of wealth and subsequent uneven economic development which disrupted the political and social order. Existing mines, however, are said to have less than five years' life. Bauxite exports are rising.

About 71 per cent of the population participates in agriculture, rice being the most important crop. Most agriculture is subsistence production. Manufacturing is limited to consumer products such as beer and cigarettes. A number of government-backed development schemes were launched in the mid-1960s but most have closed down. Sierra Leone has strong ties with neighboring Liberia and plans for an eventual economic union with that country.

M.L.

Liberia

Liberia's longest boundary is with the Atlantic Ocean to the southwest. It is bordered to the northwest by Sierra Leone, to the northeast by Guinea and to the east by the Ivory Coast. A coastal plain extends about 55 kilometers inland; beyond is a plateau covered by thick rain forest. The northern highlands feature mountains rising to over 1700 meters. Most of the country experiences the rainy season from May to October. Monrovia, the capital, receives 4650 millimeters of rain annually, and has an average temperature of 26°. The country is drained by 15 rivers, none of them navigable.

The Americo–Liberians, descendants of the founders of the republic, comprise about 5 per cent of the population, although they dominate the politics and economics of Liberia. They speak English, practice Christianity and adhere to Western patterns of social organization. The other Liberians comprise 16 ethno-linguistic groups, divided into 124 chiefdoms. The largest of these groups are the Kpelle, in the interior, and the Bassa, on the southern coast. The rural populations largely practice

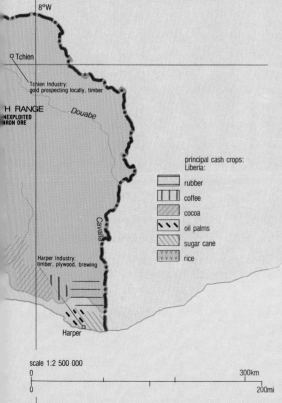

8°W

Tchien

Tchien Industry:
gold prospecting locally, timber

H RANGE
UNEXPLOITED
IRON ORE

Douabe

principal cash crops:
Liberia:

- rubber
- coffee
- cocoa
- oil palms
- sugar cane
- rice

Harper Industry:
timber, plywood, brewing

Cavalla

Harper

scale 1:2 500 000

0 ____ 300km
0 ____ 200mi

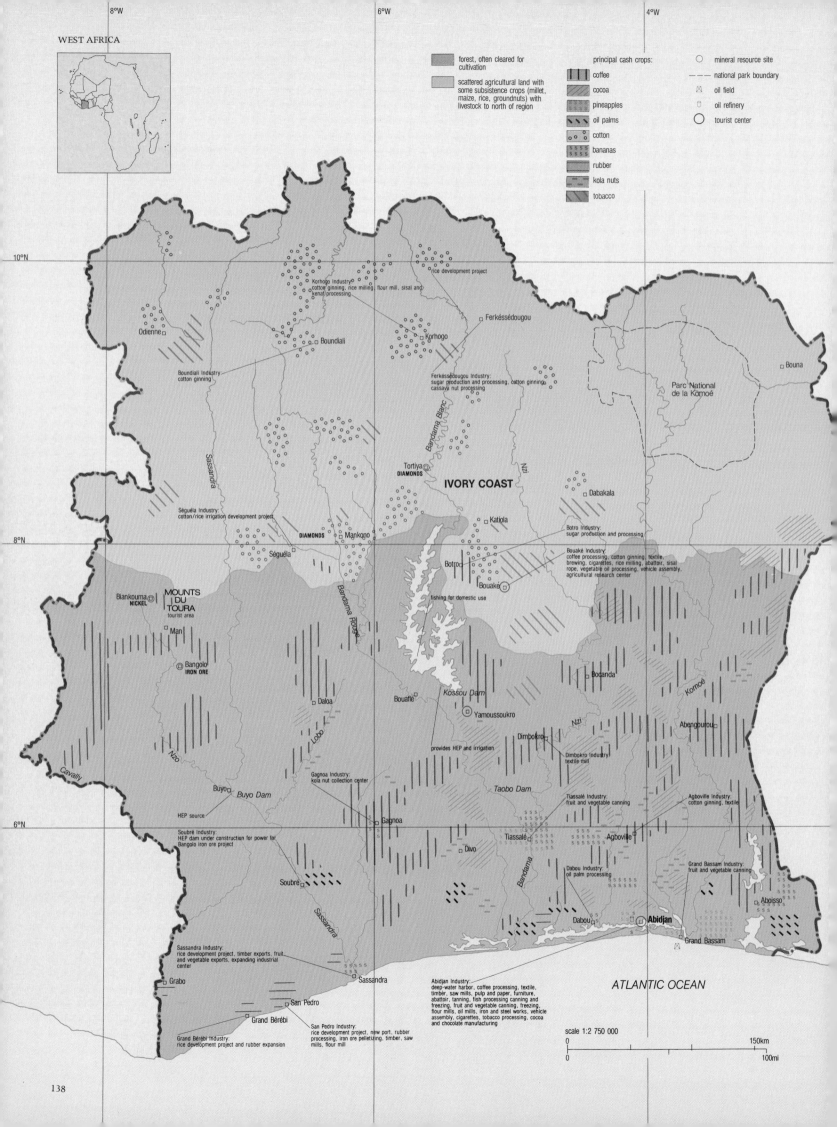

WEST AFRICA

forest, often cleared for cultivation

scattered agricultural land with some subsistence crops (millet, maize, rice, groundnuts) with livestock to north of region

principal cash crops:
coffee
cocoa
pineapples
oil palms
cotton
bananas
rubber
kola nuts
tobacco

○ mineral resource site
--- national park boundary
oil field
oil refinery
○ tourist center

8°W   6°W   4°W

10°N

rice development project

Korhogo Industry:
cotton ginning, rice milling, flour mill, sisal and kenaf processing

Odienne

Ferkéssédougou

Boundiali

Korhogo

Bouna

Boundiali Industry:
cotton ginning

Ferkéssédougou Industry:
sugar production and processing, cotton ginning, cassava nut processing

Parc National de la Komoé

Sassandra

Bandama Blanc

Nzi

8°N

Séguéla Industry:
cotton/rice irrigation development project

Tortiya
DIAMONDS

IVORY COAST

Dabakala

Botro Industry:
sugar production and processing

DIAMONDS   Mankono

Séguéla

Katiola

Botro

Bouaké Industry:
coffee processing, cotton ginning, textile, brewing, cigarettes, rice milling, abattoir, sisal rope, vegetable oil processing, vehicle assembly, agricultural research center

Bandama Rouge

Bouaké

Blankouma
NICKEL

MOUNTS
DU
TOURA
tourist area

fishing for domestic use

Man

Bocanda

Bangolo
IRON ORE

Komoé

Daloa

Bouaflé

Kossou Dam

Nzi

Abengourou

Yamoussoukro

Dimbokro

Nzo

Lobo

provides HEP and irrigation

Dimbokro Industry:
textile mill

Cavally

Buyo   Buyo Dam

Gagnoa Industry:
kola nut collection center

Taobo Dam

Tiassalé Industry:
fruit and vegetable canning

Agboville Industry:
cotton ginning, textile

6°N

HEP source

Soubré Industry:
HEP dam under construction for power for Bangolo iron ore project

Gagnoa

Divo

Tiassalé

Agboville

Grand Bassam Industry:
fruit and vegetable canning

Bandama

Dabou Industry:
oil palm processing

Soubré

Aboisso

Sassandra

Sassandra Industry:
rice development project, timber exports, fruit and vegetable exports, expanding industrial center

Dabou

Abidjan

Grand Bassam

Grabo

Abidjan Industry:
deep-water harbor, coffee processing, textile, timber, saw mills, pulp and paper, furniture, abattoir, tanning, fish processing canning and freezing, fruit and vegetable canning, freezing, flour mills, oil mills, iron and steel works, vehicle assembly, cigarettes, tobacco processing, cocoa and chocolate manufacturing

ATLANTIC OCEAN

Sassandra

San Pedro

Grand Bérébi

Grand Bérébi Industry:
rice development project and rubber expansion

San Pedro Industry:
rice development project, new port, rubber processing, iron ore pelletizing, timber, saw mills, flour mill

scale 1:2 750 000

0   150km

0   100mi

138

traditional religions; about 10 per cent of the population is Muslim. The country is considered underpopulated, with an average density of 14·5 per square kilometer.

Liberia's present-day settlement patterns began to emerge in the 15th and 16th centuries with the arrival of groups fleeing the break-up of the great Sudanic kingdoms. The first Americo–Liberians arrived from the USA in 1821 as the result of an American plan to finance the emigration and settlement of former slaves. They were joined by about 6000 Africans freed from slave ships by British and American patrols. In 1847 Liberia declared its independence. The nation in reality consisted of Monrovia and other centers of Americo–Liberian settlement, for there was no control over the interior until after 1915, when the last resistance movements were quashed.

American subsidies to Liberia decreased in the mid-19th century, and as exports also declined, Liberia looked to Europe for help, receiving loans on unfavorable terms. In 1927 the Firestone Company began its rubber plantation operations. Firestone became the dominant economic force in the country, and accordingly, Liberia's external orientation shifted back to the USA. In 1930 Liberia was internationally embarrassed when a League of Nations investigation implicated national leaders in forced labor schemes.

William Tubman, president from 1944 to 1971, was the first actively to advocate integration of the interior peoples into the political system. In 1945 they achieved representation in government, and in 1947 universal suffrage was declared. Liberia joined the Allies in World War II and became a strategic link in the supply route. Later it became a charter member of the UN. Since World War II Liberia has been able substantially to reduce its dependence on Firestone through diversification.

Tubman's successor, William Tolbert, attempted to continue Tubman's policies, but was assassinated in a military coup led by Samuel K. Doe in 1980. Tolbert's regime was accused of corruption and of failure to move

fast enough to share political power with the interior peoples.

Until the coup government in Liberia was modeled on the US structure, with a bicameral legislature, an executive branch and a supreme court. However, all power was granted to the central government, which also appointed local officials. Political power rested with the True Whig Party, which won every election since 1877.

Almost three-quarters of Liberia's population engage in agriculture, the primary food crops being rice and cassava. Per-acre rice production is low and attempts are being made to improve it. Cash crops include rubber, coffee and cocoa. Rubber accounted for about 12 per cent of Liberia's 1975 exports, with Firestone producing about 40 per cent of that amount. Liberia's forest reserves are only beginning to be developed and show great potential. Iron ore accounted for 75 per cent of 1975 exports and new discoveries continue to be made. Diamonds are also an important export. Oil prospecting has begun to pay off after 10 years of operations. Industrial development remains limited, although more advanced than most sub-Saharan African countries. The government had been developing the economy and infrastructure through a series of five-year plans, financed internally and by foreign loans and grants.

Until the recent coup, Liberia's economic and political future looked promising. Whether the promise will be fulfilled is now uncertain.

M.L.

Ivory Coast

The Ivory Coast occupies about 1 per cent of the surface of the African continent. Approximately 46 per cent of the Ivory Coast is covered with rain forest which is thickest in the southwest part of the country. The northern third of the country is wooded savanna land which extends south between the Bandama and Nzi rivers to form the Baoulé savanna. The country is largely flat, rolling land except for the region of Man, which is noted for its beautiful mountains and waterfalls. Other hilly areas are near Boungouanou, the Baoulé chain and the granite domes and inselbergs of the Odienné–Boundiali region. The sea coast is of two very distinct types divided by the estuary of the Bandama river. West of the town of Fresco the coast is rocky with cliffs and small picturesque bays and beaches (San Pedro, Sassandra, Monogaga). East of Fresco a long sandy island separates the ocean from a series of lagoons stretching 300 kilometers to the Tanoé river and the border of Ghana.

The Ivory Coast region is the meeting place of several major ethnic and linguistic groups. The original inhabitants are unknown but during the 16th to 18th centuries Mande speakers moved into the north as traders and settlers, brought by gold and kolanuts which they traded north to Mali. They founded Bornu (17th century) and such kingdoms as Kong (18th century) and Kabadougou (19th century). The Agni and Baoulé moved into the area east of the Bandama river as a result of the growth of the Asante empire in the 18th

century and other Akan political developments.

The coastal area was not hospitable to Europeans and, even though the French tried to establish themselves at Assinie in 1637 and again in 1838, they had only a nominal claim to a presence there until Arthur Verdier and his aide, Treich-Laplène, settled in eastern Ivory Coast during the 1870s and 1880s. The French explorer L. G. Binger who traveled down from the Sudan in 1887–88 was named the first governor of the colony in 1893 and such great colonialists as Maurice Delafosse and Jean Marie Clozel played a major role in the attempted "peaceful penetration" of the mostly unconquered interior of the Ivory Coast. The north of Ivory Coast was the scene of the last great struggles of the famous Malinke warrior, Samori Touré, who set up his second empire in Dabakala (1893–98), destroyed Kong (1897) and finally was captured and exiled by the French in September 1898. In 1908 Gabriel Angoulvant was named military governor and he conquered by force of arms the many peoples of Ivory Coast. The conquest and wars of resistance lasted from 1908 to 1915.

In 1903 a railroad was begun from Abidjan, though it did not reach its present terminus, Ouagadougou, Upper Volta, until 1954. It was not until 1950 that the Canal of Vridi was opened and Abidjan became a seaport with ships able to enter the lagoon. Since then the Ivorien economy has grown spectacularly and it is one of the world's leading exporters of coffee, cocoa, wood, pineapples, kola and bananas, and has rising exports of rubber, vegetable oils, palm kernels, soybean, cotton and refined oil. Ivory Coast has relied heavily on foreign investment and has made a great effort to attract foreign capital; the French and Lebanese have taken particular advantage of this.

The political situation has developed since 1944 under the astute leadership of Félix Houphouet-Boigny. Aided by such capable followers as Mamadou Coulibaly, Ouezzin Coulibaly, Joseph Anoma and many others, Houphouet-Boigny founded the Rassemblement Démocratique Africaine (RDA), then led the RDA through a series of political maneuvers culminating in the Loi Cadre (1956) and the independence of the French-speaking African countries.

Ivory Coast government is quite conservative and very pro-French. The Parti Démocratique de la Côte d'Ivoire-RDA (PDCI-RDA) is the sole political party and so long as the Vieux (as Houphouet-Boigny is called) remains at the helm (he was born in 1905), the political stance of the Ivory Coast remains clearly defined by its close cooperation with France. The Vieux has been able to maintain a remarkable stability and growth rate because of his political pragmatism and the wealth of the country. However, the external debt has reached considerable proportions and the more obvious development projects have been completed. Will the country be able to weather the passing of the Vieux or a serious bout of belt tightening? The Ivory Coast and the Ivorien people have shown a remarkable commitment to modernization and have repeatedly proved wrong the Cassandras predicting the end of the "Ivorien miracle."

J.O'S.

Ivory Coast

Official Name
République de Côte d'Ivoire

Area 322 463 sq km

Date of Independence 7 Aug 1960

Status and Name in Colonial Times
1893–1960 French colony (part of French West Africa)

Population
6 670 912 (1975 census); 7 500 000 (UN est 1979)

Annual Growth Rate
3·8% (1965–78); 2·7% (UN est 1979)

Capital City Abidjan

Population of Capital
921 682 (1975 census); 1 242 000 (est 1978)

National Language(s)
French; Malinke

Gross National Product (US dollars)
5180 million; 710 per capita (est 1977)

Local Currency
1 franc CFA = 100 centimes

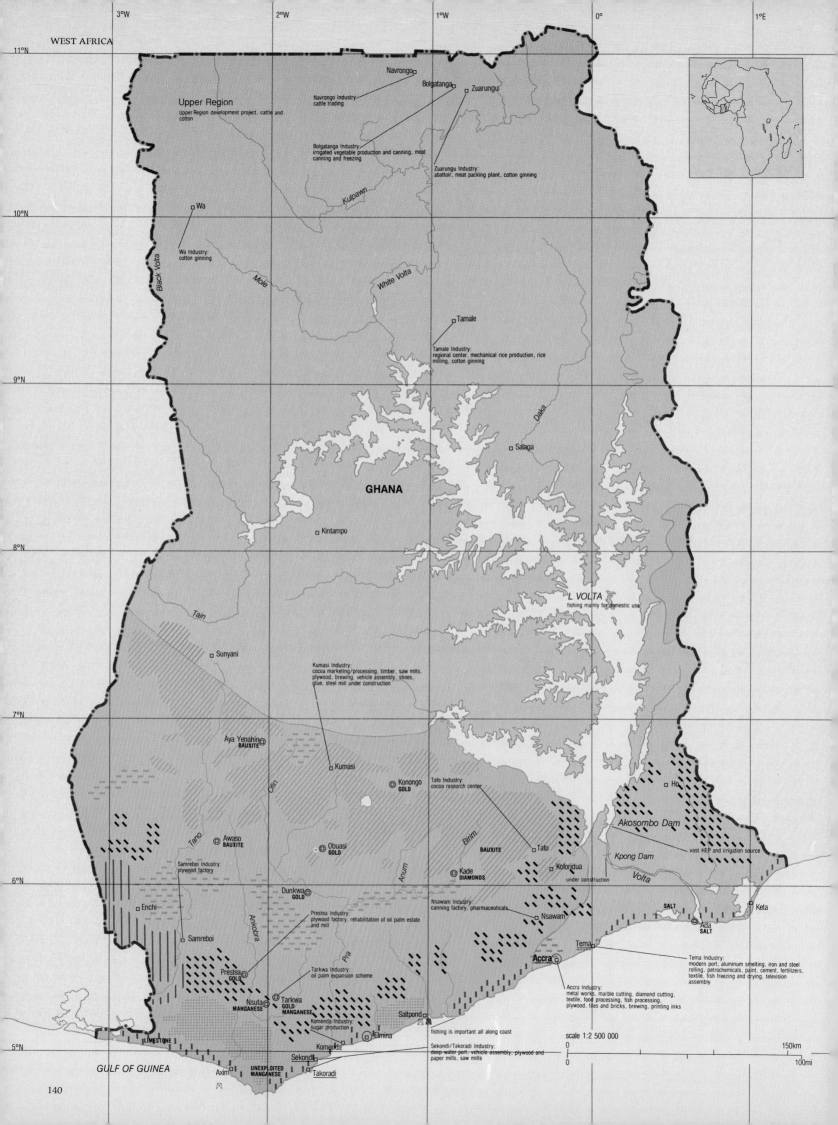

WEST AFRICA

11°N

Upper Region
Upper Region development project, cattle and
cotton

Navrongo
Navrongo Industry:
cattle trading

Bolgatanga
Zuarungu

Bolgatanga Industry:
irrigated vegetable production and canning, meat
canning and freezing

Zuarungu Industry:
abattoir, meat packing plant, cotton ginning

□ Wa
Wa Industry:
cotton ginning

10°N

Black Volta

Kulpawn

Mole

White Volta

□ Tamale
Tamale Industry:
regional center, mechanical rice production, rice
milling, cotton ginning

9°N

Daka

□ Salaga

GHANA

□ Kintampo

8°N

Tain

L VOLTA
fishing mainly for domestic use

□ Sunyani

Kumasi Industry:
cocoa marketing/processing, timber, saw mills,
plywood, brewing, vehicle assembly, shoes,
glue, steel mill under construction

7°N

Aya Yenahin
BAUXITE

Ofin

□ Kumasi

Konongo
GOLD

Tafo Industry:
cocoa research center

□ Ho

Akosombo Dam

Tano

Awaso
BAUXITE

Obuasi
GOLD

Birim

BAUXITE

□ Tafo

vast HEP and irrigation source

Kpong Dam

under construction

Volta

Samreboi Industry:
plywood factory

Ankobra

Dunkwa
GOLD

Anum

Kade
DIAMONDS

Koforidua

6°N

Enchi □

Prestea Industry:
plywood factory, rehabilitation of oil palm estate
and mill

Pra

Nsawam Industry:
canning factory, pharmaceuticals

□ Nsawam

SALT

□ Keta

□ Samreboi

Prestea
GOLD

Tarkwa Industry:
oil palm expansion scheme

Nsuta
MANGANESE

Tarkwa
GOLD
MANGANESE

Komenda Industry:
sugar production

□ Saltpond

Tema

Accra

Ada
SALT

Tema Industry:
modern port, aluminum smelting, iron and steel
rolling, petrochemicals, paint, cement, fertilizers,
textile, fish freezing and drying, television
assembly

Accra Industry:
metal works, marble cutting, diamond cutting,
textile, food processing, fish processing,
plywood, tiles and bricks, brewing, printing inks

□ Elmina

fishing is important all along coast

LIMESTONE

Komenda

Sekondi

Axim

UNEXPLOITED
MANGANESE

Takoradi

Sekondi/Takoradi Industry:
deep-water port, vehicle assembly, plywood and
paper mills, saw mills

scale 1:2 500 000

0   150km

0   100mi

5°N

GULF OF GUINEA

Ghana

Extending from the Gulf of Guinea some 640 kilometers inland, Ghana ranges from a narrow coastal plain through a tropical forest belt to the northern savanna region. In the precolonial period, large parts of the country were often integrated under the aegis of centralized states – for instance the Gonja kingdom in the north or the Asante and Akwamu states in the south.

The first contacts with Western nations were made at the coast. British colonial rule grew out of trading contacts and treaty arrangements made with the Fante states there. In the 19th century Britain gradually extended its influence and control, buying out other European trading powers, suppressing the slave trade and allying itself with the Fante against the powerful Asante state of the southern interior. Britain annexed the territory south of the Pra river in 1874, the Northern Territories by 1900 and conquered Asante by 1902. The new colony arbitrarily brought together a host of very different peoples – although Akan languages are spoken widely through the south.

Little further unity was imposed on the colony during the period of British rule. Developments in all fields were extremely uneven. Virtually all exports, such as minerals, timber and agricultural products, were produced in the southern third of the colony. Northerners on the whole participated in the colony's economic development only by migrating south as laborers for the cocoa farms and mines. As elsewhere in Africa, the economy was based on the production and extraction of primary products, with little industrial development. Nevertheless, at independence Ghana enjoyed a small foreign debt and large foreign reserves.

In most areas – education, medicine, building and communications – development was concentrated in the south. Urbanization intensified, both around the ports and mining areas of the south, and also around traditional centers like Kumasi. Virtually all secondary schools, hospitals and industry were in the southern third of the country.

Administratively, the government did little to unite the various regions. The original Gold Coast colony, British Togoland (a mandate after World War I), Asante and the Northern Territories were all administered separately. The colony was not united with Asante till 1946, and British Togoland was not added until a pre-independence plebiscite. The problems of regionalism inevitably surfaced in politics, given the administrative fragmentation and the uneven development. Both in the pre- and post-independence periods there have always been regional parties. Nkrumah's Convention People's Party (CPP) most closely approached national party status in the pre-independence period, but even then the opposition to the CPP was to some extent along regional lines.

Until the period following World War II African political activity was very much limited to the educated urban minority of the south. Such people made up the membership of the Congress of British West Africa, and the

Youth Conference, and they demanded further participation in the existing colonial system. After the war, under the pressure of rapid social and political change, politics became a demand for independence rather than for reform. The major political force was the United Gold Coast Convention (UGCC), led by lawyers and still elitist in its membership. In 1947 Kwame Nkrumah returned to the Gold Coast after 12 years in the USA and Britain, and became its secretary. Under him the UGCC began to acquire mass support. But he came into conflict with the elitist leaders and in 1949 broke away to form the Convention People's Party. The CPP was a popular party in a way the UGCC had not been, with a younger, more impatient and less educated following. Nkrumah was arrested and imprisoned after a series of strikes, but the CPP won elections under a new constitution. Nkrumah was released in 1951 to form a government, becoming prime minister in 1952 and in 1957 president of independent Ghana – the first British colony to gain independence.

Even before 1957, Nkrumah's first government had used the country's large reserves to promote development. There was much investment in agriculture and in the economy in general, and social services, education and communications were expanded. But the problems of regionalism continued. The CPP won handily in the 1954 elections but was challenged by the National Liberation Movement (NLM), a largely Asante group, immediately afterwards. The British ordered new elections in 1956. These also the CPP won; the NLM had not expanded much beyond its ethnic base. In the first years of Nkrumah's rule, he moved to strengthen the CPP and to curb regional opposition. The economy at independence was overwhelmingly in the hands of expatriate companies and at first little effort was made to change this pattern. The Volta river project – to provide electricity, irrigation and the exploitation of bauxite – was a key element in the plan for increased industrialization. The standard of living was high, and social services continued to expand, although the economy developed little independence. In foreign policy Ghana aimed at forging strong links within Africa – putting the ideals of pan-Africanism into practice – and the relationship with the Commonwealth and the USA was strong.

From about mid-1960 Nkrumah initiated major policy changes. He had long regarded himself as a socialist, and now initiated state participation in industry, banking and the import–export sector. Much of the state investment, however, was begun without sufficient capital, technicians, raw materials and planning. Inefficiency, combined with a fall in cocoa prices, led to severe shortages and virtual bankruptcy.

Nkrumah's economic policies and his increasing contacts with communist nations alienated many of his CPP followers. At the same time Nkrumah increased his personal power and a personality cult was fostered around him. The new constitution of 1960 (when Ghana became a republic) gave him enormous control over legislation and appointments in the civil service, and a one-party state was declared. There were accusations that the plebiscites that authorized these changes had been rigged. The 1965

---

forest, often cleared for cultivation

subsistence agriculture (millet, maize, sorghum, rice) livestock in north, becoming more productive to south with intensive cultivation around lake

principal cash crops:

cocoa

oil palms

coffee

kola nuts

coconuts

fruit and vegetables

○ mineral resource site

⊠ oil field

⬔ gas field

⊟ oil refinery

⊠ oil prospecting

Sekondi major port

Tema fishing port

○ tourist center

11°N

10°N

9°N

8°N

7°N

Ghana

Official Name
Republic of Ghana

Area
238 537 sq km

Date of Independence
6 Mar 1957

Status and Name in Colonial Times
British colony: The Gold Coast

Population
8 559 313 (1970 census); 11 700 000 (UN est 1979)

Annual Growth Rate
3·3% (UN est 1979)

Capital City
Accra

Population of Capital
849 000 (est 1970)

National Language(s)
English; Akan, Ewe

Gross National Product (US dollars)
4080 million; 380 per capita (est 1977)

Local Currency
1 new cedi = 100 pesewas

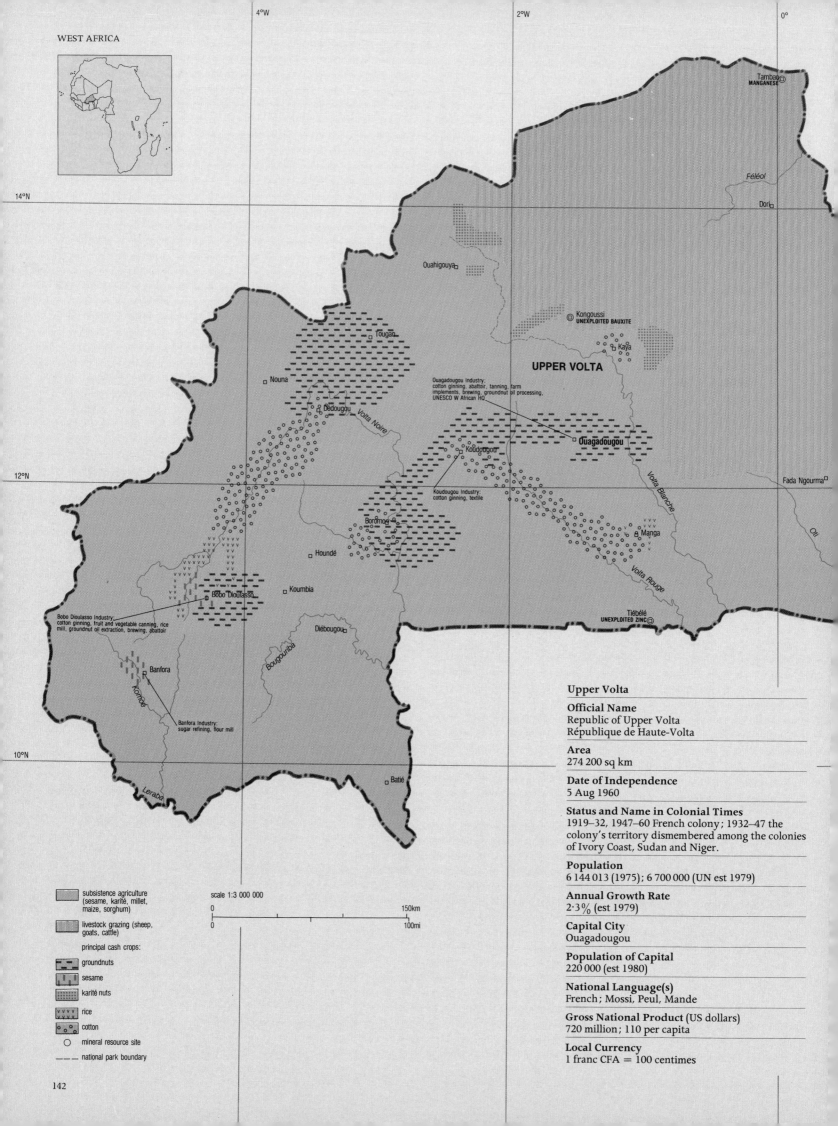

WEST AFRICA

14°N

Féléol

Tambao
MANGANESE

Dori

Ouahigouya

Tougan

Kongoussi
UNEXPLOITED BAUXITE

Kaya

UPPER VOLTA

Nouna

Dédougou

Ouagadougou Industry:
cotton ginning, abattoir, tanning, farm
implements, brewing, groundnut oil processing,
UNESCO W African HQ

Ouagadougou

Volta Noire

Koudougou

12°N

Fada Ngourma

Koudougou Industry:
cotton ginning, textile

Bordmo

Volta Blanche

Houndé

Manga

Bobo Dioulasso

Koumbia

Volta Rouge

Bobo Dioulasso Industry:
cotton ginning, fruit and vegetable canning, rice
mill, groundnut oil extraction, brewing, abattoir

Diébougou

Tiébélé
UNEXPLOITED ZINC

Banfora

Bougouriba

Komoé

Banfora Industry:
sugar refining, flour mill

10°N

Batié

Leraba

Upper Volta

Official Name
Republic of Upper Volta
République de Haute-Volta

Area
274 200 sq km

Date of Independence
5 Aug 1960

Status and Name in Colonial Times
1919–32, 1947–60 French colony; 1932–47 the
colony's territory dismembered among the colonies
of Ivory Coast, Sudan and Niger.

Population
6 144 013 (1975); 6 700 000 (UN est 1979)

Annual Growth Rate
2·3% (est 1979)

Capital City
Ouagadougou

Population of Capital
220 000 (est 1980)

National Language(s)
French; Mossi, Peul, Mande

Gross National Product (US dollars)
720 million; 110 per capita

Local Currency
1 franc CFA = 100 centimes

subsistence agriculture
(sesame, karité, millet,
maize, sorghum)

livestock grazing (sheep,
goats, cattle)

principal cash crops:

groundnuts

sesame

karité nuts

rice

cotton

mineral resource site

national park boundary

scale 1:3 000 000

0   150km

0   100mi

elections were canceled and the Preventive Detention Act was used to cope with opposition. Finally, he alienated the police and army and dismissed senior army officers. This was the final outrage. The army seized power in February 1966, while he was out of the country. He went into exile in Guinea and died in 1972.

A National Liberation Council was set up. It introduced various austerity measures and, aided by loans and gifts from abroad, achieved some economic recovery. Relations with neighboring states, strained during Nkrumah's later years, improved. The NLC

moved in 1968 to return to civil government, handing over to Dr K. A. Busia's Progress Party in October 1969. The army, however, intervened again in January 1972, under Colonel I. K. Acheampong. The economic situation continued to deteriorate. Acheampong became more and more repressive and dissatisfaction increased, articulated especially by professionals and in Asante. Under pressure to make concessions, Acheampong devised a plan for non-party civilian rule, under heavy domination by the military. This plan was widely opposed, despite narrow approval in another rigged plebiscite, and Acheampong was overthrown from within the army in July 1978.

The Chief of Staff and new head of state, Lieutenant General F. W. K. Akuffo, immediately set in motion the return to civilian rule. Despite a coup by junior officers in June 1979, the schedule of elections was maintained. Parliamentary and presidential elections were held in July 1979, resulting in the absolute majority of the People's National Party, a direct descendant of the CPP. This civilian government took over in September 1979 but the army, especially the junior officers, maintain the intention of scrutinizing its activities from behind the scenes.   I.S.

Upper Volta

Upper Volta lies between 10° and 15° north, within the bend of the Niger river, and is over 500 kilometers from its main outlet to the sea, the port-capital of Abidjan, Ivory Coast.

Three ecological zones, the sahelian, Sudanic and Guinean, belts of increasing rainfall running from east to west, cross the country. The agricultural population, 90 per cent of the total, depends on the adequacy and timely arrival of the seasonal rains which begin in April in the south and end in October.

Population densities vary greatly. The central region of the Mossi, the largest ethnic group, contains over half the total population (average density – 40 persons per square kilometer), and although only 6 per cent of the total land in the Mossi region is arable, certain overpopulated areas maintain over 190 persons per square kilometer. Upper Volta has only two major cities, Ouagadougou and Bobo Dioulasso.

The Mossi kingdoms of Ouagadougou, Yatenga and Gourma dominate in the early history of the region. Having withstood the expansion of the empires of Mali and Songhay, they were until recently little influenced by Islam, and in this century were strongly proselytized by French Catholic missionaries. Both Islam and Christianity have made strong inroads, but the majority of the people follow traditional religions. The area was annexed by the French in the 1890s when they defeated competing British and German efforts. Most of the region was integrated into the French Sudan at the turn of the century.

French administration proved schizophrenic, alternately composing and dismembering the territory until 1946. Lack of natural resources and isolation frustrated development visions. The greatest resource in 1900, as now, was surplus manpower. During World War I men were heavily conscripted as soldiers, as plantation laborers in Ivory Coast, and for forced labor within the colony. This recruitment, coupled with heavy taxation, led to widespread revolt. Thousands migrated to the Gold Coast. Representative government came to Upper Volta in 1957 with membership in the French Union in 1958. Full independence followed in 1960. Ties with France remain strong.

Upper Volta is closely tied economically to Ivory Coast, its major export customer in cereals and the residence of perhaps one million laborers from Upper Volta. Upper Volta has charted a conservative economic course since independence, based on high importation duties and limited capital investment. The discovery of manganese and phosphates in isolated regions in the east of the country brings hope of European investment for extraction, but the government development plans envision no change in the policy which has resulted in overall balance-of-payments surpluses since independence. Already the recipient of considerable foreign aid, Upper Volta relies on outside sources for new development. The sahel drought of the early 1970s set back development projections measurably.

Upper Volta has had only two heads of state since independence. Maurice Yameogo, a Mossi, served from 1960 to 1966 when a military coup ended his tenure. Then 1979 saw a return to civilian rule as the former head of the military government, General Sangoulé Lamazina, became the new popularly elected civilian president.

W.E.

Togo

Togo shares a boundary with Ghana and has had a long relationship with the peoples of Ghana. Like Ghana, Togo stretches about 800 kilometers inland from the Gulf of Guinea through coastal, forest and savanna zones, but its coastline is only 52 kilometers long. At its height the Asante empire included parts of Togo. The Ewe people live on both sides of the modern border with Ghana and the natural links of trade and kinship continue.

Generally, in West Africa, European colonization occurred where earlier commercial interests had developed. In Togo, although the French government had supported the establishment of commercial posts, German diplomatic maneuvers and the expansion of trade into the interior culminated in German colonial rule after 1884. In common with other colonial powers, the Germans found it necessary to rely on local authorities in order to govern their territories. Where obvious chiefs existed they were recognized and used to administer government directives and collect taxes. In other parts of Togo, such as in Lomé district, political organization rarely extended beyond the village level. In such areas the Germans, having no inclination at the time to study social structure, simply created "chiefs," who operated as far as possible within the traditional context. The Germans began a study of Ewe law, hoping to issue a new legal code, but were forestalled by World War I.

The beginnings of an infrastructure were laid in the German period. Railroads were built along the coast and into the interior. German goods carried in this way were traded across to the Northern Territories of the Gold Coast, overshadowing British goods in many markets. Agricultural development and most land remained in African hands.

After World War I Togo was divided between the British and the French, under a League of Nations mandate. British Togoland was administered in a similar fashion to the rest of the Gold Coast. Most traditional chiefs recognized by the Germans were in the area now administered by Britain, and they fitted neatly into the pattern of indirect rule. The impact of the mandate was more significant in the French sector. The rest of French West Africa was highly centralized and ruled directly from Dakar. Togo, however, had its own High Commissioner and financial autonomy. The mandate ensured that forced labor and conscription were severely restricted and the French were not allowed to levy protective tariffs or keep out merchants of other nations. From the beginning of the mandate there was greater African participation in government, in an advisory capacity at first.

One result of the division of German Togoland was the rise of ethnic nationalism

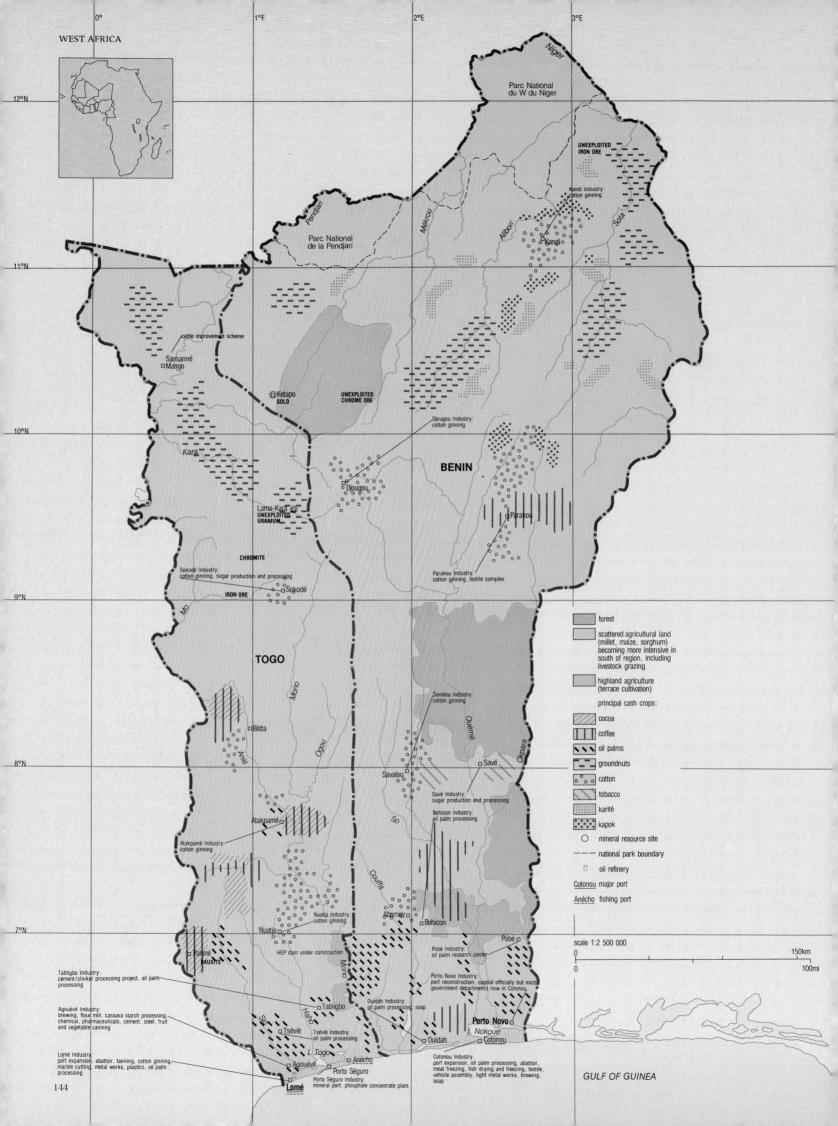

WEST AFRICA

12°N

Parc National
du W du Niger

Niger

UNEXPLOITED
IRON ORE

Kandi Industry:
cotton ginning

□Kandi

Parc National
de la Pendjari

Pendjari

Mékrou

Alibori

Sota

11°N

cattle improvement scheme

Sansanné
□ Mango

⊚Ketapo
GOLD

UNEXPLOITED
CHROME ORE

BENIN

10°N

Djougou Industry:
cotton ginning

Kara

Djougou

□Parakou

Lama-Kara
UNEXPLOITED
URANIUM

CHROMITE

Parakou Industry:
cotton ginning, textile complex

Sokodé Industry:
cotton ginning, sugar production and processing

IRON ORE

□Sokodé

9°N

forest

scattered agricultural land
(millet, maize, sorghum)
becoming more intensive in
south of region, including
livestock grazing

highland agriculture
(terrace cultivation)

principal cash crops:

TOGO

Mo

Ouémé

Okpara

cocoa

coffee

Blitta

oil palms

groundnuts

cotton

8°N

Ané

Mono

Ogou

Savalou Industry:
cotton ginning

□Savé

tobacco

karité

kapok

Savalou

Savé Industry:
sugar production and processing

Bohicon Industry:
oil palm processing

mineral resource site

national park boundary

oil refinery

Atakpamé

So

Cotonou major port

Anécho fishing port

Atakpamé Industry:
cotton ginning

Couffa

Nuatja Industry:
cotton ginning

Abomay

□Bohicon

scale 1:2 500 000

7°N

Nuatja

Palmé
BAUXITE

HEP dam under construction

Mono

Pobé Industry:
oil palm research center

□Pobé

0   150km

0   100mi

Tabligbo Industry:
cement/clinker processing project, oil palm
processing

Porto Novo Industry:
port reconstruction, capital officially but most
government departments now in Cotonou

Agouévé Industry:
brewing, flour mill, cassava starch processing,
chemical, pharmaceuticals, cement, steel, fruit
and vegetable canning

Hano

□Tabligbo

Ouidah Industry:
oil palm processing, soap

Porto Novo

Lomé Industry:
port expansion, abattoir, tanning, cotton ginning,
marble cutting, metal works, plastics, oil palm
processing

Sio

Tsévié Industry:
oil palm processing

□Tsévié

□Ouidah

L Nokoué

□Cotonou

L Togo

Agouévé

□Anécho

Cotonou Industry:
port expansion, oil palm processing, abattoir,
meat freezing, fish drying and freezing, textile,
vehicle assembly, light metal works, brewing,
soap

GULF OF GUINEA

□ Porto Séguro

Lomé

Porto Séguro Industry:
mineral port, phosphate concentrate plant

Togo

Official Name
République Togolaise
Togo Republic

Area
56 000 sq km

Date of Independence
27 Apr 1960

Status and Name in Colonial Times
1894–1918 German colony: Togoland
1919–60 joint mandate under League of Nations
and UN: British and French Togoland (British part
joined Ghana)

Population
1 997 109 (1970 census); 2 500 000 (UN est 1979)

Annual Growth Rate
2·8% (UN est 1979)

Capital City
Lomé

Population of Capital
229 400 (est 1977)

National Language(s)
French; Ewe, Mina, Dagomba, Tim, Cabrais

Gross National Product (US dollars)
700 million; 300 per capita (est 1977)

Local Currency
1 franc CFA = 100 centimes

Benin

Official name
République Populaire du Benin

Area
112 622 sq km

Date of Independence
1 Aug 1960 (as Republic of Dahomey)

Status and Name in Colonial Times
French colony (part of French West Africa)

Population
3 400 000 (est 1979)

Annual Growth Rate
2·7%

Capital City
Porto Novo

Population of Capital
104 000 (est 1975)

National Language(s)
French; Fon, Mina, Yoruba, Dendi

Gross National Product (US dollars)
660 million; 200 per capita (est 1977)

Local Currency
1 franc CFA = 100 centimes

among the Ewe. During the war all Ewe had been under British rule and a single Presbyterian church had been created, which served as a focus for the community. The drawing of the border through Ewe territory naturally aroused discontent. In the 1930s attempts by the British and French to enforce border regulations led to riots. But despite Ewe pressure the colonial powers resisted unification. At independence British Togoland (although never tightly integrated with the Gold Coast) voted to join Ghana. This problem continued to plague the independent governments of Ghana and Togo.

Togo's mandate status marked the colony for eventual independence (or at least autonomy within a French federation) long before the possibility was considered for the other French possessions. The Togolese resisted any inroads into their special status, and were in the vanguard of nationalism in French West Africa. Most political parties in the colonies were government-sponsored, but the Comité d'Unité Togolaise (CUT) was independent and anti-French. From 1950 the French were committed to increasing self-government, but hoped to retain the territory within the French sphere.

Elections leading to independence were held in 1958 and were swept by Sylvanus Olympio's CUT. Olympio then led Togo to independence in 1960. Togo retained close links with France and established economic links with other former French colonies. The problem of Ewe irredentism remained; Olympio demanded the unification of British and French Togoland, despite the plebiscite in the former. There were several attempted coups in 1961 and 1962, and the opposition Juvento Party was dissolved. In January 1963 Olympio was assassinated in a coup led by non-commissioned army officers, who invited Nicolas Grunitzky to form a government. There was a belief – both among Togolese and among anti-Nkrumah Ghanaians – that the Ghana government had collaborated in this and earlier coup attempts.

Bad relations with Ghana continued under the new government, as did dissatisfaction within the army. There was an attempted coup in 1966, followed by a successful one in 1967, when Grunitzky agreed to hand over power to the army under Lieutenant Colonel Eyadema (who had also been involved in the overthrow of Olympio). Eyadema promised to hand over power to civilian rule, but in 1969 created his own party, the Togolese People's Party, and was confirmed as head of state by an apparently huge majority in a referendum in 1972.

I.S.

Benin

Benin is physically small, economically poor and politically unstable. Squeezed between Togo and Nigeria, it has a coastline of only 125 kilometers and a hinterland stretching back 675 kilometers. Apart from the relatively fertile *terre de barre* near the coast, Benin has poor soils and there is little forest cover, the savanna reaching virtually to the Atlantic's edge.

As Dahomey, Benin became a French colony in 1894. It took its name from the kingdom which, from its capital at Abomey, 100 kilometers north of the coast, flourished by involvement in the slave trade in the late 18th and early 19th centuries. After 50 years of direct colonial rule, Dahomey was given elective representation and a territorial assembly in 1946. Universal suffrage was introduced in 1957 and increasing degrees of self-government led to independence in August 1960.

Both the population (largely concentrated in the south) and the government's exchequer are dependent for income on agriculture, which provides the main cash crops (palm produce and, increasingly, cotton). Low prices, lack of investment, inflation and a high birthrate have prevented a significant growth in real incomes since independence, although a sharp increase in food production has occurred since 1976. The small size of the domestic market has discouraged manufacturing industry, most of which has been limited to the processing of exportable commodities. The narrow range of such commodities and their low prices have kept down government revenue – over half of which comes from taxes on trade – and have contributed to a severe and chronic balance-of-payments problem: between 1960 and 1973, there were only four years in which exports covered even 50 per cent of imports.

Benin's problems arising from a lack of physical resources have, ironically, been compounded by its exceptional wealth of human resources, especially of skilled and educated manpower. This abundance, created by high rates of school attendance in the colonial period, became an embarrassment after the breakup in 1960 of the French West African Federation, of which Benin was a part and throughout which its educated elite was dispersed. The forcible repatriation of this elite led to the overstaffing of the domestic civil service (salaries for which still consume over 65 per cent of the budget). It led also to the creation of a sophisticated and demanding middle class which has resisted austerity programs, pushed up import bills, and – not least – contributed to the curious blend of high-flown rhetoric and dismal performance that characterizes Beninois politics. Gorged with programs, analyses, promises and plots, Benin still has an infant mortality rate of 185 deaths per 1000 live births and for the average citizen a life expectancy of 41 years (1973).

Since 1960, Benin has had ten heads of state and six coups d'état – more than any other African state. This instability was caused initially by the establishment of three regional parties (one in northern and two in southern and central Benin), sufficiently balanced, entrenched and exclusive to prevent the building of stable coalitions or the emergence of a one-party system. The extreme parochialism of rural Benin was, before and after independence, aggravated by intense competition for office within the urban elite (including latterly the officer corps of an army numbering only 1500). The result was an apparently endless and unfathomable sequence of realignments, coups and conspiracies.

Since 1975, Benin has officially transcended both regionalism and "bourgeois mentality" by the adoption of Marxism–Leninism and the

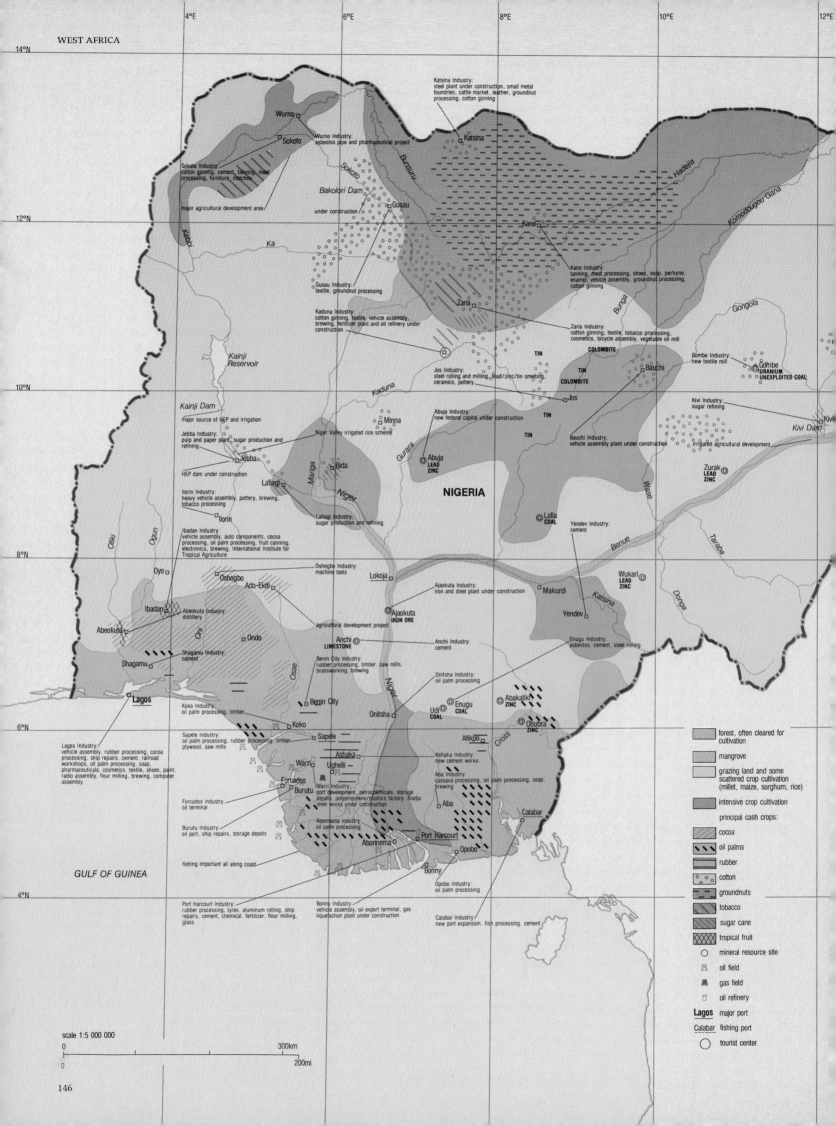

14°N

Wurno

Sokoto

Wurno Industry:
asbestos pipe and pharmaceutical project

Sokoto Industry:
cotton ginning, cement, tanning, meat
processing, furniture, matches

major agricultural development area

Bakolori Dam
under construction

Gusau

Gusau Industry:
textile, groundnut processing

Kaduna Industry:
cotton ginning, textile, vehicle assembly,
brewing, fertilizer plant and oil refinery under
construction

Katsina Industry:
steel plant under construction, small metal
foundries, cattle market, leather, groundnut
processing, cotton ginning

Katsina

Kano

Kano Industry:
tanning, meat processing, shoes, soap, perfume,
enamel, vehicle assembly, groundnut processing,
cotton ginning

Zaria

Zaria Industry:
cotton ginning, textile, tobacco processing,
cosmetics, bicycle assembly, vegetable oil mill

Gombe Industry:
new textile mill

Gombe
URANIUM
UNEXPLOITED COAL

Kebbi

Ka

12°N

Sokoto

Bunsuru

Bunga

Gongola

Hadejia

Komodougou Gana

Kainji
Reservoir

Kainji Dam
major source of HEP and irrigation

Jebba Industry:
pulp and paper plant, sugar production and
refining

Niger Valley irrigated rice scheme

HEP dam under construction

Ilorin Industry:
heavy vehicle assembly, pottery, brewing,
tobacco processing

Jebba

Mariga

Niger

Lafiagi

Lafiagi Industry:
sugar production and refining

Bida

Ilorin

Minna

Abuja Industry:
new federal capital under construction

Gurara

Abuja
LEAD
ZINC

NIGERIA

TIN

COLOMBITE

TIN
COLOMBITE

Jos Industry:
steel rolling and milling, lead/zinc/tin smelting,
ceramics, pottery

Jos

TIN

TIN

Bauchi

Bauchi Industry:
vehicle assembly plant under construction

Kivi Industry:
sugar refining

Kivi Dam

Zurak
LEAD
ZINC

Lafia
COAL

Yendev Industry:
cement

Wase

Benue

Taraba

Kaduna

10°N

Ibadan Industry:
vehicle assembly, auto components, cocoa
processing, oil palm processing, fruit canning,
electronics, brewing, International Institute for
Tropical Agriculture

Oshogbo Industry:
machine tools

Oshogbo

Ado-Ekiti

Ibadan

Abeokuta Industry:
distillery

Abeokuta

Ondo

Shagamu Industry:
cement

Shagamu

Lokoja

Ajaokuta Industry:
iron and steel plant under construction

Makurdi

Wukari
LEAD
ZINC

Yendev

Katsina

Donga

8°N

Oyo

Ofiki

Ogun

Oni

Osse

Ajaokuta
IRON ORE

Anchi
LIMESTONE

agricultural development project

Anchi Industry:
cement

Enugu Industry:
asbestos, cement, steel rolling

Benin City Industry:
rubber processing, timber, saw mills,
brassworking, brewing

Onitsha Industry:
oil palm processing

Koko Industry:
oil palm processing, timber

Lagos

Koko

Benin City

Onitsha

Udi
COAL

Enugu
COAL

Abakaliki
ZINC

Obubra
ZINC

Lagos Industry:
vehicle assembly, rubber processing, cocoa
processing, ship repairs, cement, railroad
workshops, oil palm processing, soap,
pharmaceuticals, cosmetics, textile, shoes, paint,
radio assembly, flour milling, brewing, computer
assembly

Sapele Industry:
oil palm processing, rubber processing, timber,
plywood, saw mills

Sapele

Ashaka

Afikpo

Cross

6°N

Ashaka Industry:
new cement works

Aba Industry:
cassava processing, oil palm processing, soap,
brewing

Warri Industry:
port development, petrochemicals, storage
depots, polypropylene/plastics factory, Aladja
steel works under construction

Warri

Ughelli

Aba

Calabar

Forcados Industry:
oil terminal

Forcados

Burutu

Burutu Industry:
oil port, ship repairs, storage depots

Abonnema Industry:
oil palm processing

Abonnema

Port Harcourt

Opobo

fishing important all along coast

Bonny

Opobo Industry:
oil palm processing

GULF OF GUINEA

4°N

Port Harcourt Industry:
rubber processing, tyres, aluminum rolling, ship
repairs, cement, chemical, fertilizer, flour milling,
glass

Bonny Industry:
vehicle assembly, oil export terminal, gas
liquefaction plant under construction

Calabar Industry:
new port expansion, fish processing, cement

forest, often cleared for
cultivation

mangrove

grazing land and some
scattered crop cultivation
(millet, maize, sorghum, rice)

intensive crop cultivation

principal cash crops:

cocoa

oil palms

rubber

cotton

groundnuts

tobacco

sugar cane

tropical fruit

mineral resource site

oil field

gas field

oil refinery

Lagos major port

Calabar fishing port

tourist center

scale 1:5 000 000

0   300km

0   200mi

4°E   6°E   8°E   10°E   12°E

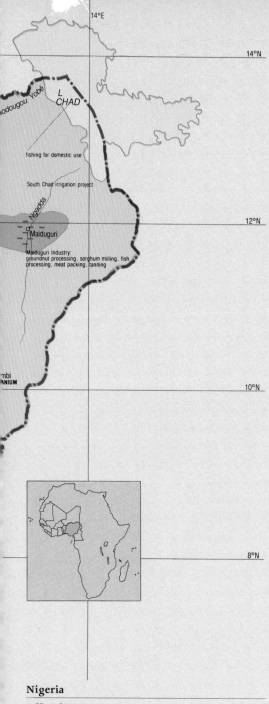

creation of the Benin People's Revolutionary Party (BPRP), led by the head of state, Colonel Kerekou, and his most trusted fellow officers. In pursuit of socialism, the BPRP has nationalized a number of commercial and financial enterprises, assumed control of produce exportation, reorganized the school system in accordance with its commitment to "African authenticity," instituted national service, and established a network of provincial, district and communal revolutionary bodies. It has also abolished examinations and religious holidays, replacing Christmas with a "Feast of Production."

Benin's cultivation of socialist-bloc countries and revolutionary rhetoric has not, however, seriously obstructed its relationship with France, which until 1976 provided a direct budgetary subsidy and is still Benin's main trading partner and source of aid. Benin remains part of the franc zone and of the West African Monetary Union (supported by the French treasury). Since its commitment to making "the Benin people master of its own fate," the government has also renewed its defense agreements with France and attended conferences of Francophone African heads of state.

Despite occasional quarrels, Benin has also sought to maintain good relations with its less radical neighbors, especially Nigeria which has provided some aid and investment. Benin, though a people's republic, is thus one closer to the Romanian than to the Albanian model, tempering a high level of rhetoric with a large element of pragmatism in its international relations and emphasizing the role of the "vanguard" rather than that of the "masses" in its domestic politics.

M.S.

Nigeria

Named for the Niger river, whose lower portion the country encloses, Nigeria is Africa's most populous nation and one of its richest. It possesses vast reserves of petroleum and natural gas, significant deposits of coal, tin and colombite and is a major producer of rubber, cocoa, peanuts, cotton, palm oil and kernels and timber.

With the longest north–south axis of any coastal West African nation, Nigeria is a land of great diversity and contrasts. The vigorous tropical monsoons which drench the southern states with 1250 to over 3500 millimeters of rain a year (with dry seasons in August and from mid-November to February) have produced coastal mangrove swamps and inland rain forest, the latter greatly modified by centuries of clearing and cultivation. While humidity is high in the southern states, temperatures generally stay between 20° and 30° day and night year round. Further north the coastal forests give way to more open plateaus, rainfall decreases, and the temperature range widens. The northern savannas receive under 1000 millimeters of rain a year during two shorter rainy seasons, with high temperatures averaging 30° to 40° and lows 15° to 25°. When the dry, dusty Harmattan wind blows out of the Sahara during the long dry season frost is not unknown in parts of the north.

Diversity is also characteristic of Nigeria's people, whose spoken languages number over 200. When united, the different cultures are, in the words of former Prime Minister Abubakar Tafawa Balewa, "a source of great strength," but cultural rivalries have also fueled recent conflicts. Most important of the ethnic groupings are the Hausa, Fulani and Kanuri of the north, the Nupe and Tiv of the middle belt, and the Yoruba, Edo (Bini), Igbo (Ibo) and Ibibio of the south. Only about a fifth of the enormous population live in large towns, but many rural areas are also thickly settled with densities of over 150 persons per square kilometer in several places. Besides the capital, the leading cities include Ibadan, Kano, Zaria, Ogbomosho and Onitsha. Most northerners are Muslim, most southerners Christian, but traditional religions and syncretism are still common.

While Nigeria's boundaries are a product of British colonization at the end of the 19th century, they circumscribe much older political, economic and cultural units. The northern half of the country corresponds to the Sokoto caliphate, a vast Islamic empire founded by the reformer Usuman dan Fodio at the beginning of the 19th century, and its smaller but much more ancient neighbor, the Kingdom of Bornu. Southwestern Nigeria contained many Yoruba kingdoms, founded ultimately from the holy city of Ife; of these the most important were Oyo, which flourished in the 18th century, and Ibadan, which flourished in the 19th. The Bendel state contains the ancient Benin empire, whose kings and craftsmen impressed a long succession of Western visitors. The Igbo, Ibibio and Ijo peoples of the southeast inhabited a multitude of small, generally egalitarian states in the precolonial era, but, like most other parts of the country, were closely linked by networks of trade routes and markets serving important internal and export trades.

These disparate peoples were brought under British control, beginning with the annexation of Lagos in 1861 and culminating with the declaration of separate protectorates over Southern Nigeria and Northern Nigeria in 1900. After subduing African resistance, the British combined the two protectorates into the Colony of Nigeria in 1914, largely to balance the administrative deficits in the north with the surpluses from the south. Despite amalgamation the two halves remained quite distinct culturally, economically and administratively.

The colonial economy until after 1945 was largely an expanded version of the precolonial; exports were dominated by cash crops produced by small farmers using traditional methods – palm products from the southeast, cocoa from the southwest, cotton and (from the 1890s) peanuts from the north. The construction of a network of motor roads and rail lines facilitated the movement of these products and stimulated increased production. The opening of new tin mines on the Jos plateau and coal mines near Enugu added minerals to the export list, but agricultural exports were still of paramount importance until after independence.

The profits from these expanding exports went largely to foreign trading companies and to supporting the colonial administration rather than to improving social services. Not

Nigeria

Official Name
Federal Republic of Nigeria

Area
923 768 sq km

Date of Independence
1 Oct 1960

Status and Name in Colonial Times
1900–60 British colony: Nigeria (Northern and Southern) with many amalgamations including British-administered UN trusteeship territory of Northern Cameroons

Population
83 400 000 (UN est 1979)

Annual Growth Rate
2·7% (1970–76); 3·3% (UN est 1979)

Capital City
Lagos (new capital planned for Abuja)

Population of Capital
1 477 000 (est 1975)

National Language(s)
English; Hausa, Fulani, Yoruba, Igbo

Gross National Product (US dollars)
33 340 million; 420 per capita (est 1979)

Local Currency
1 naira = 100 kobo

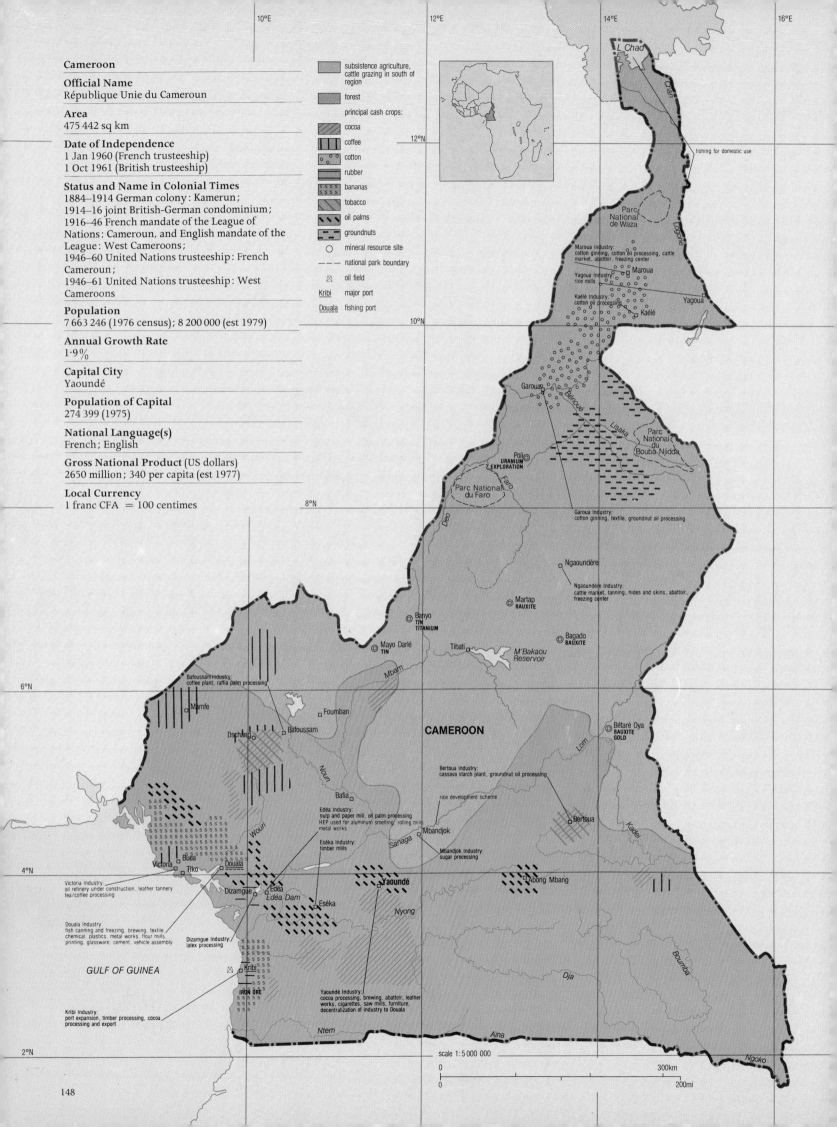

Cameroon

Official Name
République Unie du Cameroun

Area
475 442 sq km

Date of Independence
1 Jan 1960 (French trusteeship)
1 Oct 1961 (British trusteeship)

Status and Name in Colonial Times
1884–1914 German colony: Kamerun;
1914–16 joint British-German condominium;
1916–46 French mandate of the League of
Nations: Cameroun, and English mandate of the
League: West Cameroons;
1946–60 United Nations trusteeship: French
Cameroun;
1946–61 United Nations trusteeship: West
Cameroons

Population
7 663 246 (1976 census); 8 200 000 (est 1979)

Annual Growth Rate
1·9%

Capital City
Yaoundé

Population of Capital
274 399 (1975)

National Language(s)
French; English

Gross National Product (US dollars)
2650 million; 340 per capita (est 1977)

Local Currency
1 franc CFA = 100 centimes

Legend

subsistence agriculture,
cattle grazing in south of
region

forest

principal cash crops:

cocoa

coffee

cotton

rubber

bananas

tobacco

oil palms

groundnuts

○ mineral resource site

national park boundary

oil field

Kribi major port

Douala fishing port

Map labels

L Chad
Chari
Logone
fishing for domestic use
Parc National de Waza
Maroua industry:
cotton ginning, cotton oil processing, cattle
market, abattoir, freezing center
Maroua
Yagoua Industry:
rice mills
Kaélé Industry:
cotton oil processing
Kaélé
Yagoua
Garoua
Benoué
Lisaka
Parc National du Bouba Njidda
Poli
URANIUM EXPLORATION
Faro
Deo
Parc National du Faro
Garoua Industry:
cotton ginning, textile, groundnut oil processing
Ngaoundéré
Ngaoundéré industry:
cattle market, tanning, hides and skins, abattoir,
freezing center
Martap BAUXITE
Banyo TIN TITANIUM
Bagado BAUXITE
Mayo Darlé TIN
Tibati
M'Bakaou Reservoir
Mbam
Bafoussam industry:
coffee plant, raffia palm processing
Mamfe
Foumban
CAMEROON
Bétaré Oya BAUXITE GOLD
Dschang
Bafoussam
Noun
Bafia
Lom
Bertoua industry:
cassava starch plant, groundnut oil processing
Bertoua
Kadei
Edéa industry:
pulp and paper mill, oil palm processing
HEP used for aluminum smelting, rolling mill,
metal works
Eséka Industry:
timber mills
Mbandjok
Sanaga
Mbandjok Industry:
sugar processing
Victoria
Buéa
Tiko
Douala
Victoria Industry:
oil refinery under construction, leather tannery
tea/coffee processing
Dizamgue
Edéa
Edéa Dam
Eséka
Yaoundé
Abong Mbang
Nyong
Douala Industry:
fish canning and freezing, brewing, textile,
chemical, plastics, metal works, flour mills,
printing, glassware, cement, vehicle assembly
Dizamgue Industry:
latex processing
GULF OF GUINEA
Kribi
Wouri
IRON ORE
Yaoundé Industry:
cocoa processing, brewing, abattoir, leather
works, cigarettes, saw mills, furniture,
decentralization of industry to Douala
Kribi Industry:
port expansion, timber processing, cocoa
processing and export
rice development scheme
Dja
Aina
Ntem
Ngoko
Boumba

scale 1:5 000 000

0 300km
0 200mi

until after World War II did this policy alter significantly. Nevertheless, social change during the colonial period was extensive in the southern regions as jobs in government service, commerce and transportation drew many away from traditional agricultural employment. Larger cities developed in proximity to the roads, railroads and coastal ports. Much of the change in the south was facilitated by mission schools, a feature of some coastal towns in the 19th century, but now expanding rapidly in inland areas. The initiative for these schools as well as their financing and staffing came primarily from the African communities with the assistance and cooperation of foreign Protestant and Roman Catholic mission societies. Government subsidies (low until after 1945) and inspection helped improve quality.

In the northern region the rate of change was much slower because the colonial policy of indirect rule maintained conservative traditional leaders in power, causing less disruption of society. The influence of Western culture and education was also very much less in the north as a result of the government policy of excluding Christian missionaries from Islamic areas. By 1950 the north had only a fifth as many pupils in modern schools as the south, by 1960 only a tenth as many. While northern cities grew in this period, much of the expansion was due to the influx of southerners, especially Igbo.

Opposition to British rule goes back to the earliest days of imperialism, but coordinated national protest dates from the formation of the Nigerian Youth Movement in the 1930s. After World War II nationalist activity increased dramatically with the support of nascent trade unions, military veterans, urban dwellers and a growing number of educated leaders, of whom the American-educated Nnamdi Azikiwe, later the first president of Nigeria, was the most prominent. Though national in outlook, the independence movement was largely the work of southerners. Lack of education, conservativism and a regional outlook retarded northern participation. It is notable that the first prime minister of independent Nigeria, Balewa, who was a northerner, had first gained prominence as a critic of the diversity of Nigeria and of early self-government.

As a consequence of British colonial policies, Nigeria became independent as a federation of three unequally sized, self-governing regions, each dominated by a large ethnic group and with over half the population and territory of the country in the Northern Region. By 1965 political inexperience, corruption and personal, regional, political and ethnic rivalries had brought this uneasy federation to its knees. A coup d'état by junior military officers in January 1966 overthrew the civilian politicians, killing Prime Minister Balewa and the premiers of the Northern and Western Regions. Major General Aguiyi Ironsi attempted to reform and strengthen the federation, but hasty changes and a growing suspicion of domination by the Igbo of the Eastern Region led to his downfall in a new coup in July 1966. The youthful Colonel Yakubu Gowon, a Christian from a northern minority group, attempted to restore order and strengthen the increasingly fragile national unity, but appalling massacres of some 10 000–30 000 Igbo and other easterners

in the north and a constitutional stalemate left the Eastern Region leaders with the conviction that secession was their only alternative. In May 1967 the region declared its independence as the Republic of Biafra under the leadership of Oxford-educated Colonel Odumegwu Ojukwu. At first Biafran forces made significant gains, but the outcome, prolonged by international involvement, was Biafran capitulation in January 1970. The legacies of the civil war include the largest army in black Africa and a substantial military presence throughout the country, but a hearteningly low level of lingering bitterness. However, though the federation had been preserved, the issues that divided it had not been solved. Renewed charges of corruption and favoritism and the decision to postpone a return to civilian rule led to the bloodless overthrow of Gowon and his military governors in July 1975 by war-seasoned officers committed to restoring democratic institutions. Despite the assassination of the new head of state, General Murtala Muhammad, in an abortive coup in February 1976, the ruling Supreme Military Council, headed by Lieutenant General Olusegun Obasanjo, continued the transition to civilian rule. Under a new constitution the nation was divided into 19 states with a federal district in the center of the country where a new capital will be built at Abuja. Political activity was again permitted in 1978 and, under complex formulas ensuring a broad national base, elections held in mid-1979 chose a president and members of a bicameral legislature, bringing an end to 13 years of military rule.

Since independence the structure of the Nigerian economy has changed drastically as the result of petroleum production and new government policies to promote "indigenization." Since drilling its first well in 1956 Nigeria has become one of the world's major producers of petroleum, which by 1977 accounted for 90 per cent of its foreign earnings. Oil revenues have greatly increased the rate of economic growth and industrial development, despite the disruption of the civil war. Manufacturing has been expanding rapidly since the 1950s, concentrated at first in "export substitution" industries (notably textiles, rubber, brewing, metal fabrication and tobacco), later expanded into auto (Peugeot and Volkswagen), commercial vehicle, refrigerator and air conditioner assembly plants. Industries intended for the 1980s include a new petroleum refinery, direct-reduction steel plants at Warri and Port Harcourt, an iron and steel industry at Ajoakuta in Kwara State, three fertilizer plants, several new cement plants and additional vehicle-assembly plants. The steel industry is expected to stimulate tin and coal mining, the production of which had declined in the 1960s and 1970s.

As a member of OPEC, the Lomé Convention and the Economic Community of West African States (ECOWAS) Nigeria has sought to maximize its economic growth through foreign trade and, beginning in 1962, by a series of National Development Plans. While encouraging outside investment, the government has sought to limit foreign economic control by import controls and by insisting on total or partial Nigerian ownership in many economic sectors. In the case of oil

companies, of which the government has owned 55 per cent since 1974, full control is intended as soon as sufficient Nigerian technicians and managers are available.

Although agricultural exports declined from about four-fifths of total exports at independence to less than 6 per cent in 1974, some two-thirds of Nigerians continue to be employed in agriculture, which remains a mainstay of the domestic economy. The modernization of this sector is receiving greater government attention both to increase domestic food supplies and to maintain a significant volume of traditional exports. In addition to agriculture, small industries and crafts, both traditional and modern, employ many Nigerians.

D.N.

Cameroon

The most striking characteristic of the physical environment of Cameroon is its diversity. This is due in part to its latitudinal range, which extends between 2° and 13° north. Cameroon lies astride a volcanic belt which separates West and central Africa and is intermediate between the basins of the Niger and Congo rivers and Lake Chad. There is also considerable variation in altitude, most dramatically manifested by Mount Cameroon (4070 meters) situated close to the shoreline of the Bight of Biafra. In terms of the climate, vegetation and geography of Cameroon, five different environmental zones can be delineated. The most southerly is the Atlantic coastal forest plain consisting mostly of dense forest and mangrove. This zone is characterized by a high rainfall (about 3800 millimeters per year) and extends between 72 and 128 kilometers inland. Bordering the coastal plain on the east is a region of plateaus (average elevation 640 meters) and dense tropical forests extending from the Sanaga river to the Congo Basin. North of the Sanaga lies the Adamawa Plateau region. Elevations there range between 790 and 1500 meters and it can be seen as a transitional zone between northern and southern Cameroon. The fourth region is the extensive savanna and steppe of the Benue and Chad plains in the north. During the rainy season (June through October) much of this region, particularly the area around Lake Chad, becomes a vast flood plain. The fifth region is the mountainous region of the west, including Mount Cameroon and the grassfields of the Bamenda Highlands and extending northwards to the Mandara Hills.

The geographical diversity of the nation is reflected in the human population. The environmental zones have tended to result in culture areas that are based on different forms of adaptation. The coastal population has long been supported by fishing and coastal trade. The forest area is suitable for the cultivation of yams and cassava. The peoples of the Adamawa Plateau and the Benue and Chad plains cultivate maize and other cereal crops and practice pastoralism. The attractive climate and fertile soil of the Bamenda Highlands have been responsible for the great density of population in that area, and a distinctive cultural pattern can be discerned throughout the many chieftaincies there.

Human variation is reflected further in the

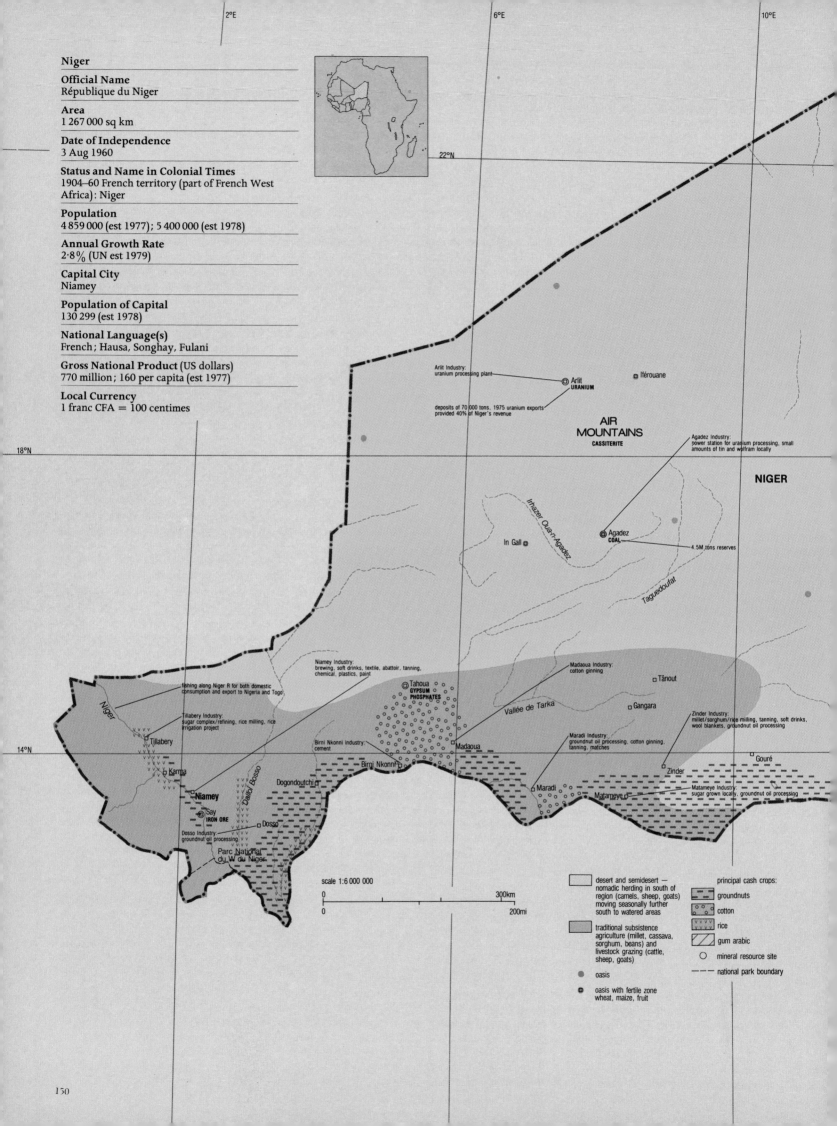

Niger

Official Name
République du Niger

Area
1 267 000 sq km

Date of Independence
3 Aug 1960

Status and Name in Colonial Times
1904–60 French territory (part of French West
Africa): Niger

Population
4 859 000 (est 1977); 5 400 000 (est 1978)

Annual Growth Rate
2·8% (UN est 1979)

Capital City
Niamey

Population of Capital
130 299 (est 1978)

National Language(s)
French; Hausa, Songhay, Fulani

Gross National Product (US dollars)
770 million; 160 per capita (est 1977)

Local Currency
1 franc CFA = 100 centimes

22°N

18°N

14°N

2°E   6°E   10°E

NIGER

AIR
MOUNTAINS
CASSITERITE

Arlit Industry:
uranium processing plant

Arlit
URANIUM

Iférouane

deposits of 70 000 tons, 1975 uranium exports
provided 40% of Niger's revenue

Agadez Industry:
power station for uranium processing, small
amounts of tin and wolfram locally

In Gall

Agadez
COAL

4.5M tons reserves

Irhazer Ouan-Agadez

Taguedoufat

Niamey Industry:
brewing, soft drinks, textile, abattoir, tanning,
chemical, plastics, paint

Madaoua Industry:
cotton ginning

Tânout

fishing along Niger R for both domestic
consumption and export to Nigeria and Togo

Tahoua
GYPSUM
PHOSPHATES

Vallée de Tarka

Gangara

Tillabery Industry:
sugar complex/refining, rice milling, rice
irrigation project

Niger

Tillabery

Birni Nkonni Industry:
cement

Madaoua

Zinder Industry:
millet/sorghum/rice milling, tanning, soft drinks,
wool blankets, groundnut oil processing

Maradi Industry:
groundnut oil processing, cotton ginning,
tanning, matches

Karma

Dallol Bosso

Birni Nkonni

Gouré

Zinder

Dogondoutchi

Maradi

Niamey

Matameye

Matameye Industry:
sugar grown locally, groundnut oil processing

Say
IRON ORE

Dosso

Dosso Industry:
groundnut oil processing

Parc National
du W du Niger

scale 1:6 000 000

0   300km

0   200mi

desert and semidesert —
nomadic herding in south of
region (camels, sheep, goats)
moving seasonally further
south to watered areas

traditional subsistence
agriculture (millet, cassava,
sorghum, beans) and
livestock grazing (cattle,
sheep, goats)

oasis

oasis with fertile zone
wheat, maize, fruit

principal cash crops:

groundnuts

cotton

rice

gum arabic

mineral resource site

national park boundary

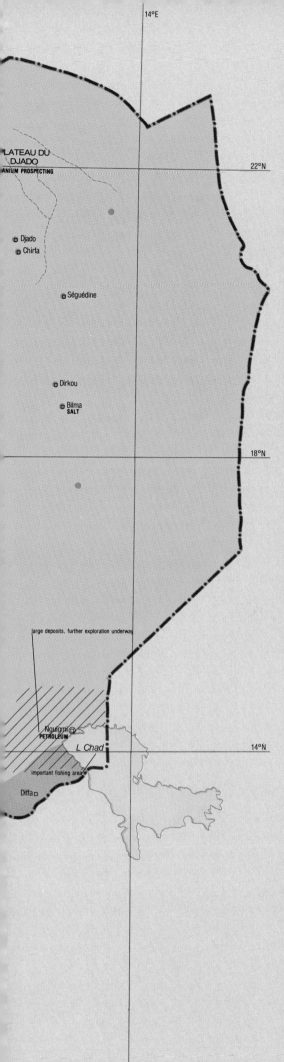

great linguistic diversity of Cameroon. The southern peoples are mostly Bantu speaking, and linguists have suggested that the Bamenda Highlands may have been the point of origin of Bantu-speaking peoples. There are also several groups of pygmies in the forests of the south, and Sudanic and Afroasiatic languages are spoken in the north. Another aspect of the cultural diversity is in the realm of religion; the north is populated largely by Muslim peoples, such as the Fulani (Foulbe or Peul), while the south is predominantly Christian.

The beginnings of present-day Cameroon lie in the rivalry between European powers vying for control of the West African coast in the late 19th century. In July 1884 the German diplomat Nachtigal established the German Kamerun Protectorate, which lasted until 1916, when a combination of British and French forces brought German rule to an end. Although German rule was harsh, its accomplishments are impressive. These include the vast and highly profitable set of plantations in the south which are now operated by the Cameroon Development Corporation. Following World War I, four-fifths of the territory of the former Kamerun Protectorate became a French mandate, and the remainder became a British mandate. The British administered their mandate, which consisted of two non-contiguous areas in the west, as an adjunct to the colonial government of Nigeria. The French, on the other hand, established a separate administration in their mandate and were effective in increasing the production of cocoa and palm. The orientations of the French and British administrations began to change after 1946, when East and West Cameroon became United Nations Trustee-ships. The people of both territories began to anticipate self-government, and political groups began to be formed as aspirations for independence were voiced. After 1948 the Union des Populations du Cameroun (UPC) advocated the reunification of the two territories and opposition to French rule. Anti-French activities intensified throughout the 1950s as the influence of the UPC spread. In 1961 a plebiscite was held in the two areas of the west which were administered by the British. The former Northern Cameroons voted to join Nigeria, and Southern Cameroons became the western state of the newly reunified Cameroon Federal Republic. The governing party was the Union Camerounaise under the leadership of M. Ahmadou Ahidjo, who became the first president. In 1966 the Union Camerounaise, a predominantly eastern party, joined forces with the Kamerun National Democratic Party (KNDP) of the west and formed the Union National Camerounaise (UNP), which has remained as the governing party until the present. Ahmadou Ahidjo continues to hold the office of president having been reelected in 1975. At present the government is stable and effective, although there is some tension between the Anglophone and Francophone sectors of the population which may have political repercussions in the future. The continued success of the government will depend largely on its ability to implement a policy of economic development, most notably in connection with Cameroon's newly discovered oil deposits. Another vital consideration is the question of who will

succeed President Ahidjo, whose status as one of the early leaders of the African independence movement has done a great deal to enhance the authority of his party and maintain the sometimes uneasy alliance between the Anglophone and Francophone populations.

R.C.

Niger

Two-thirds of Niger is covered by the Sahara, the domain of the Tuareg. Even in the remaining southern and western third the very existence of agricultural societies reposes on a delicate balance, which an invasion of locusts, drought, unfavorable timing of the rain or too rapid demographic expansion can easily, and has often, upset. In this century famines occurred in 1899–1903/04, 1913–15, 1931 and during the early 1970s.

Niger is composed of regions that constituted traditionally the outlying peripheral provinces of the more prominent central Sudanic empires and kingdoms, regions, that is, that served as refuge zones in times of upheaval. Indeed, after the defeat of the Songhay army in 1591, it was in the south (that is, among the Zerma/Songhay of present-day western Niger) that the Songhay emperors found a following ready to continue the resistance against the Moroccan occupiers. And it was to the Hausaland of modern Niger that those Hausa fled who refused to accept the new Fulani–Muslim regime established in central Hausaland (present-day Northern Nigeria) after 1804. Here, on the outer fringes of Hausaland, members of some of the dynasties, deposed by the Fulani, established the kingdoms of Maradi and Gobir/Tsibiri. They found a ready ally in the emerging and increasingly powerful state of Damagaram–Zinder which owed its wealth to the trans-Saharan trade (still profitable in the 19th century). These kingdoms posed a continuous threat to the Sokoto Caliphate.

The French conquest from 1897 onwards was a by-product of "the march towards Chad" and the desire to operate a junction between the emerging colonial empires of North, West and Equatorial Africa. It took initially the shape of the notorious Voulet–Chanoine expedition, whose undoing constitutes one of the most glorious chapters in the history of African resistance. Later the French were faced with major revolts among the Zerma/Songhay in 1905–06 and among the Tuareg in 1916–18.

The necessity of providing the French with taxes forced many of the Zerma/Songhay to engage themselves as seasonal laborers on the coast. The Hausa (who constitute nearly half of the total population), on the other hand, responded by turning to the cultivation of groundnuts. In the early 1970s the prices for groundnuts in the world market slumped catastrophically. At the same time Ghana closed its borders to migrant laborers. The damaging effects of these developments (together with the severe drought of the early 1970s) were in part offset by the boom in the mining industry. Nine years after the discovery of the first uranium deposits (in 1967), government royalties amounted to 12 billion francs CFA. Niger also contains huge deposits

Mali

Official Name
République du Mali

Area
1 204 021 sq km

Date of Independence
22 Sept 1960

Status and Name in Colonial Times
French colony (part of French West Africa): French
Sudan; 1958–60 member state of the French
Community: Mali

Population
6 035 272 (1976 census); 6 400 000 (UN est 1979)

Annual Growth Rate
2·0% (UN est 1979)

Capital City
Bamako

Population of Capital
400 022 (1976 census)

National Language(s)
French; Bambara, Fulani, Marka, Songhay,
Malinke, Tuareg

Gross National Product (US dollars)
680 million; 110 per capita (est 1977)

Local Currency
1 franc malien = 100 centimes

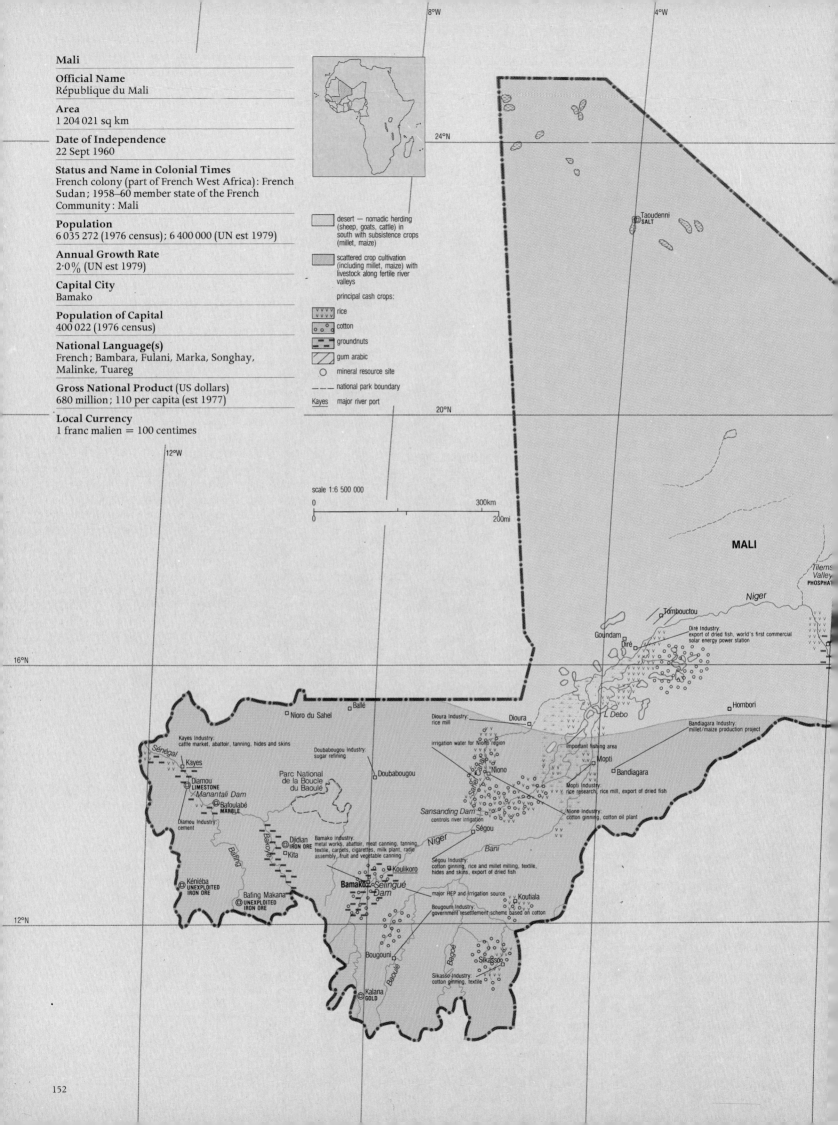

desert — nomadic herding
(sheep, goats, cattle) in
south with subsistence crops
(millet, maize)

scattered crop cultivation
(including millet, maize) with
livestock along fertile river
valleys

principal cash crops:

rice

cotton

groundnuts

gum arabic

○ mineral resource site

- - - national park boundary

Kayes major river port

scale 1:6 500 000

0 ———————— 300km
0 ———————— 200mi

MALI

Tilemsi
Valley
PHOSPHATE

Niger

Taoudenni
SALT

Tombouctou

Diré Industry:
export of dried fish; world's first commercial
solar energy power station

Goundam
Diré

L Debo

Hombori

Ballé

Nioro du Sahel

Dioura Industry:
rice mill

Dioura

Bandiagara Industry:
millet/maize production project

Kayes Industry:
cattle market, abattoir, tanning, hides and skins

Doubabougou Industry:
sugar refining

irrigation water for Niono region

important fishing area

Mopti

Sénégal

Kayes

Diamou
LIMESTONE
Manantali Dam

Bafoulabé
MARBLE

Parc National
de la Boucle
du Baoulé

Doubabougou

Niono

Mopti Industry:
rice research, rice mill, export of dried fish

Bandiagara

Diamou Industry:
cement

Bafing

Bakoye

Djidian
IRON ORE

Kita

Bamako Industry:
metal works, abattoir, meat canning, tanning,
textile, carpets, cigarettes, milk plant, radio
assembly, fruit and vegetable canning

Sansanding Dam
controls river irrigation

Ségou

Niono Industry:
cotton ginning, cotton oil plant

Niger

Bani

Kéniéba
UNEXPLOITED
IRON ORE

Bafing Makana
UNEXPLOITED
IRON ORE

Koulikoro

Bamako
*Selingué
Dam*

Ségou Industry:
cotton ginning, rice and millet milling, textile,
hides and skins, export of dried fish

major HEP and irrigation source

Koutiala

Bougouni Industry:
government resettlement scheme based on cotton

Bougouni

Baoulé

Bagoé

Sikasso

Sikasso Industry:
cotton ginning, textile

Kalana
GOLD

152

of iron, and oil prospecting is progressing apace.

Although the Zerma/Songhay constitute only about a fifth of the total population, they have always dominated the political scene. The socialist Djibo Bakary, elected Niger's first head of government in 1957, was defeated after he decided to campaign for the ''no'' vote in the 1958 referendum, concerning the continuing association of the French African territories with the French Republic. His cousin, Hamani Diori, governed for 16 years until he was toppled by a coup, engineered by Lieutenant Colonel Kountché, another Zerma, in 1974.

F.F.

Mali

Between forest in the south and desert in the north Mali bridges the sahel, which makes up much of its area. This scanty savanna is peopled by camel- or cattle-herding Tuareg and other nomads. In the arid northeast the shortness and uncertainty of the rains have meant that famines like that of 1972 are a constant possibility. The Niger river provides almost the only guaranteed perennial water. Here, apart from the settlements along the river, the sedentary population has tended to cluster in the defensible villages of the dramatic rocky outcrops around Hombori and the Bandiagara plateau, home of the Dogon. In the neck of Mali, above Tombouctou, are rich plains inhabited by a diversity of peoples: Songhay and Fulani farmers, Sorko and Bozo fishers and others. These regions have for centuries supplied the surplus agricultural products needed by the trading centers like Tombouctou on the edge of the desert. In the extreme southwest Sudanic bush gives way to stretches of forest watered by a multitude of streams. Here live the related Malinke groups of Bambara, Dyola (the famous Mandinke traders) and Khassonke and, among others, the Sarakolle and Senufo.

Unlike some states which have named themselves after ancient African kingdoms, Mali's present boundaries do include the heartland of the old Mali empire, as well as its predecessor, Ghana, and the western core of its successor, Songhay. The centuries after the fall of Songhay to a Moroccan army in 1591 were a time of disorder and movement, but also of state-formation among non-Muslim people like the Bambara and Mossi. The 19th-century *jihad* movement led to the creation of a militant Islamic state centered on Masina and the Segu empire of al-Haj 'Umar whose son, Ahmadu, was finally defeated by the French after a fierce resistance in 1892. Thus Mali's diverse peoples have had a long history of coexistence in states which, whether formally Muslim or pagan, have generally tended to combine elements of both Islam and traditional religion.

Colonial conquest produced a bitter but unsuccessful resistance from the Segu empire and later from the militant Islamic Hamalliyah movement. The Soudan Français was detached from Haut–Senegal–Niger and formed into a distinct territory in 1920. The present boundaries were drawn up by 1947. Landlocked, with a single railroad to Dakar as its only outlet to the sea, Mali was the most committed to federation of all ex-French African states but its union with Senegal only lasted from 1959 till 1960. In the great drought of the years after 1968 the radical government of Modibo Keita was otherthrown by a military coup. Natural factors – underpopulation, lack of mineral resources, together with dependence on unpredictable rains – have helped to make Mali one of the three poorest countries in the world. However, while livestock have not yet recovered from the effects of the drought, agricultural production in the staples, millet, sorghum, maize and rice, has increased, together with the production of cotton and groundnuts, and Mali is potentially self-supporting.

E.H.

4°E

24°N

20°N

ADRAR DES
IFORAS
MANGANESE

16°N

12°N

WEST CENTRAL AFRICA

The region we have chosen to call West Central Africa has no obvious geographic coherence, nor any superimposed cultural unity acquired during the colonial period. In the north the nations were part of French Equatorial Africa; the enormous nation of Zaïre, once Belgian Congo, borders former Portuguese Angola, and the enclave of Equatorial Guinea was once under Spanish rule. Geographically the variety is wide: arid semidesert in Chad, dense tropical rain forest in the Congo basin, grasslands in Angola. So from Sahara to sahel through forest to grasslands, bisected by the equator, this region contains in itself all of Africa.

The peoples of the region are as diverse as the climate. From Arabic-speaking Muslims in northern Chad, we pass south to areas where languages of the Niger–Congo family, like Zande, are spoken. But over much of the region, from the equator south, Bantu languages are universally spoken, and it is probably from a heartland in the forests that Bantu expansion commenced.

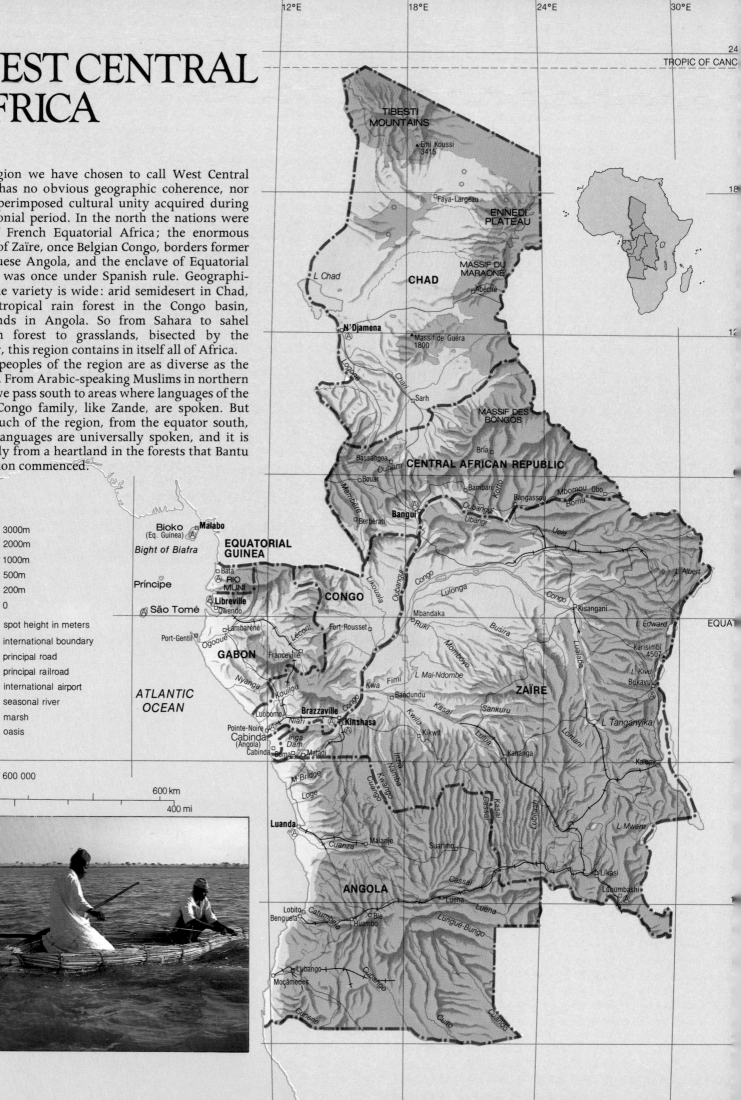

scale 1:17 600 000

3000m	
2000m	
1000m	
500m	
200m	
0	

▲ 3415   spot height in meters
—·—·—   international boundary
———   principal road
—+—+—   principal railroad
Ⓐ   international airport
········   seasonal river
  marsh
○   oasis

Right Throughout West Central Africa hunting and fishing are important in the rural economy of the forest areas where cattle cannot be kept. Here, near Kisangani (Stanleyville) on the Zaïre river in northwest Zaïre, Wagenia fishermen use wicker fish traps to catch fish in the swirling rapids.

Below Scattered throughout the rain forests of the region are settlements of pygmies, hunters who preceded the majority population of Negroid agriculturalists. The pygmies now speak the language of their neighbors, with whom they exchange game and fish for grain and vegetables. Here, on the CAR–Zaïre border, a dance takes place in a forest clearing, in front of the pygmy huts built of banana fronds.

Below right Minerals such as manganese and uranium are bringing radical change and wealth to finance modernization and further industrial development in West Central Africa. This manganese mine is at Moanda, near Franceville, in southeast Gabon.

Left Lake Chad, lying across the boundary of Nigeria and Chad, is the home of the Baduma, island dwellers who exist mainly by fishing. Papyrus boats are used for transportation on the lake.

Right Fulani (Fulbe) peoples are found across West Africa from the Atlantic coast to Cameroon and, as in this illustration, in southwest Chad. All speak a Nigritic language, although they vary greatly in physical appearance and in modes of livelihood.

Far right In southern Chad, near Léré, the main agricultural region of the country, villagers store their grain (mainly millet) in tall vermin-proof granaries.

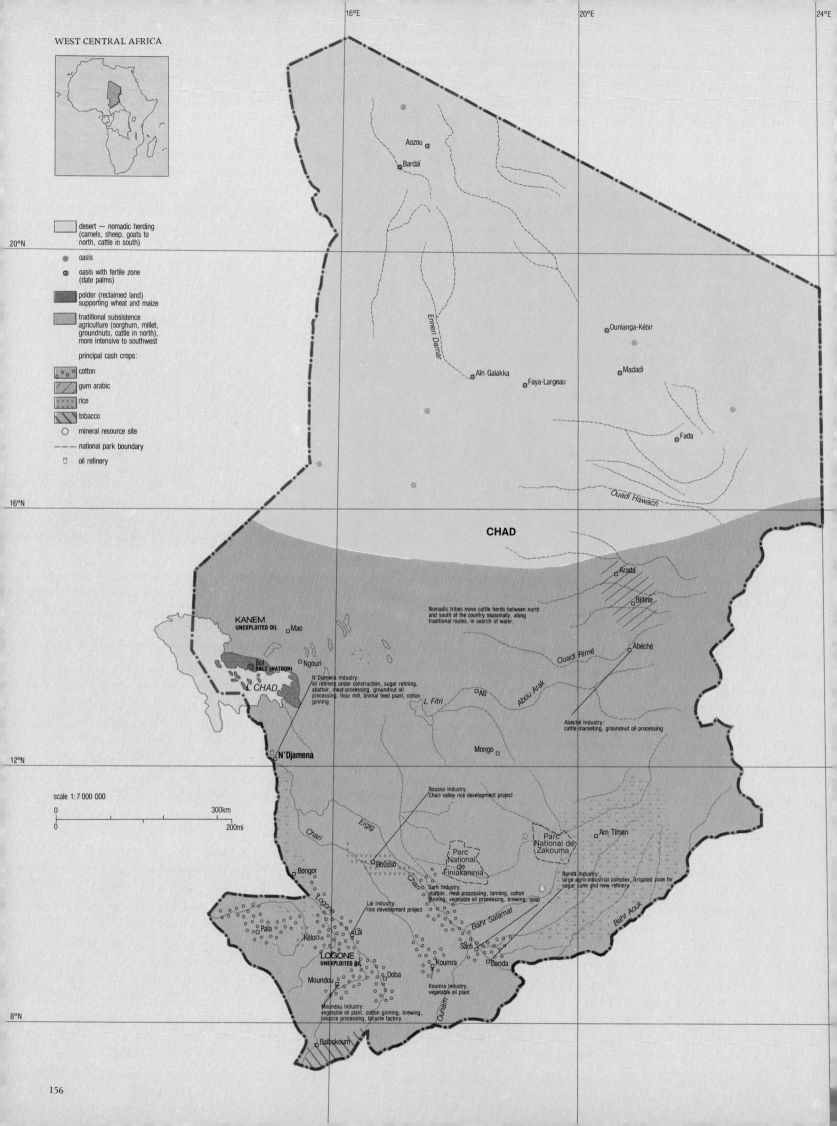

WEST CENTRAL AFRICA

desert — nomadic herding
(camels, sheep, goats to
north, cattle in south)

oasis

oasis with fertile zone
(date palms)

polder (reclaimed land)
supporting wheat and maize

traditional subsistence
agriculture (sorghum, millet,
groundnuts, cattle in north),
more intensive to southwest

principal cash crops:

cotton

gum arabic

rice

tobacco

mineral resource site

national park boundary

oil refinery

16°E   20°E   24°E

20°N

16°N

12°N

8°N

Aozou

Bardaï

Enneri Damar

Ouniangâ-Kébir

Aïn Galakka

Faya-Largeau

Madadi

Fada

Ouadi Hawach

CHAD

Arada

Biltine

Nomadic tribes move cattle herds between north
and south of the country seasonally, along
traditional routes, in search of water.

KANEM
UNEXPLOITED OIL

Mao

Abéché

Ouadi Rimé

Abou Arak

Bol
SALT (NATRON)

Ngouri

CHAD

N'Djamena Industry:
oil refinery under construction, sugar refining,
abattoir, meat processing, groundnut oil
processing, flour mill, animal feed plant, cotton
ginning

L Fitri

Ati

Abéché Industry:
cattle marketing, groundnut oil processing

N'Djamena

Mongo

Bousso Industry:
Chari valley rice development project

Ergig

Am Timan

Chari

Parc
National de
Zakouma

Parc
National
de
Finiakaninia

Bongor

Logone

Bousso

Banda Industry:
large agro-industrial complex, irrigated zone for
sugar cane and new refinery

Sarh Industry:
abattoir, meat processing, tanning, cotton
ginning, vegetable oil processing, brewing, soap

Laï Industry:
rice development project

Pala

Kélo

Laï

Bahr Salamat

Sarh

Koumra

Banda

Bahr Aouk

LOGONE
UNEXPLOITED OIL

Doba

Moundou

Koumra Industry:
vegetable oil plant

Moundou Industry:
vegetable oil plant, cotton ginning, brewing,
tobacco processing, bicycle factory

Ouham

Baïbokoum

scale 1:7 000 000

0   300km

0   200mi

156

Chad

The Republic of Chad, previously the northernmost part of French Equatorial Africa, remains one of Africa's poorest and most isolated countries. Located near the geographical center of the continent, Chad is the fifth largest state, comprising roughly the eastern half of the Lake Chad drainage basin, yet its population is less than four million. The climate ranges from full desert in the Tibesti mountains of the north to moist savanna in the Chari and Logone river valleys of the south.

Humankind has had a long and varied history in Chad as the bones of *Chadanthropus* and the rock paintings of the northern mountains attest. Within the confines of the modern state are found speakers of three of Africa's four linguistic groupings. The Central-Sudanic-speaking Sara, the most numerous group, are politically the most important. Before the time of Christ the Sao of Chad were living in cities, and from the 9th century AD large states, whose economies were based on the trans-Saharan trade of slaves and other goods, have dominated the area. The earliest and most durable of these, Kanem-Bornu, was instrumental in the introduction and spread of Islam in this part of Africa at an early date. In the 14th century Arabic-speaking people began moving into the Chad basin from the east and north, and the Bulala, Bagirmi and Wadai successfully challenged the dominance of Kanem-Bornu.

During the 19th century several European expeditions visited the Chad area. Among them, Denham and Clapperton in 1822 were the first and Heinrich Barth in the 1850s was the most important. The present boundaries of Chad were established by the Franco–British Convention of 1898, despite subsequent arrangements between Germany and France that temporarily changed the borders prior to World War I. The military conquest of Chad by the French began on 22 April 1900 when French and African forces under Commandant Lamy defeated Rabih, the ruler of Bornu, on the site of the modern capital, N'Djamena. Parts of northern and eastern Chad resisted until the eve of World War I.

In the French colonial framework Chad was neglected and ignored. Its people were used as a reservoir of manpower to build the Congo–Ocean railroad although Chad is still without its own rail system. Education was the worst in the French colonies. Despite the introduction of cotton as a cash crop in 1929, the Chadian economy has modernized only very slowly. The road network remains one of the poorest in Africa. During World War II, under the leadership of Félix Éboué, Chad rallied to the cause of the Free French and became the base for French operations against the Axis in the Sahara.

In 1946 the Chadian Progressive Party (PPT) was formed by Gabriel Lisette, a West Indian. By 1956 it became the majority party by opposing the white men and the chiefs, and Lisette became prime minister. During Lisette's absence in Paris, François Tombalbaye, a labor leader, emerged as a force within the party. Tombalbaye was able to merge the major opposition party, based among the Muslims of the north, with his Sara-based PPT. Leading this coalition Tombalbaye became Chad's first president.

As Tombalbaye's regime grew into a personal dictatorship opposition began to form. A guerrilla war began in 1965 and in April 1975 Tombalbaye was killed in a coup led by disgruntled army officers. Félix Malloum, a Chadian soldier, became president but his government was also unable to achieve national unity. In 1978 the disputing parties met at Kano in Nigeria and Goukouni Ouedeye, one of the rebels, became the new head of state. With the recent discovery of oil in Chad, real economic development is possible if political stability can be achieved.

D.E.S

Central African Republic

Placed in the center of the African continent north of the Ubangi river, the Central African Republic, formerly the French colony of Ubangi-Shari, sits astride the Chad–Congo watershed. The southern part of the country abuts the equatorial forest, but towards the north the climate becomes moist savanna. The eastern frontier follows the line of the Nile–Congo watershed, while in the west more arbitrary boundaries separate the country from Cameroon, Chad and the Congo.

Unlike the majority of African states, the boundaries of the Central African Republic correspond closely to the territory inhabited by the speakers of Ubangian languages. Not recent arrivals, the Ubangian speakers probably built the megaliths at Bouar during the last millennium BC. The large precolonial states of the Zande and Senoussi also show the importance of the region before the arrival of the white man.

Late in coming to the Ubangi basin, the first European, Georg Schweinfurth, reached the Zande states in 1870. During the rest of the 19th century and the first two decades of the 20th century the Ubangi became a bone of contention between rival European imperialisms. While the rights of the French had been recognized at the Berlin convention of 1894, the colony of Ubangi-Shari did not take its final form until after World War I.

Divided among 27 concessionary companies which ruthlessly exploited the population to gather rubber and for other forms of forced labor, the colony suffered from a population decline. This trend, begun during the slave trade, was exacerbated by the concessions, a sleeping sickness epidemic and rebellions that persisted into the 1930s. Under these conditions economic and political development was at a standstill.

Following World War II, Barthelemy Boganda founded the Movement of Social Evolution in Black Africa (MESAN). He became the advocate of a confederation of all the colonies of French Equatorial Africa into a state he called the Central African Republic. After his death in 1959 his successor, David Dacko, was forced to settle for a reduced CAR, which he led to independence on 13 April 1960.

Chad

Official Name
République du Tchad

Area
1 284 000 sq km

Date of Independence
11 Apr 1960

Status and Name in Colonial Times
French territory (one of four territories of French Equatorial Africa): Chad

Population
4 500 000 (UN est 1979)

Annual Growth Rate
2·3%

Capital City
N'Djamena (formerly Fort-Lamy)

Population of Capital
241 639 (est 1977)

National Language(s)
French; Arabic, Sara Madjingay, Tuburi, Mundang

Gross National Product (US dollars)
540 million; 130 per capita (est 1977)

Local Currency
1 franc CFA = 100 centimes

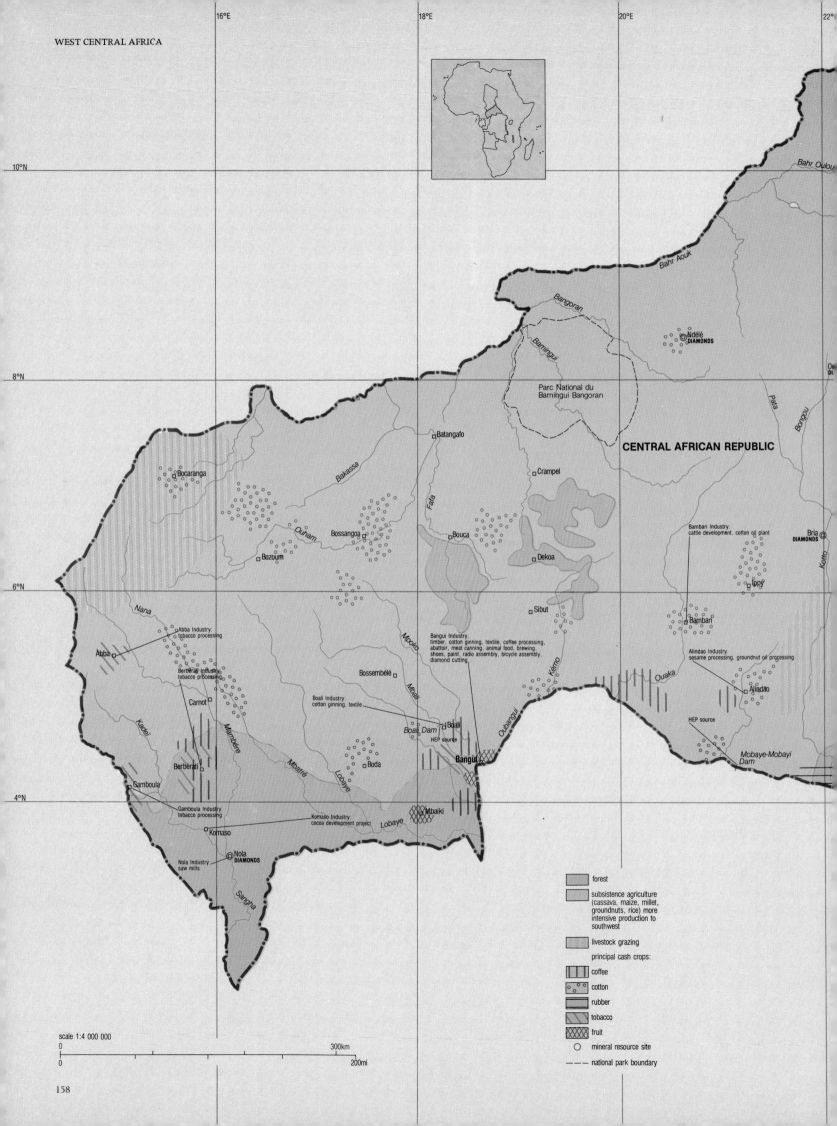

10°N

16°E

18°E

20°E

22°

Bahr Oulou

Bahr Aouk

Bangoran

Bamingui

Ndélé
DIAMONDS

8°N

Parc National du
Bamingui Bangoran

CENTRAL AFRICAN REPUBLIC

Batangafo

Bakassa

Fata

Crampel

Di

Pala

Bongou

Bocaranga

Ouham

Bossangoa

Bouca

Bambari Industry:
cattle development, cotton oil plant

Bria
DIAMONDS

Katto

Bozoum

Dekoa

6°N

Ippy

Nana

Sibut

Mpoko

Bambari

Abba Industry:
tobacco processing

Abba

Bangui Industry:
timber, cotton ginning, textile, coffee processing,
abattoir, meat canning, animal food, brewing,
shoes, paint, radio assembly, bicycle assembly,
diamond cutting

Kémo

Alindao Industry:
sesame processing, groundnut oil processing

Berbérati Industry:
tobacco processing

Bossembélé

Ouaka

Carnot

Mbaïki

Boali Industry:
cotton ginning, textile

Boali Dam

Boali

Oubangui

Alindao

Kadeï

Mambéré

HEP source

Bangui

HEP source

Berbérati

Mbaéré

Lobaye

Boda

Mobaye-Mobayi
Dam

Gamboula

4°N

Gamboula Industry:
tobacco processing

Komaso Industry:
cocoa development project

Lobaye

Mbaïki

Komaso

Nola
DIAMONDS

Nola Industry:
saw mills

Sangha

	forest
	subsistence agriculture (cassava, maize, millet, groundnuts, rice) more intensive production to southwest
	livestock grazing

principal cash crops:

	coffee
	cotton
	rubber
	tobacco
	fruit
○	mineral resource site
---	national park boundary

scale 1:4 000 000

0   300km

0   200mi

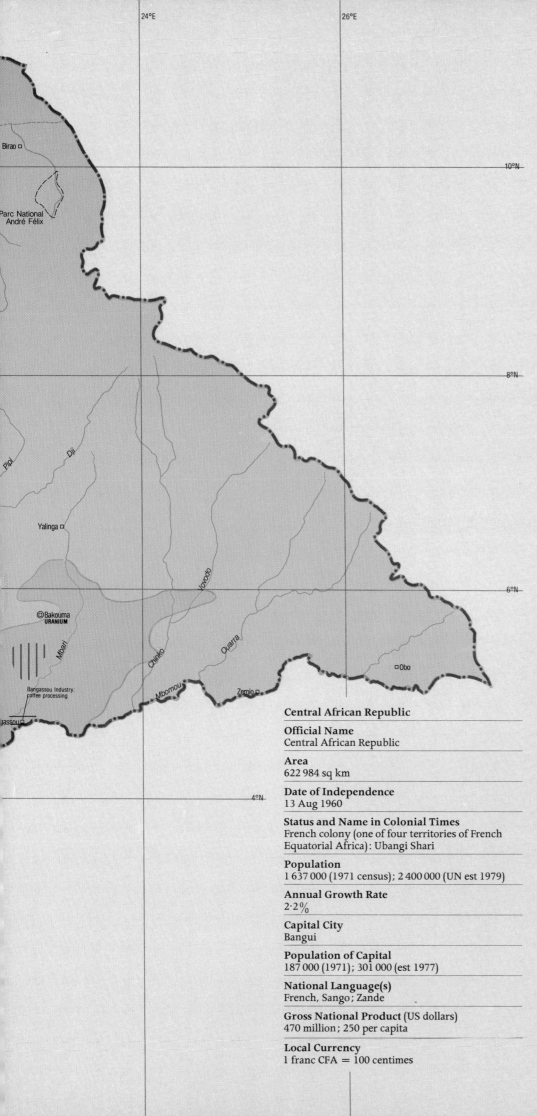

Dacko, who was not the leader that Boganda had been, was overthrown by Colonel Jean Bedel Bokassa on 31 December 1965. Bokassa gradually built a regime of personal rule that culminated in the declaration of himself as Emperor Bokassa I. The country's name was changed to the Central African Empire. Much of its production of diamonds was diverted from providing funds for foreign exchange and development in order to create the crown jewels.

Discontent grew under Bokassa, finally erupting on 18 January 1979 when soldiers gunned down at least 100 students who were protesting against Bokassa's decree that they wear uniforms despite the fact that they could not afford them. Several French-owned buildings were destroyed. On 21 September 1979 a coup returned David Dacko to power while Bokassa fled·to France. The bloodless coup was carried out with French troop support that insured Dacko's position and prevented the return of Ange Patasse who, like Dacko, was a former imperial minister and is believed to be the only CAR politician capable of rallying the various dissenting groups into a national movement.

The Central African Republic remains poorly developed, with the per capita income at $120 per annum. It does, however, have enormous potential, because of its considerable mineral resources and relative ethnolinguistic unity. Mineral deposits include iron, tin and chromium. There are extensive forests and great hydroelectric potential, both virtually untapped.

D.E.S.

Gabon

Sitting astride the equator, Gabon receives heavy rainfall and warm temperatures, both of which favor the growth of tropical rain forest. Covering almost all of the country, the dense forest rests upon an impoverished clay subsoil and a thin surface layer of humus. Rivers and streams are abundant, and many of them are connected to Gabon's major waterway, the Ogooué. Navigable from its mouth at Cape Lopez to the first set of rapids over 160 kilometers inland, the Ogooué and its affluents drain the interior plateau down an escarpment to the coastal plain. Gabon has three major ports: Libreville (the capital) on the Gabon estuary; Owendo, also on the estuary; and Port Gentil near the mouth of the Ogooué. Gabon's population is increasingly centered in urban areas, leaving much of the interior plateau virtually uninhabited.

The first inhabitants of the region were the pygmies. They were followed by Bantu-speaking peoples who moved into the region as early as 1000 AD. Europeans first sailed to the coast of Gabon in the 1470s and began trading contacts with Africans dwelling along the estuary. Slaves and ivory dominated Gabon's export trade with the West until the mid-19th century when slave exports declined in favor of timber (ebony, dyewood) and rubber. During this time of commercial transition, European merchants, missionaries and officials established permanent footholds on the Gabon estuary shore near present-day Libreville. At the same time, a large ethnic group – the Fang – began a long-term

Central African Republic

Official Name
Central African Republic

Area
622 984 sq km

Date of Independence
13 Aug 1960

Status and Name in Colonial Times
French colony (one of four territories of French Equatorial Africa): Ubangi Shari

Population
1 637 000 (1971 census); 2 400 000 (UN est 1979)

Annual Growth Rate
2·2%

Capital City
Bangui

Population of Capital
187 000 (1971); 301 000 (est 1977)

National Language(s)
French, Sango; Zande

Gross National Product (US dollars)
470 million; 250 per capita

Local Currency
1 franc CFA = 100 centimes

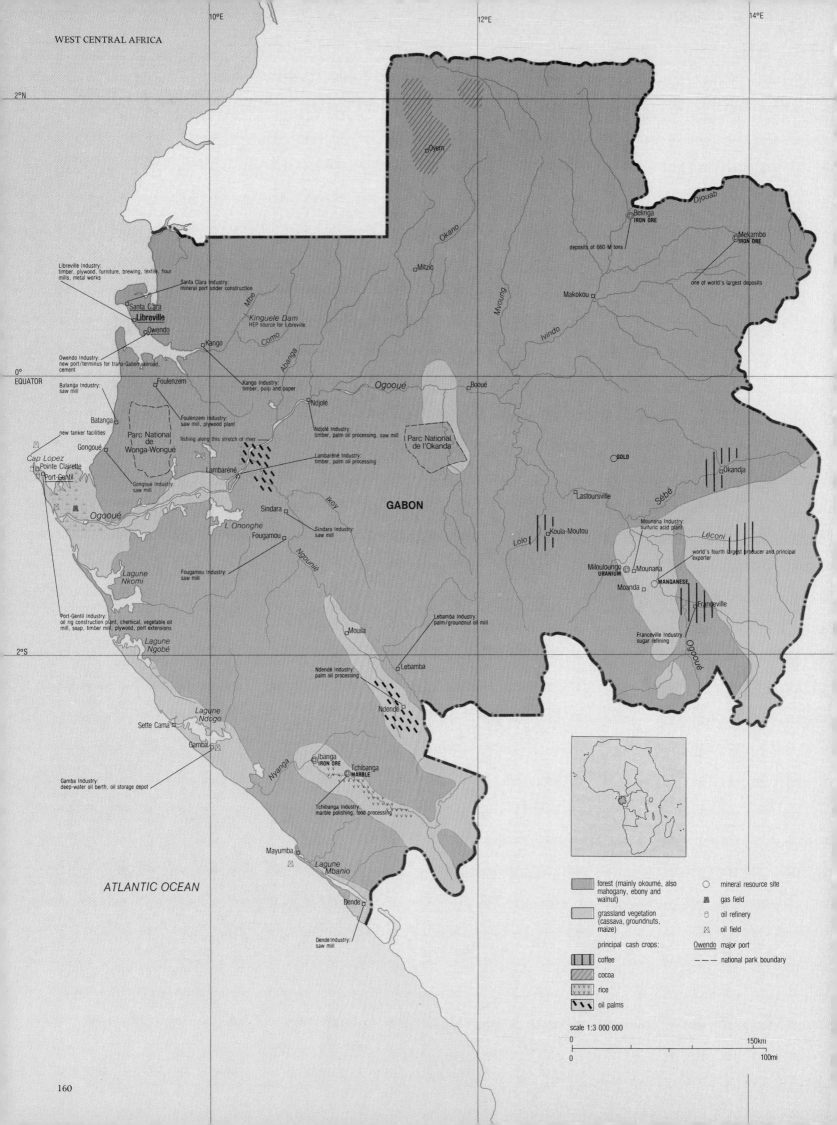

WEST CENTRAL AFRICA

10°E   12°E   14°E

2°N

Oyem

Djouab

Belinga
IRON ORE

Mekambo
IRON ORE

Mitzic

deposits of 660 M tons

one of world's largest deposits

Makokou

Libreville Industry:
timber, plywood, furniture, brewing, textile, flour
mills, metal works

Santa Clara Industry:
mineral port under construction

Mbé

Kinguele Dam
HEP source for Libreville

Santa Clara
Libreville
Owendo

Kango

Como

Abanga

Okano

Mvoung

Ivindo

0°
EQUATOR

Owendo Industry:
new port/terminus for trans-Gabon railroad,
cement

Foulenzem

Kango Industry:
timber, pulp and paper

Ogooué

Booué

Batanga Industry:
saw mill

Ndjolé

Ndjolé Industry:
timber, palm oil processing, saw mill

Parc National
de l'Okanda

Batanga

new tanker facilities

Parc National
de Wonga-Wongué

fishing along this stretch of river

Lambaréné Industry:
timber, palm oil processing

GOLD

Okandja

Gongoué

Gongoué Industry:
saw mill

Lambaréné

Sébé

Cap Lopez
Pointe Clairette
Port-Gentil

Ogooué

Sindara

Ikoy

GABON

Mounana Industry:
sulfuric acid plant

Léconi

L. Ononghé

Sindara Industry:
saw mill

Lastoursville

Fougamou

Lolo

Koula-Moutou

Lagune
Nkomi

Fougamou Industry:
saw mill

Ngounié

world's fourth largest producer and principal
exporter

Miouloungo
URANIUM

Mounana

MANGANESE

Port-Gentil Industry:
oil rig construction plant, chemical, vegetable oil
mill, soap, timber mill, plywood, port extensions

Moanda

Lagune
Ngobé

Mouila

Lebamba Industry:
palm/groundnut oil mill

Franceville

Ogooué

Franceville Industry:
sugar refining

2°S

Ndendé Industry:
palm oil processing

Lebamba

Sette Cama

Lagune
Ndogo

Ndendé

Gamba

Gamba Industry:
deep-water oil berth, oil storage depot

Nyanga

Ibanga
IRON ORE

Tchibanga
MARBLE

Tchibanga Industry:
marble polishing, food processing

Mayumba

Lagune
Mbanio

ATLANTIC OCEAN

Dende

Dende Industry:
saw mill

forest (mainly okoumé, also
mahogany, ebony and
walnut)

○ mineral resource site

grassland vegetation
(cassava, groundnuts,
maize)

⊠ gas field

⊟ oil refinery

⊠ oil field

principal cash crops:

Owendo major port

coffee

--- national park boundary

cocoa

rice

oil palms

scale 1:3 000 000

0   150km

0   100mi

160

16°E

2°N

0°
EQUATOR

2°S

Gabon

Official Name
République Gabonaise

Area
267 667 sq km

Date of Independence
17 Aug 1960

Status and Name in Colonial Times
French colony (one of the four territories of French
Equatorial Africa) with the names French Congo
(1890–1903), Gabon (within the French Congo
1903–10), Gabon (1910–60)

Population
1 027 529 (1972 census); 580 000 (UN est 1979)

Annual Growth Rate
1·0% (1970–75); 1·7% (est 1979)

Capital City
Libreville

Population of Capital
251 400 (1975)

National Language(s)
French

Gross National Product (US dollars)
3220 million; 110 per capita (est 1977)

Local Currency
1 franc CFA = 100 centimes

migration from their homeland near Cameroon
toward the dynamic commercial centers on the
estuary and the Ogooué.

France obtained colonial title to the territory
in the 1880s. The French government then
parceled out the region to commercial companies who administered and traded in their
exclusive concessions. The policy was a
commercial failure and was abandoned in the
1920s just as European companies began their
first significant purchases of okoumé timber,
an ideal wood for the manufacture of plywood.
Gabon prospered thanks to okoumé, and its
economic future was further assured by the
discovery of major deposits of oil near Port
Gentil, and manganese and uranium near
Franceville around the year of independence,
1960.

Leon M'ba was elected the first president of
Gabon in 1961. He survived an attempted coup
d'état in 1964 only because French para-
troopers intervened to maintain him in power.
French influence in Gabon has continued with
M'ba's chosen successor, President Omar
Bongo, whose major responsibility has been
the management of Gabon's rich economy to
the satisfaction of the French, who run it, and
his Gabonese constituency, who want to share
in it.

Since 1968 Gabon has been an official one-
party state under President Bongo's Parti
Démocratique Gabonaise. Gabon has been
stable politically although a growing number
of refugees from Equatorial Guinea (60 000
according to one estimate) has been a source of
past unrest in Libreville. Internationally,
Gabon is known for its reluctance to adhere to
multilateral arrangements with poor neighbors and for her commercial and political
contacts with minority-ruled southern Africa.

The economy of Gabon is dominated by the
mining sector which is operated by foreign
enterprises. Oil at OPEC prices accounts for
approximately 70 per cent of the government's
revenues, but long-term supply prospects are
unsure. With the construction of the Trans-
Gabonais railroad reaching Franceville in
1980, however, manganese and uranium
exports will rise appreciably. In 1982 the
railroad is scheduled to reach Mekambo where
the world's largest iron ore deposits await
exploitation. The railroad will also revive the
stagnant timber industry in currently inaccessible forest zones. Gabon's economy
requires a large, mostly imported, labor force.
Agricultural production is inadequate and
food is also imported. This array of Gabon's
economic strengths and failings echoes patterns reaching back to the 19th century when
foreign companies first arrived to export
Gabon's natural wealth, but found that food
and labor were in short supply.

C.C.

Equatorial Guinea

Equatorial Guinea consists of a mainland
enclave called Río Muni and five small
islands: Bioko (formerly Macías Nguema
Biyogo and Fernando Póo), Pigalu (formerly
Annobón), Corisco, Grand Elobey and Little
Elobey. Bioko, the largest of the five, was
formed by three extinct volcanoes. It is
endowed with fertile soil and high rainfall,

conditions ideal for the cultivation of high-
quality cocoa. The mainland, Río Muni, is
covered by tropical rain forest through which
the Mbini river (also known as the Benito or
Woleu river) flows westward over the interior
plateau and down an escarpment to the coastal
plain. The Muni river on the southern border
is actually an estuary fed by several rivers
including the Utanboni. The only natural
harbor is at the capital, Malaba (formerly Santa
Isabel), on Bioko. Bata is the principal town on
the mainland and its harbor was recently
improved.

When Portuguese mariners first sailed to
Bioko in 1472, they were met by the Bubi, the
indigenous inhabitants who had crossed over
from the mainland Río Muni area during the
13th century. On the mainland the Bubi were
followed by several coastward waves of Bantu
migrants, the last of whom were the Fang in
the 19th century. The Portuguese ruled Bioko
until 1778 when they surrendered the island
and their rights to the mainland to Spain, but
in 1827 Britain acquired from Spain the right
to use the island as a forward base for her
antislavery naval patrols. Britain resettled
many captured slaves there, the descendants
of whom are today called "Fernandinos." This
growing labor force was, however, insufficient to work the nascent cocoa industry on
the island and laborers were recruited in
Liberia and elsewhere in West Africa. They
were frequently mistreated and forced to
remain on the island, a practice continuing to
this day.

Spain sent troops to occupy the Río Muni
mainland in the 1920s and encountered stiff
resistance from the Fang. Most Spaniards
stayed on Bioko, acquired much of the land
and developed the intensive cultivation of
cocoa. After World War II a colonial policy of
cultural and political assimilation failed to
dampen nationalistic feelings of the African
population which supported independence
movements in the 1960s. These movements
successfully won from Spain the granting of
full independence on 12 October 1968 under
President Francisco Macías Nguema. Macías
Nguema later proclaimed himself president for
life but was deposed in 1979. His nephew,
Teodoro Obiang Nguema Mbasogo, replaced
him.

Under Macías Nguema the economy of
Equatorial Guinea contracted precipitously.
The exodus of Spanish farmers and technicians
from Bioko in 1969 helped to reduce the
cocoa crop from pre-independence levels of
35000–45000 tons to 15000 tons in 1975.
Nigeria recalled approximately 45000 agricultural workers from Bioko in 1975 and
1976 on reports of severe mistreatment and
loss of life. Conditions on the plantations in
1978 and 1979 were reported as *de facto*
slavery.

The once productive timber industry also
contracted due to political instability and the
exhaustion of accessible forest reserves. Coffee
production in Río Muni stagnated at low
levels. Mineral exploration for oil and uranium
halted under Nguema, but his successor has
reestablished trade with Spain and exploration should resume.

Described by some as a "hermit republic,"
Equatorial Guinea under Macías Nguema
earned a reputation as a flagrant violator of
human rights. Reports of political murders,

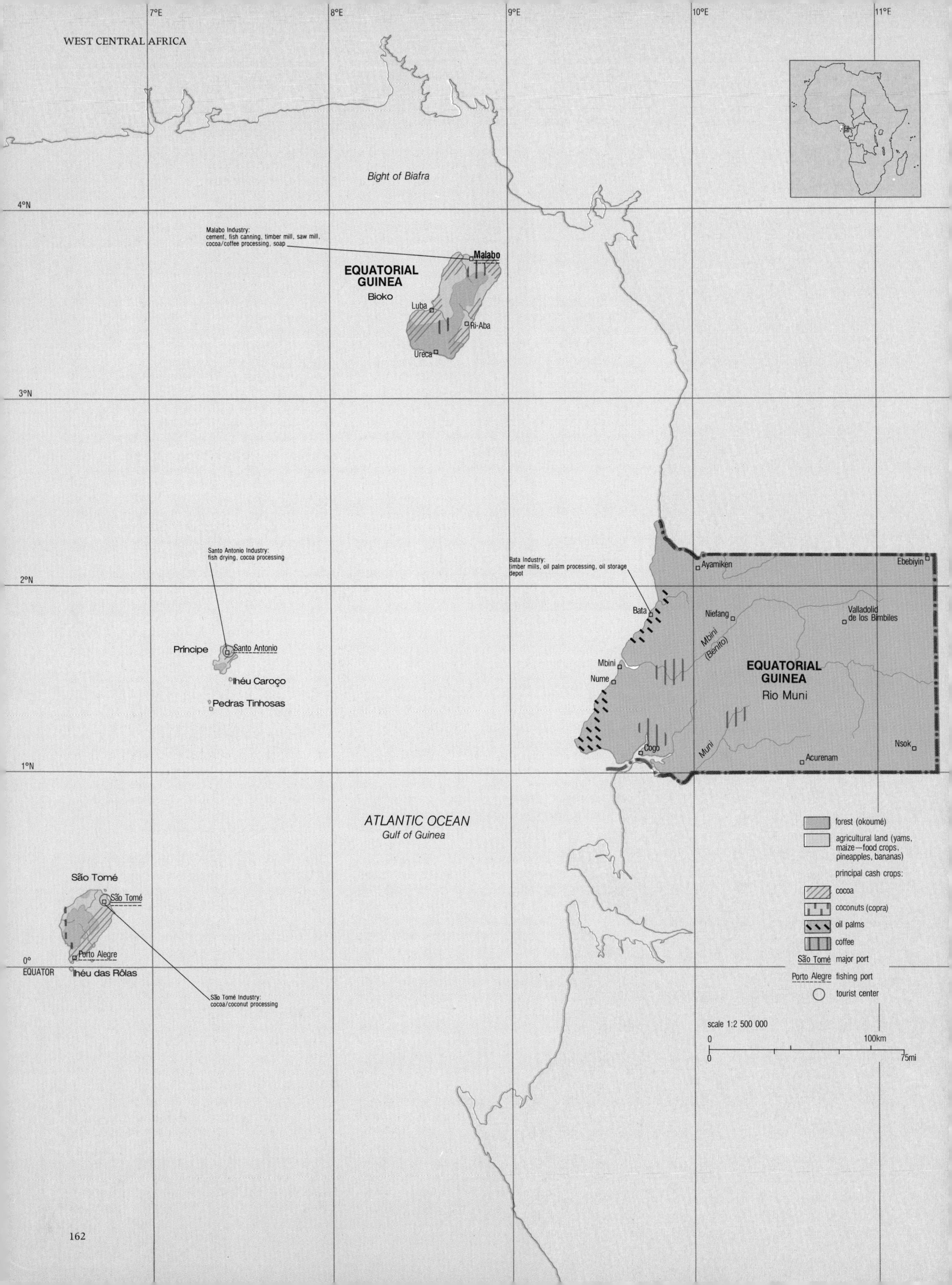

WEST CENTRAL AFRICA

Bight of Biafra

4°N

Malabo Industry:
cement, fish canning, timber mill, saw mill,
cocoa/coffee processing, soap

Malabo

**EQUATORIAL
GUINEA**

Bioko

Luba

Ri-Aba

3°N

Ureca

Santo Antonio Industry:
fish drying, cocoa processing

Bata Industry:
timber mills, oil palm processing, oil storage
depot

2°N

Ayamiken

Ebebiyin

Bata

Niefang

Valladolid
de los Bimbiles

Príncipe

Santo Antonio

Mbini
(Benito)

**EQUATORIAL
GUINEA**

Ihéu Caroço

Mbini

Rio Muni

Nume

Pedras Tinhosas

Nsok

Cogo

Muni

Acurenam

1°N

ATLANTIC OCEAN
Gulf of Guinea

| | forest (okoumé) |
| | agricultural land (yams, maize—food crops, pineapples, bananas) |

principal cash crops:

	cocoa
	coconuts (copra)
	oil palms
	coffee

São Tomé

São Tomé   major port

São Tomé

Porto Alegre   fishing port

0°   Porto Alegre

○   tourist center

EQUATOR   Ihéu das Rôlas

São Tomé Industry:
cocoa/coconut processing

scale 1:2 500 000

0   100km

0   75mi

162

Equatorial Guinea

Official Name
República de Guinea Ecuatorial

Area
28 051 sq km

Date of Independence
12 Oct 1968

Status and Name in Colonial Times
Spanish colony: Spanish Guinea (Territorios Españoles del Golfo de Guinea including Río Muni and Fernando Póo (1900–59)); 1959–68 two Spanish provinces: Equatorial Region of Spain

Population
245 989 (1960 census); 340 000 (est 1979)

Annual Growth Rate
1·8% (est 1979)

Capital City
Malabo (formerly Santa Isabel)

Population of Capital
19 869 (1960 census); 37 000 (est 1975)

National Language(s)
Spanish

Gross National Product (US dollars)
110 million; 340 per capita (est 1977)

Local Currency
1 ekuele = 100 céntimos

São Tomé and Príncipe

Official Name
Republica Democratica de São Tomé e Príncipe/Democratic Republic of São Tomé e Príncipe

Area
964 sq km

Date of Independence
12 July 1975

Status and Name in Colonial Times
1522–1975 Portuguese colony: São Tomé and Príncipe (also called Cocoa Islands)

Population
73 631 (1970 census); 82 750 (est 1977)

Annual Growth Rate
1·7%

Capital City
São Tomé

Population of Capital
17 380 (1970 census)

National Language(s)
Portuguese; Creole

Gross National Product (US dollars)
30 million; 420 per capita

Local Currency
1 dobra = 100 centavos

mass executions and religious persecution were frequent. Almost a third of the country's population (90 000) is still in exile in Cameroon, Gabon and Spain. With Macías Nguema gone, conditions have improved, but Equatorial Guinea faces a staggering task of reconstruction and development.

C.C.

São Tomé and Príncipe

The two islands of São Tomé and Príncipe are located in the Atlantic 440 and 200 kilometers respectively off the coast of northern Gabon. Part of a volcanic mountain chain extending from Mount Cameroon out into the Atlantic, the islands have fertile volcanic soil and mountainous relief. Both receive high rainfall and warm temperatures, conditions that favor the growth of dense tropical rain forests. The low-lying slopes and flatlands on the islands' perimeters are ideal for cocoa, coffee and copra production. The towns of São Tomé and Santo Antonio are the main ports. The rocky islets of Pedras Tinhosas and Rolas are also part of the islands.

When Portuguese mariners first reached the islands in 1471, they found them uninhabited. The Portuguese monarch assumed administrative responsibility for the island colonies in 1522 after they had become major entrepôts in the African slave trade to the West Indies and the site of productive sugar plantations run by Portuguese criminals and outcasts. Intermarriage between Portuguese settlers and their slave laborers produced a mestizo population which survives to this day. The Angolares, survivors of a wrecked slave ship, still inhabit the southern area of São Tomé.

The islands enjoyed great prosperity during the 16th century, but fell into a slump during the 17th as Portuguese dominance of the slave trade waned. Growing slave exports from the mainland revived the islands' role as entrepôts in the 18th century, and the pattern continued well into the 19th century. After 1860 a boom in cocoa and coffee production on the islands created a new demand for labor, which was supplied at first by the purchase of slaves from the nearby mainland and from the 1870s by contract laborers (*libertos*) from Angola. The *libertos* were treated as slaves once they reached the islands, and in 1908 Britain officially boycotted São Tomé's cocoa in protest of the conditions which the workers suffered at the hands of the planters.

Labor abuses were curbed and the boycott lifted, but conditions soon reverted to their former state. In 1953 the Portuguese governor fired on striking plantation workers, killing nearly 1000 in what is remembered today as the "Batepa Massacre." In 1960 the forerunner of the Movement for the Liberation of São Tomé and Príncipe (MLSTP) was formed at a conference in Ghana, and from their base in Gabon the MLSTP pressed Portugal for independence. Following the fall of the Caetano dictatorship in 1974, Portugal met the MLSTP and arranged for the peaceful transition to independence on 12 July 1975. President Manuel Pinto da Costa, the

country's first president, faced a colonial inheritance of widespread poverty, inadequate social facilities and a foundering economy due to the departure of the country's 3000 Portuguese planters after independence.

Once in power, the government immediately granted unrealistic wage and hours benefits to the plantation workers, a move that combined with the Portuguese exodus to reduce cocoa exports from 10000 tons before independence to just over 5000 tons in 1975. The MLSTP government has nationalized nearly all the Portuguese plantations without compensation and is now attempting to balance and diversify the country's export production. Gabon is an emerging source of aid and technical assistance, but the islands' past labor practices still hamper labor recruitment.

The MLSTP has retained ties with other liberation movements now in power in former Portuguese Africa and has succeeded in mobilizing the population in developmental programs. Politically the islands have been stable since independence, although in April 1979 the president abolished the post of prime minister, thus consolidating his own power. As a result a serious split developed in the MLSTP.

C.C.

Congo

In spite of its position, almost exactly straddling the equator, the People's Republic of the Congo presents some diversity of landscape and natural environment. This diversity is largely due to the influence of the cold Benguela Current along its coasts and of the anticyclone centered on the island of St Helena. In the north a true equatorial climate predominates, characterized by abundant rainfall (1550 to 2500 millimeters) and dense forest. The south, a savanna region, also has less rainfall (1350 millimeters) and has a long dry cool season from June through September. This geographical diversity determines the distribution of population in that in the southwest, between Brazzaville and the sea, 70 per cent of the total live on 25 per cent of the territory.

The history of the modern Congolese state begins in 1880, when the explorer Pierre Savorgnan de Brazza signed a treaty of friendship with the Makoko Iloo, king of the Teke, which bound the latter to France. The territory of the Congo did not make its appearance until 1886; in 1903 it was given the name Middle Congo (Moyen-Congo), though readjustments of the borders with Cameroon, Ubangi-Shari (the Central African Republic) and Gabon continued until just after World War II.

In the Middle Congo, as in the rest of French Equatorial Africa, French colonialism showed itself more primitive than elsewhere in Africa. In 1899 the territory was handed over to 14 concessionary companies, who shared out between them over 220 000 square kilometers and embarked on systematic plundering of the country's natural resources. Despite reforms in 1911, the abuses continued: the construction of the Congo–Ocean railroad, according to the grim formula, "cost a man a sleeper." Education was neglected until 1950.

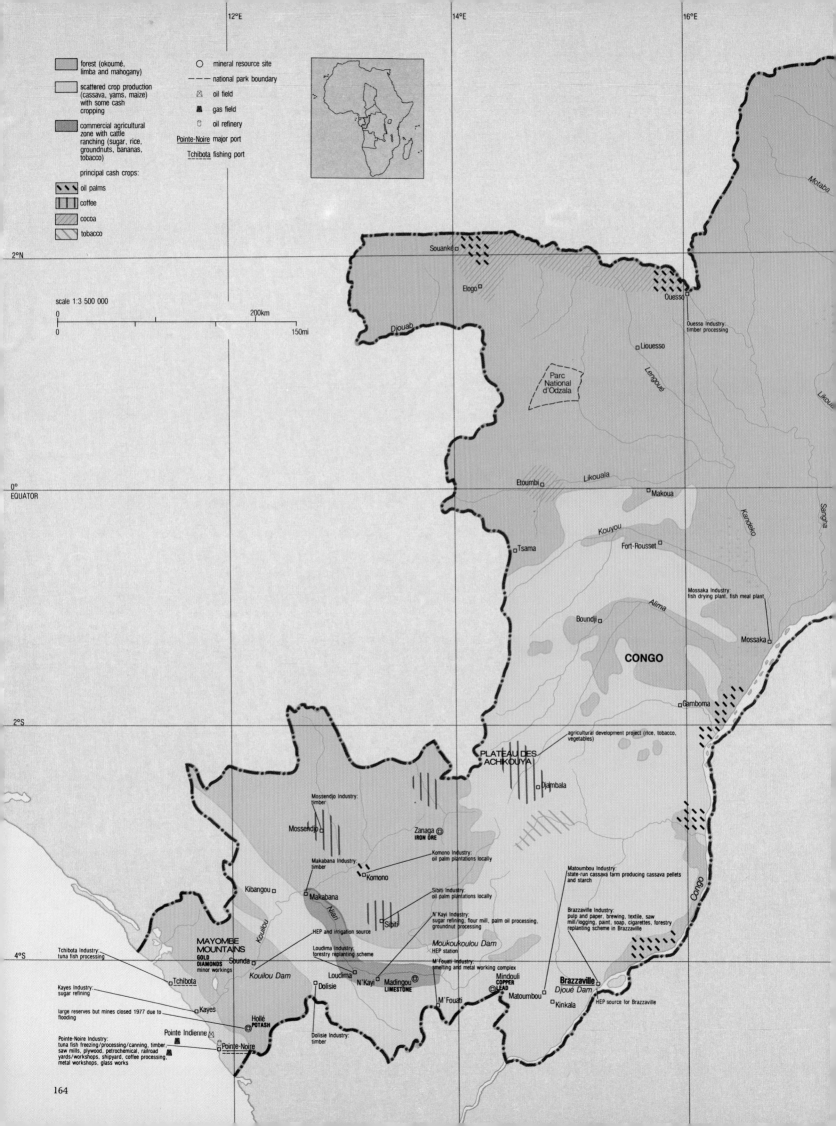

forest (okoumé, limba and mahogany)

scattered crop production (cassava, yams, maize) with some cash cropping

commercial agricultural zone with cattle ranching (sugar, rice, groundnuts, bananas, tobacco)

principal cash crops:

oil palms

coffee

cocoa

tobacco

○ mineral resource site

--- national park boundary

⊠ oil field

▲ gas field

⬚ oil refinery

Pointe-Noire major port

Tchibota fishing port

scale 1:3 500 000

0   200km

0   150mi

2°N

EQUATOR 0°

2°S

4°S

12°E   14°E   16°E

Motaba

Souanké

Elogo

Ouesso

Ouesso Industry: timber processing

Djouab

Liouesso

Lengoué

Likoue

Parc National d'Odzala

Etoumbi

Likouala

Makoua

Sangha

Kouyou

Kandeko

Tsama

Fort-Rousset

Alima

Mossaka Industry: fish drying plant, fish meal plant

Boundji

CONGO

Mossaka

Gamboma

agricultural development project (rice, tobacco, vegetables)

PLATEAU DES ACHIKOUYA

Djambala

Congo

Mossendjo Industry: timber

Mossendjo

Zanaga ◎ IRON ORE

Komono Industry: oil palm plantations locally

Makabana Industry: timber

Komono

Matoumbou Industry: state-run cassava farm producing cassava pellets and starch

Kibangou

Makabana

Niari

Sibiti Industry: oil palm plantations locally

Brazzaville Industry: pulp and paper, brewing, textile, saw mill/logging, paint, soap, cigarettes, forestry replanting scheme in Brazzaville

Sibiti

N'Kayi Industry: sugar refining, flour mill, palm oil processing, groundnut processing

HEP and irrigation source

MAYOMBE MOUNTAINS

Tchibota Industry: tuna fish processing

GOLD DIAMONDS minor workings

Loudima Industry: forestry replanting scheme

Moukoukoulou Dam HEP station

M'Fouati Industry: smelting and metal working complex

Sounda

Kouilou Dam

Loudima

N'Kayi

Madingou LIMESTONE

Mindouli COPPER ◎ LEAD

Brazzaville

Djoué Dam

Kayes Industry: sugar refining

Dolisie

M'Fouati

Matoumbou

HEP source for Brazzaville

large reserves but mines closed 1977 due to flooding

Kayes

Kinkala

Pointe-Noire Industry: tuna fish freezing/processing/canning, timber, saw mills, plywood, petrochemical, railroad yards/workshops, shipyard, coffee processing, metal workshops, glass works

Hollé ◎ POTASH

Pointe Indienne ⊠

Dolisie Industry: timber

Pointe-Noire

Tchibota

164

the Brazzaville Conference (1944) which, while condemning the idea of self-government, stimulated a real liberalization of the colonial system. Three parties contended for votes, Jean-Félix Tchicaya's Parti Progressiste Congolais (PPC), Jacques Opangault's Mouvement Socialiste Africain (MSA) and Abbé Fulbert Youlou's Union Démocratique de Défense des Intérêts Africains (UDDIA). Progress to independence was marked by persistent serious disturbances. After the proclamation of independence (15 August 1960) Abbé Youlou was elected head of state in 1961, but the new regime, moderate and corrupt, soon became very unpopular and was swept away by the popular revolution of the Glorious Three Days (13–15 August 1963).

Far from solving the problems which had appeared under the Youlou regime, this revolution plunged the Congo into a persistent crisis. Personal quarrels, ideological differences, ethnic antagonisms between northerners and southerners, the incoherence of the institutions and finally the conflict between young and old were all factors making for instability. The only permanent element has been a constant appeal to communist ideology. As early as December 1963 Pascal Lissouba, prime minister in the new government, declared himself in favor of "scientific socialism." In 1964 this was written into the charter of the National Revolutionary Movement (MNR), the only party. In 1968 the Congolese Workers' Party (Parti Congolais du Travail, PCT) replaced the MNR. The 1970 constitution made Marxism–Leninism the basis of the regime. However, since 1963 there have been innumerable demotions, plots, political murders and executions. The extreme Left, which had been very active since the fall of Youlou, was eliminated from the political scene with the murder of its spokesman, Ange Diwara, in March 1973. Marien Ngouabi, head of state since 1968, was assassinated in his turn on 18 March 1977, which brought about the execution of several figures, including Massamba-Débat, the new regime's first president of the republic.

This political situation hinders economic growth and development. Since the bulk of the state's resources is absorbed in paying its civil servants (75 per cent of the budget), it has to rely on foreign countries for productive investment. Among capitalist countries, France remains the main supplier, followed at a great distance by West Germany and the other members of the EEC; the Congo is also still a member of the franc zone. To diversify its sources of credit, the Congo also draws on the USSR and the People's Republic of China. Nevertheless the economy remains fragile. Agriculture, based on the production of foodstuffs, is still the poor relation: this adversely affects the food supply to the towns, where 33 per cent of the population live, and also fuels inflation. Transportation, visibly neglected, threatens to immobilize the economy. Industry, partially nationalized, is based mainly on the textile sector, hydroelectricity and cement. The Congo has concentrated on giving priority to export products. Wood – okoumé, limba and redwood – makes up 70 per cent of the value of exports to developed countries. The production of potassium, started in 1969, stopped completely in 1978. Oil, exploited since 1971,

has not lived up to expectations. The reserves are becoming exhausted and the financial resources obtained from hydrocarbons are not sufficient to keep the trade account in balance. The relaunching of the economy on sound foundations is now the Congo's top priority.

E.M'B.

Zaïre

The Republic of Zaïre is the third largest country on the African continent encompassing an area four times the size of France. The country's topography is dominated by the Zaïre river (formerly the Congo) which rises in the southeast, flows north across the equator, then south again, to empty finally into the Atlantic Ocean some 4700 kilometers later. The basin drained by the Zaïre is rimmed by high mountains in the east and by high plateaus in the north and south. Zaïre's borders were largely set by the Treaty of Berlin in 1885 when western European nations carved up Africa into spheres of influence. These boundaries coincide with natural boundaries (rivers, lakes, dividing lines between drainage basins) except for the southern border with Angola.

Zaïre lies astride the equator between 5° north and 13° south. The climate within three or four degrees of the equator is characterized by constant high temperatures, high humidity and heavy rainfall (1800–2200 millimeters annual average). North and south of this zone the climate becomes tropical, with alternating wet and dry seasons. Depending on the distance from the equator, the dry seasons last from three to six months. They bring cool nights along with warm days; temperatures may drop to 2° or 3° on the high plateau. At the foot of the eastern mountains, which rise to an elevation of more than 5000 meters, the climate is quite temperate. Due to its climate, lakes, mountains and national parks, this area is the part of Zaïre most favored by tourists.

Slightly more than half of Zaïre is covered by equatorial rain forest where the warm, humid soil produces tall trees and extremely dense vegetation. The forest, which includes the largest forest reserves in Africa, harbors a great wealth of flora and fauna. The plateau regions of southern Zaïre are savanna grasslands cut by forested river valleys. The lateritic soils of these regions are quickly leached and easily eroded, but with proper care they can produce a great variety of crops. The volcanic soils of eastern Kivu province are even more fertile, but are now losing their fertility.

Linguistic and archaeological evidence indicates that the ancestors of Zaïrians began migrating into the areas just east and south of the rain forest some 1500 years ago. Originating from the Niger river basin, these early pioneers arrived with a knowledge of horticulture and metalworking techniques which enabled them to supplant any possible predecessors. Since most Zaïrians today speak Bantu languages, it is thought that these pioneers were also Bantu speakers. In addition to Bantu languages some Sudanese and Nilotic languages are spoken in the north and northeast.

Although most of these people remained politically decentralized until the colonial era,

Congo

Official Name
République Populaire du Congo

Area
342 000 sq km

Date of Independence
15 Aug 1960

Status and Name in Colonial Times
French colony (one of the four territories of French Equatorial Africa) with the names French Congo (1882–86), Congo (1886–1903), Middle Congo (1903–58); Republic of the Congo (1958–60)

Population
1 500 000 (est 1979)

Annual Growth Rate
2·7% (est 1979)

Capital City
Brazzaville (Ntamo)

Population of Capital
289 700 (est 1977)

National Language(s)
French; Lingala, Monokutuba

Gross National Product (US dollars)
700 million; 500 per capita

Local Currency
1 franc CFA = 100 centimes

African reaction at first took the form of messianic movements, particularly active in the southern areas. The church, founded in 1921 by Simon Kimbangu in the Belgian Congo, won many followers here. In 1926 André Matswa founded a French Equatorial Africa Association (Amicale des Originaires de l'Afrique Equatoriale Française), which opposed the colonial regime. The year 1939 saw the appearance of the *kakist* movement inspired by Simon Pierre M'Padi, who claimed to be a successor of Kimbangu. The modern political parties made their appearance after

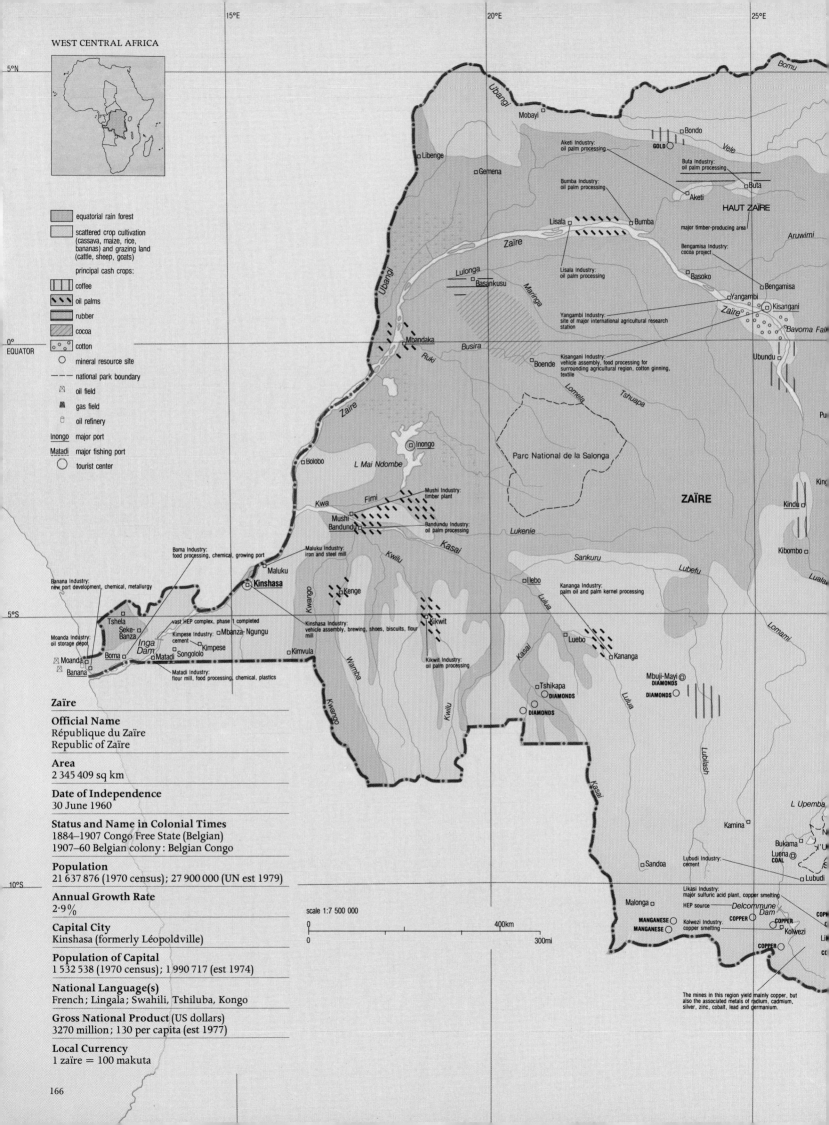

WEST CENTRAL AFRICA

Legend:

- equatorial rain forest
- scattered crop cultivation (cassava, maize, rice, bananas) and grazing land (cattle, sheep, goats)

principal cash crops:
- coffee
- oil palms
- rubber
- cocoa
- cotton

- ○ mineral resource site
- — — national park boundary
- ⊠ oil field
- ▲ gas field
- ⊡ oil refinery
- Inongo major port
- Matadi major fishing port
- ○ tourist center

Zaïre

Official Name
République du Zaïre
Republic of Zaïre

Area
2 345 409 sq km

Date of Independence
30 June 1960

Status and Name in Colonial Times
1884–1907 Congo Free State (Belgian)
1907–60 Belgian colony: Belgian Congo

Population
21 637 876 (1970 census); 27 900 000 (UN est 1979)

Annual Growth Rate
2·9%

Capital City
Kinshasa (formerly Léopoldville)

Population of Capital
1 532 538 (1970 census); 1 990 717 (est 1974)

National Language(s)
French; Lingala; Swahili, Tshiluba, Kongo

Gross National Product (US dollars)
3270 million; 130 per capita (est 1977)

Local Currency
1 zaïre = 100 makuta

scale 1:7 500 000

0 — 400km
0 — 300mi

ZAÏRE

HAUT ZAÏRE

Parc National de la Salonga

Inga Dam

Kinshasa

Industry notes:

Aketi Industry: oil palm processing
Buta Industry: oil palm processing
Bumba Industry: oil palm processing
Lisala Industry: oil palm processing
Bengamisa Industry: cocoa project
Yangambi Industry: site of major international agricultural research station
Kisangani Industry: vehicle assembly, food processing for surrounding agricultural region, cotton ginning, textile
Mushi Industry: timber plant
Bandundu Industry: oil palm processing
Maluku Industry: iron and steel mill
Boma Industry: food processing, chemical, growing port
Banana Industry: new port development, chemical, metallurgy
Moanda Industry: oil storage depot
Kinshasa Industry: vehicle assembly, brewing, shoes, biscuits, flour mill
Kimpese Industry: cement
Matadi Industry: flour mill, food processing, chemical, plastics
vast HEP complex, phase 1 completed
Kikwit Industry: oil palm processing
Kananga Industry: palm oil and palm kernel processing
Lubudi Industry: cement
Likasi Industry: major sulfuric acid plant, copper smelting
Kolwezi Industry: copper smelting
major timber-producing area

The mines in this region yield mainly copper, but also the associated metals of radium, cadmium, silver, zinc, cobalt, lead and germanium.

a number of kingdoms arose in the southern savanna region during the past 500 years. Located near the mouth of the Congo river, the Kongo kingdom dominated that area for several centuries. It established diplomatic relations with the Portuguese in the 16th century, but had fallen by the 18th century. The largest kingdoms at the time of the 19th-century European exploration were the Kuba, Lunda and Luba kingdoms which all engaged in long-distance trade.

In the 1870s King Léopold of the Belgians became interested in central Africa and succeeded in gaining title to control what eventually became Zaïre at the Berlin Conference of 1884. He used the territory for commercial purposes but was forced to cede it to the Belgian government in 1908. Thus the Belgian Congo came into being. The Belgian colonial administration concentrated on the exploitation of the natural resources of the territory by granting huge concessions to private companies for mining copper, diamonds, manganese and iron, and for establishing plantations to produce palm oil, coffee, tea, cotton and other cash crops on territory which they simply appropriated. Troops were sent to quell any local resistance to Belgian rule. The Belgian government set up a paternalistic administration to maintain order, collect taxes and assure an adequate supply of labor for the private companies. Political unrest in the late 1950s forced Belgium to grant independence precipitately in 1960.

In the general elections that preceded independence Patrice Lumumba was elected prime minister and Joseph Kasavubu was designated chief of state. When the provinces of Katanga and part of Kasai tried to secede in the months following independence United Nations troops were called in to restore order. For some years after 1960 the struggle for power among the major politicians prevented any government from establishing firm control. While the problem of the secessions was resolved in 1963, other armed insurrections followed in 1963, 1964 and 1967. Patrice Lumumba was assassinated in Katanga in 1961 and has since become a nationalist hero.

In November 1965 General Joseph Mobutu seized power in a coup. After bringing political and military stability to the country with the help of foreign mercenaries, Mobutu created a new constitution and political party in 1967 and became president. This political party, the Popular Revolutionary Movement, has since served as the only vehicle for political activity. In 1971, to help erase apparent ties to the colonial past, Mobutu changed the name of the country from Congo to Zaïre and renamed himself Mobutu Sese Seko. After running for reelection unopposed in 1978, Mobutu was nominated for another seven-year term as president. He governs essentially by decree and personal patronage.

Since independence Zaïre has maintained close economic and political ties with Belgium and its Western allies, most notably Britain, France and the USA. Almost all Zaïre's exports are bought by these countries, who in turn furnish most of its foreign aid and capital investment. These allies gave military assistance to the regime in both 1977 and 1978, after former inhabitants of Shaba province returned from Angola in an attempt to topple Mobutu's government.

The population of Zaïre is concentrated in the east between the forest and the mountains and south of the forest that stretches from Matadi near the coast through Kinshasa into East Kasai. Although there are more than 250 languages spoken, there are four dominant languages in addition to French, the official language. Lingala is spoken primarily in Kinshasa and in Equator province, Kikongo in the provinces of Lower Zaïre and Bandundu, Tshiluba in East and West Kasai provinces, and Swahili in the provinces of Upper Zaïre, Kivu and Shaba. In the late 1970s about a quarter of the population lived in urban areas.

Zaïre is famous for its great natural resources, particularly its minerals and hydro-electric potential. It ranks among the top ten countries in the world in its production of copper (6th), cobalt (1st), manganese (8th), tin (9th), gold (10th) and industrial diamonds (1st), and also produces lesser amounts of iron, zinc, silver and germanium. Since the precipitous decline of Zaïre's cash-crop production in 1974, copper alone has furnished more than 75 per cent of export earnings. The dam on the Zaïre river at Inga, scheduled for completion in 1980, will have a production capacity of 30 million kilowatts.

During the colonial period the Belgian administration concentrated on developing the mining potential and agricultural production for export. Thus the system of investment, transportation and the economic infrastructure were designed primarily to facilitate the export of raw materials. By favoring the establishment of large plantations and by forcing peasant farmers to plant a minimum acreage of food and cash crops each year the administration was able to make the colony a net exporter of food during the 1950s. In 1959 agricultural production accounted for 45 per cent of export earnings.

The political instability that followed independence disrupted the economy by precipitating the flight of the controlling foreign capital and personnel. Since 1967 Mobutu has been trying to establish national control over major industries by renegotiating the status of ownerships, by government regulation of banking procedures and by direct takeover of some companies. However, with the political instability from 1975 to 1979, the collapse of world copper prices, and the closing of the Benguela railroad through Angola, the GNP of Zaïre has been dropping each year, resulting in an indebtedness to foreign banks that exceeded 3 billion dollars in 1978. An annual inflation rate of 40 to 100 per cent accompanied the drop in production, and is reflected in the buying power of Zaïrian workers, which in 1977 was only 15 per cent of what it was in 1960.

To develop its economic potential Zaïre is seeking to revamp its system of transportation, to reestablish strong agricultural production, to reduce the rate of inflation and to train Zaïrians in business management. Since 1971 Zaïre has had its own national university to train its professional and civil service cadre. The government has administered most of the medical services and, until 1978, the educational system.

Zaïre is a country of tremendous contrasts in physical and social environments, in religion, in personal wealth, in life styles and in artistic expression. Zaïrian popular music is known

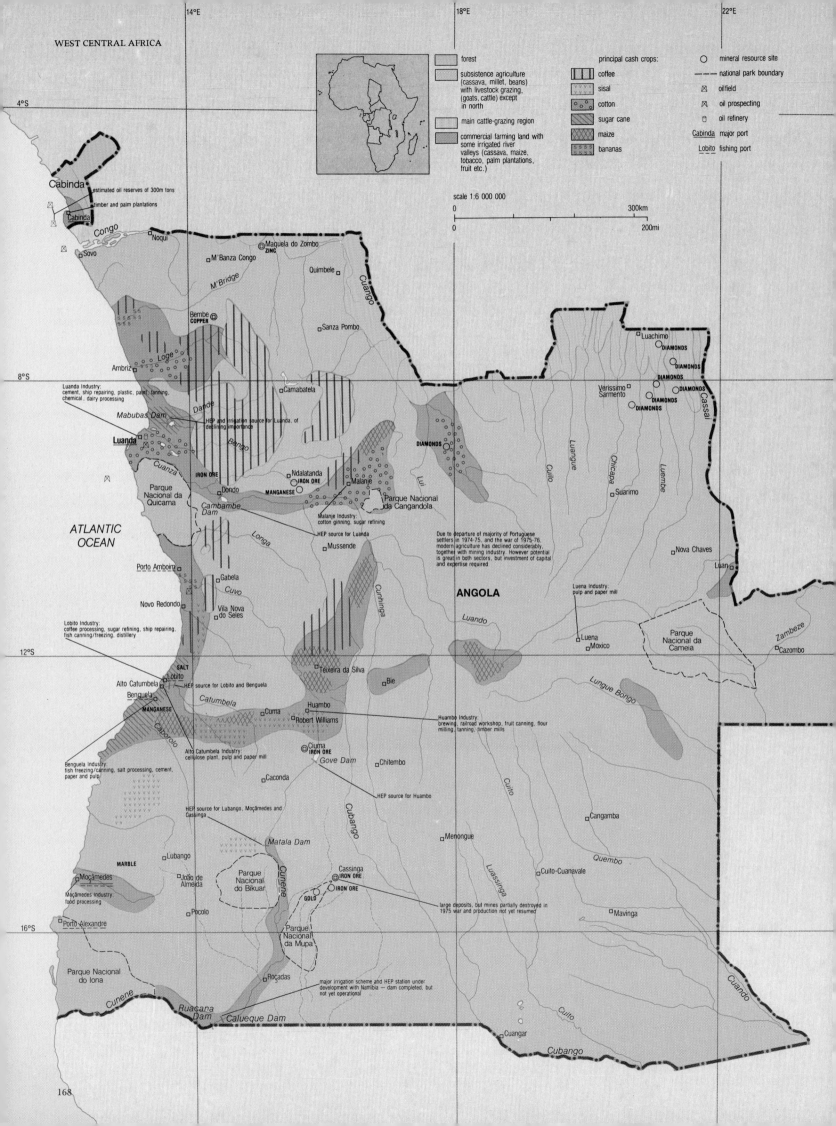

forest

subsistence agriculture
(cassava, millet, beans)
with livestock grazing,
(goats, cattle) except
in north

main cattle-grazing region

commercial farming land with
some irrigated river
valleys (cassava, maize,
tobacco, palm plantations,
fruit etc.)

principal cash crops:

coffee

sisal

cotton

sugar cane

maize

bananas

○ mineral resource site

— · — national park boundary

⊠ oilfield

⊠ oil prospecting

⊡ oil refinery

Cabinda major port

Lobito fishing port

scale 1:6 000 000

0   300km

0   200mi

Cabinda

estimated oil reserves of 300m tons

timber and palm plantations

Cabinda

Congo

Noqui

Sovo

Maquela do Zombo

ZINC

M'Banza Congo

Quimbele

M'Bridge

Cuango

Sanza Pombo

Bembe
COPPER

Loge

Ambriz

8°S

Luanda Industry:
cement, ship repairing, plastic, paint, tanning,
chemical, dairy processing

Dande

Mabubas Dam

HEP and irrigation source for Luanda, of
declining importance

Luanda

Bengo

Cuanza

IRON ORE

Parque
Nacional da
Quicama

Dondo

Cambambe
Dam

Ndalatanda
IRON ORE

MANGANESE

Malanje

Parque Nacional
da Cangandola

Malanje Industry:
cotton ginning, sugar refining

HEP source for Luanda

**ATLANTIC
OCEAN**

Longa

Mussende

DIAMONDS

Lui

Luachimo
DIAMONDS
DIAMONDS
DIAMONDS
Verissimo
Sarmento   DIAMONDS
DIAMONDS
DIAMONDS

Cassai

Luangue

Cuilo

Chicapa

Luembe

Suarimo

Nova Chaves

Luan

Due to departure of majority of Portuguese
settlers in 1974-75, and the war of 1975-76,
modern agriculture has declined considerably,
together with mining industry. However potential
is great in both sectors, but investment of capital
and expertise required

ANGOLA

Luando

Luena Industry:
pulp and paper mill

Porto Amboim

Gabela

Cuvo

Cunhinga

Novo Redondo

Vila Nova
do Seles

Lobito Industry:
coffee processing, sugar refining, ship repairing,
fish canning/freezing, distillery

12°S

SALT
Lobito

Alto Catumbela

HEP source for Lobito and Benguela

Benguela

MANGANESE

Catumbela

Caporolo

Teixeira da Silva

Bie

Cuma

Huambo

Robert Williams

Huambo Industry:
brewing, railroad workshop, fruit canning, flour
milling, tanning, timber mills

Luena
Moxico

Parque
Nacional da
Cameia

Zambeze

Cazombo

Lungue Bongo

Alto Catumbela Industry:
cellulose plant, pulp and paper mill

Benguela Industry:
fish freezing/canning, salt processing, cement,
paper and pulp

Ciuma
IRON ORE

Gove Dam

Chitembo

HEP source for Huambo

Caconda

Cuito

Cangamba

HEP source for Lubango, Moçâmedes and
Cassinga

Matala Dam

Menongue

Cubango

Quembo

MARBLE

Lubango

Moçâmedes

Parque
Nacional
do Bikuar

Cunene

João de
Almeida

Cassinga
IRON ORE

IRON ORE

Cuito-Cuanavale

Luassinga

Moçâmedes Industry:
food processing

Pocolo

GOLO

large deposits, but mines partially destroyed in
1975 war and production not yet resumed

Mavinga

16°S

Porto Alexandre

Parque
Nacional
da Mupa

Parque Nacional
do Iona

Roçadas

major irrigation scheme and HEP station under
development with Namibia — dam completed, but
not yet operational

Cunene

Ruacana
Dam

Calueque Dam

Cubango

Cuito

Cuando

Cuangar

Cubango

and appreciated throughout much of Africa. Traditional wood sculptures such as masks and figurines command high prices on the international market. It will require much patience and courage to forge a viable social and economic unit out of this diversity.

S.Y.

Angola

The center of Angola consists of a plateau undulating between 1300 and 2000 meters. This plateau is separated from the 1600-kilometer Atlantic shoreline by a sterile coastal plain ranging from 50 to 160 kilometers in width. In the north and east the plateau tilts down towards the Congo and Zambezi basins and the river boundaries with Zaïre and Zambia. In the south the border with Namibia links the Kunene and Cubango rivers. The north has higher rainfall and a few pockets of dense tropical forest. Much of the south is acacia savanna. The average annual temperature at Luanda is 23°.

The farming populations of Angola began to evolve sophisticated forms of royal government in the later Middle Ages. The 15th-century kings built their power around agricultural ceremonies at rain shrines and in important iron-smelting and salt-mining districts. In the more southerly parts of the country cattle wealth was important. In the north the famous kingdom of Kongo had a local textile industry and national shell currency.

From 1493 Angola's agrarian economy was modified by an increasingly lucrative market for agricultural slave labor. In the next 400 years two million or more Angolans were bought or captured by Portuguese, French, British, Brazilian and other ocean merchants. Portugal established a small colony in Angola as a base for its operations and garrisoned it with half a dozen forts, a few hundred slave-soldiers and assorted convict settlers. Despite 19th-century efforts to suppress the traffic, captives continued to be sold at Angolan ports till about 1910.

Efforts to build a tropical colonial economy to replace slaving were at first unsuccessful. A coffee boom in the 1890s was short-lived but coffee returned in the mid-20th century to become Angola's major export crop. Production rose to over 200 000 tons by the 1970s and Angola was the world's fourth largest producer. The major coffee zones were Uige and Kwanza. The rise in coffee prices led to a rapid growth of the plantation sector and the partial elimination of the peasant sector.

Local government activity was primarily concerned with recruiting labor at below market cost and with raising African rural taxes to be funneled into development schemes for the benefit of Europeans. Government neglect was partially compensated for by mission health and education services: Baptists in the north, Methodists in the Kwanza regions, Congregationalists in the Benguela plateau and Spiritans in the south all provided some social services as well as Christian proselytization. Secondary schooling remained negligible till the 1960s and even then mainly white.

Before 1940 Angola was popularly considered fit only for convict settlement. After 1950 coffee prosperity brought in free colonists. Government sought to settle them as peasants but the majority became urban artisans, petty officials and above all retail traders. By 1970 the immigrant population probably surpassed 300 000, almost all of them of Portuguese or Cape Verdian origin.

The influx of settlers, the alienation of coffee land and the lack of educational opportunity in the 1950s led to severe African disaffection. The early colonial politics of Angola had been squeezed out of existence by the dictatorship of Salazar and the introduction, in 1957, of his political police. By 1961 local despair was fueled by black political success in the rest of Africa. Rebellion broke out in both town and country and large-scale massacres occurred. Portugal mobilized an army some 60 000 strong to recapture the political initiative. It held Angola for a further 13 years of sporadic war.

In 1974 Portugal prepared to withdraw from its African colonies and numerous regional and international powers intervened to serve their own interests in Angola. The recent discovery of offshore mineral oil (about 9 million tons a year) brought in business with expectations of great universal wealth. The possibility of a Marxist government brought anti-Marxist military interventions. The first invasion was by Zaïre in support of the Frente Nacional de Libertação de Angola (FNLA), a predominantly northern party, with Baptist-educated cadres and urban business support in the capital. The second invasion was by South Africa which supported and armed the União para a Independencia Total de Angola (UNITA) party which dominated the highlands, had Congregational leaders and some working-class white support. The third invasion was by several thousand airlifted Cubans who supported the Movimento Popular da Libertação de Angola (MPLA), a Marxist party based on the capital and with the Methodist sphere of influence behind it. American business, government and mercenaries variously supported all three parties and business retained a firm hold on the oil wells, thereby furnishing the postwar government of the MPLA with 80 per cent of its revenue. The USSR also supported the MPLA, though it was perplexed by its acrimonious factionalism which nearly resulted in a coup d'état in 1977. France supported Zaïre and its allies, and Britain was primarily concerned with the defense of Namibia and of the Benguela railroad to Zambia, which the war nevertheless closed.

The 1975–76 war caused 90 per cent of the white-settler and expatriate population to emigrate. Only a few of their skills could be replaced by Angolans or by Cubans and other foreign-aid personnel. The war broke the transportation system as bridges were blown and vehicles and aircraft taken out of the country. Food production and distribution became difficult. Labor migration to the coffee estates decreased and unemployment in the towns contrasted with the high economic expectations of independence. All these problems had to be tackled by a new, inexperienced government which was simultaneously at war with South African-supported guerrillas who had failed, by 1979, to accept the new government. A reconciliation with Zaïre helped to lift the postwar pressure in the north in 1978.

D.B.

4°S

8°S

12°S

Angola

Official Name
People's Republic of Angola

Area
1 246 700 sq km

Date of Independence
11 Nov 1975

Status and Name in Colonial Times
Portuguese colony; 1972–75 overseas province: Angola

Population
5 646 166 (1970); 6 761 000 (est 1975)

Annual Growth Rate
2·4%

Capital City
Luanda

Population of Capital
569 113 (1970); 700 000 (est 1979)

National Language(s)
Portuguese; Umbundu, Kimbundu

Gross National Product (US dollars)
1970 million; 330 per capita (est 1977)

Local Currency
1 kwanza = 100 lwei

NORTHEAST AFRICA

Geographically this is a region of immense contrasts. Those countries that make up what is often called the "Horn" of Africa – Djibouti, Somalia and parts of eastern Ethiopia – share the Islamic faith and a way of life as nomadic herders struggling to survive in a harsh and challenging environment. Culturally all these peoples have much in common, though they have lived as separated and often warring tribes.

Sudan and Ethiopia present great contrasts, within themselves and with the Horn. Like the sahel countries to its west, Sudan is a bridge between northern Islamic Arab Africa and black "pagan" Africa. Many of its southern inhabitants are now Christians. In the highlands of Ethiopia live peoples who are an exception to most generalizations about Africa. Their ancient church links them to Egypt, and through centuries of literacy the history of the kingdoms of the Ethiopian mountains has been preserved as in few other places in Africa.

Most borders in Africa are arbitrary, and nowhere more so than here. On all sides peoples' natural affinities are cut by artificial colonial boundaries, and this continues to be the source of great misery and suffering. The Somali-speaking peoples are found also in Ethiopia and northern Kenya, and their struggle to unite goes on. In southern Ethiopia and southern Sudan linguistic groups straddle the borders with Kenya and Uganda. The Nile flowing north through Sudan links that country with Egypt. Perhaps the Islamic faith is the strongest unifying force across all these very different nations.

The Nile (seen here at the Tissisat Falls, on the Blue Nile, in Ethiopia) is the link between Mediterranean Africa and the deep interior, and the search for its source drew many Western explorers into Africa. Although cut by cataracts, it provides a highway where roads are still few or nonexistent, and despite the barrier of the Sudd swamps, the river is often the only route into the far south of Sudan.

Right In the Ethiopian highlands south of Asmera the village of Aruba, near Adigrat, is shown below carefully cultivated hillsides which must be utilized to the full in mountainous country where every scrap of soil is valuable.

Below Sudan's north is deeply arabized and Islamized, but many communities remain largely untouched. The Nuba, in the hills of southern Kordofan, are one such people. They are agriculturalists who also keep cattle, small stock and fowls. Both men and women traditionally go naked except for ornaments and body paint.

Below right Mogadisho, with a present population of 250000, is an ancient Muslim city. It was visited by the North African traveler Ibn Battuta in the 14th century, when its influence was beginning to decline. In the colonial period it was the capital of Italian Somalia and its architecture retains a distinctly Italian flavor.

Far right Cattle are of crucial importance in Dinka culture, and the young men become deeply attached to their favorite animals, taking praise names from them. Milking is carried out by women and boys, who abandon the role after passing through initiation ceremonies. Here hairdressing is seen in progress.

Below The Faron Mosque in Khartoum, capital of Sudan, lying at the junction of the White and Blue Niles. The city developed from an Egyptian garrison founded in the 1820s, and in 1885 became infamous in Europe as the scene of the death of General Gordon at the hands of the Mahdi's followers.

Below center The Dinka, speakers of an Eastern Sudanic language, are transhumant herders in the southern Sudan. From dry-season river camps they move in the rains to permanent settlements where they grow food crops like millets. At their ceremonies, and in daily life, Dinka wear only body paint.

Below right A priest of the ancient Ethiopian Church, in liturgical dress, holds two of the processional crosses which are a special feature of that church's regalia. They show Greek influence, recalling the founding of the church by missionaries from Constantinople.

Center In many parts of northeast Africa cultivation is still by digging stick or hoe, but in some areas, as in this part of Ethiopia near Asmera, oxen are used to plow the stony soil. The chief cereal crops grown are wheat and barley.

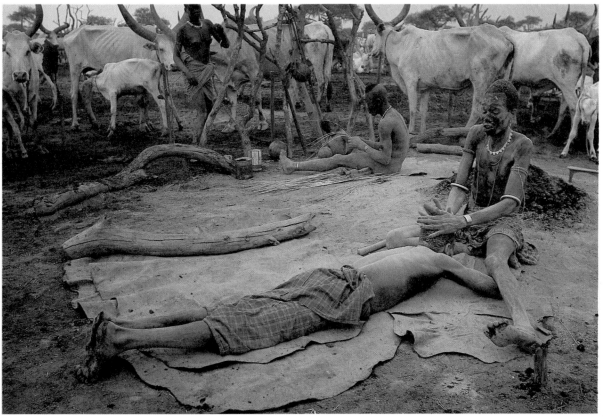

Sudan

Sudan, Africa's largest country, stretches southwards from Egypt for 2000 kilometers and westwards from the Red Sea for 1500 kilometers. Adjacent countries include Ethiopia, Kenya, Uganda, Zaïre, Central African Republic, Chad and Libya.

Lying mostly below 1000 meters, Sudan has relatively uniform relief, broken by volcanic uplands in the west, the south-central Nuba mountains, the edges of the East African highlands and the Red Sea hills. Over most of the country a tropical continental climate prevails. In the south it merges into an equatorial rainy climate; in the north, into desert. Vegetation correlates generally with rainfall to produce a transition from desert, to semidesert and steppe scrub, to short- and tall-grass savannas, to flooded grasslands, forest savannas and mist forests. Draining north-wards, the Nile and its tributaries, such as the Sobat, Blue Nile and Atbarah, bring vital water from East Africa and Ethiopia. In the south the annual floods create a vast swamp, the Sudd.

Sudan

Official Name
Jamhuryat es-Sudan Al Democratia
The Democratic Republic of the Sudan

Area
2 505 813 sq km

Date of Independence
1 Jan 1956

Status and Name in Colonial Times
1898–1955 Anglo-Egyptian Condominium: Sudan

Population
14 819 271 (1973 census); 20 900 000 (UN est 1979)

Annual Growth Rate
3·2% (UN est 1979)

Capital City
Khartoum (El Khartum)

Population of Capital
333 906 (1973 census)

National Language(s)
Arabic; English

Gross National Product (US dollars)
4910 million; 300 per capita (est 1977)

Local Currency
1 Sudanese pound = 100 piastres = 1000 millièmes

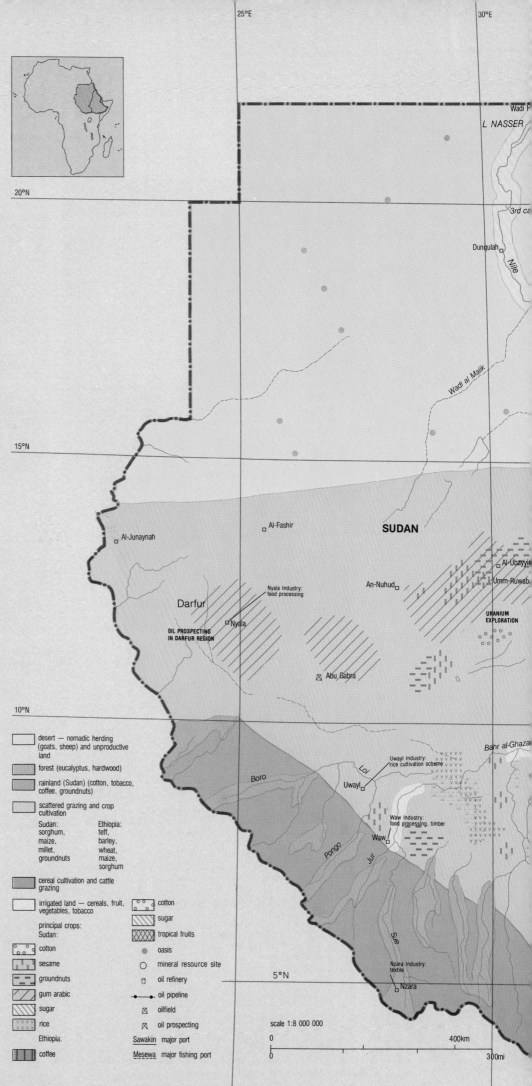

desert — nomadic herding (goats, sheep) and unproductive land

forest (eucalyptus, hardwood)

rainland (Sudan) (cotton, tobacco, coffee, groundnuts)

scattered grazing and crop cultivation

Sudan:	Ethiopia:
sorghum,	teff,
maize,	barley,
millet,	wheat,
groundnuts	maize,
	sorghum

cereal cultivation and cattle grazing

irrigated land — cereals, fruit, vegetables, tobacco

principal crops:
Sudan:

cotton

sesame

groundnuts

gum arabic

sugar

rice

Ethiopia:

coffee

cotton

sugar

tropical fruits

oasis

mineral resource site

oil refinery

oil pipeline

oilfield

oil prospecting

Sawakin major port

Mesewa major fishing port

scale 1:8 000 000

0   400km
0   300mi

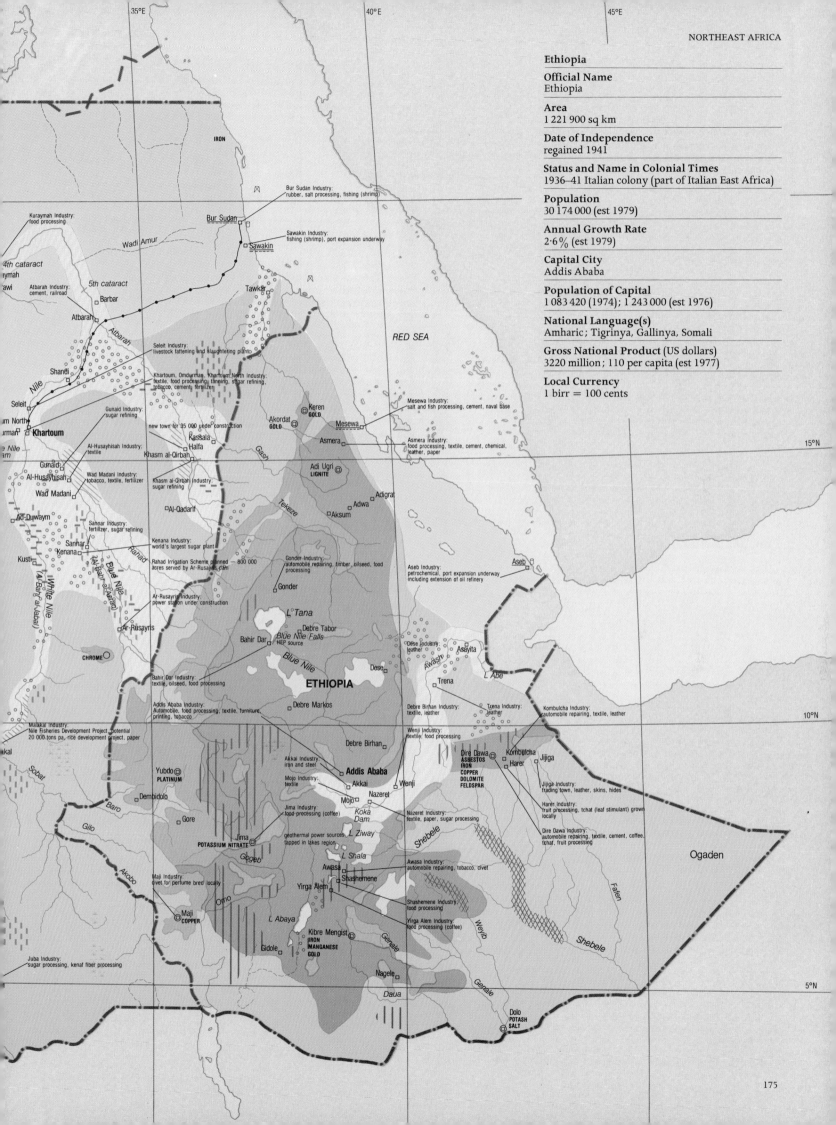

Ethiopia

Official Name
Ethiopia

Area
1 221 900 sq km

Date of Independence
regained 1941

Status and Name in Colonial Times
1936–41 Italian colony (part of Italian East Africa)

Population
30 174 000 (est 1979)

Annual Growth Rate
2·6% (est 1979)

Capital City
Addis Ababa

Population of Capital
1 083 420 (1974); 1 243 000 (est 1976)

National Language(s)
Amharic; Tigrinya, Gallinya, Somali

Gross National Product (US dollars)
3220 million; 110 per capita (est 1977)

Local Currency
1 birr = 100 cents

IRON

Bur Sudan Industry:
rubber, salt processing, fishing (shrimp)

Kuraymah Industry:
food processing

4th cataract

5th cataract

Atbarah Industry:
cement, railroad

Barbar

Atbarah

Wadi Amur

Atbara

Shandi

Seleit Industry:
livestock fattening and slaughtering plants

Nile

Seleit

um North

urman

Khartoum

Khartoum, Omdurman, Khartoum North Industry:
textile, food processing, tanning, sugar refining,
tobacco, cement, fertilizer

Gunaid Industry:
sugar refining

new town for 35 000 under construction

Rassala

Halfa

Al-Husayhisah Industry:
textile

Gunaid

Al-Husayhisah

Khasm al-Qirbah

Wad Madani Industry:
tobacco, textile, fertilizer

Wad Madani

Khasm al-Qirbah Industry:
sugar refining

Al-Qadarif

Ad-Duwaym

Sannar Industry:
fertilizer, sugar refining

Sannar

Kenana

Kenana Industry:
world's largest sugar plant

Rahad Irrigation Scheme planned – 800 000
acres served by Ar-Rusayris dam

Ar-Rusayris Industry:
power station under construction

Kusti

White Nile

(Al-Bahr al-Abyad)

Blue Nile

Rahad

(Al-Bahr al-Azraq)

Ar-Rusayris

CHROME

Sobat

Malakal Industry:
Nile Fisheries Development Project potential
20 000 tons pa, rice development project, paper

kal

Yubdo
PLATINUM

Dembidolo

Baro

Gilo

Gore

Maji Industry:
civet for perfume bred locally

Maji
COPPER

Jima
POTASSIUM NITRATE

Jima Industry:
food-processing (coffee)

geothermal power sources
tapped in lakes region

Akobo

Juba Industry:
sugar processing, kenaf fiber processing

Gidole

Omo

Gogeb

Koka
Dam

L Ziway

L Shala

Awasa

Shashemene

Yirga Alem

L Abaya

Kibre Mengist
IRON
MANGANESE
GOLD

Nagele

Daua

RED SEA

Tawkar

Keren
GOLD

Akordat
GOLD

Mesewa

Mesewa Industry:
salt and fish processing, cement, naval base

Asmera

Asmera Industry:
food processing, textile, cement, chemical,
leather, paper

Adi Ugri
LIGNITE

Gash

Adigrat

Adwa

Aksum

Tekeze

Gonder Industry:
automobile repairing, timber, oilseed, food
processing

Gonder

Aseb Industry:
petrochemical, port expansion underway
including extension of oil refinery

Aseb

L°Tana

Debre Tabor

Blue Nile Falls
HEP source

Bahir Dar

Blue Nile

Dese

Dese Industry:
leather

Awash

Asayita

L Abe

Trena

ETHIOPIA

Bahir Dar Industry:
textile, oilseed, food processing

Addis Ababa Industry:
Automobile, food processing, textile, furniture,
printing, tobacco

Debre Markos

Debre Birhan Industry:
textile, leather

Trena Industry:
leather

Kombulcha Industry:
automobile repairing, textile, leather

Wenji Industry:
textile, food processing

Debre Birhan

Akaki Industry:
iron and steel

Mojo Industry:
textile

Addis Ababa

Akaki

Wenji

Nazeret

Mojo

Nazeret Industry:
textile, paper, sugar processing

Dire Dawa
ASBESTOS
IRON
COPPER
DOLOMITE
FELDSPAR

Kombulcha

Harer

Jijiga

Jijiga Industry:
trading town, leather, skins, hides

Harer Industry:
fruit processing, tchat (leaf stimulant) grown
locally

Dire Dawa Industry:
automobile, textile, cement, coffee,
tchat, fruit processing

Shebele

Awasa Industry:
automobile repairing, tobacco, civet

Shashemene Industry:
food processing

Yirga Alem Industry:
food processing (coffee)

Genale

Ogaden

Fafen

Shebele

Dolo
POTASH
SALT

Wenib

Genale

35°E   40°E   45°E

15°N

10°N

5°N

175

Sudan is lightly populated. Half the people live in 14 per cent of the country, around the capital, the White and Blue Niles and in the south. Over 85 per cent live in rural areas, although urbanization is increasing. The rural populace consists mostly of village-dwelling farmers, but nomadic and seminomadic pastoralists occupy wide areas. The Khartoum-Umm Durman-Khartoum Bahri conurbation dominates Sudanese economic, social, political and cultural life. Important regional towns include Bur Sudan, Wad Madani, Kassala, Al-Ubayyid, Al-Qadarif, Atbarah, Nyala and Kusti.

There are at least 56 separate ethnic groups, subdivided into 597 subgroups, and 115 languages. However, most northern peoples speak Arabic and accept an Arabic cultural heritage. Other northern ethnic groups include Nubians, Beja, Funj, Nuba and Fur. Dinka, Nuer, Shilluk and other Nilotic peoples straddle the Nile in the south. Heterogeneous peoples of Equatoria and western Bahr Al-Ghazal relate linguistically and culturally to larger groups in adjacent countries; most prominent are the Azande. Southerners speak local languages, but use Arabic as a lingua franca. Northern Sudan is predominantly Muslim and two-thirds of all Sudanese practice Islam. Most southerners adhere to traditional beliefs and practices; about 4 per cent, mainly southerners, are Christian.

Only along the Nile, where successive kingdoms contacted external civilizations, is a continuous Sudanese history known. Sequestered from the north by the Sudd, equatorial Sudanese lived in tribal isolation, which until the 20th century was only interrupted by explorers and slave raiders. Somewhat less remote, Darfur usually remained independent of outside control and did not maintain close relations with the Nile valley until the 20th century.

Pharaonic Egypt effectively controlled the riverine north (Cush) from 1530 BC until the Meroïtic kingdom (c. 750 BC–350 AD) achieved periods of independent central government. Three Christian kingdoms succeeded Meroë and survived Arab penetration until the establishment of the Islamic sultanate of the Funj in 1504. Thereafter, the loose federation of tribes ruled by the Funj dynasty dominated much of north-central Sudan. In 1821 Ottoman Egypt brought Sudan under Turco-Egyptian rule which lasted until 1881 when the Sudanese revolted under Muhamad Ahmad, the Mahdi. The theocratic Mahdist state survived only until 1898 when it fell to Anglo-Egyptian conquerors.

British colonial rule was established under a nominal Anglo-Egyptian condominium. Gradually the entire country was subdued and southern and western appendages were incorporated. A coherent administration was established, a social infrastructure begun and an externally oriented commercial base laid. Sudanese nationalists, especially after World War II, pressed Britain for independence, finally attained on 1 January 1956.

After a brief period of parliamentary rule (1956–58) the army established a military dictatorship (1958–64). Another period of ineffectual parliamentary rule (1964–69) was followed by another period of military domination (1969–present). Only limited success has attended the governments' grappling with

civil war (1955–72), corruption, political instability and vacillating economic direction.

The Sudanese economy is overwhelmingly agricultural and pastoral. Rainfed subsistence farming predominates in most areas and livestock is ubiquitous. From Darfur to Kassala traditional and mechanized farming of millets, peanuts and sesame coexists with the collection of gum arabic and the nomadic herding of cattle, sheep, goats and camels. In this zone a vast agricultural potential exists for Sudan as the future granary of the Arab world.

Irrigation schemes along the central Nile system produce the bulk of commercial crops and are the focus of recent investment. Paramount is the Al-Jazirah scheme, located south of Khartoum, where cotton and wheat are supplemented by peanuts, maize, rice and vegetables. The Ar-Rahad scheme, inaugurated in 1977, will significantly extend cotton production. Diversification into sugar cane has occurred at Khashm Al-Qirba and Junayd, and is under way in Kinanah, south of Al-Jazirah. The Jonglei Canal, begun in 1978, is intended to drain the vast marshes south of Malakal, thereby saving water for irrigation and reclaiming land. Proposed projects include large plantations, mechanization, cattle ranches, disease-free zones and infrastructural improvements, all to be funded by Arab sources.

Industrial production has been generally confined to simple consumer goods and primary processing of agricultural products. Recent industrial expansion into textiles, cement and oil refining has shifted industry from the capital. Although petroleum was found in 1978, little mineral development has occurred. An inadequate transport network has hindered economic development. Bur Sudan's limited port capacity, the overburdened railroad to the interior and limited all-weather roads have been bottlenecks. Efforts to alleviate these conditions involve massive road building, especially between Khartoum and Bur Sudan, and railroad revitalization. Long-term growth has been heavily dependent upon overseas aid. Low market prices for cotton, heavy trade deficits, high inflation and a vast national debt have forced curtailment of new development projects and, at best, Sudan's economic future is uncertain.

The 17-year north–south conflict, which centered around southern opposition to northern economic neglect and political hegemony, dominated Sudanese politics. A military and political stalemate, coupled with high military costs, produced instability and toppled governments. President Jaafar Al-Nimeiri's primary accomplishment has been settling the war, mainly by agreeing to regional autonomy for the south. Another longstanding difficulty has been competition for power by religious-based parties, the Muslim Brotherhood, the Communist party and the military. Al-Nimeiri came to power in a radical coup d'état but has steadily moved right while establishing a single-party state. However, he has had to balance competing factions, such as the sectarian groups pushing for an Islamic constitution, southerners opposing it, and leftists wanting a secularized socialist society.

Internationally, Sudan has had problems with Egypt, Ethiopia, Uganda, Chad and Libya

over borders, refugees and dissident movements. Contradictorily, it has mediated African conflicts, as in Chad, and yet backed secessionist groups, as in Eritrea. Beyond Africa Al-Nimeiri has shifted from a pro-Soviet stance to alignment with conservative Saudi Arabia and Kuwait and the Western powers.

G.A.H.

Ethiopia

Northeast Africa's most populous country, Ethiopia, has long stood as a predominantly Christian society occupying protecting highlands. Its distinctive national identity, despite great cultural variation, may be attributed to a long history of political independence.

A massive complex of mountains and plateaus, dissected by a deep rift valley and surrounded by marginal lowlands, dominates Ethiopia's physical geography. The Rift Valley, bifurcating the highlands into western and eastern sectors, contains a chain of lakes. Although deeply entrenched rivers radiate from central heights in all directions, the principal drainage is to the Nile basin by the Sobat, Blue Nile and Tekeze rivers.

Climate and vegetation zones reflect the great variations in altitude. The hot lowlands include deserts and steppes around the foot of the highlands and reach up valleys and plateau slopes to 1500 meters. Above lies a cooler, moister subtropical belt extending up to 2400 to 2700 meters. This would, under natural conditions, be well forested, but instead contains pastures and fields. Above this is a still wetter temperate zone of high mountains, largely covered by grassland. Everywhere rainfall is concentrated into a main summer season, with some areas having minor rains in later winter.

Favored as an agricultural environment, the central highlands have the greatest population densities. About 90 per cent of Ethiopia's population is rural, comprising mostly farmers, who live in scatered family compounds and villages. The remainder reside in the larger cities of Addis Ababa and Asmera, in smaller highland commercial towns like Dire Dawa, Dese, Harer, and Gonder or in the Red Sea ports of Mesewa and Aseb.

Ethnically Ethiopia is a composite of over 70 groups speaking nearly 100 languages. The dominating Amhara and the Tigre comprise over a third and occupy the central and northern highlands, respectively; Galla total 35 to 40 per cent and primarily inhabit the subtropical central and southern highlands; Somalis reside in the southeast; and there are scattered Bantu and Nilotic groups. Most Amhara and Tigre and some Galla are Ethiopian Orthodox Christians, but most Galla, Somalis and others who inhabit marginal reaches are Muslims. Many others practice traditional religions.

In some form Ethiopia has had a continuous national existence for 2000 years. Descendants of Arabian Semites established an empire at Aksum in the northeast in the 3rd century BC. Converted to Christianity, the Aksumite empire withstood Islamic expansions after the 9th century, but disintegrated before the 11th century. For almost a millennium incessant conflict between Christian and Muslim princes plunged Ethiopia into anarchical political fragmentation. The empire broke up into small kingdoms in the 1600s and the ensuing decentralization and civil war lasted until the mid-19th century.

Beginning in 1855, the related historical processes of political reunification, territorial expansion and resistance to Egyptian, Sudanese and European encroachments operated intermittently to reestablish the Ethiopian empire. Attempts were made after 1889 by Emperor Menelik II to modernize and regain lost provinces, culminating in recognition of Ethiopian autonomy by regional and European powers. Emperor Haile Selassie's early reforms and modernization were interrupted by the Italian occupation of 1935–41. Then in 1952 the United Nations allowed the controversial federation of the formerly Italian Eritrea with Ethiopia. In 1960 Haile Selassie incorporated it into the empire. By the mid-1960s Eritrean resistance had transformed into a nationalist movement. Throughout the 1960s internal political opposition to Haile Selassie's rule grew, an abortive coup, student unrest and labor strikes weakening his political power by the end of the decade.

Ethiopia manifests many characteristics of underdevelopment, such as a predominant subsistence sector, limited industry, immature infrastructure, little domestic capital and undiversified exports. The economic growth rate is well under the African norm. Agriculture and livestock contribute half of gross domestic product and support 90 per cent of the people. Agriculture is almost entirely rainfed and is primarily devoted to subsistence crops – wheat, barley, sorghum, millet, maize, ensete and teff. Coffee is by far the most valuable export crop, contributing three-quarters of the total, followed by oilseeds and pulses. Peasant productivity has been hindered by simple technology, insufficient fertilizing, inadequate transport, subminimal farm sizes, exploitative tenancy arrangements with absentee owners, lack of marketing facilities and limited credit. A 1975 reform nationalized all agricultural land and restricted the size of holdings. Ethiopia has large herds, especially cattle, but derives limited commercial benefit from them.

Manufacturing is little developed; processing of agricultural products, particularly cotton, is the main industrial activity, followed by light consumer goods. Most industry is located in the Addis Ababa and Asmera regions. Mineral deposits are either little known or little mined. Some hydroelectric power is generated. Relief handicaps transportation, leaving extensive areas inaccessible to railroads and all-weather, or even seasonal, roads. Major roads radiate from Addis Ababa to the provincial centers but mostly not to borders. Railroads link Asmera to the port of Mesewa and Addis Ababa to Djibouti, which handles most foreign trade. War has distorted government finance and planning, with development projects being curtailed and trade seriously impacted.

Contemporary Ethiopian politics revolve around the transformation from empire to socialist state. The emperor was overthrown by the army in 1974. In 1975 the military abolished the empire and founded a socialist

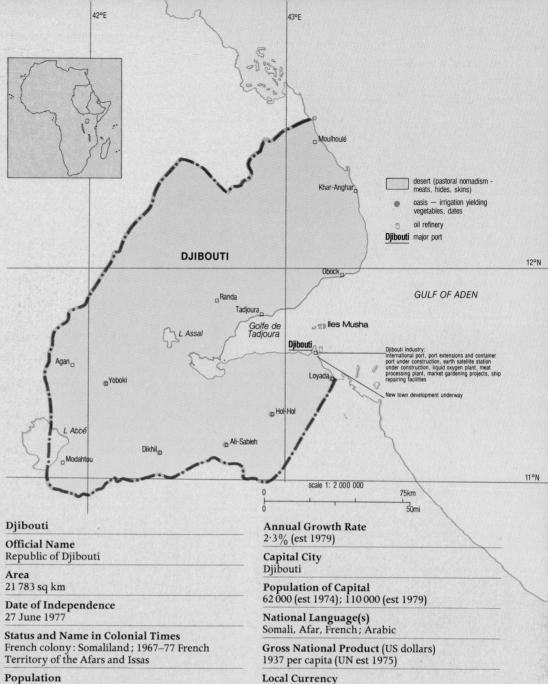

GULF OF ADEN

Djibouti

Official Name
Republic of Djibouti

Area
21 783 sq km

Date of Independence
27 June 1977

Status and Name in Colonial Times
French colony: Somaliland; 1967–77 French Territory of the Afars and Issas

Population
81 000 (est 1977); 300 000 (UN est 1979)

Annual Growth Rate
2·3% (est 1979)

Capital City
Djibouti

Population of Capital
62 000 (est 1974); 110 000 (est 1979)

National Language(s)
Somali, Afar, French; Arabic

Gross National Product (US dollars)
1937 per capita (UN est 1975)

Local Currency
1 Djibouti franc = 100 centimes

state. Since seizing power the ruling military council, the Dergue, has engaged in devastating power struggles out of which Lieutenant Colonel Mengistu Haile Mariam has emerged paramount. In 1977 and 1978 internal unrest took particularly violent forms, including assassinations and massacres, as the opposition and competing factions strove to shape events. In areas it controls, the Dergue has introduced land reform, nationalization and peasant cooperatives.

Disruptive nationality and border problems persist. In Somali-claimed Ogaden successful secessionist struggle led in 1977 to outright Somali military intervention. However, with Soviet and Cuban support Ethiopia prevailed, although guerrilla activity continues. In the mid-1970s the Eritrean rebellion escalated into a full-scale war. The Marxist Eritrean People's Liberation Front, succeeding the older Eritrean Liberation Front as the foremost nationalist military and political organization, occupied most of Eritrea before the Ethiopian military with Soviet and Cuban help dislodged them by late 1978 from virtually every town. The Eritreans still control the countryside. Elsewhere, other

ethnic movements have striven for autonomy in the absence of the army.

Paralleling its Marxist turn, Ethiopia has realigned itself with the socialist nations after being closely tied into the capitalist world under Haile Selassie. The USSR and Cuba have displaced the USA as its most supportive allies, offering economic and military assistance.

G.A.H.

Djibouti

Bordering Ethiopia and Somalia, Djibouti is strategically situated at the southern entrance to the Red Sea. The physical core of the country consists of a triangular depression, part of the East African rift system, and is marked by a complex fragmented relief of volcanic plateaus, sunken plains and lakes. Djibouti is mostly desert. Temperatures are high, rainfall low and erratic and lakes salty. Vegetation comprises seasonal grasses, thorn trees and scattered palms.

The human geography of the country is dominated by the capital, Djibouti, with its port and rail linkage to Addis Ababa. There are two ethnically distinct clan groups which are related to others across artificial boundaries: the Somalis (Issas) and Afars. Extensive migrations of nomads, who may comprise up to half the population, seasonally swell or diminish population totals. The remainder reside in Djibouti or in small towns or oases. This population is almost evenly divided between Somalis and Afars, with a small number of Arabs and Europeans also present. Most Djiboutis are Muslim.

French interest in this coast dates from 1859 and by 1896 the boundaries of French Somaliland were established. France's friendly relations with Ethiopia enabled the construction of the railroad between 1897 and 1917. Gradually the colony was granted autonomy between 1957 and 1967 when the then dominant Afars voted to continue French connections.

The national economy is based on trade through the port of Djibouti, which normally handles about half of Ethiopia's trade. Port-related activities are a major source of employment. Elsewhere the population largely subsists off animals, although small-scale agriculture exists in the oases. Fiscal subsidies are received from France and Saudi Arabia.

Until 1977 Djibouti's politics revolved around French policy decisions, first to continue the colonial connection, and then to shift, allowing Djibouti independence in June 1977. Internally the Afar–Somali rivalry continues unabated since most Somalis desire unification with Somalia, an action which Ethiopian concern over its major trade outlet has so far blocked.

G.A.H.

Somalia

Comprising a triangular wedge of dry, unproductive land, Somalia is located in the Horn of Africa where it fronts the Indian Ocean and Gulf of Aden and borders Djibouti, Ethiopia and Kenya. Somalia's poverty, irredentism and strategic position dominate its geography.

In the north and northeast some terrain is mountainous, but most consists of a low featureless plateau tilting gently southeastwards from Ethiopia. The prevailing climate features monsoon winds, hot temperatures and scarce, irregular rainfall. Droughts recur. Although low everywhere, in general rainfall increases southwards where annual totals usually exceed 330 millimeters. Shrub bush and grass comprise the primary savanna cover, which is thicker in higher areas and in the south. A general shortage of surface water presents difficulties everywhere, but towards the south the Shebele and Juba rivers drain from the Ethiopian plateau and have a regular flow.

A low population density reflects a largely nomadic or seminomadic populace. Settled agricultural and urban components make up only a quarter of the total. With the exception of Hargeysa, all major towns are situated on the coast. Only Mogadisho exceeds 100 000 residents. The Somalis, who constitute 98 per cent of the population, speak a Cushitic language, are relatively homogeneous in religion (Islam) and culture, but are often split by clan loyalties. Strongly nationalistic, Somalis have striven to incorporate their numerous kinsmen, cut off by artificial boundaries, into a single nation-state.

The Somalis first penetrated the northern coast about 1000 AD, and for the next 900 years they spasmodically pushed southwards to the Tana river, in the process driving out their Bantu and Galla predecessors. Despite some integration the essential process was the establishment of a single cultural nation in continuous occupation of a vast impoverished territory extending westward to a long frontier with Ethiopia.

Imperialist European interests mingled competitively in the last quarter of the 19th century when France staked out its claim around Djibouti, Britain assumed control of the northern regions, and Italy established a colony in the southern regions. Italy attempted unsuccessfully to colonize and develop its territory agriculturally. Britain largely ignored its protectorate until 1941, when it took control of Italian Somaliland and extended administrative and public services. In 1949 the United Nations entrusted its ex-territory back to Italy for ten years in order to prepare it for independence.

In response to Somali nationalism and despite a weak economic base and separate colonial legacies, the Italian and British territories joined together on 1 July 1960 as the independent Somali Republic. Compounding the difficult transition to unification, the new government pressed on its neighbors the principle of self-determination for all Somalis. Eventually, widespread corruption, divisive politics and other problems provoked a bloodless military coup on 21 October 1969. The Supreme Revolutionary Council renamed the country the Somali Democratic Republic and appointed Major General Mohamed Siad Barre as head of a socialist state.

Somalia has an underdeveloped economy based on livestock and agriculture, with exports of animals, bananas and hides. In most areas stock raising prevails, with goats and camels in the north and cattle and sheep in the south. Concentrated along the southern rivers is a more developed agriculture; bananas and sugar cane are the main cash crops. Fishing supports small numbers along both coasts and the knowledge and exploitation of minerals are primitive. Although tanneries and light consumer industry exist, the industrial sector consists largely of food processing. Primary development objectives in the 1970s were self-sufficiency in food supplies, especially in cereals and sugar. Communications have been improved with completion of the long north–south road in 1978 and the modernization of Mogadisho's port. However, drought, flood, inflation, war and growing foreign debt have left the economy in disarray.

Since 1969 Somalia has moved toward establishing a socialist society adapted to local conditions. Although controlled from above, popular participation in local councils and worker–management committees has been stressed. Nationalization has covered medical services, schools, banks, electricity, transportation, external trade and land. Tribalism has been steadily attacked. In 1972 a modified Roman alphabet was adopted and the Somali language became the official written medium. Formed in 1976, the Somali Socialist Revolutionary Party replaced the Supreme Revolutionary Council. However, in 1978 President Siad Barre had to overcome the first attempted coup against his government.

Throughout the 1970s bitter territorial disputes continued over those adjacent areas inhabitated by ethnic Somalis. The main confrontation has been in the Ogaden region of Ethiopia where in 1977 a secessionist movement gained control over most of the contested area. Direct Somali military intervention was followed by massive Soviet and Cuban assistance to Ethiopia, leading to the latter's victory in 1978. Local guerrilla activity persists. Soviet support for Ethiopia caused bitter Somali reaction as Somalia had been a Soviet ally. Relations were broken and the Soviets expelled in November 1977. Because of Somalia's strategic location, the USA, other Western states, and Arab countries have lent considerable political and some material support.

G.A.H.

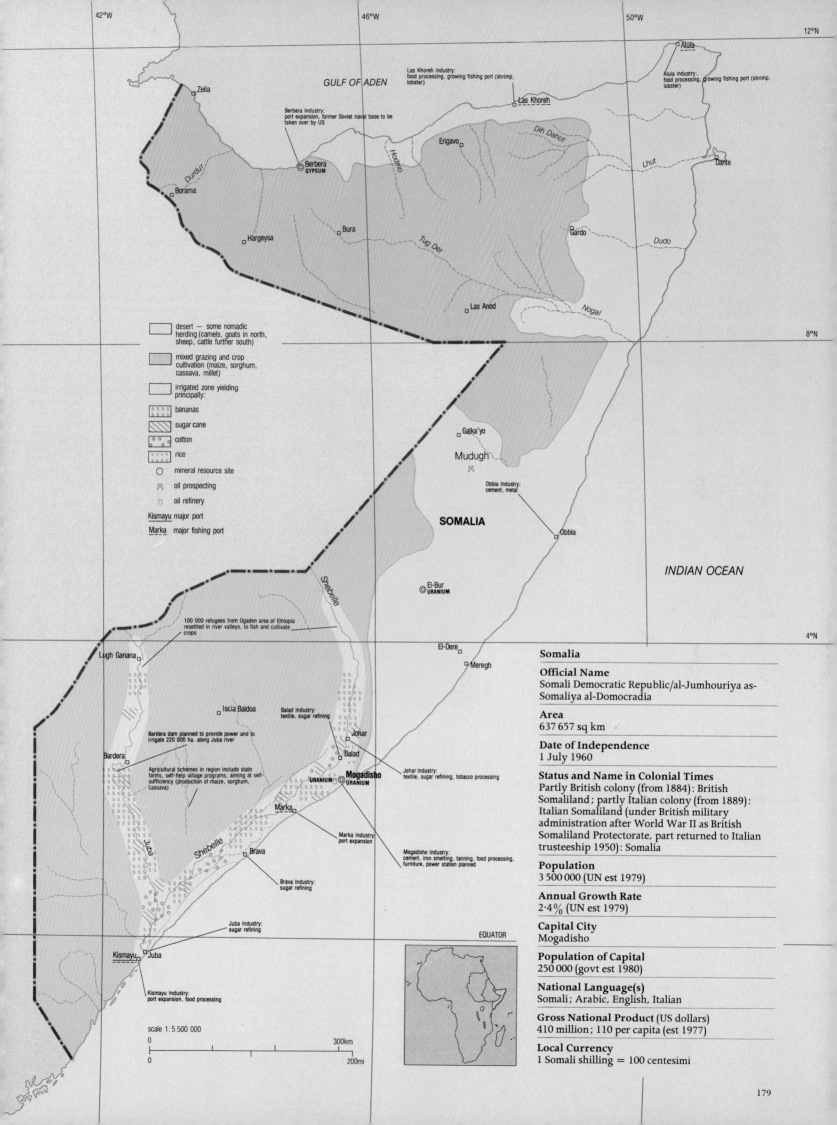

GULF OF ADEN

Zeila

Las Khoreh Industry:
food processing, growing fishing port (shrimp,
lobster)

Alula

Alula Industry:
food processing, growing fishing port (shrimp,
lobster)

Las Khoreh

Berbera Industry:
port expansion, former Soviet naval base to be
taken over by US

Dih Dahot

Erigavo

Lhut

Dante

Durdur

Berbera
GYPSUM

Hodmo

Borama

Gardo

Dudo

Hargeysa

Bura

Tug Der

Las Anod

Nogal

desert — some nomadic
herding (camels, goats in north,
sheep, cattle further south)

mixed grazing and crop
cultivation (maize, sorghum,
cassava, millet)

irrigated zone yielding
principally:

Galka'yo

s s s s
s s s s   bananas

Mudugh

sugar cane

Obbia Industry:
cement, metal

○ ○ ○
○ ○ ○   cotton

SOMALIA

v v v v
v v v v   rice

Obbia

○   mineral resource site

⊠   oil prospecting

⊟   oil refinery

INDIAN OCEAN

Kismayu   major port

Marka   major fishing port

El-Bur
URANIUM

100 000 refugees from Ogaden area of Ethiopia
resettled in river valleys, to fish and cultivate
crops

El-Dere

4°N

Lugh Ganana

Shebelle

Meregh

Iscia Baidoa

Balad Industry:
textile, sugar refining

Bardera dam planned to provide power and to
irrigate 220 000 ha. along Juba river

Johar

Bardera

Balad

Agricultural schemes in region include state
farms, self-help village programs, aiming at self-
sufficiency (production of maize, sorghum,
cassava)

Johar industry:
textile, sugar refining, tobacco processing

URANIUM

Mogadisho
URANIUM

Marka

Marka Industry:
port expansion

Mogadisho Industry:
cement, iron smelting, tanning, food processing,
furniture, power station planned

Juba

Shebelle

Brava

Brava Industry:
sugar refining

Juba Industry:
sugar refining

EQUATOR

Kismayu   Juba

Kismayu Industry:
port expansion, food processing

scale 1:5 500 000

0   300km

0   200mi

Somalia

Official Name
Somali Democratic Republic/al-Jumhouriya as-
Somaliya al-Domocradia

Area
637 657 sq km

Date of Independence
1 July 1960

Status and Name in Colonial Times
Partly British colony (from 1884): British
Somaliland; partly Italian colony (from 1889):
Italian Somaliland (under British military
administration after World War II as British
Somaliland Protectorate, part returned to Italian
trusteeship 1950): Somalia

Population
3 500 000 (UN est 1979)

Annual Growth Rate
2·4% (UN est 1979)

Capital City
Mogadisho

Population of Capital
250 000 (govt est 1980)

National Language(s)
Somali; Arabic, English, Italian

Gross National Product (US dollars)
410 million; 110 per capita (est 1977)

Local Currency
1 Somali shilling = 100 centesimi

EAST AFRICA

Above left Zanzibar, an island off the East African coast, was the Western traveler's doorway into the interior and an important slave market throughout the 19th century. From the 1820s the Omani dynasty made it their capital, and from Zanzibar Islamic religion and culture and the Swahili language spread inland.

Above The thornbush plains of East Africa are the home of many species of game, and have enabled the independent nations to develop flourishing tourist industries based on game viewing and photography, with hunting and trophy taking now illegal. But organized poaching remains a problem.

Left From the Persian Gulf and India the northeast monsoon takes craft to East Africa from November to January, and from April the southwest monsoon brings them north again. For many centuries small craft – dhows – have traded between the Gulf and the East African ports, and even smaller craft along the coast itself.

East Africa has been seen as a political and a geographical region throughout the colonial period. From the end of World War I to the granting of independence in the early 1960s Kenya, Uganda, Tanganyika and Zanzibar were all under forms of British colonial rule. English and Swahili were taught and spoken to a greater or lesser degree throughout this region.

The two tiny but densely populated nations of Rwanda and Burundi might by some be considered to have closer links with West Central Africa. Under German rule (like Tanganyika) to the end of the Great War, they were then through Belgian trusteeship associated with the Congo, and through the use of the French language with the other Francophone nations. But their geographical ties with the British territories were strong, as were their links with the other interlacustrine kingdoms of southern Uganda and western Tanganyika, with their royal courts and almost feudal organization. Over most of the region societies were organized on a much smaller scale. Agriculturalists of the highlands and cattle keepers of the high grasslands alike settled disputes and celebrated rituals under the presidency of councils of elders, without any leader who could be called a chief.

Throughout much of Kenya, and down the Rift Valley into central Tanzania, are a number of ethnic groups which, although speaking totally different languages, share a number of distinctive cultural traits. The most notable are the initiation of both young men and girls through ceremonies including circumcision for males and a comparable physical operation on females. The circumcised males enter a named age group and formerly acted as warriors.

A last distinctive feature of East Africa has been the long-standing presence of Arabs along its coasts and offshore islands, and their influence in spreading Islamic faith and culture. The very recent settlement of merchants and craftsmen from the Indian subcontinent, and farmers and businessmen from Europe, has also left a distinctive mark on East Africa which is enduring into the period of independence.

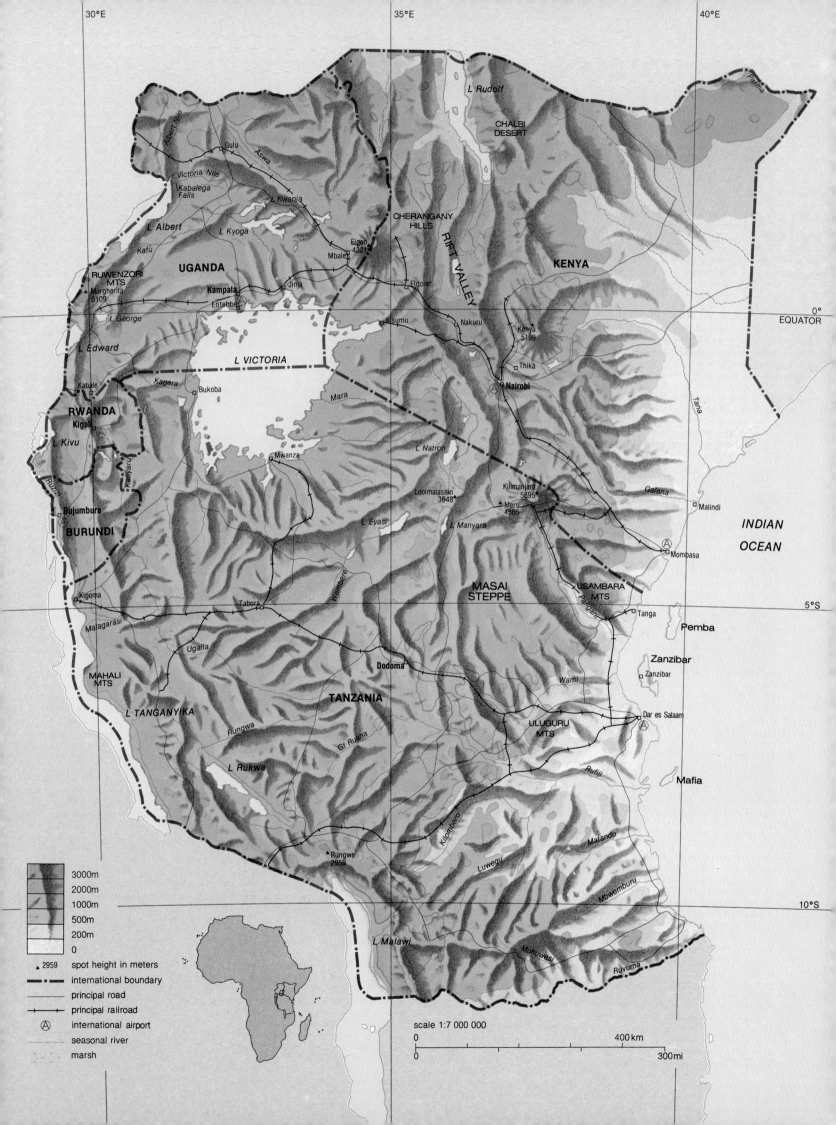

30°E　　　　　　　　　　35°E　　　　　　　　　　40°E

L Rudolf

CHALBI
DESERT

Parma

Albert Nile

Gulu

Aswa

Victoria Nile

Kabalega
Falls

L Kwania

CHERANGANY
HILLS

L Albert

L Kyoga

Kafu

UGANDA

Elgon
4321

Mbale

RIFT VALLEY

KENYA

RUWENZORI
MTS
▲ Margherita
5109

Kampala

Jinja

Entebbe

Eldoret

L George

Kisumu

Nakuru

Kenya
5199

0°
EQUATOR

L Edward

Thika

Kabale

Kagera

Bukoba

L VICTORIA

Mara

Nairobi Ⓐ

RWANDA

Kigali Ⓐ

Tana

L Kivu

Kanyaru

L Natron

Mwanza

Kilimanjaro
5895

Galana

Bujumbura

Loolmalassin
3648 ▲

▲ Meru
4565

Malindi

BURUNDI

L'Eyasi

L Manyara

**INDIAN
OCEAN**

Mombasa Ⓐ

MASAI
STEPPE

USAMBARA
MTS

5°S

Kigoma

Tabora

Wembere

Pangani

Tanga

Malagarasi

Pemba

Ugalla

Zanzibar

Zanzibar

MAHALI
MTS

Dodoma

Wami

L TANGANYIKA

TANZANIA

Dar es Salaam Ⓐ

Rungwa

ULUGURU
MTS

Gt Ruaha

Mafia

L Rukwa

Rufiji

Kilombero

Matandu

▲ Rungwe
2959

Luwegu

10°S

L Malawi

Mbwemburu

Muhuwesi

Ruvuma

3000m
2000m
1000m
500m
200m
0

▲ 2959　spot height in meters
　━━━　international boundary
　───　principal road
　┼┼┼┼　principal railroad
　Ⓐ　international airport
　─ ─ ─　seasonal river
　░░░░　marsh

scale 1:7 000 000

0　　　　　　　　　　　400 km

0　　　　　　　300 mi

Top left In a number of archaeological sites along the East African coast there are evidences of trading connections between the coast and China via the so-called silk routes. At Kunduchi, 25 kilometers north of Dar es Salaam, this 18th-century pillar-tomb features embedded Chinese plates of the late Ming period.

Top right The cattle-keeping Maasai are famous as warriors of the East African grasslands, usually pictured in ocher cloth and pigtails. From the early period of European settlement some worked as herders on cattle ranches, and they have added a raincoat and bowler, while keeping their traditional earrings.

Above Sisal has long been an important export crop in Kenya, and especially in Tanzania. During the colonial period it was chiefly grown and processed on plantations owned by European firms, but African farmers grew hedgerow sisal, which was widely used by African women for baskets and mats.

Right Somali nomads have been moving south into Kenya for many years and the northeast corner of Kenya is inhabited almost exclusively by Somali. Their mode of life in Kenya is, as in Somalia, centered around the wells and water holes where their stock, often including camels, are watered.

Far left Tea has been a valuable cash crop in Kenya for many years but it was formerly grown only on large estates. In recent years African farmers in the higher altitudes of districts like Murang'a and Nyeri have been growing tea on smallholdings and sending it for processing in cooperatively owned tea factories.

Left The Ankole of southwestern Uganda possess large herds of a native long-horned breed of cattle which are valued for their milk and meat and are also of great importance as indicators of wealth and prestige.

Kenya

Kenya's origins as a modern nation lie in its existence as a colonial territory. There were no preexisting kingdoms uniting the very disparate African societies. The Sultan of Zanzibar exercised some control over the Arab-dominated cities along the coast, but this scarcely extended even to the Bantu-speaking Africans of the coastal interior.

The physical geography of Kenya has always been a dominating factor, with altitude more important than the equatorial latitude. Outside the narrow coastal strip there is a wide belt of thorn-tree savanna, game country, which in the north becomes semidesert. In the south the land rises gradually, and the mountains of central Kenya have their base at about 1600 meters. Here, around Lake Victoria to the west, and along the coastal strip rainfall is sufficient for fairly intensive agriculture, limited in the highlands by the altitude. Elsewhere subsistence pastoralism is all that is possible. Given this situation, communities have over the centuries competed for the fertile islands in an arid sea.

Kenya had been an area of migration long before the European incursion and peoples of very diverse linguistic and ethnic origins met and mingled in the highlands and around the lake. Later comers have displaced and to some extent assimilated previous populations. In the highlands these seem to have been Cushitic-speaking peoples, for later societies speaking both Bantu and Nilotic languages exhibit a number of markedly Cushitic traits (as cycling age sets). All these societies were organized politically on a small scale, with very localized authorities. But in the 19th century there were areas where religious leaders, or successful long-distance traders, or war leaders were beginning to extend their influence and build up a wider authority. The colonial intrusion cut short this process, and migration, as for instance of Somali tribes from the northeast, was also limited or halted.

British interest in Kenya proceeded out of an earlier involvement with Zanzibar and the coastal ports, her later involvement with Uganda and the necessity of limiting German territorial ambitions. The building of the Uganda railroad (completed to Kisumu 1904) and the related arrival of white settlers – farmers and businessmen – and of Indian artisans and traders laid the scene for the complicated interactions and competing ambitions that marked colonial Kenya. The areas most desirable to Africans were also those coveted by the newcomers. The Indian migrants were legally prevented from becoming landowners (outside very strict limits) but large areas of agricultural land were alienated for white farms and plantations, and the pastoral Maasai were forcibly moved to allow room for European-owned ranches.

The small-scale African societies were not equipped to offer massive resistance to the incomers, but the degree of force needed for "pacification," and the time it took, were considerable. Many of the agricultural peoples, especially the Kikuyu, already suffering from land shortage which losses to white farmers only intensified, took work as laborers and squatters on European farms. Many more, again largely from the agricultural peoples, attended the new schools opened by Christian missionaries, and obtained education which opened up avenues of employment (however limited) in the new society. Others, especially the pastoralists, were able to continue their traditional way of life with relatively little change.

White settlers and Indians soon demanded a share in the government and by the 1920s some African groups were also making political claims. Among the Kikuyu and Luo, societies were formed which, if not yet explicitly nationalist, were at least acting as a focus for an enlarged sense of ethnic identity. In 1929 the Kikuyu Central Association sent a representative to Britain to present their land claims to the Colonial Office. His name was Jomo Kenyatta and he remained there, on and off, for nearly 20 years.

Earlier, in 1923, the British government dashed the hopes of white settlers for internal self-government by declaring that "Kenya is an African territory" and that "the interests of the African natives must be paramount." It was largely the need to curb Indian claims that meant that European aspirations also had to be limited. Africans were not represented directly in the Legislative Assembly until 1944, when one African-nominated member was appointed.

This was too little, too late. Land and labor problems, rising population and rising expectations, serious land erosion, urban unemployment, the intransigence of white settler opinion and the "petty apartheid" they imposed combined to bring matters to a head. Jomo Kenyatta had returned in 1947 and became president of the Kenya African Union (KAU), but sections of the Kikuyu were not prepared to work slowly for constitutional change. Violence erupted in the early 1950s, and in 1952 the government declared a state of emergency which was not finally lifted till 1960. Although Europeans and Asians were killed (only just over 100, including army casualties), the main victims were the Kikuyu themselves; thousands were killed in what became a civil war, in addition to those killed by the security forces, and thousands more were detained. The roots of the conflict seem to have lain in internal land-holding rivalries, as well as in the determination to regain the land alienated to whites. Kenyatta and other leaders of the KAU were tried and convicted for managing the movement, known as Mau Mau. But Kenyatta's involvement has never been satisfactorily proved, and after his release from detention in 1961 he proved an intelligent and moderate leader. In 1963 Kenya moved to a peaceful granting of independent status, and Kenyatta became prime minister. A year later, when a republic was declared, he became president, and was twice reelected, remaining in office until his death.

Since independence Kenya has continued as a relatively stable and increasingly prosperous nation. Its economic growth rate (estimated at 6·2 per cent in the decade 1964–74) makes it one of Africa's leaders. Without notable mineral resources, the diversified agricultural products and industrial sector, with a very valuable tourist industry, combine to offer continuing prospects of growth. Western capital investment continues.

Although no coups have occurred and free elections have been held, elections have latterly been confined to candidates from the ruling party (Kenya African National Union) only, the opposition party having been banned. In 1969 and again in 1975 leading politicians were murdered in circumstances that have never been explained, and a number of accidental deaths of politicians have raised queries. The increasing affluence does not reach far enough down the scale. Corruption is said to be growing and the old question of landownership remains an issue, for much of the former white highlands is still in the hands of a few people, albeit they are now Kenyan Africans. The collapse of the East African Community in 1976–77 and uneasy relations with both Uganda and Tanzania represent further difficulties.

However, when President Kenyatta died in August 1978 the selection of a new president proceeded smoothly and according to the constitution. The vice-president, Daniel arap Moi, sworn in as acting president, was later confirmed in office and was unopposed in the elections of late 1979, when a number of established politicians were rejected by the electorate. Kenya has passed its first major test as a nation, and seems set on a course which, in the context of modern Africa, offers possibilities of free and continuing development.

J.M.

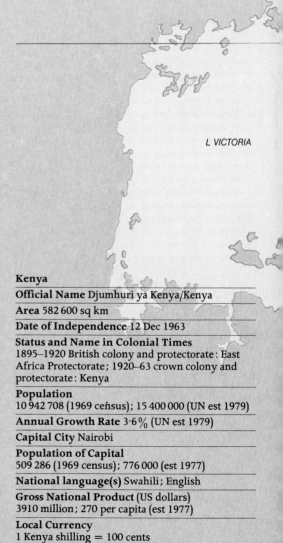

L VICTORIA

Kenya

Official Name Djumhuri ya Kenya/Kenya	
Area 582 600 sq km	
Date of Independence 12 Dec 1963	
Status and Name in Colonial Times 1895–1920 British colony and protectorate: East Africa Protectorate; 1920–63 crown colony and protectorate: Kenya	
Population 10 942 708 (1969 census); 15 400 000 (UN est 1979)	
Annual Growth Rate 3·6% (UN est 1979)	
Capital City Nairobi	
Population of Capital 509 286 (1969 census); 776 000 (est 1977)	
National language(s) Swahili; English	
Gross National Product (US dollars) 3910 million; 270 per capita (est 1977)	
Local Currency 1 Kenya shilling = 100 cents	

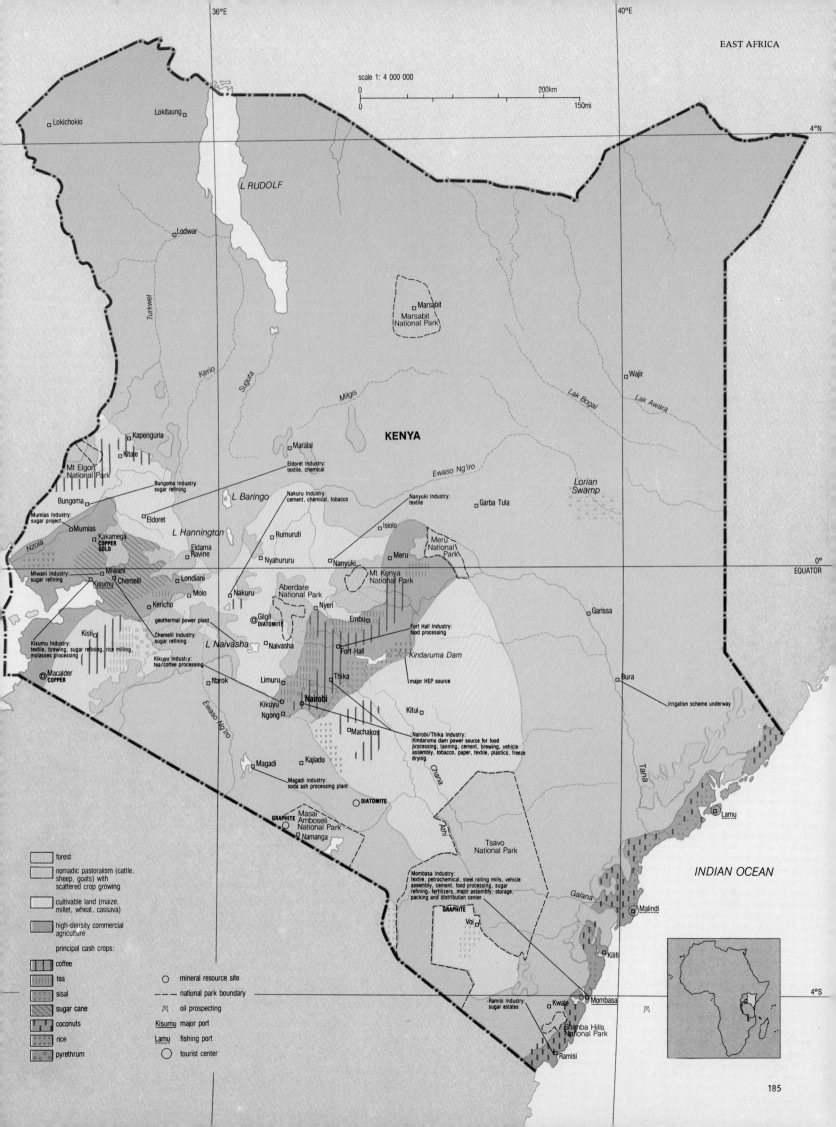

EAST AFRICA

4°N

36°E   40°E

□ Lokichokio   □ Lokitaung

L RUDOLF

□ Lodwar

Turkwel

Kerio

Suguta

Milgis

Marsabit
□ Marsabit
Marsabit
National Park

KENYA

Ewaso Ng'iro

□ Wajir

Lak Bogal

Lak Awara

Lorian
Swamp

Kapenguria
□ Kitale   □ Maralal
Mt Elgon
National Park

Eldoret Industry:
textile, chemical

Bungoma Industry:
sugar refining

□ Bungoma

Mumias Industry:
sugar project

□ Mumias

Nzoia   Kakamega
                      COPPER
                      GOLD

L Baringo

□ Eldoret

L Hannington

□ Rumuruti

Nakuru Industry:
cement, chemical, tobacco

Nanyuki Industry:
textile

□ Garba Tula

□ Isiolo

Meru
National
Park

EQUATOR

Miwani Industry:
sugar refining

□ Miwani
Kisumu □ Chemelil

Eldama
Ravine

□ Nyahururu

□ Meru

□ Londiani

□ Molo

□ Nakuru

Aberdare
National Park

Nanyuki □

Mt Kenya
National
Park

□ Garissa

Kisumu Industry:
textile, brewing, sugar refining, rice milling,
molasses processing

Kisii □

□ Kericho

geothermal power plant

Chemelil Industry:
sugar refining

Gilgil ⊙
DIATOMITE

□ Naivasha

□ Nyeri

Embu □

Fort Hall Industry:
food processing

Macalder
COPPER

Kikuyu Industry:
tea/coffee processing

L Naivasha

□ Narok

□ Limuru

Fort Hall □

□ Thika

Kindaruma Dam

major HEP source

□ Bura

irrigation scheme underway

□ Kikuyu
□ Ngong

Nairobi

□ Kitui

□ Machakos

Nairobi/Thika Industry:
Kindaruma dam power source for food
processing, tanning, cement, brewing, vehicle
assembly, tobacco, paper, textile, plastics, freeze
drying

□ Magadi   □ Kajiado

Magadi Industry:
soda ash processing plant

□ DIATOMITE

GRAPHITE

Masai
Amboseli
National Park

□ Namanga

Tana

□ Lamu

Chana

Athi

Tsavo
National Park

INDIAN OCEAN

Mombasa Industry:
textile, petrochemical, steel rolling mills, vehicle
assembly, cement, food processing, sugar
refining, fertilizers, major assembly, storage,
packing and distribution center

Galana

GRAPHITE

□ Voi

⊙ Malindi

□ Kilifi

4°S

Ramisi Industry:
sugar estates

□ Kwale

⊙ Mombasa

Shimba Hills
National Park

↕↕ Ramisi

scale 1: 4 000 000

0   200km
0   150mi

Legend:

☐ forest

☐ nomadic pastoralism (cattle,
sheep, goats) with
scattered crop growing

☐ cultivable land (maize,
millet, wheat, cassava)

☐ high-density commercial
agriculture

principal cash crops:

▦ coffee

▦ tea

▦ sisal

▦ sugar cane

▦ coconuts

∨∨∨ rice

⊙⊙⊙ pyrethrum

○ mineral resource site

--- national park boundary

⋈ oil prospecting

<u>Kisumu</u> major port

<u>Lamu</u> fishing port

⊙ tourist center

185

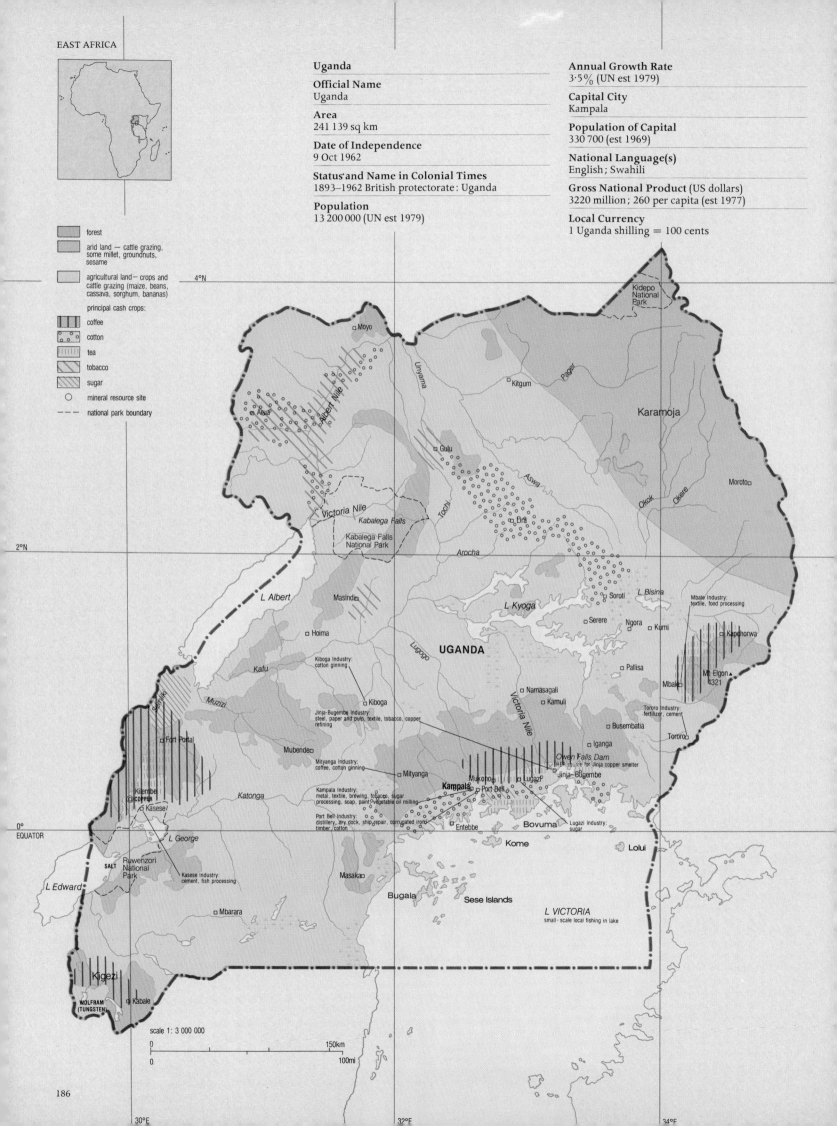

EAST AFRICA

Uganda

Official Name
Uganda

Area
241 139 sq km

Date of Independence
9 Oct 1962

Status and Name in Colonial Times
1893–1962 British protectorate : Uganda

Population
13 200 000 (UN est 1979)

Annual Growth Rate
3·5 % (UN est 1979)

Capital City
Kampala

Population of Capital
330 700 (est 1969)

National Language(s)
English ; Swahili

Gross National Product (US dollars)
3220 million ; 260 per capita (est 1977)

Local Currency
1 Uganda shilling = 100 cents

forest

arid land — cattle grazing,
some millet, groundnuts,
sesame

agricultural land — crops and
cattle grazing (maize, beans,
cassava, sorghum, bananas)

principal cash crops:

coffee

cotton

tea

tobacco

sugar

○ mineral resource site

--- national park boundary

4°N

2°N

0°
EQUATOR

Kidepo
National
Park

Moyo

Kitgum

Pager

Unyama

Karamoja

Arua

Albert Nile

Gulu

Aswa

Moroto

Victoria Nile

Kabalega Falls

Okok

Okere

Kabalega Falls
National Park

Lira

L Albert

Arocha

Masindi

L Bisina

Soroti

Mbale Industry:
textile, food processing

Hoima

L Kyoga

Serere

Ngora

Kumi

Kapchorwa

Kafu

Namasagali

Pallisa

Mt Elgon
4321

Lugogo

UGANDA

Kamuli

Mbale

Kiboga Industry:
cotton ginning

Kiboga

Tororo Industry:
fertilizer, cement

Jinja-Bugembe Industry:
steel, paper and pulp, textile, tobacco, copper
refining

Semliki

Fort Portal

Muzizi

Mubende

Busembatia

Iganga

Tororo

Mityanga Industry:
coffee, cotton ginning

Mityanga

Victoria Nile

Owen Falls Dam
HEP source for Jinja copper smelter

Kampala Industry:
metal, textile, brewing, tobacco, sugar
processing, soap, paint, vegetable oil milling

Mukono

Lugazi

Jinja-Bugembe

Kilembe
COPPER

Kasese

Katonga

Kampala

Port Bell

Port Bell Industry:
distillery, dry dock, ship repair, corrugated iron
timber, cotton

Entebbe

Bovuma

Lugazi Industry:
sugar

Kasese Industry:
cement, fish processing

Ruwenzori
National
Park

SALT

L George

Kome

Loloi

L Edward

Masaka

Bugala

Sese Islands

L VICTORIA
small-scale local fishing in lake

Mbarara

Kigezi

WOLFRAM
(TUNGSTEN)

Kabale

scale 1: 3 000 000

0   150km

0   100mi

186

Uganda

The territory of Uganda was defined during the 19th-century scramble for Africa. It contains a wide range of indigenous linguistic and political groupings. The eastern border largely consists of the mountainous western shoulder of the Kenyan Rift Valley and is dominated by the volcanic range of which Mount Elgon is the highest peak. To the southwest lies the Ruwenzori range and the mountains of Kigezi. Between these heights of over 3000 meters lies 84 per cent of Uganda's land, an extensive plateau with an elevation between 1000 and 1600 meters. This drains into the convoluted central Lake Kyoga and the vast Lake Victoria which forms the border with Tanzania to the south. Lakes Albert and Edward, forming the basin of the upper Nile, sketch in the line of the western frontier with Zaïre. Thus, 17 per cent of Uganda's territory is lakes.

Uganda's equatorial climate varies little; temperature depends mainly on altitude. Rainfall patterns define ecology and agriculture. The savanna-like northeast of Karamoja, which, with some parts of southeast Ankole, gets less than 760 millimeters per year, relies on cattle husbandry and an annual sorghum crop. Some areas near Lake Victoria receive over 2000 millimeters and have a three-month dry season. But for most of central and west Uganda permanent cultivation of bananas and cash crops of coffee and tea are made possible by plentiful and regular rainfall. Only 7 per cent of Ugandans live in towns with a population of over 1000; more than half of these are in the capital, Kampala.

In the first millennium AD the region was a melting-pot for Nilotic-speaking cattle herders and Bantu-speaking agriculturalists from which the interlacustrine kingdoms emerged in the 14th and 15th centuries. Bunyoro was the first, acting as a stimulant for the creation of Buganda, Ankole and Toro, centralized kingdoms with elaborate kingship rituals that contrasted with the more diffuse political systems of Karamoja, Busoga, West Nile, Teso and Kigezi. By the 19th century Buganda had risen to preeminence.

Egyptian interests in the headwaters of the Nile drove the Buganda Kabaka to accept missionaries to his partially Islamized court in the 1870s. The rise of a Christian elite, threatening the delicate balance between king and chiefs, led to martyrdoms in 1885. The power struggle between the converts of the British Protestants and the French White Fathers finally involved the Imperial British East Africa Company in a costly war. A bankrupt company handed over to British administrators in 1893, leaving the numerically strong Buganda kingdom with its Christian chiefs the most powerful African polity in the Uganda Protectorate.

Ganda political and religious dominance was translated into economic power through extensive cotton plantations employing both tenants and migrant labor from Rwanda. The Kampala royalist riots of the 1940s indicated growing peasant discontent against land-owners but, aside from concern over Indian and European control of markets, no common

cause united Bugunda with the rest of the protectorate. Thus, when political parties were formed at the end of the 1950s, Buganda attempted to secede, the king having suffered exile from 1953 to 1955 for his reaction to the proposed East African Federation. After the success of the nationalist leader Benedicto Kiwanuka, a Catholic Ganda commoner, and his Democratic Party, in the face of the official Buganda boycott of elections in 1961, Britain agreed to federal status for the kingdoms.

A coalition between the Uganda People's Congress led by Milton Obote and the chauvinist Kabaka Yekka Party of the king defeated the protectorate-wide Democratic Party before independence in October 1962. With the Kabaka as President of the Republic of Uganda, this uneasy alliance survived until February 1966. After a unanimous vote condemning the Obote government for gold-smuggling, the constitution was suspended. Troops stormed the Kabaka's palace and he was replaced as head of state by Milton Obote. The constitutional existence of the kingdoms was abolished in 1967 and the power of Buganda broken.

The process of centralization and modernization continued with the Common Man's Charter of 1969, the banning of opposition parties and a new state socialism with 60 per cent government control of commercial enterprises, banking and plantations. By 1970, Obote had consolidated his position with a state security system and a one-party state giving greater representation to his own region, the Nilotic-speaking north. In January 1971 his sacked chief of staff, Major General Idi Amin, seized power in his absence at the Singapore Commonwealth Conference.

The coup was greeted by Britain but it was followed by legislation restricting civil rights. The first systematic ethnic killings began in January 1972 with the elimination of Obote's Langi and Acholi support in the army. Lugbara officers were murdered in February 1974 and it is estimated that the State Research Bureau, Military Intelligence Unit, Public Safety Unit and Military Police have killed from 50 000 to 300 000 Ugandan civilians. In July 1976 Britain severed diplomatic relations.

The systematic killing of educated Ugandans (those of Benedicto Kiwanuka and Archbishop Janani Luwum are the most infamous murders), coupled with the expulsion of Asians in August 1972, left the economy without technological and managerial expertise. A low level of capital inflow, shortage of foreign exchange, transportation difficulties and declining imports rapidly followed. After 1973 cash-crop production fell on average 10 to 15 per cent per year and many farmers reverted to subsistence farming. Exports of coffee (of which Uganda was once the world's fifth largest producer), tea, cotton and sugar all declined catastrophically. When Kenya refused to continue petrol supplies in 1976 until 52 million shillings' worth of debts were paid, two million bags of coffee piled up and the economy was within weeks of total collapse. Imports fell to 1199 million shillings in 1976 and were restricted to countries offering credit facilities. British aid ceased, though payments from the STABEX fund of the Lomé Convention continued and it was largely due to aid from Libya and some other

Arab states that foreign exchange reserves reached even the level of 60 million dollars in 1976.

To disguise Uganda's internal collapse, Amin embarked on the risky venture of invading Tanzanian territory up to the Kagera river. President Nyerere's forces repulsed the invaders and slowly advanced upon Kampala. In April 1979 Amin fled to Libya and leaders of the Ugandan National Liberation Front (UNLF) returned from exile to form a National Consultative Council initially headed by Professor Yusufu Lule. Continuing factionalism within the UNLF remains a serious obstacle to the vital task of rebuilding Uganda's devastated political and economic life. Godfrey Binaisa, who within a few months replaced Lule as interim head of state, relied heavily on the presence of the Tanzanian expeditionary force to contain the threat of total anarchy. Until constitutional government and the rule of law have been reestablished there seems little chance of Uganda's receiving the massive injections of foreign aid necessary to revive the economy. The election of Obote as president in December 1980 may form the basis of recovery.

I.L.

Rwanda

The territory of Rwanda represents the small expansion, under colonial rule, of an ancient precolonial kingdom. The Nile–Congo crest, running from north to south, provides an asymmetric backbone, which drops down to Lake Kivu in the west and to the central plateau of rugged hills in the east. The eastern border with Tanzania is a wide strip lying at an elevation of about 300 meters and marked by swampy lakes and the Kagera river basin. The northern border with Uganda is dominated by the Virunga volcanoes, still active in the early 20th century.

The central plateau has an average temperature of 19° but an impressive daily variation of 14°. Annual temperature variations are slight and there are two wet and two relatively dry seasons, June through September being dusty with only a rare shower. Offering the spectacle of endless hills, huts and banana groves, Rwanda has the highest population density in Africa, particularly in some of the northern provinces which have traditionally produced cash crops on the rich volcanic soils. There are well over half a million cattle, mostly in east-central Rwanda. Only along the Nile–Congo crest does the untouched forest survive to provide one of the few habitats for gorillas. Sorghum, maize, manioc, sweet potatoes, beans, coffee and tobacco are grown in gardens around and in banana plantations. Despite manuring and mixed crops intermittent famines have occurred in the last century. Depopulation by death or emigration has not checked the erosion and exhaustion of most of the country's poor, thin soil.

The population comprises 14 per cent Tutsi, 85 per cent Hutu and 1 per cent Twa. The Tutsi are descendants of Cushitic-speaking herdsmen who settled in the southeast from the 13th century onwards. A typical interlacustrine state, Rwanda developed a powerful kingship and army, but by the 19th century society showed signs of stratification into a cattle-owning and a peasant caste. German indirect rule left the polity little changed but the Belgians, from 1916, began reforms of chieftaincies, resulting in the abolition of feudal relations in the 1950s. However, access to political office remained a Tutsi prerogative.

The publication in 1957 of the Bahutu Manifesto spelled the end of Tutsi control. The creation of democratic machinery, nonexistent under the Belgian League of Nations mandate, was speeded up by United Nations' pressure on the Trust Territory. Parti du Mouvement de l'Émancipation Hutu (PARMEHUTU) and Union Nationale Rwandaise (UNAR) were formed on social justice and nationalist platforms respectively. A dramatic peasant revolt in November 1959 ultimately pushed PARMEHUTU, under the leadership of Gregoire Kayibanda, to power on 28 January 1961. The king, *mwami* Kigeri Ndahindurwa, went into exile.

Raids by UNAR-backed rebels resulted in a repression of Tutsi in which some 5000 to 8000 died at the end of 1963. Ethnic conflict simmered and again erupted in February 1973 with the expulsion of Tutsi from institutes of higher education. The government of Gregoire Kayibanda was removed in a bloodless coup by General Juvenal Habyarimana on 5 July 1973. The northern region, traditionally beyond the jurisdiction of the old Rwandan court, now provided three-quarters of army majors and held the three major portfolios. In July 1975 National Revolutionary Movement for Development (MRND) was set up as a party dedicated to the elimination of regionalism. Military rule led to an easing in ethnic tension, improved relations with Zaïre and Burundi and a swing away from socialist tendencies in the economy.

Rwanda's economic problems remain land-hunger, the landlocked situation, lack of a railroad and overdependence on Belgium. Mining of cassiterite (tin ore) and wolframite (tungsten ore) is controlled by four Belgian companies, though the European Investment Bank has granted a loan of 325 million francs for a tin foundry near Kigali. Development of the less populated marshy plains in the east is under way with reclamation schemes for tea and rice plantations developed by Taiwan and China. The coffee crop earns the country an average of 5000 to 6000 million Rwandan francs, and tobacco, cotton and pyrethrum are important. Manufacturing industry is rudimentary, though transistor radios are made, and hydroelectric schemes are well advanced. Foreign aid accounts for 40 per cent of the budget.

In 1977 Tanzania, Burundi and Rwanda joined together in the Kagera river basin scheme to exploit the mineral and hydro-electric potential of the region. Methane gas is already being exploited in Lake Kivu. Promising cooperative endeavors in agriculture, sponsored by the Catholic Church, contribute to the very slow rate of urbanization. However, Rwanda's dependence on its neighbors for transportation facilities acts as a brake on economic growth.

I.L.

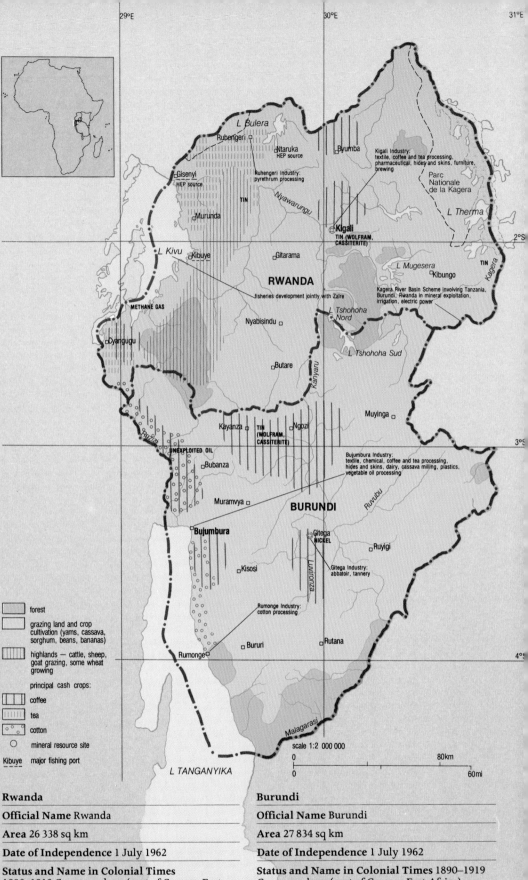

Rwanda	Burundi
Official Name Rwanda	**Official Name** Burundi
Area 26 338 sq km	**Area** 27 834 sq km
Date of Independence 1 July 1962	**Date of Independence** 1 July 1962
Status and Name in Colonial Times 1890–1919 German colony (part of German East Africa); 1919–62 part of Ruanda-Urundi, administered by Belgium as League of Nations mandate, later UN Trust Territory: Ruanda	**Status and Name in Colonial Times** 1890–1919 German colony (part of German East Africa); 1919–62 part of Ruanda-Urundi, administered by Belgium as League of Nations mandate, later UN trust territory: Urundi
Population 4 820 000 (est 1978)	**Population** 4 300 000 (est 1979)
Annual Growth Rate 2·9% (est 1977)	**Annual Growth Rate** 2·4% (est 1979)
Capital City Kigali	**Capital City** Bujumbura (formerly Usumbura)
Population of Capital 89 950 (est 1977)	**Population of Capital** 157 100 (est 1976)
National Language(s) French, Rwanda	**National Language(s)** Rundi; French, Swahili
Gross National Product (US dollars) 580 million; 130 per capita (est 1977)	**Gross National Product** (US dollars): 520 million; 130 per capita
Local Currency 1 franc rwandais = 100 centimes	**Local Currency** 1 Burundi franc = 100 centimes

Burundi

Burundi's territory corresponds roughly with that of an ancient precolonial kingdom centered on the old capital of Gitega. Most of this tiny country is rolling plateau, 1500 to 2000 meters above sea level, where a rich volcanic soil supports the second highest population density in Africa (after Rwanda). A western backbone of mountains runs north into Rwanda and drops down into Lake Tanganyika, the northern tip of which provides the only natural exit for an otherwise landlocked transportation system. The average temperature on the southwestern lake shore is 23°, dropping to 20° at the 2000-meter-high crest of the Nile–Congo divide. Average rainfall throughout the country is 1200 millimeters.

Burundi was divided from neighboring states by both natural and political factors. Lake Tanganyika and the northern drainage river, the Ruzizi, running into Lake Kivu, provide a natural border with Zaïre. The irregular northern border follows the Kanyaru river and reflects the changing fortunes of the precolonial kingdoms of Gisaka and Rwanda, ancient enemies of Burundi. The long eastern border with Tanzania corresponds in the south with the edge of the plateau and in the north with the divisions of German colonial administration and the limits of Rundi political authority.

The population, similar to Rwanda, is made up of a Hutu majority (84 per cent), a Tutsi minority (15 per cent) and a few pygmoid Twa. Political authority in the precolonial state was held by the Tutsi who provided the king, *mwami*, and princes, *ganwa*. Struggles for power between Tutsi lineages allowed German military rule to be imposed in the 1890s. After World War I Burundi ceased to be politically linked with Tanganyika, and became a Belgian-administered Trusteeship Territory mandated by the League of Nations and loosely connected to the Congo. Belgium retained this mandate under the United Nations after World War II.

As a product of rapid Belgian decolonization, Union et Progrès National (UPRONA), under the leadership of Prince Louis Rwagasore, came to power in 1961. After his death the king, *mwami* Mwambutsa, attempted to maintain parity in political office between Tutsi and Hutu. In 1966 Colonel Michel Micombero seized power and the monarchy was abolished. The government was ruled by a military junta representing a minority within the Tutsi, a leadership drawn from the southern Bururi province of Tutsi-Hima.

Systematic exclusion of the Hutu from positions of responsibility in the state resulted in an abortive Hutu-led coup in April 1972. This occasioned a massive repression of Hutu, partly spontaneous, partly a planned genocide of all educated Hutu by military and paramilitary forces. Most deaths occurred in the pogrom of May 1972, but some 20 000 were killed in Ngozi province in May 1973. The total death toll amounted to around 200 000; in some areas all literate Hutu died, down to the level of local church catechists. Some 120 000 Hutu fled to neighboring countries, their raids

often provoking further killing inside Burundi.

In July 1974 a new constitution was passed, stressing national unity and banning appeals or reference to ethnic differences. On 1 November 1976 Lieutenant Colonel Bagaza seized power in a bloodless coup after Colonel Micombero had dismissed all cabinet members. With an all-Tutsi army, the coup merely transferred power to another Tutsi minority and has not altered the regional, ethnic and lineage basis of Burundi political life.

The country has a one-commodity economy – an 80 per cent dependence on coffee. The crop has yielded an annual average of 2500 million francs in exports but has been subject to the vicissitudes of rainfall and commodity prices. In 1975 the newly introduced tea crop gave 64·7 million francs in exports. The pastoral culture has restrained any development of cattle ranching; hides and skins, exported since the 19th century, yielded 59·5 million francs in 1975. Manufacturing industry (textiles, cement and insecticides) is rudimentary. Poor infrastructure – only 200 kilometers of some 6000 kilometers of roads are tarred – and civil strife have made Burundi one of the poorest countries in Africa.

In 1972 China gave a 20 million dollar loan, repayable 1982–91, and this has been supplemented by loans from the World Bank. In September 1976 Burundi, Rwanda and Zaïre joined together in the Economic Community of the Great Lakes Countries (CEPGL). Since the 1973 Rwanda coup, relations with Rwanda have steadily improved and some Hutu refugees have begun returning. The already overloaded transportation systems, however, keep international trade to a minimum.

I.L.

Tanzania

The United Republic of Tanzania goes back to 1964, when the newly independent territories of Tanganyika and Zanzibar formed one nation. Zanzibar, an island lying off the East African coast, has ancient links with both Arabia and the African mainland. Tanganyika took its name from the lake on its western border, which includes the lowest point on the African continent (some 358 meters below sea level). In the northeast Mount Kilimanjaro is the highest point (5895 meters) on the continent. Much of the mainland is a vast savanna plateau, 1000 to 1500 meters above sea level, with areas of higher altitude, higher rainfall and higher fertility on its borders. The plateau is cut by the eastern arm of the Great Rift Valley and falls gradually to the Indian Ocean coast. Rainfall over the plateau seldom exceeds 1000 millimeters a year and is often less, but except for periodic shortage of water there are few natural obstacles to population movements.

Within Tanzania (which may be the original home of the human race) are spoken languages from all four language families of Africa. The hunting Sandawe speak a "click" (Khoisan) language. There are Cushitic-speaking groups like the Burungi and Nilotic-speaking pastoralists like the Maasai, but the majority for some centuries have been Bantu-speaking agriculturalists. Politically, organization

ranged from centralized chiefdoms to small-scale, chiefless societies; so-called tribes were fluid groupings.

During the 19th century long-distance trade increased, involving both inland and coastal peoples. Ivory and slaves were the most valuable commodities. Traders from the coast carried with them the concept of *ustaarabu* (Arab culture and Islamic beliefs) and the Swahili language. Through Zanzibar contacts with the outside world increased, especially after Sultan Seyyid Said moved his capital from Muscat to Zanzibar in 1840. French, American, German and British interests competed for trade, and from about 1860 Christian missionaries and Western explorers passed through Zanzibar to the mainland. Germany ultimately annexed the mainland area south of British East Africa (later Kenya). Agreements made in 1886 and 1890 ratified this division and Zanzibar came under a British protectorate.

German administration was resisted in several areas, and it was not until the end of the century that even minimal government was established. Railroads were built, German settlers encouraged and new cash crops introduced. Literate Swahili-speaking *akidas* from the coast, and later men educated at mission schools, were used as subordinate staff in government offices. Swahili became the language of government business. This had the indirect effect of encouraging the spread of Islam. Christian missions were also active. In 1905–07 the Maji Maji rebellion affected almost the whole of the center and south of the colony, one of the most serious challenges to a colonial power in all Africa.

During World War I civilians throughout the whole German colony suffered from the depredations of both sides. The campaign ended only with the war and unsettled conditions continued for a number of years. The mainland (except for Rwanda and Burundi in the extreme northwest) became a British mandate. British interests took over the more profitable German enterprises and Asian business interests also increased. British policy, under the mandate, was that Tanganyika was "primarily a black man's country," and extensive white settlement was not encouraged. Indirect rule, on the Nigerian model, was the aim. Tanganyika was a very large and a very poor country; development of any kind was slow and came unevenly, with cash crops such as coffee (in Kilimanjaro and Bukoba) and cotton (in Sukuma) bringing prosperity to some areas while other parts were scarcely touched.

In Zanzibar, little affected by the war, the British administration increasingly took power out of the hands of the Sultan and the Arab elite, but passed on little to the black African majority. Slavery was slowly abolished, being ended by 1911. The prosperity of the islands (Pemba as well as Zanzibar) was largely based on cloves, grown on Arab-owned plantations by African labor, with marketing and export largely in Asian hands.

African political associations emerged relatively slowly. The proto-organization was the Tanganyika Territory African Civil Service Association, founded in 1922; in the late 1920s came the Tanganyika African Association (TAA). They set a precedent for a supra-tribal rather than a tribal organization. In World

War II an estimated 87000 Africans were conscripted. As in the 1914–18 conflict, missionaries were interned and church and educational work affected.

Change came faster in the postwar period and the main agent was the Tanganyika African National Union (TANU), founded in 1954. It built on the framework of the TAA, and a leading figure in making the move to an explicitly political association was a young teacher recently returned from study in Edinburgh, Julius Nyerere. Over the next few years TANU gained mass support. Ultimately independence came rather rapidly. TANU candidates contested and decisively won an election held in 1958/59 and five ministers were chosen from their ranks. Further elections were held in September 1960. Nyerere was asked to form a government and independence was agreed on for December 1961. At independence Nyerere resigned from the office of prime minister to build up TANU's local strength. After his return the nation was declared a republic and he was elected president.

The years from 1954 to 1961 were by no means plain sailing, but the violence which occurred elsewhere was almost completely absent. Among the factors that contributed to rapid and peaceful change were the territory's status as a United Nations' Trust Territory, its relative poverty of resources, the tradition of supra-tribal organizations and the widespread use of Swahili. Tanganyika significantly lacked any one dominating ethnic group and its most economically advanced groups lived far from the capital. Nyerere himself was a Zanaki, a small group in the eastern lake region.

Zanzibar was granted independence in 1963, with power passing to the Sultan and the Arabs, the traditional ruling class. A violent revolution in January 1964 killed or sent into exile a fifth of the Arab population. Power was eventually seized by the leader of the Afro–Shirazi Party, Abeid Karume, who later in 1964 became First Vice-President of the new United Republic of Tanzania. Despite the union, Zanzibar has remained somewhat separate and isolated; the amalgamation, in 1977, of the Afro–Shirazi Party and TANU may herald a slow change.

Tanzania's reputation as a radical and anticapitalist regime, though it has deeper roots, goes back to the Arusha Declaration of 1967, with its assertion of egalitarianism and national self-reliance. These doctrines are being worked out in the policy of *Ujamaa* (African socialism) and the setting-up of largely communal *ujamaa* settlements. In 1976 it was claimed that up to 65 per cent of the population lived in such settlements. Problems remain for a large and poor country, further pauperized by its intervention in Uganda in 1978–79. Despite these difficulties President Nyerere's personal reputation remains high.

J.M.

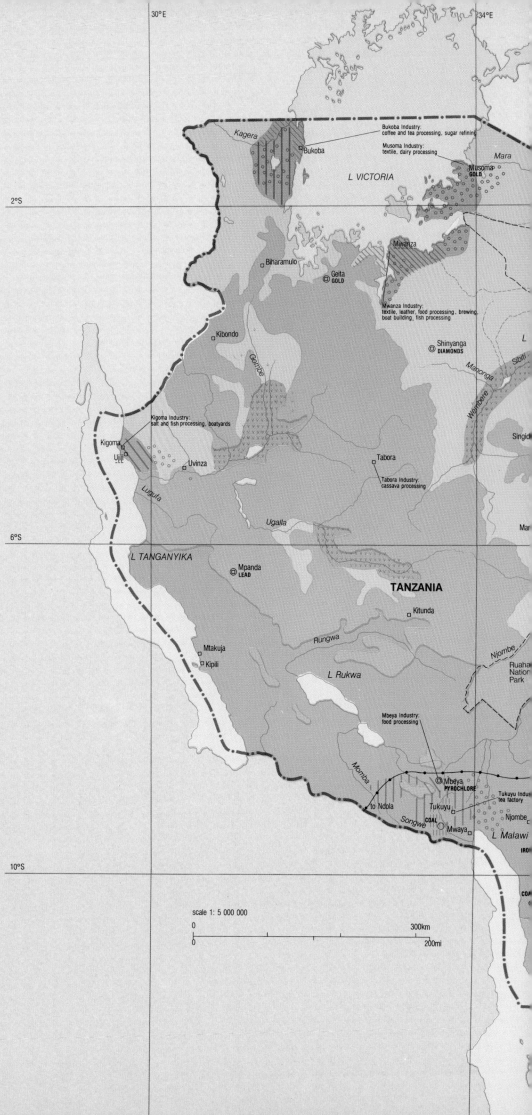

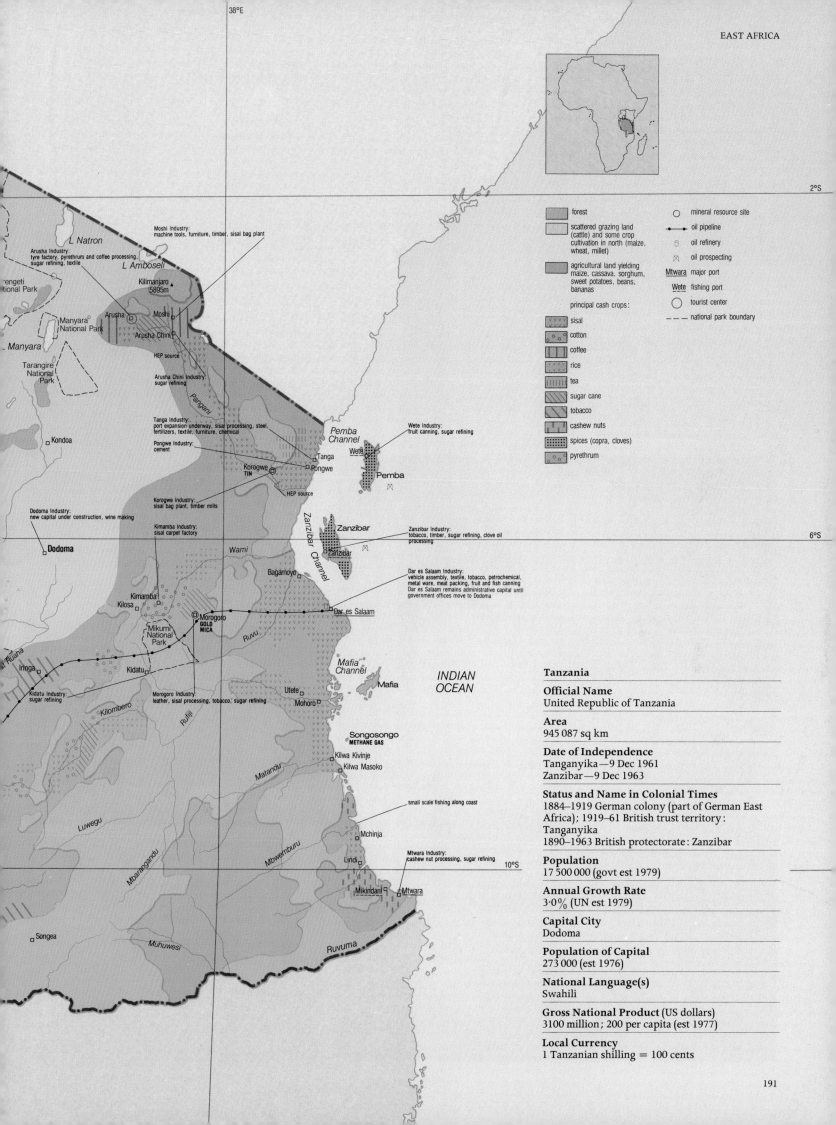

38°E

2°S

6°S

10°S

L. Natron

L. Amboseli

Arusha Industry:
tyre factory, pyrethrum and coffee processing,
sugar refining, textile

Moshi Industry:
machine tools, furniture, timber, sisal bag plant

Kilimanjaro
5895m

Serengeti
National Park

Manyara
National Park

Manyara

Arusha

Moshi

Tarangire
National
Park

Arusha Chini

HEP source

Arusha Chini Industry:
sugar refining

Kondoa

Pangani

Tanga Industry:
port expansion underway, sisal processing, steel,
fertilizers, textile, furniture, chemical

Pongwe Industry:
cement

Pemba
Channel

Wete Industry:
fruit canning, sugar refining

Wete

Tanga

Pongwe

Pemba

Korogwe
TIN

HEP source

Korogwe Industry:
sisal bag plant, timber mills

Dodoma Industry:
new capital under construction, wine making

Kimamba Industry:
sisal carpet factory

Zanzibar

Zanzibar Industry:
tobacco, timber, sugar refining, clove oil
processing

Dodoma

Wami

Zanzibar

Kimamba

Kilosa

Mikumi
National
Park

Bagamoyo

Zanzibar Channel

Dar es Salaam Industry:
vehicle assembly, textile, tobacco, petrochemical,
metal ware, meat packing, fruit and fish canning
Dar es Salaam remains administrative capital until
government offices move to Dodoma

Morogoro
GOLD
MICA

Ruvu

Dar es Salaam

Iringa

Gt Ruaha

Kidatu

Kidatu Industry:
sugar refining

Morogoro Industry:
leather, sisal processing, tobacco, sugar refining

Kilombero

Mafia
Channel

Mafia

INDIAN
OCEAN

Utete

Mohoro

Rufiji

Kilwa Kivinje

Kilwa Masoko

Songosongo
METHANE GAS

Luwegu

Matandu

small scale fishing along coast

Mbwemburu

Mchinja

Kilombero

Lindi

Mtwara Industry:
cashew nut processing, sugar refining

Mbarangandu

Mikindani

Mtwara

Songea

Muhuwesi

Ruvuma

Legend

- ▨ forest
- ▨ scattered grazing land (cattle) and some crop cultivation in north (maize, wheat, millet)
- ▨ agricultural land yielding maize, cassava, sorghum, sweet potatoes, beans, bananas

principal cash crops:
- sisal
- cotton
- coffee
- rice
- tea
- sugar cane
- tobacco
- cashew nuts
- spices (copra, cloves)
- pyrethrum

- ○ mineral resource site
- •—•—• oil pipeline
- oil refinery
- oil prospecting
- Mtwara major port
- Wete fishing port
- ○ tourist center
- – – – national park boundary

Tanzania

Official Name
United Republic of Tanzania

Area
945 087 sq km

Date of Independence
Tanganyika—9 Dec 1961
Zanzibar—9 Dec 1963

Status and Name in Colonial Times
1884–1919 German colony (part of German East
Africa); 1919–61 British trust territory:
Tanganyika
1890–1963 British protectorate: Zanzibar

Population
17 500 000 (govt est 1979)

Annual Growth Rate
3·0% (UN est 1979)

Capital City
Dodoma

Population of Capital
273 000 (est 1976)

National Language(s)
Swahili

Gross National Product (US dollars)
3100 million; 200 per capita (est 1977)

Local Currency
1 Tanzanian shilling = 100 cents

SOUTHEAST CENTRAL AFRICA

Southeast Central Africa includes the three former British colonies which for a few years formed the Central African Federation, and the former Portuguese territory once often known as "Portuguese East." The Zambezi river system drains water from all four countries and economic development in the Zambezi valley, notably the Cabora Bassa dam, is of potential benefit to the region. The landlocked nations of the former CAF have historical economic links with Mozambique which were strengthened in the colonial period by their use of railroad and harbor facilities in the Portuguese colony.

Rivers and lakes are important features in all these countries. The forested highlands of Malawi are exceptional in the more general landscape of open woodland, with agricultural potential dictated by altitude and by rainfall. Cattle keeping has been of less importance and subsistence agriculture (with hunting and fishing) was almost everywhere the mode of livelihood. All the African peoples of this region speak Bantu languages, and in many areas there were no sharp divisions between ethnicities. Identity was defined by residence and by loyalty to a chief or headman, and could be changed. Most people lived in small-scale communities, but Zimbabwe was once the site of the Monomotapa empire and later smaller states. The Lozi kingdom of southwest Zambia survived into the colonial period.

Mineral wealth has been important in all these nations. In Zambia the copper of the north led to early and rapid urbanization and industrialization. In all four countries large numbers of men earned their families' living as migrant laborers in the mines and towns of South Africa as well as in their own or neighboring territories.

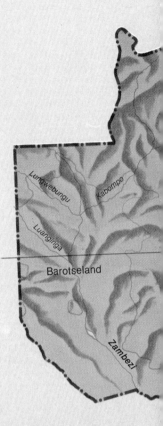

Left The Victoria Falls (named by David Livingstone) are on the Zambezi river between Zambia and Zimbabwe, south of the town of Livingstone.

Below Tea is an important cash crop grown on large estates in the highlands of Mozambique (as here at Gurue) and in Malawi.

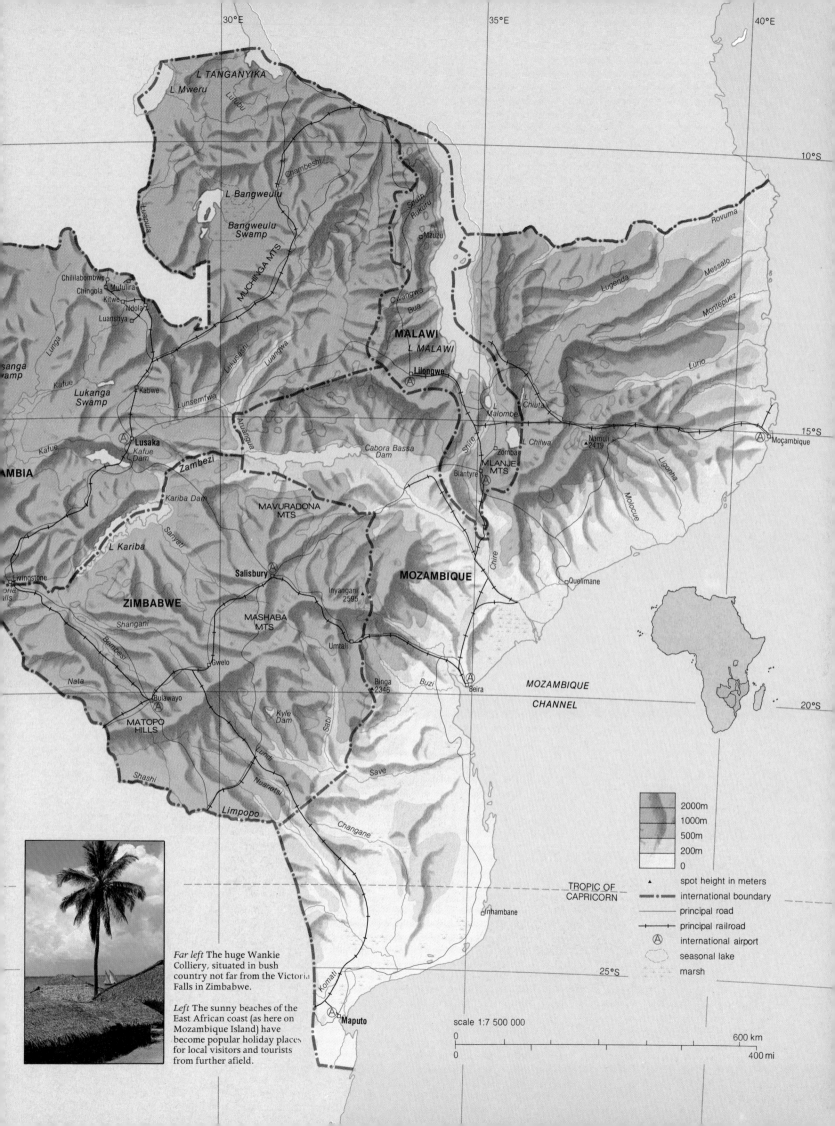

30°E
35°E
40°E

10°S
15°S
20°S
25°S

L TANGANYIKA
L Mweru
L Bangweulu
Bangweulu Swamp
Luapula
Lufubu
Luapula
Chambeshi
MUCHINGA MTS
South Rukuru
Mzuzu
Rovuma
Lugenda
Messalo
Montepuez
Chililabombwe
Chingola
Mutulira
Kitwe
Ndola
Luanshya
Owangwa
Bua
MALAWI
L MALAWI
Lilongwe
Lurio
Lunga
Kafue
Lukanga Swamp
Luangwa
Likusashi
Luangwa
L Chiuta
L Malombe
Namuli
2419
Moçambique
Lusaka
Kafue Dam
Acuangua
Lunsemfwa
Kabwe
Cabora Bassa Dam
Shire
Zomba
L Chilwa
MLANJE MTS
Blantyre
Ligonha
Molocue
ZAMBIA
Kafue
Zambezi
Kariba Dam
L Kariba
Sanyati
MAVURADONA MTS
Chire
Quelimane
Livingstone
Victoria Falls
ZIMBABWE
Salisbury
Inyangani 2595
MOZAMBIQUE
Shangani
MASHABA MTS
Bambesi
Nata
Gwelo
Umtali
Binga 2346
Buzi
Beira
MOZAMBIQUE CHANNEL
Shashi
Kyle Dam
Sabi
MATOPO HILLS
Bulawayo
Lundi
Nuanetsi
Save
Limpopo
Changane
TROPIC OF CAPRICORN
Inhambane
Komati
Maputo

Far left The huge Wankie Colliery, situated in bush country not far from the Victoria Falls in Zimbabwe.

Left The sunny beaches of the East African coast (as here on Mozambique Island) have become popular holiday places for local visitors and tourists from further afield.

scale 1:7 500 000

0   600 km
0   400 mi

2000m
1000m
500m
200m
0

▲ spot height in meters
── ∙ ── international boundary
── principal road
──┼── principal railroad
Ⓐ international airport
seasonal lake
marsh

Zambia

The outlines of the nation-state known as Zambia only emerged with the advent of British colonial rule at the end of the 19th century. Prior to that, Zambia was a crossroads of tribal migrations and regional trade. These intertribal contacts produced a rich mixture of ethnic groups, and by the mid-1800s had stimulated the growth of several large kingdoms, notably the Lozi in the west and the Bemba in the north. Colonial rule severely restricted the earlier patterns of movement, but did not end them altogether. New migration patterns arose, as people were forced to seek employment in the mines and on the farms in Zimbabwe, South Africa, Tanzania, Zaïre and particularly within Zambia itself. Massive and continuing labor migration has given Zambia the largest percentage of urban population among independent African states, current estimates placing it at nearly 40 per cent of the total.

Migration has never been impeded by Zambia's geographical characteristics. Most of the country is over 1000 meters in elevation, rising to about 1500 meters in the northeast. The country is primarily open woodland, giving way to a more arid landscape in the southwest. Rainfall occurs from late November to April, averaging about 1000 millimeters per year, but increasing in the northern sections of the country. The soils are sandy and light structured, but have supported very diverse agricultural systems as people have adapted their cropping methods to the soils and rainfall peculiar to their regions. Until the 1950s subsistence agriculture dominated, primarily because the African economy was suppressed in favor of white settler production. Since 1964, however, government policy in encouraging agriculture at all levels has demonstrated that intensive production is possible throughout the country, although the long dry season and low population density do not facilitate full utilization of existing arable land. Zambia's lakes and rivers provide abundant fish harvests, produced primarily by small-scale enterprise.

Colonial interest in Zambia was an adjunct of British involvement in Rhodesia, now Zimbabwe. African rulers became the extension of the colonial administration at the most local levels. Prior to World War I a railroad from the Rhodesian border, crossing at Victoria Falls, was extended through central Zambia to the copper-producing region of Shaba province, Zaïre. White settlers began to confiscate land along the railroad, and European farms were also established in the Eastern and Northern provinces. Many of these farms were only marginally productive prior to the mid-1930s, when demand for food from the copper industry stimulated serious agricultural output. Thereafter European desire for highly productive land increased and a number of Africans were forcibly resettled. Much of the best land still remains in the hands of European farmers or has been transferred to wealthy Zambians.

Although copper had been mined in precolonial times, a modern industry was not fully developed until stimulated by technological breakthroughs in the mid-1920s and increased world economic demand after the Depression. The copper mines were owned by American and British companies and only a small part of the revenue earned by them remained within the country. Thousands of Africans were drawn to the mines as temporary workers, but increasingly they formed the nucleus of today's large urban population.

The mining economy, with its large number of European workers, eventually led to their demands for a greater role within the government. After years of African opposition, the whites triumphed in 1953 with the creation of the Federation of Rhodesia and Nyasaland. To the African population, federation epitomized the worst forms of racial discrimination, economic exploitation and colonial hypocrisy.

In early 1960 the United National Independence Party (UNIP) was formed, under the leadership of Kenneth Kaunda. Unlike earlier reformist parties, UNIP demanded an end to the Federation and the granting of immediate independence to the country under African rule. Constant pressure from Kaunda and his followers and similar demands within Malawi forced the British to call several elections which were won by UNIP. At the end of 1963 the Federation was dissolved and less than a year later Zambia became fully independent. Kaunda has remained the head of a UNIP government since 1964, being reelected in three subsequent elections.

Since 1964 Zambia has shown a remarkable degree of political stability, despite extremely serious economic strains caused by the Rhodesian Unilateral Declaration of Independence (UDI) in 1965, the reorientation of Zambia's export economy toward the north, the severe depression of copper prices from 1975 into 1979 and liberation wars in neighboring countries. Kaunda has been able to play off rival political factions and to create for the country a philosophy (known as Humanism) of Christian socialism. In theory, the country has progressively moved to distribute political and bureaucratic authority to all levels. In practice, however, centralization of responsibility remains.

Economically, Zambia has moved to gain greater control over her mineral resources, manufacturing sector and service network. In 1969 the country acquired 51 per cent ownership in its copper mines. Later, Zambian management was established within the industry, all these moves being necessitated by copper's central role as a source of both internal and external revenue. Over 90 per cent of Zambia's foreign exchange comes from copper exports, and prior to 1975 copper revenues contributed about 45 per cent of internal revenues. When events outside Zambia created very unstable copper prices, the country entered a prolonged depression in 1975. The price of copper fell to half the previous year's high and, as a result, for several years the government realized no tax revenue from mining operations. For two years the mines even ran at a loss and only the potential for severe labor unrest persuaded the government not to close them altogether during this period. The decline in tax revenues has resulted in a major cutback in development planning and projects throughout the

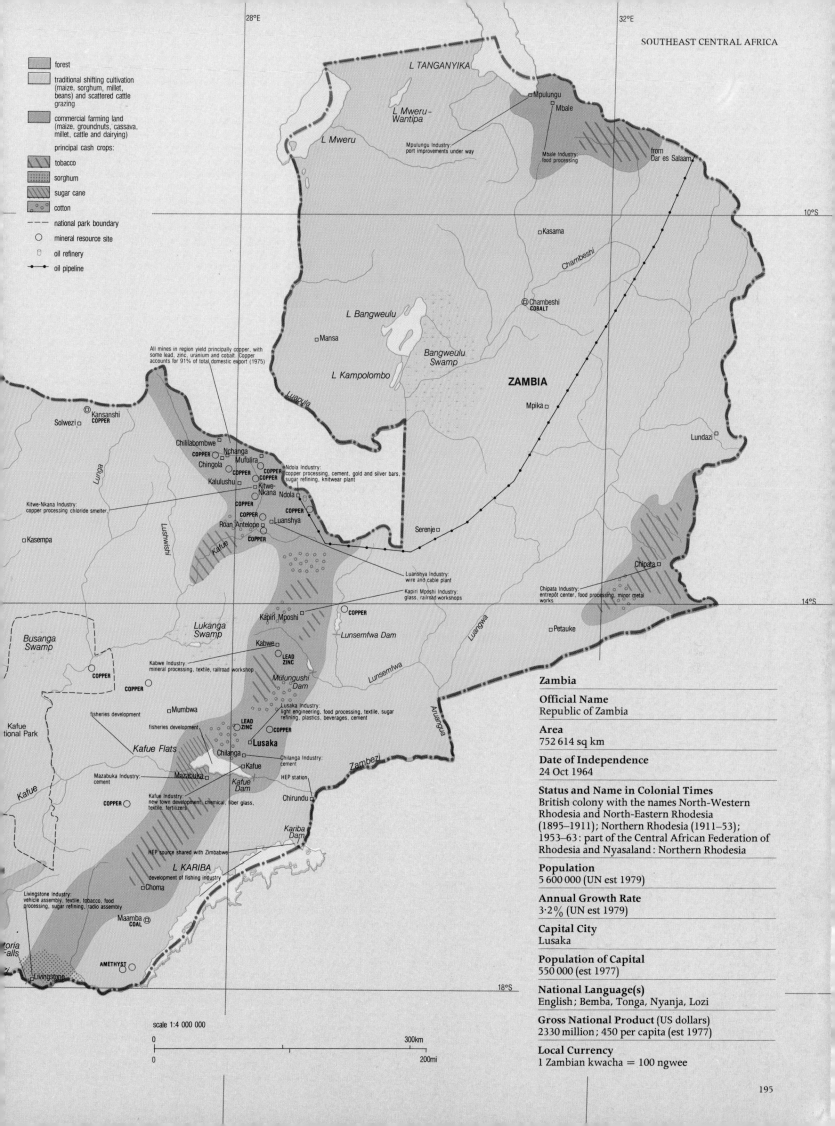

Legend

- forest
- traditional shifting cultivation (maize, sorghum, millet, beans) and scattered cattle grazing
- commercial farming land (maize, groundnuts, cassava, millet, cattle and dairying)

principal cash crops:
- tobacco
- sorghum
- sugar cane
- cotton

- national park boundary
- mineral resource site
- oil refinery
- oil pipeline

L TANGANYIKA

L Mweru-Wantipa

L Mweru

Mpulungu
Mbale

Mpulungu Industry: port improvements under way

Mbale Industry: food processing

from Dar es Salaam

Kasama

Chambeshi

ZAMBIA

L Bangweulu

Bangweulu Swamp

L Kampolombo

Mansa

Chambeshi
COBALT

Mpika

Lundazi

All mines in region yield principally copper, with some lead, zinc, uranium and cobalt. Copper accounts for 91% of total domestic export (1975)

Luapula

Kansanshi
COPPER

Solwezi

Chililabombwe
Nchanga
Mufulira
COPPER
Chingola
COPPER
COPPER
Kalulushu
Kitwe-Nkana
Ndola

Ndola Industry: copper processing, cement, gold and silver bars, sugar refining, knitwear plant

Lunga

Kitwe-Nkana Industry: copper processing chloride smelter.

Luswishi

COPPER

Roan Antelope
COPPER
Luanshya
COPPER

Kasempa

Kafue

Luanshya Industry: wire and cable plant

Kapiri Mposhi Industry: glass, railroad workshops

Serenje

Chipata

Chipata Industry: entrepôt center, food processing, minor metal works

COPPER

Lukanga Swamp

Kapiri Mposhi

Lunsemfwa Dam

Lunsemfwa

Luangwa

Petauke

Busanga Swamp

Kabwe
LEAD ZINC

Kabwe Industry: mineral processing, textile, railroad workshop

COPPER

COPPER

Mulungushi Dam

Kafue Flats

Mumbwa

fisheries development

fisheries development

Lusaka Industry: light engineering, food processing, textile, sugar refining, plastics, beverages, cement

LEAD ZINC
COPPER

Lusaka

Kafue National Park

Kafue

Chilanga
Kafue
Chilanga Industry: cement

Mazabuka Industry: cement
Mazabuka
Kafue Dam
HEP station

Kafue Industry: new town development, chemical, fiber glass, textile, fertilizers

COPPER

Chirundu

Zambezi

Kariba Dam

HEP source shared with Zimbabwe

L KARIBA

development of fishing industry

Choma

Livingstone Industry: vehicle assembly, textile, tobacco, food processing, sugar refining, radio assembly

Maamba
COAL

Victoria Falls

AMETHYST

Livingstone

scale 1:4 000 000

0 — 300km

0 — 200mi

Zambia

Official Name
Republic of Zambia

Area
752 614 sq km

Date of Independence
24 Oct 1964

Status and Name in Colonial Times
British colony with the names North-Western Rhodesia and North-Eastern Rhodesia (1895–1911); Northern Rhodesia (1911–53); 1953–63: part of the Central African Federation of Rhodesia and Nyasaland: Northern Rhodesia

Population
5 600 000 (UN est 1979)

Annual Growth Rate
3·2% (UN est 1979)

Capital City
Lusaka

Population of Capital
550 000 (est 1977)

National Language(s)
English; Bemba, Tonga, Nyanja, Lozi

Gross National Product (US dollars)
2330 million; 450 per capita (est 1977)

Local Currency
1 Zambian kwacha = 100 ngwee

195

country and also in extensive foreign borrowing. The economy has also suffered from Zambia's stand against Rhodesia, particularly the closure of the border with Rhodesia in 1973 in a move to bring further political and economic pressure against the white minority regime. The support for the Zimbabwe nationalists has also resulted in repeated Rhodesian attacks on Zambia.

These hardships are very real and immediate, yet Zambia has been able to devote substantial sums of money to the expansion of educational and health facilities, roads and communications systems, and a bureaucracy and para-state sector which has grown steadily since independence. Benefits of modernization are not evenly distributed throughout the population. The urban-based elite of political, governmental and mine workers absorbs and controls a disproportionate amount of the resources, while the rural and urban poor must make do with far less. The terms of trade for rural areas have not improved since independence and may have even gone against rural producers. There is a growing consciousness of these discrepancies and the ineffectiveness of a guiding political philosophy which promises more than its spokesmen can or are willing to fulfill.

W.R.

Zimbabwe

Zimbabwe, or Rhodesia as it was formerly known, is a colonial creation, but its borders make more sense than those of most African nations. Its territory roughly coincides with the distribution of Shona-speaking peoples, who comprise about 75 per cent of the total population. The largest non-Shona group is the Nguni-speaking Ndebele, in southwestern Zimbabwe. However, this region, too, is historically Shona territory.

Zimbabwe's main geographical handicap is lack of access to the sea; but its borders tend to follow natural features. The Zambezi river, which has historically divided culture regions, forms a logical boundary with Zambia on the north. The less formidable Limpopo river and its tributaries define the southern border. The Mozambique border runs down a string of ranges known collectively as the Eastern Highlands, a major watershed. The western, Botswana border is the most arbitrary, but it runs through a sparsely populated region that offers few possibilities for either development or conflict.

Zimbabwe lies entirely within the tropics, but its climate is ameliorated by its inland position and its altitude, mostly over 1000 meters. The central plateau extends from southwest to northeast. It and the Eastern Highlands are the most developed parts of the country, as well as the regions of greatest European settlement. Rainfall blows in from the east, drenching the Eastern Highlands and diminishing as the moist air moves west. Agriculture is most intensive in the well-watered highland areas, with most of the rest of the country given over to extensive livestock production. The country's rich and diversified mineral deposits are, coincidentally, also concentrated in the highland regions, which thus contain the biggest towns,

the richest farms, the most industry and the most highly developed infrastructure.

Archaeologists trace man's occupation of Zimbabwe back 100 000 years, and the country is rich in Stone Age remains, notably impressive rock paintings. The Iron Age began around the 2nd century AD, evidently introduced by the forebears of the Shona, who were – and are – primarily agriculturalists. By the 12th century the Shona were building in stone, initiating a unique African architectural tradition that left Great Zimbabwe and more than 400 other megalithic sites scattered around the country.

In the mid-15th century the Shona founded the Munhumutapa, or Monomotapa, empire in the north. The southwestern-based Changamire, or Rozvi, empire eclipsed Munhumutapa in the late 17th century, and dominated most of the area of modern Zimbabwe through the 18th century. After Changamire disintegrated in the early 19th century, more than 100 small, autonomous Shona states emerged. A wave of Nguni invasions, emanating from South Africa, deposited two intrusive state systems in Zimbabwe: Mzilikazi's Ndebele kingdom around present Bulawayo, and Soshangane's Gaza kingdom along the present Mozambique border, due east of the Ndebele. These new societies differed from the Shona in their greater emphasis on cattle keeping and in their more aggressive military orientations. Both states preyed upon the Shona for cattle and captives, but their territorial conquests were limited.

The Portuguese penetrated Zimbabwe from the northeast in the 16th century, but were expelled by the Changamire in the late 17th century. European interest revived in the mid-19th century when hunters, traders, prospectors and missionaries began entering from South Africa. These new intruders dealt first with the Ndebele kingdom on the southern approaches. The British negotiated with the Ndebele in the 1880s, then conquered them militarily in the 1890s. Though the Shona were treated as nonentities in this process, many joined the Ndebele in a spectacular but futile anti-British revolt in 1896.

Under a Royal Charter, Cecil Rhodes's British South Africa Company (BSAC) began colonizing Zimbabwe in 1890, completing the task in 1897, when it suppressed the African revolt with imperial military aid. A year later the BSAC administration granted limited representation to the tiny settler community. White political power grew steadily in Rhodesia, as it became known, until 1923, when the BSAC turned its administration over to the British Colonial Office. Britain immediately gave the settlers almost total self-government, though it retained some reserve powers, particularly over African affairs. The local government effectively excluded Africans from political participation by setting difficult franchise standards, and quickly institutionalized territorial segregation to ensure European economic supremacy.

Africans organized against government policies as early as the 1920s, but mass movements grew only in the late 1950s, when white political domination threatened to become permanent through the economic success of the Federation of Rhodesia and Nyasaland (formed in 1953). African oppo-

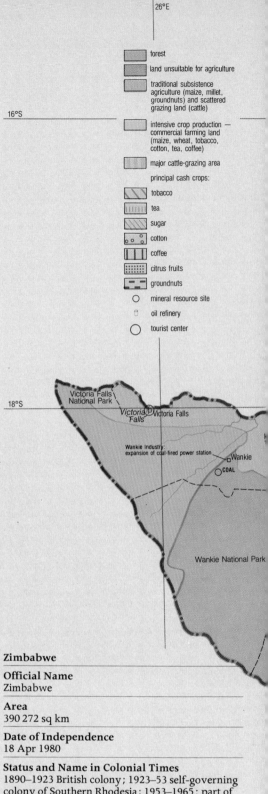

Zimbabwe

Official Name
Zimbabwe

Area
390 272 sq km

Date of Independence
18 Apr 1980

Status and Name in Colonial Times
1890–1923 British colony; 1923–53 self-governing colony of Southern Rhodesia; 1953–1965: part of the Central African Federation of Rhodesia and Nyasaland; 1965–79 illegal independence: Rhodesia; 1979–80 British colony: Zimbabwe Rhodesia

Population
7 600 000 (UN est 1979)

Annual Growth Rate
3·5% (UN est 1979)

Capital City
Salisbury

Population of Capital
610 000 (est 1978)

National Language(s)
English; Shona, Ndebele

Gross National Product (US dollars)
3360 million; 500 per capita (est 1977)

Local Currency
1 dollar = 100 cents

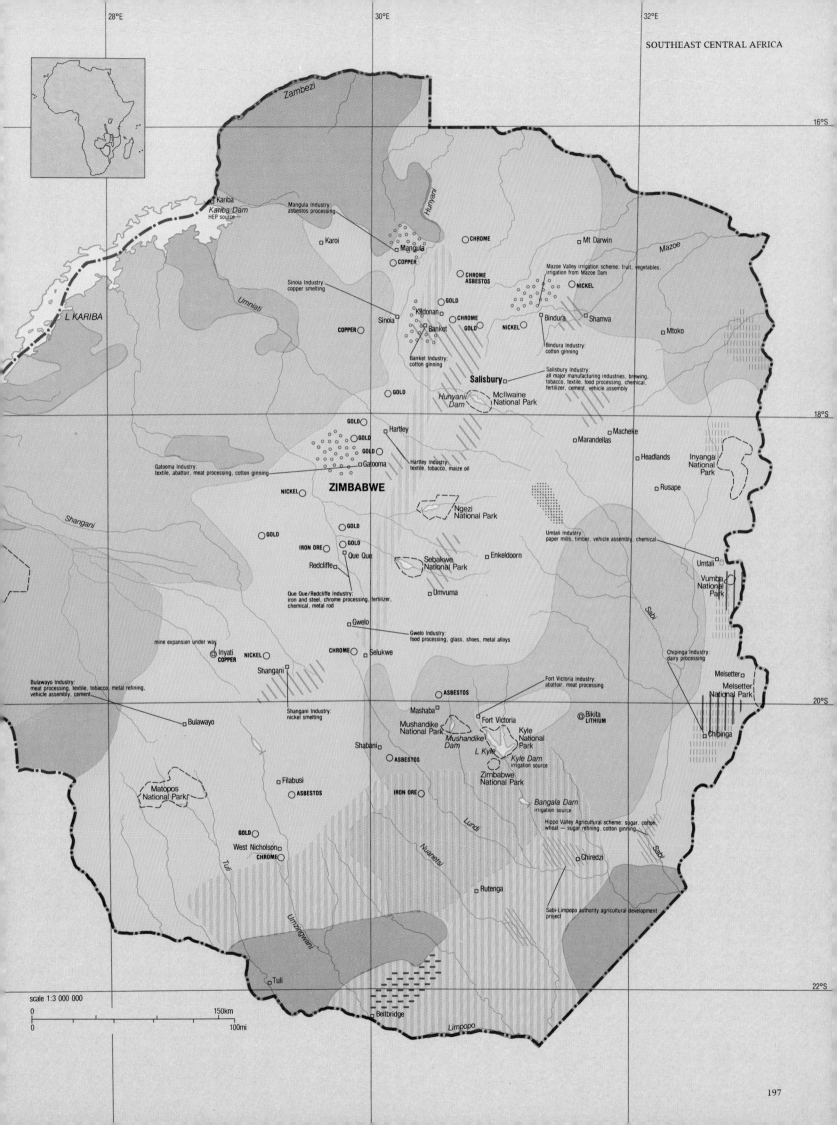

28°E
30°E
32°E
16°S
18°S
20°S
22°S

Zambezi

Kariba
Kariba Dam
HEP source

Mangula Industry:
asbestos processing

□ Karoi

○ Mangula
○ **COPPER**

○ **CHROME**

□ Mt Darwin

Mazoe

Mazoe Valley irrigation scheme: fruit, vegetables,
irrigation from Mazoe Dam

○ **CHROME
ASBESTOS**

Hunyani

Sinoia Industry:
copper smelting

○ **GOLD**

○ **NICKEL**

○ Kildonan
Sinoia
COPPER ○

○ **CHROME**
○ Banket
GOLD

○ **NICKEL**

Bindura
□ Shamva

□ Mtoko

Umniati

Banket Industry:
cotton ginning

Bindura Industry:
cotton ginning

Salisbury

Salisbury Industry:
all major manufacturing industries, brewing,
tobacco, textile, food processing, chemical,
fertilizer, cement, vehicle assembly

L KARIBA

○ **GOLD**

*Hunyanii
Dam*

McIlwaine
National Park

□ Macheke

○ **GOLD**
□ Hartley

Hartley Industry:
textile, tobacco, maize oil

□ Marandellas

□ Headlands

*Inyanga
National
Park*

○ **GOLD**

○ **GOLD**

○ **GOLD**
Gatooma

□ Rusape

Gatooma Industry:
textile, abattoir, meat processing, cotton ginning

ZIMBABWE

Shangani

○ **NICKEL**

*Ngezi
National Park*

○ **GOLD**

○ **GOLD**

Umtali Industry:
paper mills, timber, vehicle assembly, chemical

□ Umtali

○ **GOLD**
○ **IRON ORE**
○ Que Que

*Sebakwe
National
Park*

□ Enkeldoorn

*Vumba
National
Park*

Redcliffe

Que Que/Redcliffe Industry:
iron and steel, chrome processing, fertilizer,
chemical, metal rod

□ Umvuma

□ Gwelo

Gwelo Industry:
food processing, glass, shoes, metal alloys

mine expansion under way

◎ Inyati
COPPER

○ **NICKEL**

○ **CHROME** □ Selukwe

Chipinga Industry:
dairy processing

□ Shangani

□ Melsetter

*Melsetter
National Park*

Bulawayo Industry:
meat processing, textile, tobacco, metal refining,
vehicle assembly, cement

Shangani Industry:
nickel smelting

○ **ASBESTOS**

Fort Victoria Industry:
abattoir, meat processing

□ Bulawayo

□ Mashaba

○ Fort Victoria

◎ Bikita
LITHIUM

□ Chipinga

*Mushandike
National Park*

*Mushandike
Dam*

*Kyle
National
Park*

□ Shabani

○ **ASBESTOS**

L Kyle

Kyle Dam
irrigation source

□ Filabusi

○ **ASBESTOS**

*Matopos
National Park*

○ **IRON ORE**

*Zimbabwe
National Park*

Bangala Dam
irrigation source

Lundi

Hippo Valley Agricultural scheme: sugar, cotton,
wheat — sugar refining, cotton ginning

○ **GOLD**

West Nicholson
○ **CHROME**

Tuli

Nuanetsi

□ Chiredzi

Sabi

□ Rutenga

Sabi-Limpopo authority agricultural development
project

Umzingwani

□ Tuli

Beitbridge

Limpopo

scale 1:3 000 000

0 ——— 150km
0 ——— 100mi

sition in the northern territories (present Zambia and Malawi) scuttled the Federation, helping to force a reassessment of Rhodesia's own constitutional future. Britain refused to grant Rhodesia independence until adequate provisions were made for eventual majority rule. White opposition to this goal led the Salisbury government unilaterally to declare independence (UDI) in 1965.

UDI made Rhodesia's status an international issue, and the UN began enacting economic sanctions. Sanctions disrupted Rhodesia's trade, but they ultimately proved counterproductive in the face of South Africa and Portugal's noncooperation. Rhodesia diversified its own comparatively developed economy, substituting more mixed agricultural products for tobacco and building up new secondary industries to supply formerly imported goods.

After UDI African nationalist leaders alternately negotiated with the white minority regime for a new constitution and denounced the very principle of negotiated settlement. Armed opposition erupted in 1966 but became militarily significant only in late 1972. A full-scale civil war developed between government forces and guerrillas based in Zambia and Mozambique. In early 1978 Ndabaningi Sithole, Abel Muzorewa and other nationalists joined the Salisbury government as a first step in an internally negotiated plan promising to deliver majority rule after an election in 1979. By 1979 Joshua Nkomo and Robert Mugabe of the Patriotic Front ranked as the top opposition leaders based outside the country. A British initiative at the 1979 Commonwealth Conference led to negotiations in London at which all parties reached an agreement as to how the country should proceed towards independence. A ceasefire, monitored by British and Commonwealth observers, was arranged and a British governor assumed temporary control in Salisbury. Elections held early in 1980 led to a sweeping victory for the Patriotic Front and Mugabe became the first prime minister of independent Zimbabwe.

K.R.

Mozambique

Mozambique has a long Indian Ocean shoreline of over 2000 kilometers, but much of the country consists of a 300-kilometer-wide coastal strip lying below the continental escarpment. In the center Mozambique's territory extends inland along the Zambezi valley to reach Zimbabwe and Zambia. The southern tip of the Malawi rift valley system drives a wedge into Mozambican territory. The northern section of Mozambique, east of Lake Malawi, is over 500 kilometers broad and comprises some temperate upland above 800 meters on which hardwoods can grow. In the Zambezi basin and the south land is low-lying and sometimes swampy, with malarial mosquitoes and tsetse flies. Temperatures are high and rainfall is governed by the monsoons.

Mozambique's early history, from about the 3rd century AD, is dominated by the growth of tropical farming and stock raising in small scattered Iron Age communities. From the 10th century the country's economy developed growing outside links, first with the mining

zones of the high plateau in the interior and secondly with the maritime trading nations in the Indian Ocean. From 1000 to 1500 the Shona miners of Zimbabwe sold their gold in Mozambique to Muslim seafarers from the Swahili cities of East Africa and from India. Between 1500 and 1870 gold was bought by Portuguese merchants and settlers who penetrated the Zambezi valley. From 1870 the major growth of mining occurred in South Africa and large numbers of Mozambicans regularly went there as mine laborers. In exchange for recruitment rights to miners, British mining and other imperial interests agreed to use Portuguese rail and harbor services, especially in Lourenço Marques (now Maputo) and Beira. These facilities were built in the 1890s after Britain and Portugal had acrimoniously agreed to partition southeastern Africa between themselves.

After Portuguese sovereignty over Mozambique had been agreed to in Europe large areas were rented out again by Portugal. Private enterprises with various terms of reference and varied patterns of international shareholder control were established. These companies only slightly modified the slave-like status of workers usual in 19th-century Mozambique. Before 1890 Mozambican slaves went mainly to Brazil, the Cape of Good Hope and the Indian Ocean islands. After 1890 forced labor was used widely for government projects as well as in private enterprise. African crops were taxed in kind, migrant labor suffered imposts and levies and the wives of migrant laborers were commonly compelled to plant crops of cotton or rice. One important tropical plantation crop which developed was sugar. Violent demonstrations of government force were met by equally violent bouts of organized resistance over the element of labor compulsion in the domestic economy. By the 1950s Mozambique had eliminated its land concession companies but not its migrant labor recruiters.

In the 1960s the economy of Mozambique began to alter rapidly. White immigrants came in increasing numbers, attaining a maximum of around 160000 by 1970. Some of the migrants were little more skilled or educated than their depressed colonial subjects. Their presence heightened black aspirations for a more equitable return for labor and a restoration of lands transferred to European ownership. Anticolonialism and nationalism grew and were encouraged by the accession to independence of neighboring Tanzania. In 1964 war broke out in northern Mozambique. Portugal was able to contain the uprising for about seven years by fairly draconian policies. By about 1971 Portugal could hold out no longer and the war spread into central Mozambique so rapidly that in 1974 the Portuguese army sued for peace and overthrew its own metropolitan government in Lisbon.

After 1974 Mozambique was governed by a multiracial party called Frente de Libertação de Moçambique (FRELIMO). The two major problems were postwar economic reconstruction at home and the Rhodesian civil war abroad. Economic reconstruction was made difficult by the exodus of Mozambique's colonial administrators, planners, entrepreneurs and businessmen – predominantly Portuguese, South African and Indian – who

left the country around the time of independence (June 1975). Mozambique therefore had rapidly to upgrade its own government personnel and recruit a large but disparate community of international expatriates. This emergency reconstruction took place against a background of rapidly escalating war on the northwestern border. The Rhodesian war made reconstruction more difficult by disrupting communications, siphoning off planning and political expertise, and creating large refugee communities to be cared for within Mozambique.

The largest single development project of the 1970s was the £350 million Cabora Bassa dam on the Zambezi, designed to supply two million kilowatts of electricity to South Africa. Despite its large scale, the immediate benefits to Mozambique were limited. Mozambique had to buy energy back from South Africa and agricultural, transportation, industrial and flood-control advantages had not materialized by 1979.

The most intractable problem concerned agriculture. Postwar Mozambique had to reabsorb into agriculture large numbers of migrant workers who were no longer wanted in the South African mines. The drop in migration alone demanded the creation of about 50 000 new jobs in the first five years of independence. New transportation and marketing systems were required for such peasant crops as cashew nuts of which Mozambique is a leading world supplier. A policy had to be developed on mechanization or non-mechanization of settler estates transferred to the government. Some plantation industries, such as copra and sugar, carried on under colonial patterns of management, but a policy of agriculture within village communes was more generally adopted. The search for politically viable and economically feasible patterns of land management led to shortfalls in food production which had to be met from external sources.

Colonial Mozambique had comparatively low levels of social service for its black population. Health facilities in rural areas were rare and in urban areas were expensive. Missionaries and part-time army personnel provided some health cover. Education grew in the 1960s but before independence secondary education was predominantly white and university education almost wholly white. A large variety of missions provided an assortment of rural social facilities while the Portuguese Catholic Church met settler religious demands. The Mozambican churches were deeply divided by the colonial war and their relations with the FRELIMO government have ranged from close cooperation to open antagonism. After independence mission health facilities were supplemented or replaced by secular aid programs. Education became an all-government responsibility with a rapid growth in both urban and rural sectors.

Mozambique has one of the most open and varied patterns of foreign policy in Africa. It has a longstanding relationship with China, but also trades with the USSR. Its closest collaborator in Africa is Tanzania, but it is also inextricably integrated into the southern African economies. It recruits expatriates from such diverse sources as North Korea, the USA, Scandinavia, Poland, Portugal and Britain. Although policy is informed by a Marxist

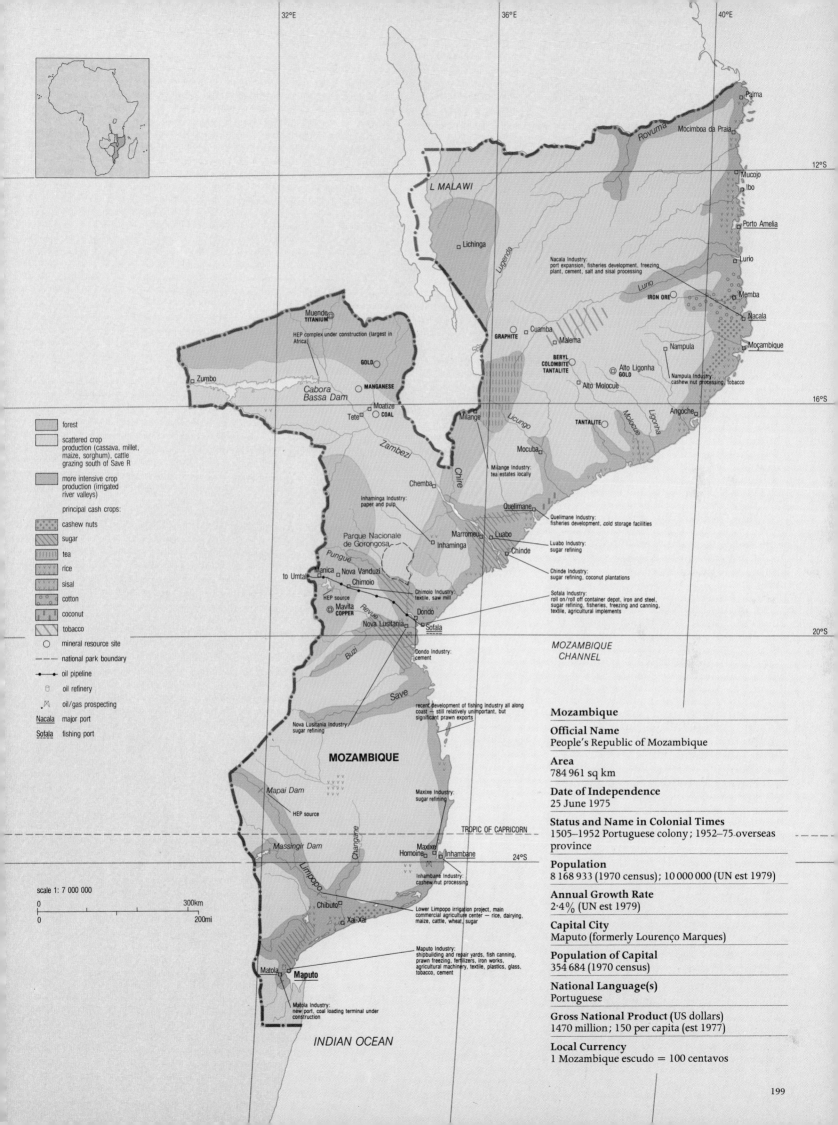

32°E   36°E   40°E

Palma
Rovuma
Mocimboa da Praia
12°S
Mucojo
Ibo
L MALAWI
Porto Amelia
Lichinga
Lurio
Nacala Industry:
port expansion, fisheries development, freezing
plant, cement, salt and sisal processing
Lurio
Memba
IRON ORE
Muende
TITANIUM
Nacala
HEP complex under construction (largest in
Africa)
GRAPHITE
Cuamba
Moçambique
GOLD
Malema
Nampula
BERYL
COLOMBITE
TANTALITE
Alto Ligonha
GOLD
Nampula Industry:
cashew nut processing, tobacco
Zumbo
MANGANESE
Alto Molocué
Cabora
Bassa Dam
16°S
Moatize
Angoche
Tete
COAL
Milange
Licungo
TANTALITE
Mocuba
Milange Industry:
tea estates locally
Chemba
Zambezi
Chire
Quelimane
Inhaminga Industry:
paper and pulp
Quelimane Industry:
fisheries development, cold storage facilities
Parque Nacionale
de Gorongosa
Marromeu
Luabo
Inhaminga
Chinde
Luabo Industry:
sugar refining
Pungue
Chinde Industry:
sugar refining, coconut plantations
to Umtali
Manica
Nova Vanduzi
Chimoio
Chimoio Industry:
textile, saw mill
Sofala Industry:
roll on/roll off container depot, iron and steel,
sugar refining, fisheries, freezing and canning,
textile, agricultural implements
HEP source
Revue
Dondo
Mavita
COPPER
Nova Lusitania
Sofala
20°S
Buzi
Dondo Industry:
cement
MOZAMBIQUE
CHANNEL
Save
recent development of fishing industry all along
coast — still relatively unimportant, but
significant prawn exports
MOZAMBIQUE
Nova Lusitania Industry:
sugar refining
Mapai Dam
Maxixe Industry:
sugar refining
HEP source
TROPIC OF CAPRICORN
Massingir Dam
Maxixe
Homoine
Inhambane
24°S
Changane
Inhambane Industry:
cashew nut processing
Limpopo
Chibuto
Lower Limpopo irrigation project, main
commercial agriculture center — rice, dairying,
maize, cattle, wheat, sugar
Xai-Xai
Maputo Industry:
shipbuilding and repair yards, fish canning,
prawn freezing, fertilizers, iron works,
agricultural machinery, textile, plastics, glass,
tobacco, cement
Matola
Maputo
Matola Industry:
new port, coal loading terminal under
construction
INDIAN OCEAN

Legend

- forest
- scattered crop production (cassava, millet, maize, sorghum), cattle grazing south of Save R
- more intensive crop production (irrigated river valleys)

principal cash crops:
- cashew nuts
- sugar
- tea
- rice
- sisal
- cotton
- coconut
- tobacco

○ mineral resource site
--- national park boundary
•─• oil pipeline
☐ oil refinery
⚹ oil/gas prospecting
Nacala major port
Sofala fishing port

scale 1: 7 000 000

0   300km
0   200mi

Mozambique

Official Name
People's Republic of Mozambique

Area
784 961 sq km

Date of Independence
25 June 1975

Status and Name in Colonial Times
1505–1952 Portuguese colony ; 1952–75 overseas province

Population
8 168 933 (1970 census); 10 000 000 (UN est 1979)

Annual Growth Rate
2·4 % (UN est 1979)

Capital City
Maputo (formerly Lourenço Marques)

Population of Capital
354 684 (1970 census)

National Language(s)
Portuguese

Gross National Product (US dollars)
1470 million ; 150 per capita (est 1977)

Local Currency
1 Mozambique escudo = 100 centavos

199

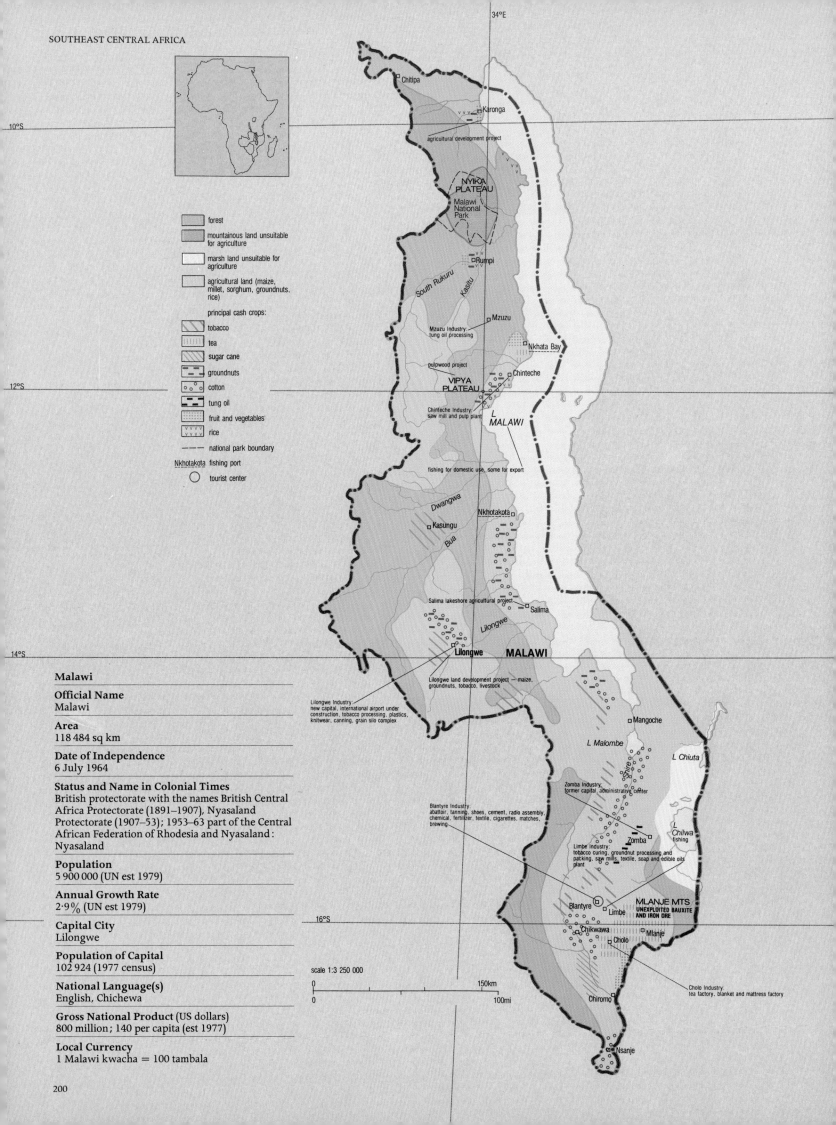

34°E

10°S

forest

mountainous land unsuitable
for agriculture

marsh land unsuitable for
agriculture

agricultural land (maize,
millet, sorghum, groundnuts,
rice)

principal cash crops:

tobacco

tea

sugar cane

groundnuts

cotton

tung oil

fruit and vegetables

rice

national park boundary

Nkhotakota fishing port

○ tourist center

Chitipa

Karonga

agricultural development project

NYIKA
PLATEAU

Malawi
National
Park

Rumpi

South Rukuru

Kasitu

Mzuzu
Mzuzu Industry:
tung oil processing

Nkhata Bay

pulpwood project

Chinteche

VIPYA
PLATEAU

Chinteche Industry:
saw mill and pulp plant

*L
MALAWI*

12°S

fishing for domestic use, some for export

Dwangwa

Nkhotakota

Kasungu

Bua

Salima lakeshore agricultural project
Salima

Lilongwe

14°S

Lilongwe
Lilongwe land development project — maize,
groundnuts, tobacco, livestock

MALAWI

Lilongwe Industry:
new capital, international airport under
construction, tobacco processing, plastics,
knitwear, canning, grain silo complex

Mangoche

L Malombe

L Chiuta

Shire

Zomba Industry:
former capital, administrative center

Blantyre Industry:
abattoir, tanning, shoes, cement, radio assembly,
chemical, fertilizer, textile, cigarettes, matches,
brewing

Zomba

*L
Chilwa*
fishing

Limbe Industry:
tobacco curing, groundnut processing and
packing, saw mills, textile, soap and edible oils
plant

16°S

Blantyre
Limbe

MLANJE MTS
**UNEXPLOITED BAUXITE
AND IRON ORE**

Chikwawa
Cholo
Mlanje

Cholo Industry:
tea factory, blanket and mattress factory

Chiromo

Nsanje

scale 1:3 250 000

0 ——— 150km

0 ——— 100mi

Malawi

Official Name
Malawi

Area
118 484 sq km

Date of Independence
6 July 1964

Status and Name in Colonial Times
British protectorate with the names British Central
Africa Protectorate (1891–1907), Nyasaland
Protectorate (1907–53); 1953–63 part of the Central
African Federation of Rhodesia and Nyasaland:
Nyasaland

Population
5 900 000 (UN est 1979)

Annual Growth Rate
2·9% (UN est 1979)

Capital City
Lilongwe

Population of Capital
102 924 (1977 census)

National Language(s)
English, Chichewa

Gross National Product (US dollars)
800 million; 140 per capita (est 1977)

Local Currency
1 Malawi kwacha = 100 tambala

ideology, poverty dictates pragmatism in both domestic and foreign affairs.

D.B.

Malawi

Situated along the southern continuation of the rift valley system, Malawi is definitely a colonial creation. Its small size and irregular borders reflect late 19th-century big-power politics, rather than any geographical or economic rationale. Except for the narrow shore line around Lake Malawi and the Shire river valley, the country is part of the central African plateau. It has an average elevation of between 750 and 1200 meters, with high mountain ranges (1800 to 3000 meters) in both the north and the south. Rainfall occurs mainly between November and April, most areas receiving between 750 and 1000 millimeters annually; amounts of up to 2000 millimeters occur along the higher mountain ranges. Over half the land area is suitable for agriculture which at present supports 90 per cent of the country's population. Fishing is a major source of income for people along the shores of lakes Malawi and Chilwa and the Shire river. These freshwater sources also hold high potential for hydroelectric production. The country is one of the most densely populated in Africa, although the distribution is uneven, with nearly 90 per cent of the total population contained within the southern and central regions. Most of the infrastructure is likewise located in these two regions.

The fertility of Malawi's soils has attracted people for hundreds of years. The Chewa-speaking people of the central area have over 350 years of documented history, with political units ranging in size from clans to kingdoms. During the 19th century the pace of change rapidly accelerated, as slave traders, African immigrants and finally European traders and missionaries entered Malawi. Many of the pre-19th-century societies were conquered or greatly disrupted by these events and historians have tended to describe much of Malawi's subsequent history in terms of these changes. Despite the impact of new peoples and ideas, the strong cultural identity and solidarity (based upon an agricultural economy) of rural Malawians have provided the framework for developments over the past 150 years.

Capitalism was far more disruptive than African or missionary invaders, and from the mid-1890s the colonial administration favored European settlers and foreign capital at the expense of African agricultural and economic development. Taxation drove thousands of men out of their villages to work on the white plantations and mines of South Africa, and the railroad in the southern part of the country was expressly built to benefit white farmers in the Shire Highlands. Where Europeans settled, land alienation quickly followed, establishing a pattern of landless laborers which continues to this day.

The message of Christian egalitarianism, mixed with widespread deprivation and the recruitment of porters from Malawi for use in World War I in East Africa, resulted in a short but significant revolt by Africans in early 1915. Led by John Chilembwe, a mission-educated teacher, the revolt sought to depose the British rulers and resolve the social crisis caused by colonial rule. However, the revolt failed to win overwhelming support and was quickly suppressed.

Following Chilembwe's attempt to overthrow the British, Malawians with a mission education turned to more adaptive methods of accommodation with the authorities. Reformist associations provided the basis for the establishment of the Nyasaland African Congress in 1944. Congress was largely ineffective in its early years in attracting widespread support for its reformist efforts with the government. However, the move by local whites and the British government towards the creation of the Federation of Rhodesia and Nyasaland in the early 1950s became a focus for effective political protest. At the same time, colonial development policy aroused opposition from rural farmers who disliked the restrictions upon their agricultural methods and the discriminatory crop-pricing arrangements which favored white farmers. The African elite's political demands and rural discontent merged into a full nationalist movement with the return of Dr Hastings Banda in 1958, following 40 years of self-imposed exile. He provided the charismatic leadership needed to challenge both the Federation and British colonial rule. In 1959 the Malawi Congress Party (MCP) was formed to fight for total independence. Under strong pressure from Malawians and Zambians, the Federation was dissolved in 1963. The following year Malawi was granted full independence, with Banda as president.

At independence, Malawi was one of the poorest countries in the world, with a per capita annual income of less than US $40. The question of internal economic and social development and its direction and leadership were central issues. Banda's position was to move slowly, not disrupting the economy or cutting Malawi's ties with the white-ruled states to the south. However, several of the younger ministers in Banda's government, who happened to be from areas neglected during the colonial era, supported a strong stand against white-dominated southern Africa and called for a rapid Africanization of the Malawian bureaucracy. The political struggle quickly came to a head, and in September 1964 several of Banda's opponents resigned from the government. In the southern part of the country Henry Chipembere led an armed revolt, aimed at toppling Banda, but this was put down by early 1965. Banda had survived the first and only major challenge to his rule and he set about consolidating his power and position. Opponents of Banda's national policies have been forced into exile. Strict cultural norms have been established and deviation from them has resulted in imprisonment or suppression. For example, in 1970, 1972 and again in 1976 thousands of Jehovah's Witnesses fled into neighboring countries after constant harassment in Malawi. In 1971 Banda had himself declared president for life, confirming his dominant role in every aspect of Malawi's affairs.

Malawi's economic development maintains the capitalist orientation of the past. A plantation economy prevails, producing tobacco, cotton, tea and groundnuts for export. These estates account for less than 5 per cent of the total land area, but are responsible for over 50 per cent of the country's exports (1977 estimate). White emigrants from Rhodesia (Zimbabwe) have been taken on as managers of some of the larger plantations which are owned by multinational corporations and elite Malawians. Industry is virtually nonexistent, as is mineral production. A manufacturing sector has emerged, linked especially to the processing of agricultural products, but this sector accounts for only a small proportion of Malawi's GDP. As in agriculture, major manufacturing interests are privately owned, including several holdings by the president.

Banda's policy of controlled economic growth has resulted in an outward stability, but only benefits already well-established Malawians. As long as the country continues to rely upon large plantation production and extensive overseas borrowing, any development is unlikely greatly to assist the rural poor. The most prestigious development project has been the construction of a new capital at Lilongwe, financed by South African loans, and intensive agricultural inputs in the region surrounding the new capital, largely financed by the World Bank. Malawi's limited financial and social resources have generally been used to reinforce the economic dominance of national and foreign elites. Despite a population equal in size to that of Zambia, Malawi has only a third of the number of health and medical personnel and they are predominantly concentrated in the urban areas. Infant mortality and tuberculosis are among the highest of any African nation, both indicators reflecting negatively on the rural population's living standards.

W.R.

SOUTHERN AFRICA

The enormous potential in almost every sphere of the southern African region is paradoxically a source of its major problems, since uneven development of this potential has exacerbated difficulties that the region shares with its northern neighbors. The industrial wealth of the Republic of South Africa contrasts dramatically with the struggling rural economies of Botswana and Lesotho. As the zone's largest and richest country, the Republic exercises a powerful economic hegemony over its neighbors, even though the zone's black African populations are implacably opposed to the Republic's political policies. The tensions that this situation causes, both within the Republic's borders and beyond, have yet to be resolved. Moreover, its extensive mineral and industrial resources make the Republic a key factor not only in the development of the African continent, but also in global political strategies.

The balance of power and numbers among the southern African peoples is also unique. The original Khoisan inhabitants were expelled or exterminated by the migration of Bantu-speaking peoples from the northeast and white settlers from the south. Shock waves from the 19th-century *Mfecane* (scattering of the peoples) affected every Bantu group in southern Africa directly or indirectly, and a strong cultural similarity exists between most of these groups. The politically dominant white minority in the Republic and Namibia is sizable and long established. Effective power lies with the descendants of Dutch settlers who have evolved their own distinctive culture and language – Afrikaans.

The political prospects for the region also hinge upon the Republic. Historically the whites have controlled not only the industrial and mineral wealth but also the most productive land. With proper management of human and agricultural resources most of the zone's populations could feed themselves, but the continued degradation of the African lands through overpopulation, overgrazing and soil erosion poses a serious threat to future political stability and economic progress.

Left The hilly terrain of the Transkei lies near the southeastern coast of South Africa. Rivers, descending abruptly from the central plateau, are too seasonal in flow to be of major economic importance, but reliable rainfall and an equable climate make the soil productive. In 1976 the area became part of the autonomous Xhosa territory of the Transkei.

Above White-clad Xhosa youths take part in an initiation ceremony in a Transkei village. Traditional institutions still survive in the rural Transkei and many Xhosa who work in the adjacent industrial centers of East London and Port Elizabeth try to maintain village behavioral sanctions even in the urban environment.

Above Groote Schuur, lying below the spectacular pinnacle of Devil's Peak, is the Cape Town residence of South Africa's premier. It stands on the site of the "great barn" in which Jan van Riebeeck stored grain from his first experimental farm in the Cape. Reconstructed after a disastrous fire, the house is in the Cape Dutch style of the early homesteads in the Cape.

Above right Cape Town lies spread out on the lower slopes of Table Mountain (997 meters). Much of the city's modern foreshore is reclaimed land and its harbor was again expanded in the 1970s.

Right Welwitschia bainesii grows only in the 80-kilometer-wide coastal strip of the Namib Desert. A botanical curiosity, its bizarre form and adaptation to its almost waterless environment have fascinated botanists. Its graceless, straplike leaves grow to a length of about 2 meters before being eroded away by sand and wind. The plant may live for 2000 years.

Far left Herero women in western Botswana dress in the fashion introduced into the area last century by the Rhenish Missionary society.

Left Founded in 1886 after the discovery of gold in the nearby Witwatersrand, Johannesburg is the commercial capital of South Africa. Skyscrapers dominate the regular layout and straight streets of the city center.

Below left The low veld area of the eastern Transvaal is a major citrus-growing zone. Much of the fruit is exported. A system of reservoirs and irrigation channels is necessary to ensure adequate water for the trees.

Below A high percentage of the world's gem-quality diamonds comes from blue rock "pipes" located in or near long-extinct volcanoes in South Africa. Kimberley, in the northern Cape Province, and Cullinan, east of Pretoria in the Transvaal, are the principal diamond-mining centers. As in gold mining, most of the underground workers are Africans. Here rock is drilled before being transported to the surface where it is crushed to release the diamonds.

South Africa

The topography of South Africa is dominated by a central plateau of varying elevations which stretches over the country. The interior plateau or high veld, roughly comprising the Orange Free State and Transvaal, is gently undulating grassland, broken occasionally by highland areas. Most of the country's mineral wealth is concentrated in this region. In the western half of the plateau, the elevation is around 900 meters and is dominated by a dry flatland known as the Karoo that merges with the Namib and Kalahari deserts. On the southeastern edge of the plateau is a major mountain chain, the Drakensberg, which stretches from the eastern Transvaal southwest into the Cape province. It is a major barrier to communication between the coastal and interior regions. In the southwestern Cape there are ranges that rise to heights of 1800 to 2250 meters. The interior plateau is in a wind belt, which brings in rain from the Indian Ocean. In the eastern plateau region, rainfall is heaviest during the summer months, while the western Cape rainfall peaks during the winter. There are no navigable rivers in South Africa. Two major rivers, the Orange, and its tributary, the Vaal, flow from east to west. Hundreds of smaller rivers such as the Umzimvubu, Great Fish, Kei, Pongola, Umgeni and Tugela flow into the Indian Ocean. The Limpopo river forms much of the northern boundary of the country.

The peoples of South Africa represent many races, languages, religions, customs and life styles. As defined by the government, there are four main groupings of people: Africans, Europeans, Coloreds and Asians. The largest grouping is the African, the majority of whom are Bantu-speakers. They comprise four major language groups. The largest, Nguni-speakers, includes Zulu, Xhosa, Ndebele and Swazi. The next largest is Tswana-speakers, which includes Tswana, Pedi and Southern Sotho. The two other groups are the Venda and Shangaan-Tsonga. The ancestors of the present-day Africans may have begun settling in small groups south of the Limpopo river as early as the 3rd century AD. Most were cattle keepers or agriculturalists. By the 15th century Bantu-speaking people were living as far south as the Fish river. Over the centuries, African societies have interacted with each other so much that it has become difficult to distinguish them with precision.

European settlement dates from the mid-17th century when, in 1652, the Dutch East India Company established a supply station at Table Bay for ships rounding the Cape of Good Hope. The Dutch settlers were augmented by French and German immigrants as well as slaves from Malaya and East and West Africa. From that early period the European settlers began intermixing with their slaves and the indigenous inhabitants, thereby creating a mixed group called the Coloreds, who have historically lived principally in the western Cape.

In later decades, as some of the settlers took up cattle keeping, they began to move gradually eastward in search of grazing land beyond official Dutch control. In the process they came into contact and conflict first with Khoisan (or Khoikhoi) and then with Xhosa peoples, who resisted settler encroachment on their land.

In 1806 England wrested control of the Cape from Holland, thereby triggering a rivalry with the Dutch settlers or Boers. In 1820 the British settled a large group of English colonists in the eastern Cape. In the 1830s groups of Boers, reacting to the British abolition of slavery, deteriorating economic conditions, wars with Africans and resentment over British imperial control, moved off on the "Great Trek" into the South African interior and founded two republics, the Orange Free State and Transvaal. In order to prevent the Boers from laying claim to any coastline, the British annexed Natal in 1842.

In 1860 the British introduced Indians to Natal as indentured laborers on sugar plantations. At the turn of the century they were joined by a group of Indian merchants. Today about 70 per cent of Asians are Hindu and 20 per cent are Muslim. The majority live around the Durban area.

Just prior to the time the Boers were trekking into the interior, African societies were undergoing traumatic changes because of the widespread dispersal of African peoples in the wake of a revolutionary upheaval called the *Mfecane*. The *Mfecane* originated in Natal when a small clan, the Zulu, led by an imaginative military leader, Chaka, created a major kingdom based on raiding. Zulu expansionism ignited a chain reaction of violent conflict, population dispersion, migration and devastation which reshuffled African peoples throughout the whole of southern Africa. Despite the unsettled nature of the region, African societies resisted European expansion on a variety of fronts until the early 20th century.

The discovery of gold and diamonds in the last third of the 19th century dramatically transformed the political and economic character of southern Africa as the region's economy changed from one almost wholly based on agriculture to one predominantly industrial and urban. For Africans the period spelled the entrenchment of European rule; they were increasingly forced off their land to seek work in European areas as migrant laborers. For Europeans, the mineral discoveries provoked greater antagonism and conflict between the British and the Boer republics, resulting in two wars (1880–81, 1899–1902). The British won the latter one, the Anglo–Boer War, which signaled the end of Boer political independence.

In 1910 the four colonies of Natal, Cape of Good Hope, Orange Free State and Transvaal joined together in the Union of South Africa. Its European parliament was initially dominated by two political parties, the South African Party and the National Party, but in 1933, the two merged to form the United Party, which dominated political life until 1948, when the Nationalist Party (NP), representing extreme Afrikaner nationalism, won power. During this period, Africans for the most part were excluded from participating in the political life of the country and parliament passed numerous pieces of legislation that cemented the economic and political dominance of the whites.

Since assuming power, the NP has moved to

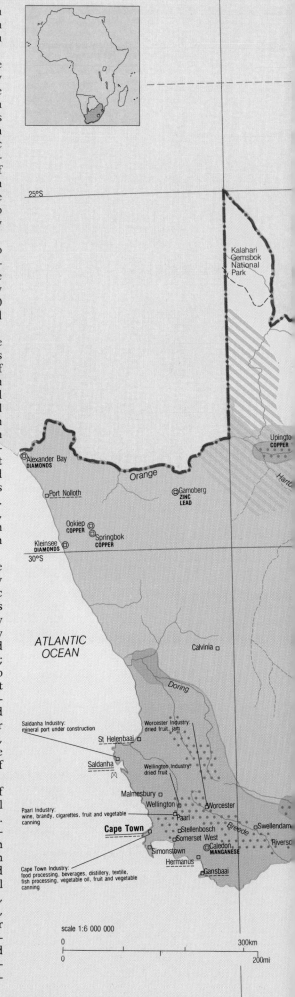

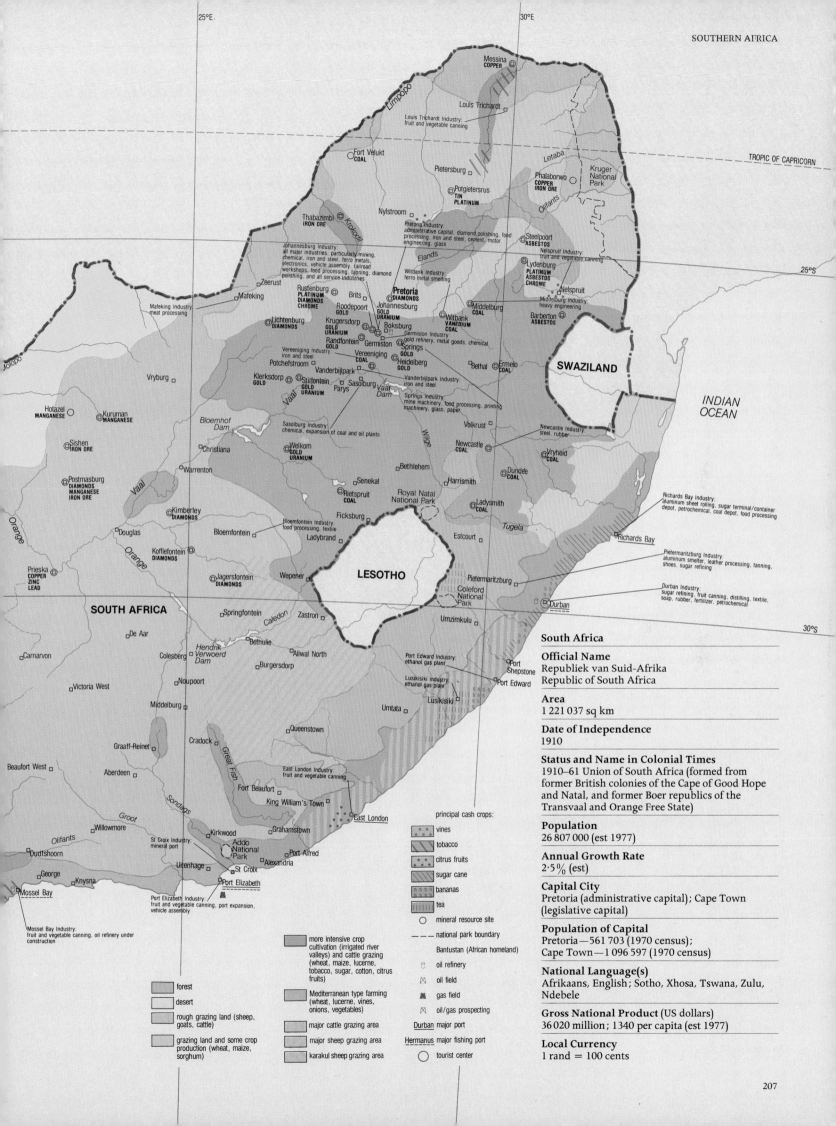

25°E
30°E

Messina
COPPER

Limpopo

Louis Trichardt

Louis Trichardt Industry:
fruit and vegetable canning

TROPIC OF CAPRICORN

Fort Velukt
COAL

Pietersburg

Letaba

Kruger
National
Park

Phalaborwo
COPPER
IRON ORE

Potgietersrus
TIN
PLATINUM

Olifants

Nylstroom

Pretoria Industry:
administrative capital, diamond polishing, food
processing, iron and steel, cement, motor
engineering, glass

Thabazimbi
IRON ORE

Krokodil

Johannesburg Industry:
all major industries, particularly mining,
chemical, iron and steel, ferro metals,
electronics, vehicle assembly, railroad
workshops, food processing, tanning, diamond
polishing, and all service industries

Elands

Steelpoort
ASBESTOS

Nelspruit Industry:
fruit and vegetable canning

25°S

Zeerust

Witbank Industry:
ferro metal smelting

Lydenburg
PLATINUM
ASBESTOS
CHROME

Mafeking

Mafeking Industry:
meat processing

Rustenburg
PLATINUM
DIAMONDS
CHROME

Brits

Pretoria

Middelburg Industry:
heavy engineering

Nelspruit

Roodepoort
GOLD

Middelburg
COAL

Lichtenburg
DIAMONDS

Johannesburg
GOLD
URANIUM

Witbank
VANADIUM
COAL

Barberton
ASBESTOS

Krugersdorp
GOLD
URANIUM

Boksburg

Vryburg

Randfontein
GOLD

Germiston

Springs
GOLD

Germiston Industry:
gold refinery, metal goods, chemical

SWAZILAND

Vereeniging Industry:
iron and steel

Vereeniging
COAL

Heidelberg
GOLD

Bethal

Ermelo
COAL

INDIAN
OCEAN

Potchefstroom

Vanderbijlpark

Klerksdorp
GOLD

Stilfontein
GOLD
URANIUM

Sasolburg

Parys

Vaal
Dam

Vanderbijlpark Industry:
iron and steel

Hotazel
MANGANESE

Kuruman
MANGANESE

Bloemhof
Dam

Springs Industry:
mine machinery, food processing, printing
machinery, glass, paper

Volkrust

Newcastle Industry:
steel, rubber

Sishen
IRON ORE

Sasolburg Industry:
chemical, expansion of coal and oil plants

Welkom
GOLD
URANIUM

Vaal

Wilge

Newcastle
COAL

Vryheid
COAL

Christiana

Bethlehem

Dundee
COAL

Warrenton

Senekal

Harrismith

Richards Bay Industry:
aluminum sheet rolling, sugar terminal/container
depot, petrochemical, coal depot, food processing

Postmasburg
DIAMONDS
MANGANESE
IRON ORE

Rietspruit
COAL

Royal Natal
National Park

Ladysmith
COAL

Tugela

Kimberley
DIAMONDS

Ficksburg

Estcourt

Richards Bay

Douglas

Orange

Bloemfontein Industry:
food processing, textile

Bloemfontein

Ladybrand

Pietermaritzburg

Pietermaritzburg Industry:
aluminum smelter, leather processing, tanning,
shoes, sugar refining

Koffiefontein
DIAMONDS

Orange

LESOTHO

Coleford
National
Park

Durban Industry:
sugar refining, fruit canning, distilling, textile,
soap, rubber, fertilizer, petrochemical

Prieska
COPPER
ZINC
LEAD

Jagersfontein
DIAMONDS

Wepener

Pietermaritzburg

Durban

SOUTH AFRICA

Springfontein

Caledon

Zastron

Umzimkulu

30°S

De Aar

Bethulie

Carnarvon

Colesberg

Hendrik
Verwoerd
Dam

Aliwal North

Burgersdorp

Port Edward Industry:
ethanol gas plant

Port
Shepstone

Victoria West

Noupoort

Lusikisiki Industry:
ethanol gas plant

Port Edward

Middelburg

Umtata

Lusikisiki

Queenstown

Graaff-Reinet

Cradock

Great Fish

East London Industry:
fruit and vegetable canning

Beaufort West

Aberdeen

Fort Beaufort

King William's Town

Sondags

King William's Town

principal cash crops:

South Africa

Official Name
Republiek van Suid-Afrika
Republic of South Africa

Olifants

Willowmore

Groot

East London

vines

Area
1 221 037 sq km

Oudtshoorn

St Croix Industry:
mineral port

Kirkwood

Grahamstown

tobacco

Date of Independence
1910

George

Knysna

Addo
National
Park

Port Alfred

citrus fruits

Status and Name in Colonial Times
1910–61 Union of South Africa (formed from
former British colonies of the Cape of Good Hope
and Natal, and former Boer republics of the
Transvaal and Orange Free State)

Uitenhage

St Croix

Alexandria

sugar cane

Mossel Bay

Port Elizabeth

bananas

Population
26 807 000 (est 1977)

Port Elizabeth Industry:
fruit and vegetable canning, port expansion,
vehicle assembly

tea

Annual Growth Rate
2·5% (est)

mineral resource site

Capital City
Pretoria (administrative capital); Cape Town
(legislative capital)

Mossel Bay Industry:
fruit and vegetable canning, oil refinery under
construction

national park boundary

Population of Capital
Pretoria—561 703 (1970 census);
Cape Town—1 096 597 (1970 census)

Bantustan (African homeland)

more intensive crop
cultivation (irrigated river
valleys) and cattle grazing
(wheat, maize, lucerne,
tobacco, sugar, cotton, citrus
fruits)

oil refinery

oil field

National Language(s)
Afrikaans, English; Sotho, Xhosa, Tswana, Zulu,
Ndebele

gas field

forest

oil/gas prospecting

Gross National Product (US dollars)
36 020 million; 1340 per capita (est 1977)

desert

Mediterranean type farming
(wheat, lucerne, vines,
onions, vegetables)

Durban major port

rough grazing land (sheep,
goats, cattle)

major cattle grazing area

Hermanus major fishing port

Local Currency
1 rand = 100 cents

grazing land and some crop
production (wheat, maize,
sorghum)

major sheep grazing area

karakul sheep grazing area

tourist center

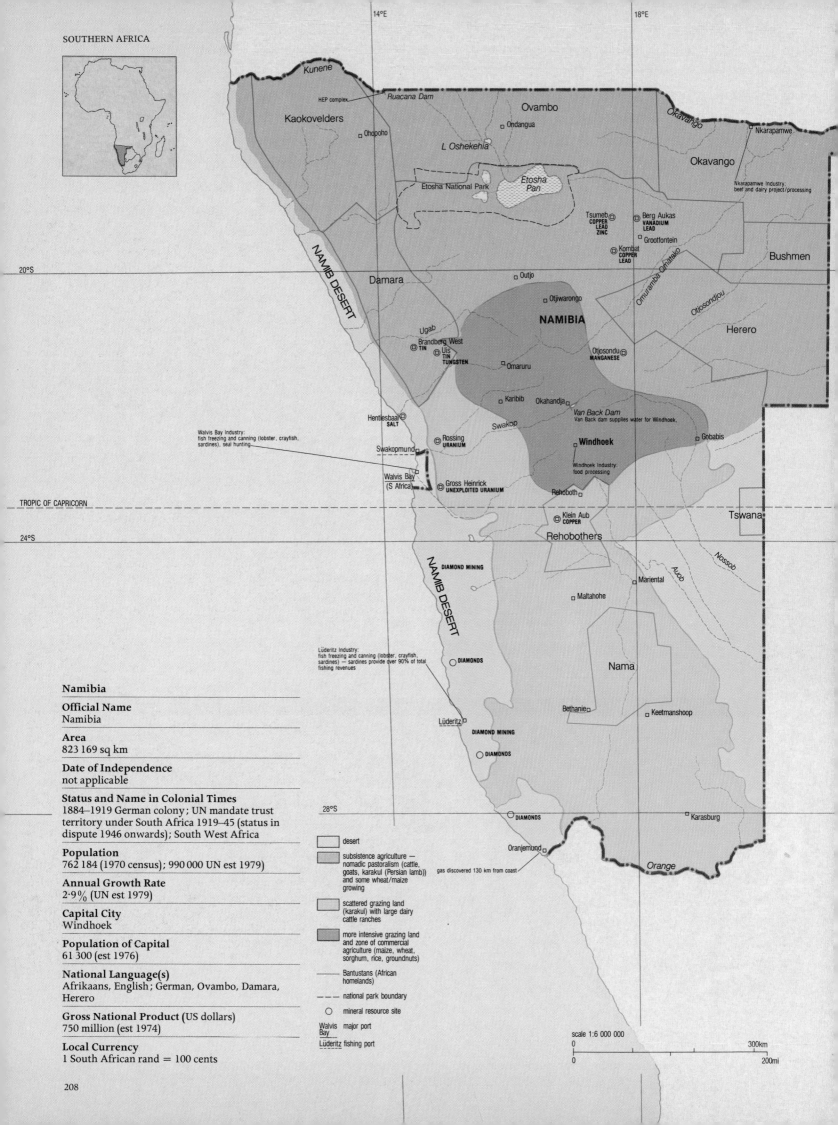

SOUTHERN AFRICA

14°E   18°E

Kunene

HEP complex.   *Ruacana Dam*

Kaokovelders   Ovambo   *Okavango*

□ Ohopoho   □ Ondangua   □ Nkarapamwe

L Oshekehia   Okavango

Etosha National Park   *Etosha Pan*   Nkarapamwe Industry: beef and dairy project/processing

Tsumeb ⊙   ⊙ Berg Aukas
COPPER   VANADIUM
LEAD   LEAD
ZINC   □ Grootfontein   Bushmen

⊙ Kombat
COPPER
LEAD

20°S   Damara   □ Outjo   *Omuramba Omatako*

□ Otjiwarongo   *Otjosondjou*

NAMIBIA   Herero

Ugab   Otjosondu ⊙
MANGANESE
Brandberg West ⊙
TIN   Omaruru □
Uis ⊙
TIN
TUNGSTEN

□ Karibib   Okahandja □   *Van Back Dam*
Van Back dam supplies water for Windhoek.

Hentiesbaai ⊙   *Swakop*   □ Gobabis
SALT

Rossing ⊙   **Windhoek**
URANIUM

Walvis Bay Industry:
fish freezing and canning (lobster, crayfish,   Swakopmund ⊙   Windhoek Industry:
sardines), seal hunting.   food processing

Walvis Bay   Gross Heinrich ⊙
(S Africa)   UNEXPLOITED URANIUM

TROPIC OF CAPRICORN   Rehoboth □

Klein Aub ⊙
COPPER   Tswana □

24°S   Rehobothers

NAMIB DESERT

DIAMOND MINING   □ Mariental

□ Maltahohe   *Auob*   *Nossob*

Nama

Lüderitz Industry:
fish freezing and canning (lobster, crayfish,   ⊙ DIAMONDS
sardines) — sardines provide over 90% of total
fishing revenues

Bethanie □   □ Keetmanshoop

Lüderitz ⊙
DIAMOND MINING

⊙ DIAMONDS

Namibia

Official Name
Namibia

Area
823 169 sq km

Date of Independence
not applicable

28°S   □ Karasburg

Status and Name in Colonial Times
1884–1919 German colony; UN mandate trust
territory under South Africa 1919–45 (status in
dispute 1946 onwards); South West Africa   Oranjemund □   ⊙ DIAMONDS

gas discovered 130 km from coast   *Orange*

Population
762 184 (1970 census); 990 000 UN est 1979)

Annual Growth Rate
2·9% (UN est 1979)

	desert

Capital City
Windhoek

subsistence agriculture —
nomadic pastoralism (cattle,
goats, karakul (Persian lamb))
and some wheat/maize
growing

Population of Capital
61 300 (est 1976)

scattered grazing land
(karakul) with large dairy
cattle ranches

National Language(s)
Afrikaans, English; German, Ovambo, Damara,
Herero

more intensive grazing land
and zone of commercial
agriculture (maize, wheat,
sorghum, rice, groundnuts)

Gross National Product (US dollars)
750 million (est 1974)

Bantustans (African
homelands)

national park boundary

Local Currency
1 South African rand = 100 cents

○ mineral resource site

Walvis
Bay   major port

Lüderitz   fishing port

scale 1:6 000 000

0   300km
0   200mi

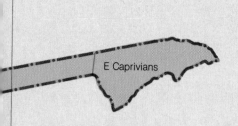

E Caprivians

consolidate its control politically. Appealing primarily to Afrikaners, who comprise 60 per cent of the white population, the NP has built up an overwhelming majority of seats in the whites-only parliament. Two minor parties, the New Republic Party (formerly the United Party) and the Progressive Federal Party, constitute an official opposition. Their appeal is largely to English-speaking voters. In 1961, after a referendum, South Africa declared itself a republic and withdrew from the British Commonwealth.

The most controversial aspect of NP rule has been its implementation of a policy known as apartheid or separate development, which is designed to order race relations. Apartheid doctrine calls for separating the races into ethnic units defined in terms of language, culture and traditions; these units are entitled to self-determination within prescribed geographical areas. According to the theory of apartheid, mixing or integrating the races leads to conflict and loss of cultural identity, so the ultimate goal is to create ten independent homelands or Bantustans for African ethnic groups and one homeland for whites. In the Bantustans, Africans are to satisfy their political and economic aspirations, but if they work in the white area, they are to have very few rights. In pursuit of this policy, the South African government has granted independence to Transkei (1976), Bophuthatswana (1977) and Venda (1979). However, no country outside of South Africa has recognized them and most of the other Bantustans have rejected offers of independence. Because Asians and Coloreds do not have geographical homelands, the government has created for them separate representative councils with limited legislative powers. Most Africans, Coloreds and Asians reject the system of apartheid and do not support the government-created political institutions.

In reality, the Bantustans, which take up less than 13 per cent of the land, are not viable economically and serve primarily as labor reservoirs for the white-dominated economy. They have few mineral resources and a limited industrial base; thus most Africans are compelled to be migrant workers in the white areas. Subsistence agriculture is practiced, and much of the land has been severely eroded because of overstocking and overgrazing.

In pursuing its goal of separating the races, the government has undertaken the massive relocation of hundreds of thousands of people, mostly blacks, who have been forcibly moved from one area to another in urban areas or from urban areas to the Bantustans. Despite the government's intention of removing Africans from white areas, over half live on white farms or in the urban areas.

Africans have historically opposed the racially discriminatory policies of the South African government. The first major African nationalist group, the African National Congress (ANC), was founded in 1912 and worked for many decades promoting political and economic equality for Africans. During the period after World War II, it was especially active in organizing major nonviolent protests against government policies. In 1959 a split within the ANC resulted in the formation of another group, the Pan Africanist Congress (PAC). In 1961, as African protests escalated, the South African government declared both groups illegal and forced them underground and into exile. Despite the fact that many African leaders such as Albert Luthuli, Nelson Mandela and Robert Sobukwe have been imprisoned and banned, the ANC and PAC continue to organize resistance to the government inside and outside the country. In order to quell dissent, the government has passed an array of security legislation which severely restricts any African political opposition.

With the ANC and PAC declared illegal, many younger Africans turned to support other organizations, such as the South African Students' Organization and the Black People's Convention. But in 1977 these organizations as well as many others were banned and a young black leader, Steve Biko, was killed in prison. The government has not allowed any movements to take their place. The only significant black movement that is allowed to operate legally is *Inkatha*, a cultural organization, which is led by Chief Gatsha Buthelezi, head of the KwaZulu Bantustan.

South Africa has the most industrialized economy on the African continent. Since World War II, its manufacturing sector has undergone spectacular growth and has become the leading sector of the economy. It contributes three times as much to the GNP as mining and agriculture combined. The primary industries in the manufacturing sector are the motor industry, iron and steel (which is dominated by the state-owned corporation ISCOR), clothing and textiles, engineering and metalworking, chemicals, food, beverages and tobacco. Most industries are concentrated in four areas: the southern Transvaal or Witwatersrand, Durban–Pinetown, Port Elizabeth–Uitenhage, and the western Cape. These areas account for four-fifths of industrial net output and employment. In recent years, in an attempt to control the flow of Africans from the Bantustans to white industrial areas, the government has attempted to decentralize industry by offering incentives to industries to locate in or near the Bantustans. However, this attempt has largely been unsuccessful.

Although mining has become of secondary importance to manufacturing, it has been of critical significance over the last century. It still accounts for about two-thirds of all exports and 12 per cent of the GDP, and it provides the catalyst for industrial development and agricultural growth. Gold and diamonds still figure significantly in the mining sector, with gold accounting for over 50 per cent of mineral output. Since World War II, there has been great expansion in the production of vanadium, nickel, copper, coal, antimony, iron ore, asbestos, fluorspar, manganese, chrome and limestone. To facilitate export of minerals, two new harbors, Saldanha Bay north of Cape Town and Richard's Bay north of Durban, have been created.

Although its importance has diminished over the years, the agricultural sector remains a cornerstone of the economy. Because only 15 per cent of land is arable and rainfall is sporadic, farmers rely heavily on irrigation and in white farming areas, agriculture is highly mechanized and export-oriented. The most important pastoral product is wool, which is the country's second leading export after gold. Different crops are important in different regions. In the southwestern Cape, wine and fruit are the major products. In Natal, sugar cane predominates, while on the high veld, it is maize and wheat, citrus fruits, tobacco, and dairy and cattle ranching.

The South African economy generates great wealth, but it is distributed unequally between whites and blacks. Whites control the economy and have structured the system so that they maintain a privileged position, while unskilled positions are reserved for black workers. Most sectors of the economy remain dependent on cheap, unskilled black labor. For instance, the mineral industry employs 700 000 persons; 90 per cent are Africans and most of them are foreign migrant workers, who come to the mines on short-term contracts. Most farm work is also done by black workers on a seasonal or contractual basis. In the western Cape, Coloreds provide most of the labor, while Africans form the bulk of the labor force elsewhere.

R.E.

Namibia

Namibia, formerly known as South West Africa, has a long Atlantic coastline and its territorial neighbors are Angola, Botswana and South Africa. It also extends to Zambia along the 30- by 440-kilometer Caprivi Strip. The Namib Desert's shifting sand dunes and salt pans extend inland from the coast. The central plateau has elevations up to 2485 meters and on its eastern side is the Kalahari Desert. Wells, boreholes and over 10 000 dams supplement intermittent rivers.

Namibia's population density is among the world's lowest. The African peoples are classified into 12 ethnic groups speaking Bantu and Khoisan languages. The northern third of Namibia is reserved for the Ovambo, a Bantu-speaking people (418 300), Okavango (61 400), East Caprivians and Kaokovelders, totaling about 518 000. Other African peoples numbering more than 40 000 each are the Damaras, the Hereros and the Namas. The Khoisan Bushmen number 27 500. The south has urban and rural areas and scattered African home areas. Windhoek, the capital, contains almost half the 100 000 whites.

Namibia has a litigious history. The harsh environment and lack of obvious economic potential initially inhibited British and South African annexation. German missions established in the 1840s provided a continuing link before Bismarck formally acquired the area in 1884. The German colonial period was marked by unrest, most notably the 1904 Herero rebellion. When, following World War I, the League of Nations and Treaty of Versailles divested Germany of its colonial empire, South West Africa was made a Class C Mandate. On 2 December 1920 the Union of South Africa proceeded to administer the region.

Following World War II the prospect of decolonization prompted the South African Nationalist regime in 1949 unilaterally to extend its sovereignty to Namibia. Whites were represented in the Cape Town parliament. In 1966 the United Nations and the International Court of Justice called for South African withdrawal but by 1969 South Africa had extended its security, apartheid and Bantustan policies to Namibia.

The white National and Federal parties of Namibia are opposed by the clandestine Southwest Africa People's Organization (SWAPO), which stands for majority rule. Guerrilla and industrial action increased after 1966. Between 1971 and 1973 the South African government under Vorster pursued a policy of dialogue with the UN Secretary-General Waldheim. Following the 1974 Portuguese coup and Portugal's withdrawal from Angola and Mozambique, South Africa reappraised its subordinate state system. "Tribal" elections were held, which did not achieve credibility because of a SWAPO boycott and intensified guerrilla activity. After South Africa's unsuccessful 1976 intervention in Angola, Vorster and Botha turned to ensuring Namibia's successor regime would incorporate whites and be friendly to South Africa. The Turnhalle Conference of August 1976 promised independence on 31 December 1978, but it did not include SWAPO's leader, Sam Nujoma. Violence erupted between ethnic groups and in March the moderate Herero leader, Clemens Kapuuo, was assassinated. During mid-1978, following an American initiative, a fragile multilateral compromise was achieved between whites, SWAPO and South Africa, including free elections and withdrawal of South African troops. The only outstanding issue was the sovereignty of Walvis Bay, which South Africa claims will remain under its control after independence. However, as Vorster resigned from office later that year, he announced that South Africa would pursue its own internal settlement.

Since the mid-1950s trade statistics have been incorporated into South Africa and the Southern African Customs Union. Secrecy surrounds economic information. Mining provides about 60 per cent of the GDP. De Beers Consolidated Mines owned 98·3 per cent of the 1·6 million carats of the predominantly gem-quality diamonds extracted in 1972. In 1975 Namibia was the world's sixth largest diamond producer. Tsumeb Corp, the largest employer, mines copper, lead and zinc. Uranium, tin, salt, vanadium, tungsten and gold are also mined. The mining sector during the 1970s appeared to be growing at a 10 per cent annual rate, but the white-to-black pay ratio remains about 23 to 1.

Cattle, goat and sheep grazing, subsistence millet and maize cultivation and migratory labor are the African's major economic pursuits. Around Windhoek farming activities include agriculture, livestock, sheep, Karakul (Persian lamb) and mohair goats. Ostrich feathers are a growing concern. The limited processing and manufacturing sectors include dairy products, meat, hides and wool. Farming provides about 17 per cent of the GDP. Fishing and canning are based at Luderitz and Walvis Bay. About 90 per cent of Namibia's production is for export. Its major trading partner, South Africa, receives half its exports and provides 90 per cent of its imports. Major overseas customers are the USA, West Germany, Britain and Japan. At least a third of the GDP accrues to foreigners in the form of repatriated profits and dividends.

Infrastructure development since the 1960s included blacktopping 3000 kilometers of the 32000 kilometers of road. The South African Railways and Harbours Administration subsidizes the 2340-kilometer rail system. Air services connect Windhoek with Europe and South Africa. Luderitz and the disputed Walvis Bay are the ocean ports, the latter handling about 90 per cent of the traffic.

O.P.

Botswana

Botswana is a landlocked tableland surrounded by the territories of Zimbabwe, South Africa and Namibia. Roughly parallel to its southeastern border is a plateau about 1300 meters in elevation, which divides the country into two distinct sectors. The smaller, eastern sector covers part of the Limpopo river watershed; it contains the most fertile land and is home to 80 per cent of Botswana's people. The huge western sector is mostly too dry for dependable agriculture, but even its Kgalagadi Desert has sufficient vegetation to support large animal life. Rainfall throughout the country is sparse and erratic. Droughts are frequent, even in the east, making more efficient collection of surface water a top national priority.

Botswana has few significant resources and even these were little exploited until after independence. Livestock products dominated the colonial economy and they remain the most important source of cash income. Post-independence prospecting has found substantial deposits of diamonds, nickel, copper and sulfur, which the government is developing commercially. Another post-independence development is the tourist industry, built around the country's still-abundant wildlife resources, particularly in the northern regions.

About 98 per cent of Botswana nationals are ethnic Tswana – members of the western branch of Sotho-speaking Bantu peoples. Most other Botswanans are San-speaking Sarwa (Bushmen). Botswana's modern history began in the early 18th century when the first Tswana people, the Kwena, entered from South Africa. The Ngwato and Ngwaketse soon broke away from these original Kwena, and the Tawana later broke from the Ngwato. By the late 19th century these four groups and four other Tswana societies dominated the country.

During the early 19th century South Africa's *Mfecane* disturbances sent refugees and marauding Bantu bands through eastern Botswana, and the Ndebele settled in southwestern Zimbabwe, from which they continued to harass the Tswana. Meanwhile, Afrikaners occupied the Transvaal, making life harder for both local and neighboring Tswana communities. Afrikaner pressures pushed the Kgatla into Botswana in 1871.

By the 1880s these external pressures were clearly imperiling the security of Botswana's peoples, and international imperialist forces were closing in around the country. The leading Tswana rulers appealed to Britain for help against Afrikaner encroachments. A British military expedition arrived in 1884, and a year later the Bechuanaland Protectorate was declared over southern Botswana. Northern Botswana was soon added. The protectorate's southern border severed Botswana's Tswana from the bulk of the Tswana peoples, most of whom lived within a separately created British colony which was later incorporated into the present Cape Province of South Africa. Cecil Rhodes's land-hungry British South Africa Company threatened to absorb the Bechuanaland Protectorate into its domain in the 1890s, but another Tswana appeal to Britain forestalled this development.

When South Africa was unified in 1910, Britain provided for Botswana's eventual incorporation into the Union of South Africa. This provision lapsed when South Africa left the Commonwealth in 1961, and Botswana was then transformed into a more orthodox colony. Prior to then, however, a High Commissioner based in South Africa was the fundamental law-making authority for Botswana, Lesotho and Swaziland, and Botswana's administrative capital was at Mafeking, outside its own territory. Local administration was built upon indirect rule through traditional authorities.

In 1961 executive and legislative councils were created, and major political changes followed swiftly. When self-government was granted in 1965, Seretse Khama became chief minister. Independence was attained a year later and Khama became president. Botswana's subsequent history has been a struggle for economic independence from its powerful white-ruled neighbor. The country's communications lifeline is the Zimbabwe-owned railroad connecting Mafeking and Bulawayo through eastern Botswana. A large part of the male labor force works in South Africa. Khama's government rejects South Africa's apartheid system, but it cannot risk economic strangulation by transforming its principles into hostile relations with its neighbors. Despite these external problems and the country's limited resources, Botswana has remained patient and tranquil and its government still functions democratically.

K.R.

Lesotho

Lesotho is a mountainous country, and is the only nation in the world with all its land situated more than 1000 meters above sea level. Three-quarters of Lesotho is dominated by the rugged and lightly populated Maloti mountains. Its highest mountain, Thabana-Ntlenyana in the Drakensberg range, at 3481 meters, is the highest in southern Africa. The western quarter of the country consists of the so-called lowlands, which are actually high plains about 1500 to 1600 meters above sea level. Most of Lesotho's administrative headquarters and towns, population and best agricultural lands are in the lowlands area. Lesotho is completely surrounded by South Africa, a fact that heavily influences its

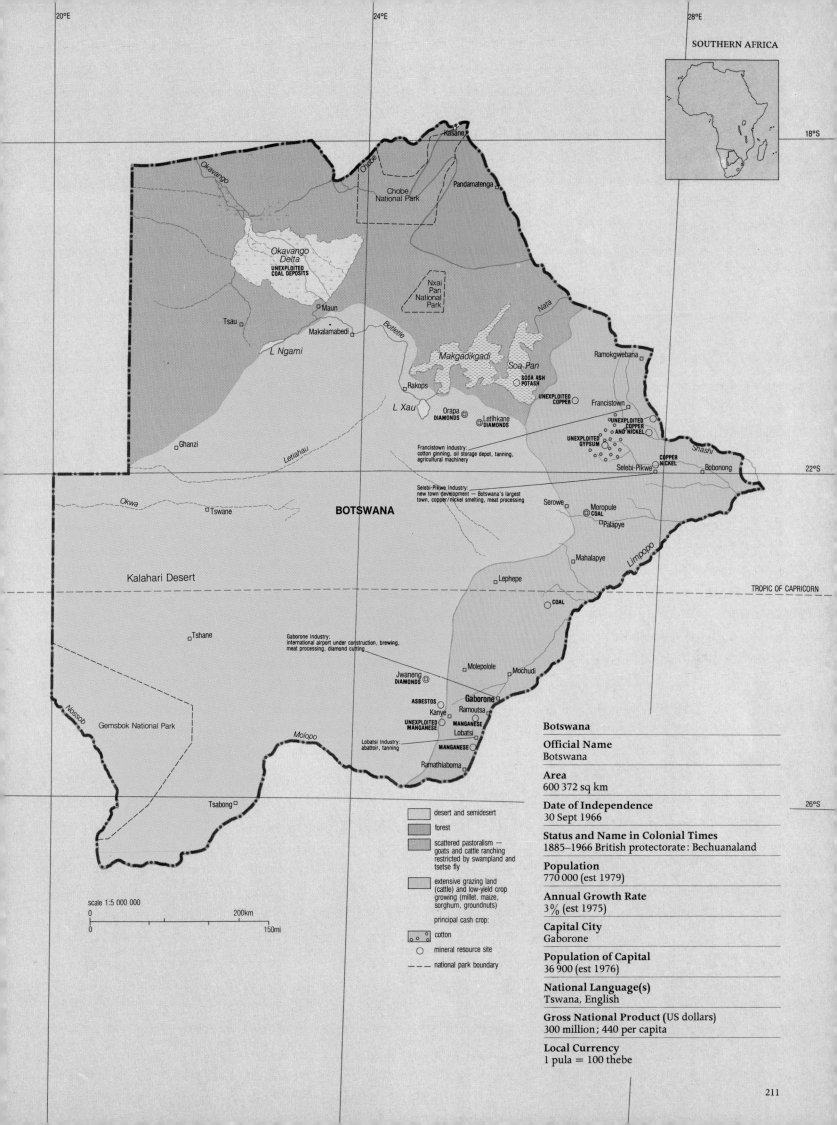

SOUTHERN AFRICA

20°E · 24°E · 28°E · 18°S · 22°S · 26°S

Okavango

Kasane

Chobe

Pandamatenga

Chobe
National Park

Okavango
Delta
**UNEXPLOITED
COAL DEPOSITS**

Nxai
Pan
National
Park

Nata

Maun

Tsau

Makalamabedi

Botletle

Makgadikgadi

L Ngami

Ramokgwebana

Soa Pan

**SODA ASH
POTASH**

Rakops

**UNEXPLOITED
COPPER**

Francistown

L Xau

Orapa
DIAMONDS

Letlhkane
DIAMONDS

**UNEXPLOITED
COPPER
AND NICKEL**

**UNEXPLOITED
GYPSUM**

Shashi

Francistown Industry:
cotton ginning, oil storage depot, tanning,
agricultural machinery

Ghanzi

Letiahau

**COPPER
NICKEL**

Selebi-Pikwe

Bobonong

Selebi-Pikwe Industry:
new town development — Botswana's largest
town, copper/nickel smelting, meat processing

Serowe

Moropule
COAL

Okwa

Tswane

BOTSWANA

Palapye

Limpopo

Mahalapye

Lephepe

TROPIC OF CAPRICORN

Kalahari Desert

COAL

Tshane

Gaborone Industry:
international airport under construction, brewing,
meat processing, diamond cutting

Molepolole

Mochudi

Jwaneng
DIAMONDS

Nossob

Gemsbok National Park

ASBESTOS

Kanye

Gaborone

Ramoutsa

Molopo

**UNEXPLOITED
MANGANESE**

MANGANESE

Lobatsi

Lobatsi Industry:
abattoir, tanning

MANGANESE

Ramathlaboma

Tsabong

Legend

	desert and semidesert
	forest
	scattered pastoralism — goats and cattle ranching restricted by swampland and tsetse fly
	extensive grazing land (cattle) and low-yield crop growing (millet, maize, sorghum, groundnuts)

principal cash crop:

cotton

○ mineral resource site

- - - national park boundary

scale 1:5 000 000

0 — 200km
0 — 150mi

Botswana

Official Name
Botswana

Area
600 372 sq km

Date of Independence
30 Sept 1966

Status and Name in Colonial Times
1885–1966 British protectorate: Bechuanaland

Population
770 000 (est 1979)

Annual Growth Rate
3% (est 1975)

Capital City
Gaborone

Population of Capital
36 900 (est 1976)

National Language(s)
Tswana, English

Gross National Product (US dollars)
300 million; 440 per capita

Local Currency
1 pula = 100 thebe

present economic and political position.

The modern nation of Lesotho was created in the early 19th century largely through the creative leadership of Moshoeshoe I, who forged together remnants of Sotho-speaking groups which had been torn apart during the *Mfecane*, a series of inter-African wars which affected much of southern Africa between about 1820 and 1830. Using the mountains of Lesotho as defensive fortresses and exhibiting considerable military and diplomatic skills, Moshoeshoe was able to consolidate and expand the Sotho state.

The greatest threat in subsequent decades came from the Boers who trekked into Sotho territory in the 1830s and created a rival state, the Orange Free State. Though the Sotho were initially able to contain the Boers, disputes over land led to wars in 1858 and 1865, which ended in the Orange Free State possessing large tracts of fertile land previously held by the Sotho. In order to stave off further Boer raids, Moshoeshoe successfully appealed in 1868 for British protection. Basutoland (as it was called) was initially administered by the Cape Colony, but after a Sotho rebellion in 1880–81, the British reassumed responsibility for the territory.

Basutoland was administered as a High Commission Territory, but the British had limited objectives and spent little money on development. Thus, from the late 19th century, Basutoland's prosperous economy declined dramatically and thousands of Sotho men were forced annually to seek employment as migrant workers on South African mines and farms. As much as possible, the British allowed traditional chiefs and headmen to rule without interference. In 1903 a National Council was created as an advisory body, but since it was dominated by chiefs, it was later opposed by such nationalist organizations as the Progressive Association and *Lekhotla la Bafo* (Council of Commoners).

Modern Lesotho politics have been dominated by three parties: the Basutoland Congress Party (BCP), formed in 1952 and led by Ntsu Mokhehle, the Basutoland National Party (BNP), founded in 1958 by Chief Leabua Jonathan, and the Marema Tlou Party, established in 1957 to advance the cause of the Basotho monarchy. The last of these now supports Moshoeshoe II.

In 1960, when the British government granted a new constitution, it established a directly elected council. The BCP won the first election in 1960, but the BNP won the next election in 1965. Thus when Britain granted Lesotho its independence in 1966, Chief Jonathan became the first prime minister. In the 1970 election, when it became apparent that the BCP would win a majority of seats in parliament, Chief Jonathan declared a state of emergency, voided the election results and suspended the constitution. Mokhehle and other BCP leaders were detained but later released. In 1974 the political conflict again erupted into violence when some supporters of the BCP attempted a coup. The coup attempt was put down and the government killed and jailed numerous BCP members. Mokhehle and other opposition leaders fled the country. Chief Jonathan still retains control over Lesotho, but in recent years he has attempted a reconciliation with some elements of the opposition.

Because Lesotho is totally surrounded by South Africa, its foreign policy has been conditioned by this relationship. Although Chief Jonathan initially favored a policy of dialogue with South Africa, since 1972 he has been an outspoken critic of South Africa's system of apartheid.

Lesotho is economically one of the world's least developed countries. Per capita GNP is about $160. The vast majority of the resident population is engaged in agriculture, but only one-eighth of the land is cultivable. Much of the land is severely eroded by overgrazing, and productivity is very low. Lesotho has over half a million cattle and over two and a half million sheep and goats. The latter provide the basis for a thriving wool industry. In the last decade the Lesotho government has attempted to develop other sectors of the economy. A number of small manufacturing industries have been created and tourism has been successfully promoted. Diamonds are mined but on a small scale. A potential resource is water which could be utilized by South Africa for irrigation and hydroelectric power.

Only about 25 000 Lesotho citizens can find wage employment in Lesotho. Because of the dearth of employment opportunities and the depressed state of agriculture, many of the rest are forced to seek employment in South Africa. Over 110 000 men are employed in mines in South Africa, and a large number of men and women, around 60 to 70 thousand, work on farms and in industry. These workers send back remittances which help to sustain the Lesotho economy. Because many adult males are migrants who are away from home for substantial parts of the year, this has had a detrimental effect on the family structure.

R.E.

Swaziland

Swaziland is one of the smallest nations of Africa. It is bounded on the north, west and south by South Africa and on the east by Mozambique. It is divided into three zones geographically: the mountainous high veld in the west which averages 1050 to 1200 meters in height, the rolling grasslands of the middle

veld (450 to 600 meters) and the bush savanna, of the low veld (150 to 300 meters) which covers the southern and eastern regions. Running the length of the low veld and separating Swaziland from Mozambique is the Lebombo range, a rolling plateau 450 to 825 meters in height. There are four main river systems, the Komati and the Umbeluzi in the north, the Great Usuthu in the middle and the Ngwavuma in the south. Most industry and agriculture, as well as almost half of the country's population, are in the middle veld.

The precolonial history of Swaziland was dominated by the Dlamini clan. Led by its founder, Dlamini, this Nguni-speaking clan moved into southern Africa during the latter part of the 16th century, settling south and west of what is now Delagoa Bay, east of Swaziland. There they stayed for almost two centuries, when their leader, Ngwane III, brought them into what is now Swaziland. During the 19th century the Swazi nation, under the leadership of a series of outstanding military and political leaders, was a major force in the region, dominating and controlling an area much larger than present-day Swaziland. The Swazi derived their name from one of these leaders, Mswati II.

In the latter half of the 19th century the Swazi were able to retain their independence despite pressures from Boer and British settlers and the Zulu. However, one ruler, Mbandzeni (1874–89), acceded to European pressures for mineral and land concessions and gave away large tracts of land. This was contrary to Swazi customary law. Later attempts to reclaim the land were rebuffed, but since independence the Swazi nation has been slowly buying back land. Nevertheless over 40 per cent of the country is still owned by Europeans, who have an influential role in the economy.

In 1903, after a brief period of administration by the Transvaal (1894–1903), Swaziland was brought under British rule. During the colonial period, the traditional system of rule was left virtually intact, leaving

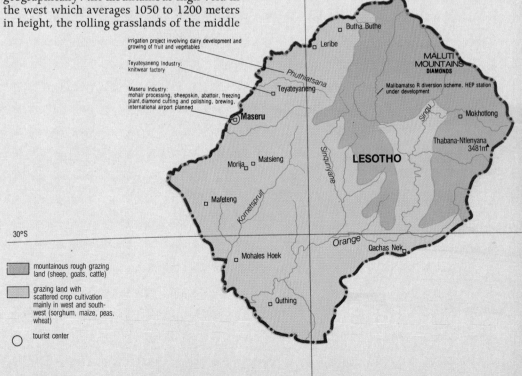

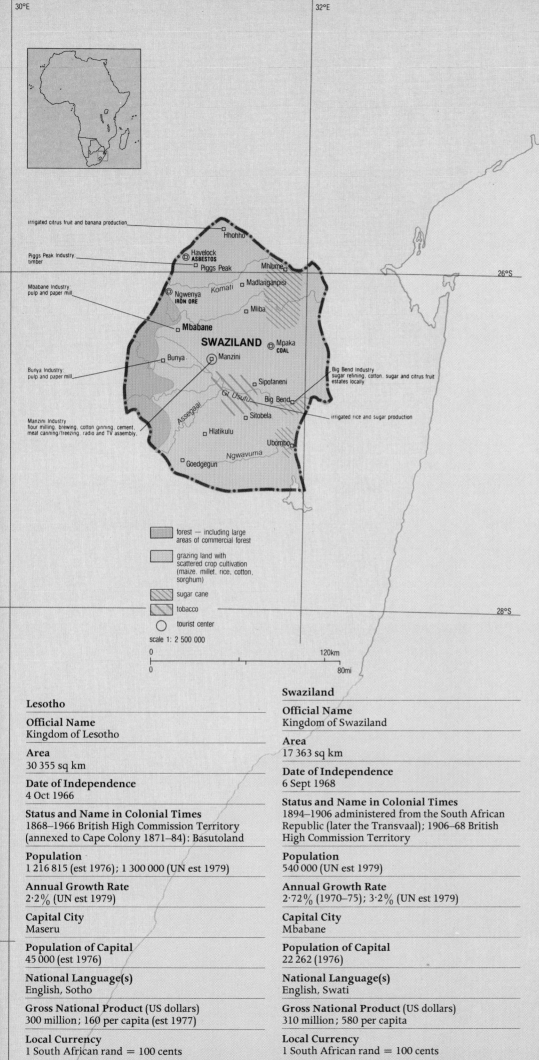

irrigated citrus fruit and banana production

Piggs Peak Industry:
timber

Mbabane Industry:
pulp and paper mill

Bunya Industry:
pulp and paper mill

Manzini Industry:
flour milling, brewing, cotton ginning, cement,
meat canning/freezing, radio and TV assembly

Hhohho

Havelock
ASBESTOS
Piggs Peak

Mhlume

Madlanganpisi

Komati

Ngwenya
IRON ORE

Mliba

Mbabane

SWAZILAND

Mpaka
COAL

Bunya

Manzini

Big Bend Industry:
sugar refining, cotton, sugar and citrus fruit
estates locally

Sipofaneni

Gt Usutu

Big Bend

Assegaai

Sitobela

irrigated rice and sugar production

Hlatikulu

Ubombo

Goedgegun

Ngwavuma

26°S

28°S

forest — including large
areas of commercial forest

grazing land with
scattered crop cultivation
(maize, millet, rice, cotton,
sorghum)

sugar cane

tobacco

tourist center

scale 1: 2 500 000

0   120km

0   80mi

Lesotho

Official Name
Kingdom of Lesotho

Area
30 355 sq km

Date of Independence
4 Oct 1966

Status and Name in Colonial Times
1868–1966 British High Commission Territory
(annexed to Cape Colony 1871–84): Basutoland

Population
1 216 815 (est 1976); 1 300 000 (UN est 1979)

Annual Growth Rate
2·2% (UN est 1979)

Capital City
Maseru

Population of Capital
45 000 (est 1976)

National Language(s)
English, Sotho

Gross National Product (US dollars)
300 million; 160 per capita (est 1977)

Local Currency
1 South African rand = 100 cents

Swaziland

Official Name
Kingdom of Swaziland

Area
17 363 sq km

Date of Independence
6 Sept 1968

Status and Name in Colonial Times
1894–1906 administered from the South African
Republic (later the Transvaal); 1906–68 British
High Commission Territory

Population
540 000 (UN est 1979)

Annual Growth Rate
2·72% (1970–75); 3·2% (UN est 1979)

Capital City
Mbabane

Population of Capital
22 262 (1976)

National Language(s)
English, Swati

Gross National Product (US dollars)
310 million; 580 per capita

Local Currency
1 South African rand = 100 cents

Swazi government in the hands of the royal family. In 1921 the present *nqwenyama* (lion), Sobhuza II, began his reign. He rules with the advice of an inner council of advisers and the Swazi National Council, which is comprised of all adult Swazi males. Sobhuza is the longest-reigning monarch in the world and his reign is synonymous with modern Swazi history.

Modern Swazi political activity dates from around 1960, when a small group of younger, educated Swazi founded the Swaziland Progressive Party. Later it split into three factions, the most important being the Ngwane National Liberatory Congress (NNLC) led by Dr Ambrose Zwane. In 1964 Swazi royalists founded the Imbokodvo (grindstone) National Movement and allied themselves with the European Advisory Council, which was established in 1921 to advance the interests of the small European community. In pre-independence elections in 1964 for a legislative council, Imbokodvo swept all seats.

The constitution with which Swaziland entered independence in 1968 reserved substantial power for the monarchy, although it retained a parliamentary system. The Imbokodvo party controlled all seats, but in the 1972 election the opposition NNLC won three seats, drawing support from younger, urbanized and working-class voters. A year later Sobhuza, claiming the constitution did not reflect Swazi traditions of government, dissolved political parties and suspended the constitution. Since then the principal opposition leader, Dr Zwane, has been periodically detained. The king appointed a royal commission to make recommendations for a new constitution. It reported in 1975, but in March 1977 Sobhuza suspended parliament and announced that representatives were to be selected by *tinkhundla* (traditional local councils), according to Swazi traditions. In 1976 Colonel Maphevu Dlamini succeeded Makhosini Dlamini as prime minister. He is also head of the small Swazi army.

Being a landlocked nation, Swaziland is primarily dependent on South Africa for external trade and markets, but since independence it has been able to develop a prosperous and diversified economy. However, most Swazi are still subsistence farmers and pastoralists. Cattle are highly valued as a source of wealth, although only a small percentage are bred for the market. The leading export crop is sugar, but citrus products and pineapples are also leading money earners. Three major mining operations – iron ore, asbestos and coal – provide substantial revenue, as does the timber industry, which has become highly profitable. A tourist industry has been developed which relies heavily on visitors from South Africa. The development of small industry is a recent occurrence and most of it is centered at Matsapha.   R.E.

AFRICA IN THE INDIAN OCEAN

These islands have one thing in common: their difference from anywhere else. They are neither "African" like Zanzibar nor "Asiatic" like Sri Lanka. A meeting point of different worlds, the islands form a world of their own. The breakup of the old continent of Gondwanaland many millions of years ago, volcanic eruptions, the slow accumulation of corals, above all, the great tropical ocean itself, have created this unique phenomenon. Isolated from the continental land masses for so long, the island world has evolved a rich diversity of flora and fauna.

Man's arrival on the islands had to wait for his ability to navigate across vast oceanic distances, a relatively recent human achievement. It is now almost certain that the first men in the island world landed in Madagascar about 2000 years ago and that they came from Indonesia, perhaps by way of India and Africa. Archaeological evidence shows the early settlers to have been in possession of fire and to have had the use of iron. If these proto-Malagasy knew of the existence of the other islands, there is no evidence of their having settled on any of them.

Next to arrive were Swahili-speaking Muslim sailors of mixed Arabic–Negro origins. They settled in the Comoros from about 1400 AD and from there spread in small numbers to the coast of Madagascar. Arab navigators had certainly sighted the other islands but they remained uninhabited until the arrival of Europeans in the 17th century.

In striking contrast to continental Africa then, the peoples making up the present-day insular nations are all descended from immigrants. However, a categoric distinction must be made between, on the one hand, Madagascar and the Comoros which had been populated and had developed societies and cultures of their own before the coming of Europeans and, on the other hand, Réunion, Mauritius and Seychelles, which had no precolonial history and whose creole societies and cultures have been entirely created under European colonial rule.

Top Fishing and inter-island trade are traditional aspects of Seychellois life. Tourists are increasingly attracted to the islands' warm, clear seas, sandy beaches and healthy climate.

Above Rice growing in Madagascar on the flooded-field system is a reminder of the Asiatic origins of Malagasy culture. Grown extensively on the island's central plateau, wet and dry rice occupies about half the total land under crops.

Left Sugar accounts for about 90 per cent of Mauritius's export trade. Descendants of imported Indian laborers own many of the smallholdings on which the crop is grown and hand-cutting of the sugarcane is still common.

Above right The lemurs are primitive primates virtually confined to Madagascar. Several purely arboreal species, threatened by the destruction of their forest environment, are listed by the International Union for Conservation of Nature and Natural Resources in the Red Data Book.

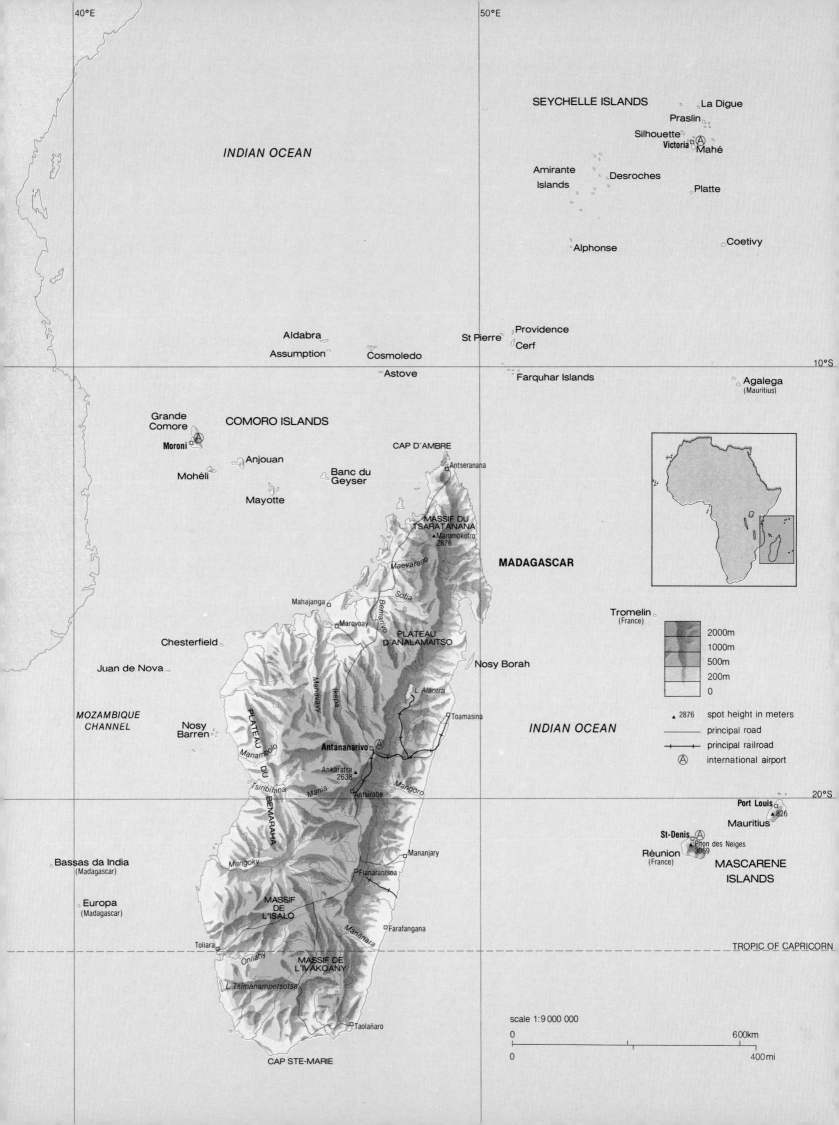

40°E

50°E

INDIAN OCEAN

SEYCHELLE ISLANDS
La Digue
Praslin
Silhouette
Victoria Ⓐ Mahé

Amirante
Islands
Desroches
Platte

Coetivy

Providence
Aldabra
St Pierre
Cerf
Assumption
Cosmoledo
Astove
Farquhar Islands

10°S

Agalega
(Mauritius)

Grande
Comore
COMORO ISLANDS
CAP D'AMBRE
Moroni Ⓐ
Antseranana

Anjouan

Mohéli
Banc du
Geyser
MASSIF DU
TSARATANANA
▲Maromokotro
2876

Mayotte

MADAGASCAR

Maevarano

Sofia

Mahajanga

Marovoay
PLATEAU
D'ANALAMAITSO

Chesterfield
Nosy Borah

Juan de Nova
L. Alaotra

*MOZAMBIQUE
CHANNEL*
Nosy
Barren
Toamasina

INDIAN OCEAN

Antananarivo Ⓐ

Ankaratra ▲
2638
Antsirabe

Mangoro

20°S

Port Louis
▲826

Mauritius

St-Denis Ⓐ
Piton des Neiges
3069
Réunion
(France)

Bassas da India
(Madagascar)

Mananjary

MASCARENE
ISLANDS

Fianarantsoa

Europa
(Madagascar)

MASSIF
DE
L'ISALO

Mangoky

Farafangana

Toliara

Onilahy

Mananara

TROPIC OF CAPRICORN

MASSIF DE
L'IVAKOANY

L. Tsimanampetsotsa

Taolañaro

CAP STE-MARIE

Tromelin
(France)

2000m
1000m
500m
200m
0

▲ 2876   spot height in meters
────────   principal road
─┼─┼─┼─   principal railroad
Ⓐ   international airport

scale 1:9 000 000

0   600km

0   400mi

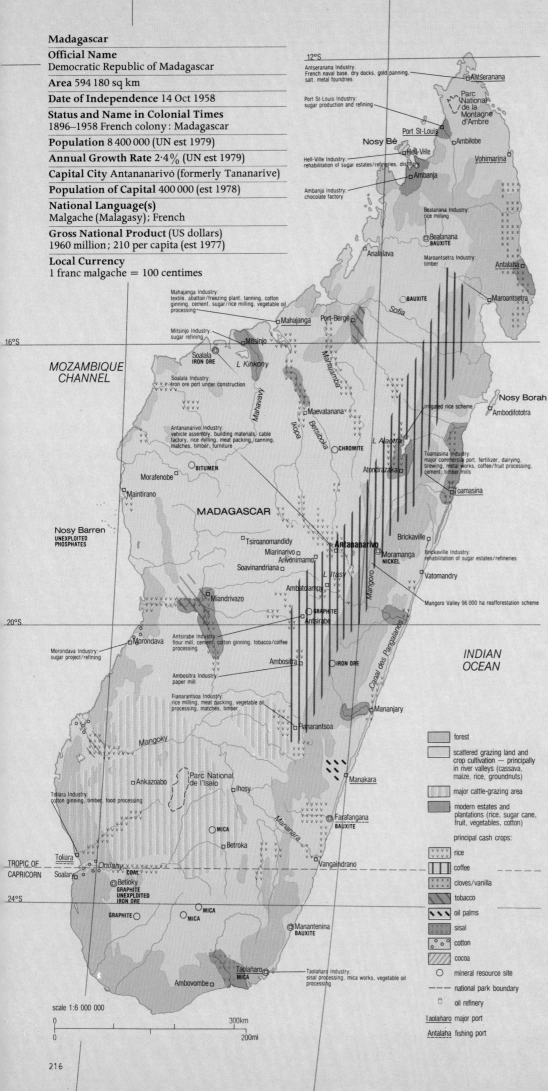

Madagascar

Official Name
Democratic Republic of Madagascar

Area 594 180 sq km

Date of Independence 14 Oct 1958

Status and Name in Colonial Times
1896–1958 French colony: Madagascar

Population 8 400 000 (UN est 1979)

Annual Growth Rate 2·4% (UN est 1979)

Capital City Antananarivó (formerly Tananarive)

Population of Capital 400 000 (est 1978)

National Language(s)
Malgache (Malagasy); French

Gross National Product (US dollars)
1960 million; 210 per capita (est 1977)

Local Currency
1 franc malgache = 100 centimes

MOZAMBIQUE CHANNEL

INDIAN OCEAN

scale 1:6 000 000

forest

scattered grazing land and crop cultivation — principally in river valleys (cassava, maize, rice, groundnuts)

major cattle-grazing area

modern estates and plantations (rice, sugar cane, fruit, vegetables, cotton)

principal cash crops:

rice

coffee

cloves/vanilla

tobacco

oil palms

sisal

cotton

cocoa

mineral resource site

national park boundary

oil refinery

<u>Taolañaro</u> major port

<u>Antalaha</u> fishing port

Madagascar

Madagascar, 1580 kilometers long and 580 kilometers broad, dwarfs the rest of the island world. A small continent in its own right, Madagascar basically comprises two coastal plains and a central plateau arranged in parallel north to south. Almost entirely within the tropics, Madagascar is warm and, except for the extreme southwest, wet most of the year round. The east coast is subject to the rain-bearing southeast trade wind and tropical cyclones, while the north and west of the island are affected by a local monsoon. The central plateau, relatively drier and much cooler, is the most densely populated and developed part of the country. Forests cover approximately 10 per cent of Madagascar. Centuries of assault on them by fire and iron have left large tracts of country bare and eroded by the torrential rains to a brick-like, infertile laterite. On the plateau, marshes have been transformed into rice fields using the Asiatic flooded-field method of cultivation. The savanna country supports large herds of cattle. The large rivers are not used much for navigation but river and lake fishing is extensive and good. On the west coast, estuaries provide natural harbors and the large continental shelf offers good fishing. In the north the splendid bay of Diégo-Suarez was developed as a French naval base. The east coast is straight but has one important man-made harbor: the port of Tamatave, the outlet for the plateau and linked by rail to Tananarive, the capital and principal town.

The inhabitants of Madagascar, never very numerous, spread throughout the island and formed a number of kingdoms and clans occasionally at war with one another but retaining the essential cultural and linguistic unity of the original Asiatic settlers. Later arrivals, a few Arabs and numerous Negro slaves, were integrated into the overall Malagasy society affecting but not changing

Réunion

Official Name
La Réunion

Area
2510 sq km

Date of Independence
not applicable

Status and Name in Colonial Times
1642–1946 French territory; 1946– French overseas *département*

Population
494 700 (est 1978)

Annual Growth Rate
1·4% (UN est 1979)

Capital City
Saint-Denis

Population of Capital
103 513 (1974)

National Language(s)
French; Creole

Gross National Product (US dollars)
1199 per capita (UN est 1975)

Local Currency
1 French franc = 100 centimes

its basic structure. It was a predominantly self-sufficient agrarian society based on a subsistence peasantry ruled by clan leaders. Around 85 per cent of the Malagasy still live on the land.

Political unification under the Hova, a people of the central plateau, gathered momentum under Adrianapoinimerina (1785–1810). His son, Radama I (1810–28), completed the unification of the island and, playing on Franco–British rivalry, kept Madagascar independent. An enlightened monarch, Radama encouraged European customs and modernization. The Bible was translated into Malagasy and Protestant missionaries from Britain provided the Malagasy language with a good written form. The reign of Radama marks the apogee of precolonial Madagascar. There followed unstable years in which periods of isolation and xenophobic attitudes alternated with periods when foreign influence was welcomed. Colonial intrigues escalated. France declared a protectorate over the island in 1885 and when this was recognized by Britain in 1890 France was left free to conquer Madagascar in 1895, depose the monarchy and impose colonial rule.

French colonialism restructured the economy through the enforced cultivation of cash crops, notably coffee, for export and the importation of French manufactured goods. The plantations diverted land and labor from food production and Madagascar had to import rice. French settlers did not come in large numbers, although Indians and some Chinese established themselves as retail traders. A few Malagasys were trained to fulfill secondary functions in administration and commerce. Roads, railroads and ports were built to handle trade. On the whole the Malagasys transferred their traditional respect and loyalty for the elders to the new French

rulers, but resentment lingered on, especially among those peoples of the plateau who had been deprived of their dominant positions. This resentment, spurred on by the disorganization of France during World War II, erupted into a widespread but badly organized anti-French uprising in 1947. French repression was swift and thorough; by 1948 over 11 000 Malagasys had been killed. In the 1950s the French fostered an alternative, more moderate, nationalism based on the traditional underdog clans of the coastal regions, to whom they transferred political power in 1960. This followed General de Gaulle's return to power in France and an overwhelming "yes" in Madagascar for membership of the French Communauté.

The new Malagasy Republic had a constitution modeled on that of the Fifth Republic, and President Tsiranana and his Social Democratic Party (PSD) kept the country closely tied to France. Practically all the modern sector of the economy remained in French hands; French influence in education and the media increased; France kept its large naval base at Diégo-Suarez and its air force base near Tananarive; French advisers staffed the administration; France looked after external security and could intervene in internal matters; foreign policy was guided by Paris. In May 1972, however, a student protest escalated into a general uprising against the regime. A turbulent period ensued with a power struggle between Left and Right factions in the armed forces. As the radicals got the upper hand most foreign-owned interests were nationalized. Relations with France were put on an entirely new footing with closure of the French bases, departure of the advisers and the country's withdrawal from the franc zone in 1973.

Captain Ratsiraka emerged as the strong man in the Council of the Revolution to become the president of the new Democratic Republic of Madagascar, established by the constitution of 1976. The new regime kept some of the gains made by the Left while reassuring the bourgeoisie. Traditional Malagasy institutions – notably the *Fokolona*, self-governing village councils – are emphasized in the plans for modernizing the economy. In foreign policy Madagascar adopts a "progressive" position, spearheading anti-South African moves at the OAU, protesting against the militarization of the Indian Ocean and maintaining good relations with China as well as the USSR and the West.

J.H.

Mauritius and Réunion

Mauritius and Réunion, frequently called "the twin sister islands," are about the same size, are not far apart, have the same volcanic origins, and are subject to more or less the same tropical climatic conditions. There are, however, important variations which have contributed to the different fortunes of the two islands. On the whole, geography has been more generous to Mauritius. Réunion is extremely mountainous and has a much smaller proportion of good level agricultural

Mauritius

Official Name Mauritius

Area 1865 sq km

Date of Independence
12 Mar 1968

Status and Name in Colonial Times
1598–1710 Dutch colony; 1715–1810 French colony: Île de France; 1810–1968 British colony

Population
930 000 (UN est 1979 including dependencies)

Annual Growth Rate 1·31%

Capital City
Port Louis

Population of Capital
142 901 (est 1977)

National Language(s)
English; Creole, French, Urdu, Tamil, Chinese, Gujarati

Gross National Product (US dollars)
690 million; 760 per capita (est 1977)

Local Currency
1 Mauritian rupee = 100 cents

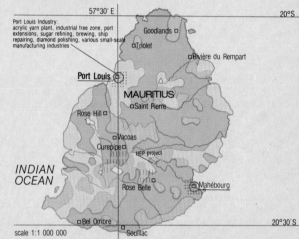

land. The fertile volcanic soils of Mauritius are not washed away by the torrential rains down the steep mountain slopes as in Réunion. Communication and transportation have always been much easier in and with Mauritius. The two good natural harbors and the necklace of coral reefs creating lagoons and splendid beaches around Mauritius contrast with Réunion's abrupt, rocky, forbidding coastline.

The French took possession of and settled in Réunion in 1642. The Dutch established a colony in Mauritius in 1638, but the few settlers were unable to conquer the natural environment. They abandoned the island in 1710. In 1715 the French from Réunion moved in and by importing slaves from Madagascar and Africa were able to cut down the forests and make a permanent settlement. The French East India Company initially used Réunion and Mauritius as supply bases on the long route to India, but the islands soon became plantation colonies in their own right. Mauritius, in particular, acquired great significance as a trade entrepôt, and as a base from which British shipping might be harassed during the long Franco–British duel for the control of the Indian Ocean. This culminated in the British conquest of the islands in 1809–10. Réunion was returned to France after the Napoleonic wars, but Mauritius,

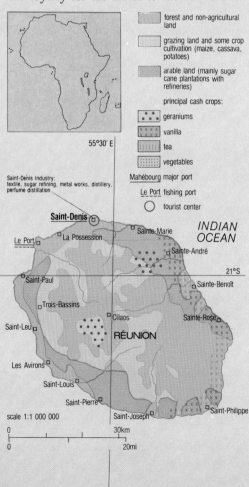

which then included the Seychelles, became a British Crown Colony. Under British rule the sugar plantations were extended, with large numbers of Indian indentured laborers replacing the Africans in the sugar fields after the abolition of slavery. The ethnic composition of the population was thus permanently altered. A colonial partnership was established between the few British civil servants and the well-established French creole sugar planters which lasted to the end of World War II.

From 1947 Mauritius was led through gradual stages of self-government, and in spite of some ethnic violence, into independence in 1968. Coalitions, dominated by the moderate Labour Party of the British-groomed Sir Seewosagur Ramgoolam, the prime minister, have been in power in a Westminster-modeled system of government ever since. Universal suffrage with the vote at 18, a free and very vocal press, very high rate of literacy, the abolition of malaria, the rudiments of a welfare state and a relatively high GNP per capita have been achieved within economic and social structures that have remained basically colonial. Tourism and the manufacture of textile goods for export have not substantially diminished the dominance of sugar, although, together with extensive government employment and a belated but successful demographic policy, they have eased the very serious unemployment problem. This has been insufficient, however, to prevent the mass appeal of the radical Third World Mauritius Militant Movement (MMM). The government's ambiguous position over South Africa, which is an important trade partner, and its partial collaboration in the takeover by Britain of the Chagos islands, a part of Mauritius, for the US military base on Diego Garcia, leave the administration open to attacks from the MMM opposition. Other characteristics of foreign policy – membership of the Commonwealth, the OAU, association with the European Common Market and strong links with France and India – reflect the

country's ethnic composition and are more generally supported.

Sugar also came to dominate Réunion. But less favorable natural conditions and the inability to import cheap Indian labor on the same scale as Mauritius have kept production well behind the sister island. Relative neglect from Paris, culminating in the near collapse of the economy during World War II, led to the island becoming a department of France in 1946. Massive transfers of capital and the extension of French laws to Réunion transformed the infrastructure of the economy, and the social and educational conditions, but failed to pull Réunion out of underdevelopment. The apparent prosperity of Réunion is artificial, being based on aid and the salaries of civil servants. The island produces only a small fraction of what it consumes. Without large-scale emigration to France its unemployment problem would be catastrophic. The hub of the French military, political and cultural presence in the region, Réunion remains the most dependent part of the island world. This situation is being exploited in the internal and international political context by the well-organized communist opposition.

J.H.

Comoro Islands

The four islands of the Comoros archipelago – Grande Comore, Anjouan, Mayotte and Mohéli – lie about 300 kilometers west of the northern tip of Madagascar. The four principal islands are volcanic in origin, but there are also numerous coral islets. The climate is generally warm, with a six-month rainy season, and, except on parts of Grande Comore, the land supports abundant tropical vegetation. Traditional human pursuits are the cultivation of rice, maize and tropical fruits, fishing and inter-island trade.

Precolonial Comoros was not a nation. The

original Swahili-speaking Muslim settlers of these four islands were organized into sultanates almost continuously at war with one another. A rigid caste-like distinction was maintained between the "Arabic" rulers and landowners and the serf-like Negroid peasants. In 1841 France, as part of its policy of expansion into Madagascar, obtained the island of Mayotte by a treaty with the local sultan. Large numbers of Christianized Malagasys came to settle on Mayotte under French rule, thus differentiating it ethnically from the rest of the Muslim archipelago. From Mayotte France gradually extended its rule over the other islands by signing treaties of protectorate with the ruling sultans. Cash crops of spices and essential oils were introduced but the French made no great effort to transform the traditional societies of the islands. From 1919 to 1946 the Comoros were administered as part of the colony of Madagascar but French rule on the islands remained distant and indirect. Becoming a *Territoire d'Outre Mer* of France (TOM) in 1946, the Comoros decided by referendum in 1958 to retain that status.

Receptive to developments taking place in Madagascar, the archipelago as a whole voted for independence in 1974. Mayotte, however, also voted overwhelmingly against independence as a part of a Comoros state. Changing its policy, France then decided against allowing the Comoros to go into independence as one entity. Upon this, Grande Comore, Anjouan and Mohéli declared themselves independent unilaterally and formed the state of Comoros (5 June 1975) which was admitted as a member of the United Nations and of the OAU. Ahmed Abdallah became the president of the new state but was overthrown by a Left-wing coup headed by Ali 'Soilih on 3 August 1975. 'Soilih was pledged to recover Mayotte from French imperialism, but without French financial and technical aid, unable to export its products, "progressive" Comoros was in a precarious position. 'Soilih was unable to cope with the deteriorating econ-

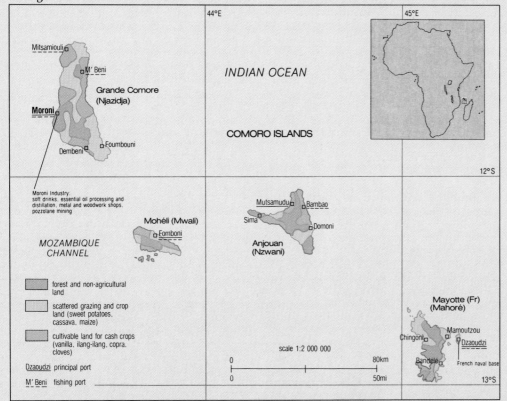

forest and non-agricultural land

scattered grazing and crop land (sweet potatoes, cassava, maize)

cultivable land for cash crops (vanilla, ilang-ilang, copra, cloves)

Dzaoudzi principal port

M' Beni fishing port

Moroni Industry: soft drinks, essential oil processing and distillation, metal and woodwork shops, pozzolane mining

scale 1:2 000 000

Comoro Isands

Official Name
État Comorien

Area
1862 sq km (2236 sq km including Mayotte)

Date of Independence
6 July 1975 (unilateral declaration of independence); 1 Jan 1976 French recognition of independence (exc. Mayotte)

Status and Name in Colonial Times
French colony (subject to governor-general of Madagascar 1919–46): Les Comores

Population
320 000 (est 1977 excluding Mayotte); Mayotte (Mahoré) 40 000 (est 1976)

Annual Growth Rate
2·1%

Capital City
Moroni (on Grand Comore)

Population of Capital
140 000 (est 1976)

National Language(s)
Swahili; Arabic, French

Gross National Product (US dollars)
70 million; 180 per capita (est 1979)

Local Currency
1 franc CFA = 100 centimes

Seychelles

Official Name
Seychelles

Area
308 sq km

Date of Independence
June 1976

Status and Name in Colonial Times
1756–94 French colony: Séchelles; 1794–1965
British colony (a dependency of Mauritius
1814–1903): Seychelles; 1965–76 part of British
Indian Ocean Territory

Population
61 900 (1977 census)

Annual Growth Rate
2·2% (1970–76)

Capital City
Victoria (on Mahé)

Population of Capital
23 000 (1977 census)

National Language(s)
English, French

Gross National Product (US dollars)
580 per capita (UN est 1975)

Local Currency
1 Seychelle rupee = 100 cents

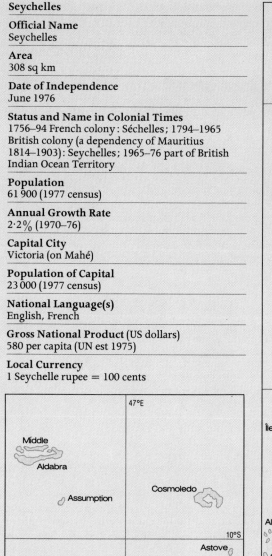

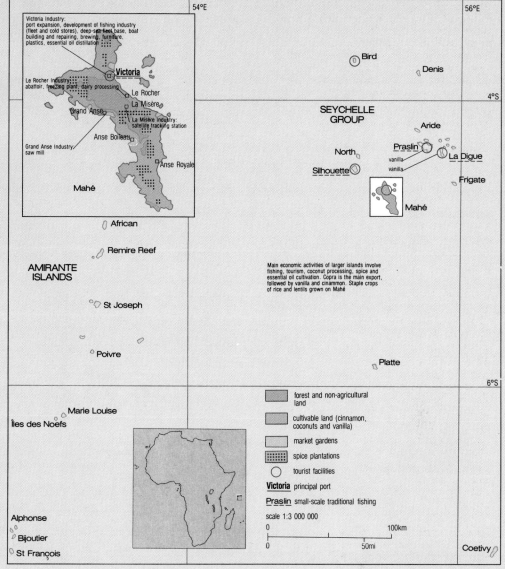

omic situation and the combined opposition of traditional Right-wing religious groups and the followers of Abdallah. He was ousted and lost his life in a countercoup led by the mercenary Bob Denard. Abdallah, who had taken refuge in France, returned to resume the presidency and try to reestablish the political unity of the archipelago through agreements with Mayotte and Paris. The probability of reunification is not very high, at least in the near future. The people of Mayotte have voted against it on several occasions and have expressed their wish to be a French Overseas Department (DOM). Strategically located on the oil route of the supertankers, between "progressive" Madagascar and Mozambique, the island has come to occupy a significant place in France's military deployment in the region.

J.H.

Seychelles

The 92 islands and islets making up the Seychelles archipelago, spread out over 700 000 square kilometers of the Indian Ocean, fall into two distinct categories: the larger mountainous islands of very ancient granite formation and the small, low-lying, much younger coral islands. Mahé, the principal

island, lies at the center of the archipelago, 900 kilometers northeast of Madagascar. Unlike the volcanic rocks of Mauritius the granite base of the Seychelles main islands does not weather into good soils. Rain, heavier and more frequent than in Mauritius, washes the poor soils of the Seychelles down mountainsides as steep as those of Réunion, leaving a hard laterite as infertile as Madagascar's. With a more equatorial than tropical climate, tempered by the oceanic location and by altitude, the Seychelles, in contrast to Mauritius and Réunion, are fortunate to be outside the cyclone zone. This, together with the coral formations, magnificent beaches and great variety of the numerous islands, has given the Seychelles an even better natural environment than Mauritius for the development of a tourist industry now that air transport has taken the islands out of their relative isolation. The capital, Victoria, on Mahé, stands on a fine natural harbor.

Although formally annexed by France in 1744, the Seychelles were not settled until the 1770s. Slaves from Mauritius were introduced to work the spice plantations. A dependency of Mauritius from 1810, the Seychelles were ceded with Mauritius to Britain at the end of the Napoleonic wars. Anti-slave-trade activities by the British navy brought liberated African slaves to the Seychelles, increasing the labor force for the copra plantations. Although

the change of colonial rulers affected it, it did not alter the basic creole French society, language and culture of the islands, the British administration grafting itself at the top of creole society. Roman Catholicism remained the majority religion. In 1903 Seychelles was formally constituted a colony separate from Mauritius. Fishing and agriculture continued as the most important activities, with exports dominated by coconut products.

Britain, after delays and hesitations prompted by military considerations, belatedly launched Seychelles into independence in 1976. A large airport had been opened to bring in international tourism, diversify the economy from copra plantations and make the islands viable without financial dependence. A presidential system, based on an unlikely coalition of Right and Left parties, hurriedly brought together under the sponsorship of Britain as precondition for independence, governed the country for a year before the anglophile President Mancham was overthrown in a bloodless coup organized by the OAU-supported Seychelles People's United Party of Prime Minister Albert René. The new regime has adopted a "progressive" stance in foreign policy while continuing to welcome foreign investments and tourists, mostly from Europe, which have transformed the country and on which it now depends.

J.H.

Flags-Symbols of Nationhood

Egypt

Libya

The flags of the independent African states are a colorful and symbolic assemblage. A few – Ethiopia, Liberia and Tunisia among them – have been in use since the 19th century. The majority, however, were designed in the late 1950s or 1960s to celebrate their countries' attainment of independence. Contemporary symbolism tends therefore to dominate historical association, though certain of the former French territories (Cameroon, Senegal, Mali, Ivory Coast) have adopted variations on the tricolor theme.

The pan-African colors of green, red and yellow are widely favored. Green generally represents the actual or hoped-for fertility of the land; red the struggle for independence; yellow mineral wealth or the sun as a general symbol of beneficence. A black stripe or star sometimes appears to symbolize the African people.

Cape Verde Islands

Mauritania

Sierra Leone

Liberia

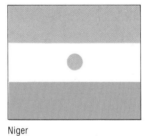

Ivory Coast

Ghana

Cameroon

Niger

Mali

Chad

Congo

Zaïre

Angola

Sudan

Uganda

Rwanda

Burundi

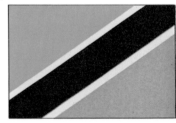

Tanzania

South Africa

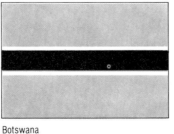

Botswana

Lesotho

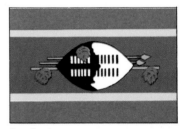

Swaziland

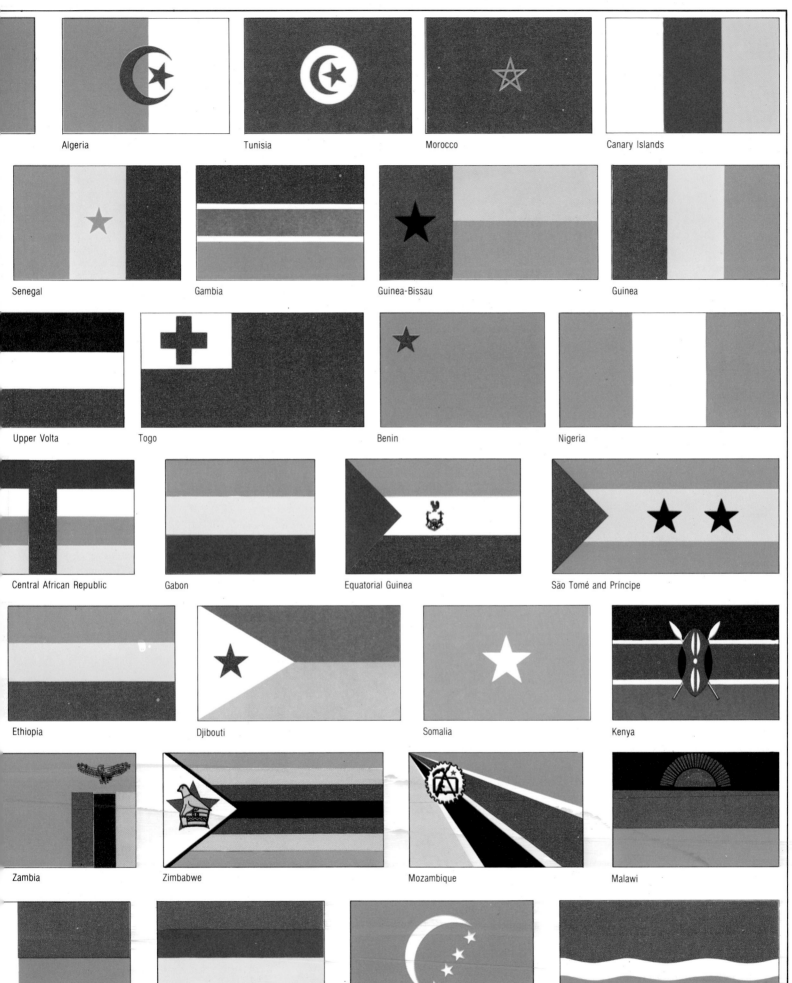

Algeria

Tunisia

Morocco

Canary Islands

Senegal

Gambia

Guinea-Bissau

Guinea

Upper Volta

Togo

Benin

Nigeria

Central African Republic

Gabon

Equatorial Guinea

São Tomé and Príncipe

Ethiopia

Djibouti

Somalia

Kenya

Zambia

Zimbabwe

Mozambique

Malawi

Madagascar

Mauritius

Comoro Islands

Seychelles

AFRICA IN THE WORLD

Many African nations have attained independence in the last two decades and thus have become members of various international bodies. There are now 49 members of UNO, which when founded in 1945 could include only four nations from Africa – Egypt, Ethiopia, Libya and South Africa. The Republic of South Africa remains a member, although relations with other African states, within and outside the Assembly, are often strained.

Organization of African Unity (OAU)
This is a grouping set up by African states themselves and includes all member-states of the United Nations with the exception of South Africa. It was founded at the Conference of Addis Ababa in

1963, with the stated aim of promoting "unity and international cooperation among African States" and of eradicating "all forms of colonialism in Africa." Its full assembly meets once a year in the capital of the member-state that provides that year's chairman – usually the head of state.

League of Arab States
Several African nations also belong to the League of Arab States (Arab League), "a voluntary organization of sovereign Arab states," founded in 1945. In addition to the North African nations of Egypt, Libya, Tunisia, Algeria and Morocco, three other states, Sudan, Somalia and Mauritania, belong to the Arab League and so form an important bridge

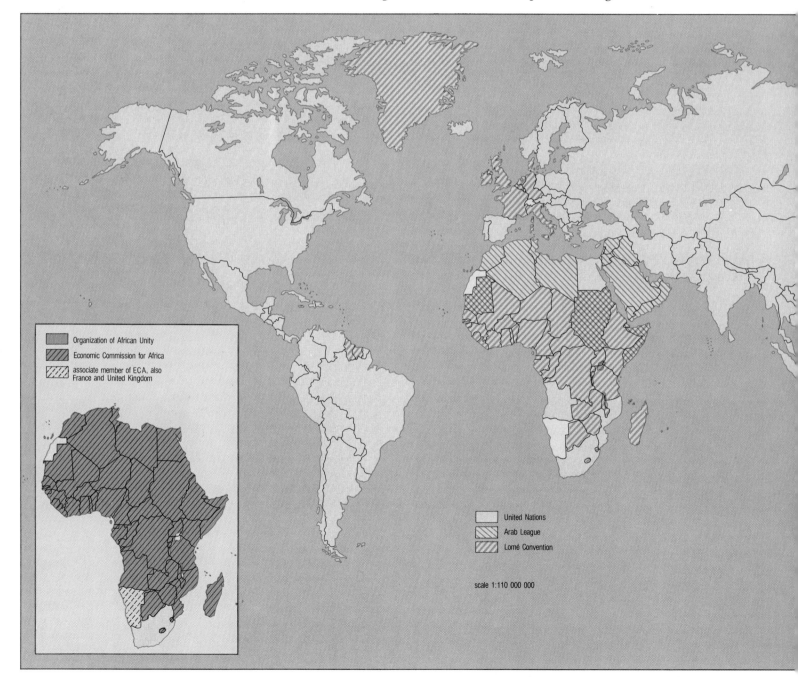

Organization of African Unity

Economic Commission for Africa

associate member of ECA, also France and United Kingdom

United Nations

Arab League

Lomé Convention

scale 1:110 000 000

President Kaunda of Zambia (left) conversing with Prime Minister Mugabe of Zimbabwe at the 1980 meeting of the Organization of African Unity in Freetown, Sierra Leone.

between black Africa and Arab Africa. In March 1977 an Afro–Arab summit was held in Cairo, comprising member countries of both the Arab League and the OAU. One result of this summit has been a decision by the oil-rich Arab states to give increased aid to the nations of black Africa.

Economic Commission for Africa (ECA)

All the sovereign African nations belong also to the Economic Commission for Africa, which has its headquarters in Addis Ababa. This includes the Republic of South Africa which was, however, suspended in 1963 and thus is no longer a functioning member. France, Britain and Namibia are associate members of the ECA.

Lomé Convention

The Lomé Convention is another and newer grouping which has very important economic implications for Africa. It involves almost 50 nations of Africa, the Caribbean and the Pacific (known as ACP countries) and the nine member nations of the European Economic Community (EEC). It was signed at Lomé, Togo, on 28 February 1975 and came into force on 1 April 1976. At precisely that time an earlier agreement, the Yaoundé Convention, which had been in force between 19 African countries and six EEC countries, lapsed.

All the independent nations of sub-Saharan Africa, with the exceptions of South Africa, Namibia and Zimbabwe, are members or potential members of the Lomé Convention. In its more limited role the Lomé Convention regards all countries of the ACP as a single customs area, with provision made for products manufactured or processed in part in one ACP country to pass through processes in another without tax complications. Its aims thus include trade cooperation, as well as export stabilization and financial and technical cooperation.

But in its extended role the Lomé Convention is concerned with the development of ACP countries within a global context. Industrial cooperation leading to industrial development is to be furthered by offering mutual access to technology and the adaptation of technology to local needs and conditions. Whether in fact these aims will be met is still a matter for discussion and negotiation.

United Nations Agencies

African nations also participate in and benefit from the activities of the various United Nations agencies. There are regional offices in various locations in Africa. Thus the Food and Agricultural Organization (FAO) has its regional office in Accra, the World Health Organization (WHO) in Brazzaville, and the International Labor Organization (ILO) in Addis Ababa. The more recently formed United Nations Environment Protection Agency (UNEP) is in Nairobi. The United Nations Educational, Scientific and Cultural Organization (UNESCO) is divided into two sections – Education, and Science and Technology. For sub-Saharan Africa the regional offices are, respectively, in Dakar and Nairobi. Both UNESCO offices for the Arab states are in Cairo.   J.M.

LIST OF CONTRIBUTORS

L.A.   'Ladipo Adamolekun is Dean of the Faculty of Administration at the University of Ife, Ile-Ife, Nigeria.

D.B.   David Birmingham is Professor of History at the University of Kent, Canterbury.

M.B.   Mark Bray is a lecturer in education at the Centre of African Studies, University of Edinburgh.

R.C.B.   R. C. Bridges is senior lecturer in history at the University of Aberdeen.

C.C.   Christopher Chamberlin, who completed a Ph.D. in African history at the University of California, Los Angeles, now works on the research staff of a United States Senator.

P.C.   Peter Clarke has taught African history at the University of Ibadan, Nigeria, and sociology of religion at King's College, London.

R.C.   Richard Curley is an associate professor of anthropology at the University of California, Davis.

S.D.   Susan Denyer has lived in East and West Africa, and published on art and architecture in Africa.

W.E.   William Eaton is a research analyst in the Library of Congress, Washington, D.C.

R.E.   Robert Edgar is a professor of history in the African Studies Program at Howard University, Washington, D.C.

C.E.   Christopher Ehret is a professor of history at UCLA.

F.F.   Finn Fuglestad is on the staff of the Historisk Institutt, University of Trondheim, Norway.

C.F.   Christopher Fyfe is Reader in History at the University of Edinburgh's Centre of African Studies.

T.G.   Thomas F. Glick is a professor of geography at Boston University, Massachusetts.

G.A.H.   Gerry A. Hale is a professor of geography at UCLA.

E.H.   Elizabeth Hodgkin, who has taught in Sudan and done fieldwork in Mali, is now at the Centre for West African Studies, University of Birmingham.

J.H.   Jean Houbert, a Mauritian by birth, is a lecturer in the Department of Politics at the University of Aberdeen.

E.J.   Emrys Jones is Professor of Geography at the London School of Economics and Political Science.

G.K.   Gerhard Kubik is a cultural scientist specializing in African and Afro-American studies and a lecturer at the University of Vienna.

I.L.   Ian Linden was recently a professor of history at the University of Hamburg and is now a freelance writer living in England.

M.L.   Mark Lipschutz, who completed a Ph.D. in African history at UCLA, now works in educational administration there.

J.M.M.   Joseph M. McCarthy is a professor of education at Suffolk University, Boston, Massachusetts.

E.M'B.   Elikia M'Bokolo is on the staff of the École des Hautes Études en Sciences Sociales, Paris.

J.M.   Jocelyn Murray is house editor at the International African Institute, London.

D.N.   David Northrup is a professor of history at Boston College, Boston, Massachusetts.

J.O'S.   John O'Sullivan is a professor of history at Tuskegee Institute, Tuskegee, Alabama.

O.P.   Oliver Pollak is a professor of history at the University of Nebraska, Omaha.

K.R.   Kent Rasmussen completed a Ph.D. in African history at UCLA and writes on central and southern Africa.

W.R.   William Rau completed a Ph.D. in African history at UCLA and later worked as an adult education organizer in Zambia.

C.D.R.   C. Duncan Rice is Professor of History and Dean of Hamilton College, Clinton, New York.

D.E.S.   Douglas E. Saxon has completed fieldwork and is writing up his research for the degree of Ph.D. at UCLA.

M.S.   Martin Staniland is a professor at the Center for International Studies, University of Pittsburgh, Pennsylvania.

J.C.S.   J. C. Stone is senior lecturer in geography and secretary of the African Studies Group at the University of Aberdeen.

I.S.   Inez Sutton is a lecturer in history at the University of Ghana, Legon.

J.E.G.S.   J. E. G. Sutton is Professor of Archaeology at the University of Ghana, Legon.

J.B.W.   Jerome B. Weiner is a professor of history at Old Dominion University, Norfolk, Virginia.

A.W.   Ann Williams is a lecturer in history at the University of Aberdeen.

S.Y.   Stanley Yoder is completing a Ph.D. degree at UCLA after periods of fieldwork in Zaïre.

LIST OF ILLUSTRATIONS

Abbreviations: t = top, tl = top left, tr = top right,
c = center, b = bottom etc. AH = Alan Hutchison
Library, London; JH = John Hillelson Agency, London;
MH = Michael Holford, Loughton, England;
WF = Werner Forman Archive, London.

All maps by Lovell Johns, Oxford.

225

BIBLIOGRAPHY

General and Reference Works
For the most up-to-date information see the current edition of the two yearbooks on Africa published annually by Europa Publications Ltd., London: *Africa South of the Sahara* and *The Middle East and North Africa*. C. Legum (ed.), *Africa Contemporary Record: Annual Survey and Documents* (London) provides an annual review of current issues affecting Africa.
For general historical background to the continent, see the *Cambridge History of Africa* (J. D. Fage and R. Oliver eds.) and the UNESCO *General History of Africa*, both at an advanced stage of preparation. The volumes published in the *Cambridge History* are:
Vol. 2 (ed. J. D. Fage): *From c. 500 BC–AD 1050* (1979)
Vol. 3 (ed. R. Oliver): *From c.1050–c.1600* (1977)
Vol. 4 (ed. R. Gray): *From c.1600–c.1790* (1975)
Vol. 5 (ed. J. E. Flint): *From c.1790–c.1870* (1977).
Among several useful one-volume general histories are:
B. Davidson, *Africa: History of a Continent*. London 1966.
J. D. Fage, *A History of Africa*. London 1978.
G. P. Murdock, *Africa: Its Peoples and Their Culture History* (New York 1959) contains an index of tribal names which, though not without error, is the most convenient way of locating many African ethnic groups. For a cartographical approach see J. D. Fage, *An Atlas of African History* (2nd ed. London 1978) and C. McEvedy, *The Penguin Atlas of African History* (Harmondsworth 1980). R. V. Tooley, *Collectors' Guide to Maps of the African Continent and Southern Africa* (London 1969) contains numerous plates illustrating the progress of cartographic knowledge of Africa.
R. I. Rotberg (ed.), *Africa and Its Explorers: Motives, Methods and Impact* (2nd ed. Harvard (Mass.) 1974) and the diaries of the explorers themselves, many of which have been republished in abridged or selected versions, trace the advance of European knowledge of the continent.
M. Lipschutz and R. K. Rasmussen, *A Dictionary of African Historical Biography* (London and Chicago (Ill.) 1978) contains an extensive bibliography on notable African figures to 1960.

Part One: The Physical Background
The Geography of Africa
C. Buckle, *Landforms in Africa*. London 1978.
J. I. Clarke (ed.), *An Advanced Geography of Africa*. Amersham 1975.
J. F. Griffiths, *Climates of Africa*. Amsterdam 1972.
A. T. Grove, *Africa*. 3rd ed. Oxford 1978.
A. M. O'Connor, *The Geography of Tropical African Development*. 2nd ed. Oxford 1978.
P. Richards (ed.), *African Environment, Problems and Perspectives*. London 1975.

Part Two: The Cultural Background
Languages and Peoples
J. H. Greenberg, *The Languages of Africa*. The Hague 1970.
J. Hiernaux, *The People of Africa*. London 1974.
G. P. Murdock, *Africa: Its Peoples and Their Culture History*. New York 1959.

Religions
A. Hastings, *A History of African Christianity 1950–1975*. Cambridge 1979.
I. M. Lewis (ed.), *Islam in Tropical Africa*. Revised ed. London 1980.
J. S. Mbiti, *Concepts of God in Africa*. London 1970.
G. Moorehouse, *The Missionaries*. London 1973.
G. Parrinder, *Religion in Africa*. London 1969.
H. Sawyerr, *God: Ancestor or Creator? Aspects of Traditional Belief in Ghana, Nigeria and Sierra Leone*. London 1970.
J. Trimingham, *The Influence of Islam upon Africa*. London 1968.

Early Man in Africa
J. D. Clark (ed.), *Atlas of African Prehistory*. Chicago (Ill.) 1967.
—— *The Prehistory of Africa*. London 1970.
S. Cole, *Leakey's Luck*. London 1975.
J. Harlan, J. M. J. de Wet and A. B. L. Stemler (eds.), *Origins of African Plant Domestication*. The Hague 1976.
G. L. Isaac and E. R. McCown (eds.), *Human Origins: Louis Leakey and the East African Evidence*. Berkeley (Cal.) 1976.
R. Oliver and B. M. Fagan, *Africa in the Iron Age*. Cambridge 1975.
D. W. Phillipson, *The Later Prehistory of Eastern and Southern Africa*. London 1977.
D. Pilbeam, *The Evolution of Man*. London 1970.
T. Shaw, *Nigeria: Its Archaeology and Early History*. London 1978.
P. L. Shinnie (ed.), *The African Iron Age*. Oxford 1971.

Kingdoms and Empires
P. Garlake, *The Kingdoms of Africa*. Oxford 1978.
R. Gray and D. Birmingham (eds.), *Pre-Colonial African Trade*. London 1970.
M. Shinnie, *Ancient African Kingdoms*. New York 1966.
J. Vansina, *Kingdoms of the Savanna*. Madison (Wisc.) 1966.

Europe in Africa
J. Duffy, *Portuguese Africa*. Cambridge (Mass.) 1961.
J. D. Hargreaves, *Prelude to the Partition of West Africa*. London 1963.
—— *West Africa Partitioned*, vol. 1: *The Loaded Pause 1885–1889*. London 1974.
W. M. Macmillan, *Bantu, Boer and Briton*. 2nd ed. Oxford 1964.

The African Diaspora
R. Bastide, *African Civilisations in the New World*. New York 1972.
P. Curtin, *The Atlantic Slave Trade. A Census*. Madison (Wisc.) 1969.
J. E. Flint and I. Geiss, "Africans Overseas," pp. 418–57 in J. E. Flint (ed.), *Cambridge History of Africa*, vol. 5. Cambridge 1977.
I. Geiss, *The Pan-African Movement*. New York 1974.
L. Jones, *Blues People*. New York 1963.
M. Kilson and R. Rotberg (eds.), *The African Diaspora. Interpretive Essays*. Cambridge (Mass.) 1976.
W. Rodney, "Africa in Europe and the Americas," pp. 578–622 in R. Gray (ed.), *Cambridge History of Africa*, vol. 4. Cambridge 1975.

The Growth of Cities
J. Gugler and W. B. Flanagan, *Urbanisation and Social Change in West Africa*. Cambridge 1978.
W. A. Hance, *Population, Migration and Urbanisation in Africa*. New York 1970.
K. Little, *Urbanisation as a Social Process*. London 1974.
A. L. Mabogunje, *Urbanisation in Nigeria*. London 1968.
H. Mmer (ed.), *The City in Modern Africa*. London 1967.

Vernacular Architecture
K. B. Andersen, *African Traditional Architecture*. Oxford 1978.
J. Beguin *et al.*, *L'Habitat au Cameroun*. Paris 1952.
S. Denyer, *African Traditional Architecture*. London 1978.
R. Gardi, *Indigenous African Architecture*. New York 1973.
H. Haselberger, *Bautraditionen der Westafrikanischen Negerkulturen*. Vienna 1964.
P. Oliver, *Shelter in Africa*. London 1971.
L. Prussin, *Architecture in Northern Ghana*. Berkeley and Los Angeles (Cal.) 1969.

African Arts
U. Beier, *Contemporary Art in Africa*. London 1971.
W. Fagg, *Tribes and Forms in African Art*. London 1965.
L. Holy, *Art of Africa: Masks and Figures from Eastern and Southern Africa*. London 1967.
M. Leiris and J. Delange, *African Art*. London 1968.
M. Trowell, *African Design*. London 1960.
F. Willett, *African Art*. London 1971.

Music and Dance
A. M. Jones, *Studies in African Music*. 2 vols. London 1959.
—— *Africa and Indonesia: The Evidence of the Xylophone and Other Musical and Cultural Factors*. 2nd ed. Leiden 1971.
G. Kubik, "Patterns of Body Movements in the Music of Boys' Initiation in South-east Angola," pp. 253–74 in J. Blacking (ed.), *The Anthropology of the Body* (A.S.A. Monograph 15). London 1977.
—— *Angolan Traits in Black Music, Games and Dances of Brazil*. Lisbon 1979.
—— *Theory of African Music. Nine Essays*. Urbana (Ill.) 1980.
A. Lomax, *Folk Song Style and Culture*. Washington (D.C.) 1968.
J. H. Kwabena Nketia, *The Music of Africa*. London 1975.
P. Oliver, *Savannah Syncopators. African Retentions in the Blues*. New York 1970.

Education and Literacy
G. N. Brown and M. Hiskett (eds.), *Conflict and Harmony in Education in Tropical Africa*. London 1975.
P. H. Coombs and M. Ahmed, *Attacking Rural Poverty: How Nonformal Education can Help*. Baltimore (Md.) 1974.
P. H. Coombs, R. C. Prosser and M. Ahmed, *New Paths to Learning*. New York 1973.
L. Mallasis, *The Rural World: Education and Development*. London 1976.
A. A. Mazrui, *Political Values and the Educated Class in Africa*. London 1978.
J. Simmons, *The Education Dilemma: Policy Issues for Developing Countries in the 1980s*. New York 1980.
F. C. Ward (ed.), *The School Leaver in Developing Countries*. London 1976.
World Bank, *Education Sector Review*. Washington (D.C.) 1980

Part Three: The Nations of Africa
North Africa
S. Amin, *The Maghreb in the Modern World; Algeria, Tunisia, Morocco*. Harmondsworth 1970.
Annuaire de l'Afrique du Nord. Paris annually.
D. Gordon, *North Africa's French Legacy, 1954–1963*. London 1963.

Egypt
J. Berque, *Egypt; Imperialism and Revolution*. London 1972.
M. Heikal, *The Road to Ramadan*. London 1975.
P. M. Holt (ed.), *Political and Social Change in Modern Egypt*. London 1968.
J. Lacouture, *Nasser: A Biography*. London 1973.
R. Mabro, *The Egyptian Economy 1952–1972*. London 1974.
P. Mansfield, *Nasser's Egypt*. Harmondsworth 1967.
S. Radwan, *Capital Formation in Egyptian Industry and Agriculture 1882–1967*. London 1975.

Libya
J. A. Allan, K. S. McLachlan and E. Penrose (eds.), *Libya: Agriculture and Economic Development*. 2nd ed. London 1978.
E. E. Evans-Pritchard, *The Sanusi of Cyrenaica*. London 1940.
R. First, *Libya: The Elusive Revolution*. London 1974.
M. Khadduri, *Modern Libya: A Study in Political Development*. Baltimore (Md.) 1963.
R. Mabro, "Labour Supplies and Labour Stability; A Case Study of the Oil Industry in Libya," *Oxford University Institute of Economics and Statistics Bulletin*, 32 (1970).
J. Wright, *Libya*. London 1969.

Algeria
F. Fanon, *Les Damnés de la terre*. Paris 1961.
A. Horne, *A Savage War of Peace; Algeria 1954–1962*. London 1977.
M. Lacheraf, *L'Algérie nation et société*. Paris 1965.
M. Lebajoui, *Vérités sur la révolution algérienne*. Paris 1970.
D. and M. Ottaway, *Algeria: The Politics of a Socialist Revolution*. Berkeley (Cal.) 1970.

Tunisia
D. E. Ashford, *Morocco-Tunisia: Politics and Planning*. Syracuse (N.Y.) 1965.
H. Bourguiba, *La Tunisie et la France*. Paris 1954.
G. Duwaji, *Economic Development in Tunisia*. New York 1967.
F. Garas, *Bourguiba et la naissance d'une nation*. Paris 1956.
M. Guen, *La Tunisie indépendente face à son économie*. Paris 1961.
C. A. Micaud, *Tunisia: The Politics of Moderation*. New York 1964.
M. Nerfin, *Entretiens avec Ahmed Ben Salah*. Paris 1974.

Morocco
R. Bidwell, *Morocco under Colonial Rule*. London 1973.
D. H. Dwyer, *Image and Self-Image: Male and Female in Morocco*. New York 1978.
E. Gellner, *Saints of the Atlas*. Chicago (Ill.) 1969.
J. P. Halstead, *Rebirth of a Nation: The Origins and Rise of Moroccan Nationalism, 1912–1944*. Cambridge (Mass.) 1967.
J. Waterbury, *Commander of the Faithful*. New York 1970.
—— *North for the Trade: The Life and Times of a Berber Merchant*. Berkeley and Los Angeles (Cal.) 1972.

Canary Islands
J. Mercer, "The Canary Islanders in Western

Mediterranean Politics," pp. 159–76 in *African Affairs*, 78 (1979).

R. Pélissier, *Los Territorios Españoles de Africa*. Madrid 1964.

Western Sahara

J. Mercer, *Spanish Sahara*. London 1975.

F. E. Trout, *Morocco's Saharan Frontiers*. Geneva 1969.

West Africa

J. F. A. Ajayi and M. Crowder (eds.), *History of West Africa*. 2 vols. London 1971, 1974.

J. D. Hargreaves, *West Africa: The Former French States*. Englewood Cliffs (N.J.) 1967.

Cape Verde Islands

A. A. Mendes Corrêa, *Ultramar Português. II: Ilhas de Cabo Verde*. Lisbon 1954.

A. Hodge, "Cape Verde under the PAIGC," pp. 43–47 in *Africa Report*, 22 (May–June 1977).

J. M. McCarthy, *Guinea-Bissau and Cape Verde Islands: A Comprehensive Bibliography*. New York and London 1977.

Mauritania

A. G. Gerteiny, *Mauritania*. London and New York 1967.

Introduction à la Mauritanie (Préface de D. G. Lavroff). Paris 1979.

Senegal

J. L. Balans, *Autonomie locale et intégration nationale au Sénégal*. Paris 1976.

L. Busch, *Guinea, Ivory Coast and Senegal: A Bibliography on Development*. Monticello (Ill.) 1973.

M. Crowder, *Senegal: A Study in French Assimilation Policy*. London 1962.

J. C. Gautron, *L'Administration sénégalaise*. Paris 1971.

S. Gellar, *Structural Changes and Colonial Dependency: Senegal, 1885–1945*. Beverly Hills (Cal.) 1976.

W. G. Johnson, *Emergence of Black Politics in Senegal: The Struggle for Power in the Four Communes, 1900–1920*. Stanford (Cal.) 1971.

I. L. Markovitz, *Léopold Sédar Senghor and the Politics of Negritude*. 1969.

L. Porgès, *Bibliographies des régions du Sénégal: complément pour la période des origines à 1965 et mise à jour 1966–1973*. Paris 1977.

E. J. Schumacher, *Politics, Bureaucracy and Rural Development in Senegal*. Berkeley (Cal.) 1975.

F. G. Snyder, *Law and Population in Senegal: A Survey of Legislation*. Leiden 1977.

Gambia

B. Berglund, *Gambia*. Uppsala 1975.

H. A. Gailey, *A History of the Gambia*. London 1964.

—— *Historical Dictionary of the Gambia*. Metuchen (N.J.) 1975.

M. Haswell, *The Nature of Poverty: A Case History of the First Quarter-Century after World War II*. London 1975.

G. Innes, *Kaabu and Fuladu: Historical Narratives of the Gambian Mandinka*. London 1976.

Guinea-Bissau

J. Barreto, *Historia da Guiné, 1418–1918*. Lisbon 1938.

H. Bienen, "State and Revolution: The Work of Amilcar Cabral," pp. 555–75 in *Journal of Modern African Studies*, 15 (Dec. 1977).

J. M. McCarthy, *Guinea-Bissau and Cape Verde Islands: A Comprehensive Bibliography*. New York and London 1977.

A. Teixeira da Mota, *Guiné Portuguesa*. 2 vols. Lisbon 1954.

B. I. Obichere, "Reconstruction in Guinea-Bissau: From Revolutionaries and Guerrillas to Bureaucrats and Politicians," pp. 204–19 in *A Current Bibliography on African Affairs*, 8 (1975).

Guinea

L. Adamolekun, *Sékou Touré's Guinea: An Experiment in Nation Building*. London 1976.

—— "The Socialist Experience in Guinea," in C. Rosberg and T. M. Callaghy (eds.), *African Socialism: A New Assessment*. Berkeley (Cal.) 1979.

W. Attwood, *The Reds and the Blacks: A Personal Adventure*. London 1967.

W. Derman, *Serfs, Peasants and Socialists*. Berkeley (Cal.) 1973.

R. W. Johnson, "Sékou Touré and the Guinean Revolution," pp. 350–65 in *African Affairs*, 69 (Oct. 1970).

C. Rivière, "Mutations sociales en Guinée," pp. 62–84 in *Rev. Franç. Études Polit. Afr.*, 43 (July 1969).

S. Soriba, *La Guinée sans la France*. Paris 1977.

J. Suret-Canale, *La République de Guinée*. Paris 1970.

Sierra Leone

W. Barrows, *Grassroots Politics in an African State: Integration and Development in Sierra Leone*. New York 1976.

J. R. Cartwright, *Political Leadership in Sierra Leone*. Toronto 1978.

J. I. Clarke, *Sierra Leone in Maps*. London 1966.

T. S. Cox, *Civil–Military Relations in Sierra Leone: A Case Study of African Soldiers in Politics*. Cambridge (Mass.) 1976.

C. Fyfe, *A History of Sierra Leone*. London 1962.

S. A. Jabati, *Agriculture in Sierra Leone*. New York 1978.

A. P. Kup, *Sierra Leone: A Concise History*. Newton Abbot 1975.

R. G. Saylor, *The Economic System of Sierra Leone*. Durham (N.C.) 1968.

A. B. C. Sibthorpe, *History of Sierra Leone*. 4th ed. New York 1971.

L. Spitzer, *Creoles of Sierra Leone: Responses to Colonialism, 1870–1945*. Madison (Wisc.) 1974.

G. J. Williams, *Bibliography of Sierra Leone, 1925–1967*. New York 1971.

Liberia

K. Y. Best, *Cultural Policy in Liberia*. Paris 1974.

C. A. Cassell, *Liberia: History of the First African Republic*. Vol. 1 (of 2 vols.) New York 1970.

C. S. Clapham, *Liberia and Sierra Leone: An Essay in Comparative Politics*. Cambridge 1976.

R. W. Clower et al., *Growth without Development: An Economic Survey of Liberia*. 1966.

R. W. Davis, *Ethnohistorical Studies on the Kru Coast*. Newark (N.J.) 1976.

D. E. Dunn, *Foreign Policy of Liberia during the Tubman Era, 1944–1971*. London 1979.

R. M. Fulton, "Selected Bibliography on Rural Liberia," in *Rural Africana*, 15 (1971).

S. E. Holsoe, *Bibliography on Liberia*. 3 vols. Newark (N.J.) 1971–76.

J. G. Liebenow, *Liberia: The Evolution of Privilege*. 1969.

M. Lowenkopf, *Politics in Liberia: The Conservative Road to Development*. Stanford (Cal.) 1976.

W. Siegmann, "Bibliography of Ethnographic Studies in Liberia," in *Rural Africana*, 15 (1971).

C. M. Wilson, *Liberia: Black Africa in Microcosm*. New York 1971.

Ivory Coast

M. Rémy, *The Ivory Coast Today*. Paris 1976.

A. R. Zolberg, *One-Party Government in the Ivory Coast*. 2nd ed. Princeton (N.J.) 1969.

Ghana

A. A. Boahen, *Ghana: Evolution and Change in the Nineteenth and TwentiethCenturies*. London 1975.

K. Dickson, *A Historical Geography of Ghana*. Cambridge 1969.

K. Nkrumah, *The Autobiography of Kwame Nkrumah*. Edinburgh 1957.

M. Oppenheimer and R. B. Fitch, *Ghana, End of an Illusion*. New York 1966.

E. Reynolds, *Trade and Economic Change on the Gold Coast 1807–1874*. London 1974.

W. E. F. Ward, *A History of Ghana*. 4th ed. London 1967.

I. Wilks, *Asante in the Nineteenth Century: The Structure and Evolution of a Political Order*. London 1975.

Upper Volta

D. M. McFarland, *Historical Dictionary of Upper Volta*. London and Metuchen (N.J.) 1978.

Togo

R. Cornevin, *Histoire du Togo*. 3rd ed. Paris 1969.

R. Cornevin, J.-C. Froelich and P. Alexandre, "Les Populations du Nord-Togo," Part 10 of *Ethnographical Survey of Africa*. Paris 1963.

Benin

R. Cornevin, *Histoire du Dahomey*. Paris 1962.

S. Decalo, *Historical Dictionary of Dahomey*. Metuchen (N.J.) 1976.

M. J. Herskovits, *Dahomey: An Ancient West African Kingdom*. 2 vols. Evanston (Ill.) 1938 (reprinted 1967).

D. Ronen, *Dahomey between Tradition and Modernity*. Ithaca (N.Y.) 1975.

Nigeria

D. B. Abernethy, *The Political Dilemma of Popular Education: An African Case*. Stanford (Cal.) 1969.

M. Crowder, *The Story of Nigeria*. 4th ed. London 1978.

R. O. Ekundare, *An Economic History of Nigeria 1860–1960*. New York 1973.

J. Hatch, *Nigeria: A History*. London 1971.

R. K. Udo, *Geographical Regions of Nigeria*. Berkeley and Los Angeles (Cal.) 1970.

G. Williams, *Nigeria: Economy and Society*. London 1977.

Cameroon

M. W. and V. H. DeLancey, *A Bibliography of Cameroon*. New York 1975.

T. Eyongetah and R. Brain, *A History of the Cameroon*. London 1974.

W. Johnson, *The Cameroon Federation: Political Integration in a Fragmentary Society*. Princeton (N.J.) 1970.

V. T. LeVine, *The Cameroons: From Mandate to Independence*. Berkeley (Cal.) 1964.

E. Mveng, *Histoire du Cameroun*. Paris 1963.

Niger

S. Baier and P. Lovejoy, "The Desert-Side Economy of the Central Sudan," pp. 531–81 in *International Journal of African Historical Studies*, 8:4 (1975).

S. Bernus and P. Gouletquer, "Du cuivre au sel. Recherches ethno-archéologiques sur la région d'Azelik," pp. 7–68 in *Journal de la Société des Africanistes*, 46 (1976).

F. Fuglestad, "UNIS and BNA. The Role of Traditionalist Parties in Niger, 1948–60," pp. 113–35 in *Journal of African History*, 16:1 (1975).

—— and R. Higgot, "The 1974 Coup d'État in Niger: Towards an Explanation," pp. 383–98 in *Journal of Modern African Studies*, 13:3 (1975).

F. Lancrenon and P. Donaint, *Le Niger*. Paris 1972.

J. Nicolaisen, *Ecology and Culture of the Pastoral Tuareg*. Copenhagen 1963.

G. Nicolas, *Dynamisme social et appréhension du monde au sein d'une société hausa*. Paris 1975.

Y. Poncet, *Cartes ethno-démographiques du Niger*. Niamey 1973.

J. Rouch, *Les Songhay*. Paris 1954.

Y. Urvoy, *Histoire des populations du Soudan Central (Colonie du Niger)*. Paris 1936.

Mali

S. M. Cissoko, *Tombouctou et l'empire Songhay: épanouissement du Soudan nigerien aux XVᵉ–XVIᵉ siècles*. Dakar 1975.

K. Ernst, *Tradition and Progress in the African Village: The Non-Capitalist Transformation of Rural Communities in Mali*. Leiden 1976.

A. S. Kanya-Forstner, *The Conquest of the Western Sudan*. Cambridge 1969.

N. Levtzion, *Ancient Ghana and Mali*. London 1973.

West Central Africa

G. Nachtigal, *Sahara and Sudan*. 4 vols. London 1974–.

R. I. Rotberg, *A Political History of Tropical Africa*. London 1966.

J. Suret-Canale, *Afrique noire occidentale et centrale l'ère colonial 1900–1945*. 3 vols. 2nd ed. Paris 1968.

—— *French Colonialism in Tropical Africa 1900–1945*. London 1971.

Chad

J. Cabot (ed.), *Atlas pratique du Tchad*. Paris 1972.

R. Jaulin, *La Mort Sava*. Paris 1967.

J. Le Cornec, *Histoire politique du Tchad 1900 à 1962*. Paris 1963.

D. E. Saxon, "Saharan and Chadic Interactions," in *Papers of the African Studies Association Annual Meeting*. Los Angeles (Cal.) forthcoming.

M. Vernhes and J. Bloch, *Guerre coloniale au Tchad*. Lausanne 1972.

Central African Republic

P. Kulck, *Central African Republic*. London 1971.

P. Pean, *Bokassa 1ᵉʳ*. Paris 1977.

D. E. Saxon, "Linguistic Evidence for the Eastward Spread of Ubangian Speakers," in C. Ehret and M. Posmansky (eds.), *Linguistics and Archaeology in African History*. Berkeley and Los Angeles (Cal.) forthcoming.

D. E. Saxon, C. Ehret et al., "Some Thoughts on the Early History of the Nile–Congo Watershed," in *Ufahamu*, 5:2 (1974).

Gabon

J. Bouquerel, *Le Gabon*. Paris 1970.

C. Chamberlin, "The Fang Migration into Central Gabon during the Nineteenth Century: A New Interpretation," pp. 429–56 in *International Journal of African Historical Studies*, 11:3 (1978).

K. D. Patterson, *The Northern Gabon Coast to 1875*. Oxford 1975.

B. Weinstein, *Gabon: Nation Building on the Ogooué*. Cambridge (Mass.) 1966.

Equatorial Guinea

S. Cronjé, *Equatorial Guinea: The Forgotten Dictatorship*. London 1976.

M. Liniger-Goumaz, *Guinea Ecuatorial: bibliografia general*. Berne 1974.

R. Pélissier, *Études hispano-guinéennes*. Paris 1969.

São Tomé and Príncipe

Secretary General of the United Nations, *Assistance to São Tomé and Príncipe: A Report*. New York 1978.

L. Wisenberg, "Mini-State with Maxi Problems," *Africa Report*, 21 (1976).

Congo

H. Bertrand, *Le Congo: Formation économique et mode de développement économique*. Paris 1975.

C. Coquery-Vidrovitch, *Le Congo au temps des grandes*

compagnies concessionnaires, 1898–1930. Paris–La Haye 1972.
T. Obenga, *La Cuvette congolaise, les hommes et les structures.* Paris 1976.
G. Sautter, *De l'Atlantique au fleuve Congo, une géographie du sous-peuplement.* Paris–La Haye 1966.
M. Sinda, *Le Messianisme congolais et ses incidences politiques.* Paris 1972.
M. Soret, *Histoire du Congo Brazzaville.* Paris 1978.
J. Vansina, *The Tio Kingdom of the Middle Congo, 1880–1892.* London 1973.
J.-M. Wagret, *Histoire et sociologie politiques de la République du Congo-Brazzaville.* Paris 1963.

Zaïre
R. Anstey, *King Leopold's Legacy.* Oxford 1966.
R. Cornevin, *Histoire du Congo.* 3rd ed. Paris 1970.
R. Lemarchand, *Political Awakening in the Congo: The Politics of Fragmentation.* Berkeley (Cal.) 1965.
R. Slade, *King Leopold's Congo.* London 1962.
J. Vansina, *Introduction à l'ethnographie du Congo.* Kinshasa 1966.

Angola
D. Birmingham, *Trade and Conflict in Angola.* Oxford 1966.
W. G. Clarence-Smith, *Slaves, Peasants and Capitalists in Southern Angola.* Cambridge 1979.
B. Davidson, *In the Eye of the Storm.* London 1972.
J. Marcum, *The Angolan Revolution.* 2 vols. Cambridge (Mass.) 1969, 1978.
D. Wheeler and R. Pélissier, *Angola.* London 1971.

Northeast Africa
T. J. Farer, *War Clouds on the Horn of Africa: A Crisis for Détente.* New York 1976.
A. Moorehead, *The Blue Nile.* London 1962.

Sudan
W. Adams, *Nubia: Corridor to Africa.* Princeton (N.J.) 1977.
T. Barnett, *The Gezira Scheme: An Illusion of Development.* London 1977.
M. O. Beshir, *Revolution and Nationalism in the Sudan.* London 1974.
S. A. El-Arifi, "Pastoral Nomadism in the Sudan," pp. 89–103 in *East African Geographical Review,* 13 (1975).
S. Hale, "Sudan's North–South 'Civil War': Religion or Class?" pp. 157–82 in Suad Joseph and B. L. K. Pillsbury (eds.), *Muslim–Christian Conflict: Economic, Political, and Social Origins.* Boulder (Col.) 1978.
J. H. G. Lebon, *Land Use in Sudan.* Bude 1965.
D. Roden, "Regional Inequality and Rebellion in the Sudan," pp. 498–516 in *Geographical Review,* 64:4 (Oct. 1974).
A. Sylvester, *Sudan under Nimeiri.* London 1977.

Ethiopia
P. Gilkes, *The Dying Lion: Feudalism and Modernization in Ethiopia.* London 1975.
A. Hiwet, *Ethiopia from Autocracy to Revolution.* London 1975.
J. Markakis, *Ethiopia: Anatomy of a Traditional Polity.* Oxford 1974.
—— and N. Ayele, *Class and Revolution in Ethiopia.* London 1978.
W. A. Shack, *The Central Ethiopians: Amhara, Tigrina and Related Peoples.* London 1974.
J. Shepherd, *The Politics of Starvation.* New York 1975.
R. Valdés Vivó, *Ethiopia's Revolution.* New York 1978.
M. Wolde-Mariam, *An Introductory Geography of Ethiopia.* Addis Ababa 1972.

Djibouti
S. Y. Abdi, "The Mini-Republic of Djibouti: Problems and Prospects," pp. 35–40 in *Horn of Africa,* 1:2 (1978)
M. Galaud, "French Territory of the Afars and the Issas," pp. 195–98 in Committee for the World Atlas of Agriculture, *World Atlas of Agriculture: Volume 4: Africa.* Novara 1976.
T. A. Marks, "Djibouti: France's Strategic Toehold in Africa," in *African Affairs,* 73 (1974).
N. A. Shilling, "Problems of the Political Development in a Ministate: The French Territory of the Afars and Issas," pp. 613–34 in *Journal of Developing Areas,* 7:4 (July 1973).
V. Thompson and R. Adloff, *Djibouti and the Horn of Africa.* Stanford (Cal.) 1968.

Somalia
T. W. Box, "Nomadism and Land Use in Somalia," pp. 222–28 in *Economic Development and Culture Change,* 19:2 (1971).
U. Funaioli, "Somalia," pp. 516–27 in Committee for the World Atlas of Agriculture, *World Atlas of Agriculture: Volume 4: Africa.* Novara 1976.
I. M. Lewis, *The Modern History of Somaliland: From Nation to State.* New York 1965.

—— "The Somali Conquest of the Horn of Africa," pp. 213–30 in *Journal of African History,* 1:2 (1960)

East Africa
E. A. Alpers, *Ivory and Slaves in East Central Africa.* London 1975.
M. F. Hill, *Permanent Way. The Story of the Kenya and Uganda Railway.* 2nd ed. London 1961.
J. S. Kirkman, *Men and Monuments of the East African Coast.* London 1964.
A. Moorehead, *The White Nile.* Revised ed. London 1971.
B. A. Ogot and J. A. Kieran (eds.), *Zamani. A Survey of East African History.* Revised ed. (by B. A. Ogot) Nairobi 1974.
R. Oliver, *The Missionary Factor in East Africa.* Revised ed. London 1965.
R. Oliver et al. (eds.), *A History of East Africa.* 3 vols. Oxford 1963–75.

Kenya
G. Bennett, *Kenya: A Short Political History.* London 1963.
E. Huxley, *White Man's Country. Lord Delamere and the Making of Kenya.* 2 vols. 2nd ed. London 1953.
J. Kenyatta, *Facing Mount Kenya. The Tribal Life of the Agikuyu.* London 1938.
J. Murray-Brown, *Kenyatta.* London 1972.
C. Rosberg and J. Nottingham, *The Myth of Mau Mau. Nationalism in Kenya.* Stanford (Cal.) 1966.

Uganda
D. E. Apter, *The Political Kingdom in Uganda.* Princeton (N.J.) 1961.
J. Beattie, *The Nyoro State.* Oxford 1971.
M. S. M. Kiwanuka, *The Kings of Buganda.* Nairobi, Dar es Salaam and Kampala 1971.
D. Martin, *General Amin.* London 1974.
F. Welbourn, *Religion and Politics in Uganda 1951–1962.* Nairobi 1965.

Rwanda and Burundi
R. Lemarchand, *Rwanda and Burundi.* London 1970.
I. Linden, *Church and Revolution in Rwanda.* Manchester 1977.
W. R. Louis, *Ruanda–Urundi 1884–1919.* Oxford 1963.
J. J. Maquet, *Le Système des relations sociales dans le Rwanda ancien.* (English translation. *The Premise of Inequality in Ruanda.* Oxford 1961.)

Tanzania
J. Iliffe, *Tanganyika under German Rule, 1905–1912.* Cambridge 1969.
—— *A Modern History of Tanganyika.* Cambridge 1979.
M. Lofchie, *Zanzibar: Background to Revolution.* London 1965.
A. Roberts (ed.), *Tanzania before 1900.* Nairobi 1968.

Southeast Central Africa
E. A. Alpers, *Ivory and Slaves in East Central Africa.* London 1975.
R. Gray, *The Two Nations: Aspects of the Development of Race Relations in the Rhodesias and Nyasaland.* London 1960.
R. Palmer and N. Parsons (eds.), *The Roots of Rural Poverty in Central and Southern Africa.* Berkeley (Cal.) 1977.

Zambia
D. Hywel Davies (ed.), *Zambia in Maps.* New York 1972.
J. A. Hellen, *Rural Economic Development in Zambia 1890–1964.* Munich 1968.
International Labour Office, Jobs and Skills Programme for Africa, *Narrowing the Gaps: Planning for Basic Needs and Productive Employment in Zambia.* Addis Ababa 1977.
C. S. Lombard and A. H. C. Tweedie, *Agriculture in Zambia since Independence.* Lusaka 1972.
A. Martin, *Minding Their Own Business: Zambia's Struggle against Western Control.* Harmondsworth 1975.
W. E. Rau, *A Bibliography of Pre-Independence Zambia: The Social Sciences.* Boston (Mass.) 1978.
A. Roberts, *A History of Zambia.* London 1976.
W. Tordoff (ed.), *Politics in Zambia.* Manchester 1974.

Zimbabwe
M. Akers (ed.), *Encyclopedia Rhodesia.* Salisbury 1973.
R. Cary and D. Mitchell, *African Nationalist Leaders in Rhodesia: Who's Who.* Johannesburg 1977.
M. O. Collins (ed.), *Rhodesia: Its Natural Resources and Economic Development.* Salisbury 1965.
G. Kay, *Rhodesia: A Human Geography.* London 1970.
H. Kuper, A. J. B. Hughes and J. van Velsen, *The Shona and Ndebele of Southern Rhodesia.* London 1954.
H. D. Nelson et al., *Area Handbook for Southern Rhodesia.* Washington (D.C.) 1975.
O. and K. Pollak, *Rhodesia/Zimbabwe: An International Bibliography.* Boston (Mass.) 1977.
R. K. Rasmussen, *Historical Dictionary of Rhodesia/Zimbabwe.* Metuchen (N.J.) 1979.
L. Vambe, *From Rhodesia to Zimbabwe.* London 1976.

Mozambique
K. Middlemass, *Cabora Bassu.* London 1975.
E. Mondlane, *The Struggle for Mozambique.* Harmondsworth 1969.
M. D. D. Newitt, *Portuguese Settlement on the Zambesi.* London 1973.
J. Paul, *Mozambique: Memoirs of a Revolution.* Harmondsworth 1975.

Malawi
H. Dequin, *Agricultural Development in Malawi.* 2nd ed. Munich 1970.
I. Linden, *Catholics, Peasants and Chewa Resistance in Nyasaland.* Berkeley (Cal.) 1974.
C. McMaster, *Malawi – Foreign Policy and Development.* New York 1974.
B. Pachai, *Malawi: The History of the Nation.* London 1973.
—— (ed.), *The Early History of Malawi.* London 1972.
G. Shepperson and T. Price, *Independent African.* Edinburgh 1958.

Southern Africa
J. Halpern, *South Africa's Hostages: Basutoland, Bechuanaland, and Swaziland.* Harmondsworth 1965.
R. Stevens, *Lesotho, Botswana and Swaziland; The Former High Commission Territories in Southern Africa.* London 1967.
M. Wilson and L. M. Thompson, *Oxford History of South Africa.* 2 vols. (Vol. 1 to 1870: Vol. 2 1870–1966). Oxford 1969, 1971.

South Africa
R. W. Johnson, *How Long Will South Africa Survive?* London 1977.
B. Magubane, *The Political Economy of Race and Class in South Africa.* 1979.
L. M. Thompson and J. Butler (eds.), *Change in Contemporary South Africa.* Berkeley (Cal.) 1975.

Namibia
H. Bley, *South-West Africa under German Rule.* London 1971.
P. Duignan and L. H. Gann, *South West Africa – Namibia.* New York 1978.
R. First, *South West Africa.* Harmondsworth 1963.
R. Vigne, *A Dwelling Place of Our Own. The Story of the Namibian Nation.* London and Cambridge (Mass.) 1973.

Botswana
Botswana Notes and Records. (Published annually by the Botswana Society.) Gaborone 1968–.
I. Schapera, *The Tswana.* London 1953. Reprinted, with supplemental bibliography, 1971.
A. Sillery, *Botswana: A Short Political History.* London 1974.
P. Smit, *Botswana: Resources and Development.* Pretoria n.d.

Lesotho
D. Ambrose, *The Guide to Lesotho.* 2nd ed. Johannesburg 1976.
H. Ashton, *The Basuto; A Social Study of Traditional and Modern Lesotho.* 2nd ed. London 1967.
G. Haliburton, *Historical Dictionary of Lesotho.* Metuchen (N.J.) 1977.
P. Sanders, *Moshoeshoe Chief of the Sotho.* London 1975.

Swaziland
H. Kuper, *The Swazi, A South African Kingdom.* London and New York 1963.
—— *Sobhuza II: Ngwenyama and King of Swaziland.* London 1978.
J. S. M. A. Matsebula, *A History of Swaziland.* Johannesburg 1972.

Africa in the Indian Ocean
Annuaire des pays de l'océan indien vol. 1 (1974), vol. 2 (1975). Marseilles 1977.
J. Auber, *Histoire de l'océan indien.* Tananarive 1954.
A. Toussaint, *Histoire de l'océan indien.* Paris 1961.

Madagascar
R. Archer, *Madagascar depuis 1972.* Paris 1976.
C. Cadoux, *La République Malgache.* Paris 1969.
H. Deschamps, *Madagascar.* Paris 1976.

Mauritius and Réunion
M. Debré, *Une Politique pour la Réunion.* Paris 1974.
Government of Mauritius, *Mauritius Economic Review 1971–1975.* Port Louis 1976.
—— *Mauritius Five Year Plan 1975–1980.* Port Louis 1976.
M. Robert, *La Réunion.* Paris 1976.
A. Toussaint, *Histoire de l'île Maurice.* Paris 1971.
—— *Histoire des îles Mascareignes.* Paris 1972.

Seychelles
Republic of Seychelles, *First National Development Plan 1977 to 1981.* Mahé 1977.

GAZETTEER

236